Kiplinger's
Practical Guide
to Your
Money

Kiplinger's

Third Edition

Practical Guide to Your Money

KEEP MORE OF IT, MAKE IT GROW, ENJOY IT, PROTECT IT, PASS IT ON

From the Editors of
Kiplinger's Personal Finance

Dearborn™
Trade Publishing
A **Kaplan Professional** Company

President, Dearborn Publishing: Roy Lipner
Vice President and Publisher: Cynthia A. Zigmund
Senior Acquisitions Editor: Mary B. Good
Cover Design: Design Solutions
Typesetting: the dotted i

Published by Dearborn Trade Publishing
A Kaplan Professional Company

Printed in the United States of America

05 06 07   10 9 8 7 6 5 4 3 2 1

Library of Congress Cataloging-in-Publication Data

Kiplinger's practical guide to your money : keep more of it, make it grow, enjoy it, protect it, pass it on / from the edtiors of Kiplinger's personal finance.—3rd ed.
    p.   cm.
   Rev. ed. of: Kiplinger's practical guide to your money : keep more of it, make it grow, enjoy it, protect it, pass it on / Ted Miller. ©2002.
   Includes index.
   ISBN 1-4195-1752-X (7.25x9 pbk.)
   1. Finance, Personal.   I. Miller, Theodore J. Kiplinger's practical guide to your money.
II. Kiplinger's personal finance magazine.
HG179.M492 2005
332.024—dc22

                                          2005019994

Contents

Contents

Contents

Introduction

I f ever there was a subject prone to information overload, personal finance is it. Advice on managing your money comes at you in a torrent from countless sources—magazines, books, newspapers, the Internet, radio and television, and—increasingly—from companies trying to sell you their financial products.

The dilemma most people face isn't having enough information, but having too much. The challenge is culling it to find advice that is accurate, clear, trustworthy, untainted by commercial interests, and—yes—practical.

The dictionary defines "practical" as "useful," "disposed to action," and "not theoretical or abstract." Those words sum up very well the advice we offer in every chapter of this book. We at *Kiplinger's Personal Finance* magazine know that financial strategies that are overly complex and time-consuming just won't be implemented by busy Americans with other priorities—such as earning a living, raising children, and helping in their community.

So we cut through the information clutter on your behalf, focusing on time-proven ways to make your money grow, enabling you to achieve the financial independence you seek. This book will help you set realistic goals and design ways to reach them. It is a complete personal-finance manual, with treatment of budgeting, saving and investing, buying a home and car, insurance, getting ready for retirement, and the basics of estate planning. There are, of course, entire books written on each of these subjects—including some excellent ones from us. But I think you'll be pleasantly surprised to find that most of what you really need to know is included in this book.

Our no-nonsense approach to money management has evolved over 58 years in the pages of *Kiplinger's Personal Finance* magazine. It is straightforward, down-to-earth, and free of tricks and gimmicks.

When *Kiplinger's* magazine was founded in 1947, it was the first periodical that wrote extensively about personal finance for the American family. It was a pioneer in urging Americans to invest in growth stocks rather than low-yielding savings accounts and bonds. It deciphered the mysteries of life insurance, becoming an early champion of high-coverage, low-premium term insurance for young families with children to protect. It introduced its readers to a new way of investing through "investment trusts"—now known as mutual funds—that brought the benefits of portfolio management and diversification to small investors.

We at *Kiplinger's* have always cautioned our readers against the temptation of get-rich-quick schemes and exotic investment techniques—commodities, options, limited partnerships, etc.—that tend to enrich brokers more than investors. We are also skeptical of Initial Public Offerings of stock, because in our experience, you can usually buy the same shares later for a lower price, after the hype is gone and the company has settled down to its normal business. We preach the beauty of diversification, with holdings of bonds leavening the short-term risks of stocks. And we never bought into the breathless euphoria in the late 1990s over the "dot-com" stocks of the Internet boom, which crashed and burned in early 2000. We told our readers that speculators and naïve investors were paying an outrageous price for start-up companies that had little prospect of ever being profitable.

Kiplinger subscribers who followed this advice fared relatively well in the humbling bear market from 2000 to 2002, and were poised to benefit from the market recovery in 2003–2004. Why? Because they were holding a broad array of quality stocks, not over-heavy in the slumping tech sector, and they also had offsetting holdings in CDs, bonds, and money-market funds.

We think your goal should be to get rich slowly—a very achievable goal if you follow some simple rules.

We've never believed in stock market timing, because we don't think anyone can time the peaks and valleys very well, especially in the increasing volatility of today's global markets. That's why *Kiplinger's* was an early advocate of the investment technique called "dollar cost averaging," the disciplined investing of money in markets that will be, at one time or another, low, high, and in between. That's just one of the effective strategies that's explained in this book.

The first decade of this century—the new millennium—is already proving to be a fascinating, challenging time, fraught with peril but equally rich in opportunities for the well prepared and well informed. There is more market turbulence than ever before. Competition among nations is heightening, thanks to an accelerating flow of goods and capital. The workplace is roiled by changes in demographics, technology, regulation, and new ways of managing people and business structures. Loyalty between employers and employees continues to diminish, boosting the rate of job and career changes. Social Security—while always "being there" for future retirees—won't be nearly as good a deal as it is for today's seniors. Lucrative corporate pensions continue to give way to 401(k)s and IRAs, funded largely by employees themselves.

All of this means that people must take more individual responsibility for their own futures, with continuous education, retraining, strategic job changes, and—at every step along the way—smart financial planning.

Americans have never before faced so many choices of how to manage their money. The options are so many that some folks are dismayed and paralyzed, not knowing where to start. This book will give you the confidence to get started, or if you're already under way, a reality check on whether your plan is sound. Either way, you'll have the confidence of knowing that you're walking a path that has led thousands of others to financial security over five decades.

On behalf of my colleagues at Kiplinger, I wish you the best of good fortune on the journey ahead.

Knight Kiplinger

KNIGHT A. KIPLINGER
Washington, D.C.

Take Charge of Your Money

Part I

First, Take Charge of Your Money

Chapter 1

The world is mesmerized by money. A rack full of newspapers and magazines and a truckload of newsletters devote themselves entirely to chronicling the use and abuse of money. Cable TV beams money-related programming day and night. The Internet is jammed with money-minded Web sites. Scribes pen countless books about money (this one, for instance). Money is a top-ten topic of family conversation, too. It's a well-reported fact that married couples fight more about money than about sex. A recent edition of *Bartlett's Familiar Quotations* lists 98 entries for the word *money,* a mere 39 for *sex.*

Considering that the subject occupies so much of our time and attention, isn't it amazing that so many people have barely a clue about how to handle their own money? Amazing maybe, but no mystery: Americans typically manage to navigate 12, 16, or more years of very fine formal education without ever learning how to balance a checkbook, size up a stock, or resist a fast-talking salesman of bad financial ideas. Diploma in hand, you may be able to explain the fine points of difference between Milton and Chaucer, between demographics and psychographics, or between protons and leptons but draw a blank when it comes to the differences between, say, money-market funds and money-market deposit accounts.

You are not alone.

The purpose of this book is to fill in the blanks by suggesting ways to use the money you have to live better today and build a more secure future at the same time. Along the way it will attempt to explain

To find out where your money is going, fill out the cash-flow worksheet on the opposite page.

many things, some of which you will already be familiar with, or think you are. The book does have a plan—a logical beginning, middle, and end—but it's written with the expectation that you'll skip the subjects you know in order to concentrate on the ones you don't know.

Where Are You Now?

If you've been around awhile and feel comfortably on top of your regular income and outgo, then maybe you can safely skip this chapter, for instance. On the other hand, if you have to admit that you're barely making it from payday to payday, or if you're not exactly drowning but have the distinct feeling that you're treading water while others swim merrily by, then here is where you'll find the means to get moving.

One thing you need to do is take a financial inventory. That means sorting out the money and other assets that are all yours from those that someone else has a claim on—in other words, finding out what you own and what you owe. This isn't hard to do. You add up the value of everything you own, then you subtract from it the total of all your debts. The result is your net worth, and the form on pages 8 and 9 will walk you through the steps.

Before you check out the form, though, it will be helpful to perform another little piece of self-analysis. Taking some time to record what you do with the money that passes through your hands on a day-to-day basis will pay off in valuable information about the state of your financial affairs. It's the first step in getting them under control.

If you haven't been paying much attention to where your money goes, fill in the cash-flow form on the opposite page. You'll have exact figures for some expenses—mortgage or rent, for example, and insurance premiums—and you can estimate others on a monthly basis. Go over your canceled checks, paid bills, and credit card statements. Hang on to cash-register receipts from stores, cleaners, gas stations, and restaurants. The more actual expenditures you can pinpoint, the more you'll know about your spending habits when you're through.

No matter how this exercise comes out, you're going to be confronted with the evidence of your spending and forced to make some judgments about it. You'll find yourself in one of three situations.

YOUR CASH FLOW

INCOME	TOTAL FOR YEAR	MONTHLY AVERAGE
Take-home pay	$ _____	$ _____
Dividends, capital gains, interest	_____	_____
Bonuses	_____	_____
Other	_____	_____
Total income	$ _____	$ _____

EXPENDITURES		
Mortgage or rent	$ _____	$ _____
Taxes not withheld from pay	_____	_____
Food	_____	_____
Utilities and fuel	_____	_____
Insurance premiums	_____	_____
Household maintenance	_____	_____
Auto (gas, oil, maintenance, repairs)	_____	_____
Other transportation (bus, parking)	_____	_____
Loan payment	_____	_____
Credit card interest	_____	_____
Medical bills not covered by insurance	_____	_____
Clothing and care	_____	_____
Savings and investments	_____	_____
Charity	_____	_____
Recreation and entertainment	_____	_____
Miscellaneous	_____	_____
Total expenditures	$ _____	$ _____

SUMMARY		
Total income	$ _____	$ _____
Minus total expenditures	_____	_____
Surplus (+) or deficit (−)	$ _____	$ _____

ARE INCOME AND EXPENDITURES ROUGHLY IN BAL-ANCE? Making it from one year to the next without getting into a hole may be something of a feat these days, but before you start patting yourself on the back, check your totals again. How much did you put into savings compared with what you spent on recreation, gifts, or clothing? Out-of-whack entries in those or other categories of discretionary spending could mean trouble's brewing. There's more to good money management than balancing the books. You have to balance your priorities, too.

DID YOU MAKE MORE THAN YOU SPENT? This isn't necessarily a good sign, either. Because your cash-flow statement includes savings and investments, you shouldn't have any money left over. What may at first look like a surplus is probably just a failure to remember some spending. Go over the numbers again.

DID YOU SPEND MORE THAN YOU MADE? This is the clearest sign of trouble ahead. You've either been dipping into savings, borrowing money, or buying on

---

NO MONEY LEFT TO SAVE

Q: I'd like to start saving some money, but after I've made the mortgage payment, the car payment, bought the groceries, and had a little fun (and I do mean a little), all the money is gone. Is there any hope for people like me?

A: There are at least a couple of avenues you can investigate.

Do you get an income-tax refund each year? If so, take a trip to your company's human resources office and adjust your withholding to reflect more closely the taxes you'll owe for the year. If you tend to get a $500 refund, you can increase your take-home pay by more than $40 a month by changing your withholding.

When was the last time you reshopped your homeowners and auto insurance policies? Premiums charged by different companies for the same level of coverage in the same city can vary by hundreds of dollars a year.

There's one more step: When you've freed up the cash from these other sources, authorize your bank to take it out of your checking account automatically each month and transfer it to savings or a mutual fund account. Out of sight, out of mind—until you begin to notice how the money is adding up.

credit. You can get away with it for a while, and there are times when it's smart to borrow or when you have no choice. But as a regular practice, it's bad money management that will cost you in the long run.

Go over your cash-flow statement carefully, looking for places where your money might be dribbling away. As you proceed with this chapter, you should begin to spot some ways to plug the leaks.

How Much Are You Worth?

Now you have a picture of how you're handling the money that comes your way on a regular basis. But performing a cash-flow analysis for a single year doesn't give you much information about the cumulative impact on your financial worth of all the cash that's been flowing through your hands day after day for all of your adult life. A net-worth statement will show you this, and a form for creating one is on pages 8 and 9. Here's how to use it.

ADD UP ASSETS. Start with cash: what you have on hand, what's in your checking account, and what you may have squirreled away elsewhere. Next list money in savings accounts and certificates of deposit. (If you own U.S. savings bonds and want to be finicky about it, check their current values with a bank or go online (http://www.publicdebt.treas.gov) to get them. But you could spend the better part of a day at that little exercise if you own more than, say, a dozen bonds bought over a period of years. You might settle for a ballpark estimate of the value, which is somewhere between what you paid for them (half their face value) and what they're worth today.

Premium payments on a whole-life insurance policy add to your net worth by increasing the policy's cash value (the amount you'd get if you cashed it in). Your insurance agent or a table in the policy can tell you the current cash value. Ditto for the surrender value of any annuities you own.

Settling on figures to enter as the current value of your pension and profit-sharing plans is tricky. A pro-

Go over your cash-flow statement carefully, looking for places where your money might be dribbling away.

YOUR NET WORTH

ASSETS

Cash in checking accounts	$ _____
Cash in savings accounts	_____
Certificates of deposit	_____
U.S. savings bonds (current value)	_____
Cash value of life insurance	_____
Equity in pension, 401(k), and profit-sharing plans	_____
Market value of IRA or Keogh plan	_____
Surrender value of annuities	_____
Market value of house or apartment	_____
Market value of other real estate	_____
Market value of securities	_____
Stocks	_____
Bonds	_____
Mutual fund shares	_____
Other	_____
Current value of durable possessions	
Automobiles	_____
Household furnishings	_____
Household appliances and equipment	_____
Furs and jewelry	_____

gram that will provide you with retirement income is surely an important asset, but it's difficult (although by no means impossible) to put a present-day dollar value on income you're supposed to receive in the future. For purposes of this statement, include in your net worth only the amount you could withdraw in cash if you quit your job today. Your human resources office should be able to provide that figure. If you have an individual retirement account (IRA), 401(k) plan, or Keogh, list its current balance.

Your home is likely to be your biggest asset, so it's especially important that the value you assign to it be accurate. Don't list what it cost you or take a wild guess

Precious metals _____

Collectibles _____

Recreation and hobby equipment _____

Loans receivable _____

Interest in a business _____

Other assets _____

Total Assets $ _____

LIABILITIES

Current bills outstanding $ _____

Credit card balances _____

Car loans

Taxes due _____

Balance due on mortgages _____

Other loans _____

Other liabilities _____

Total Liabilities $ _____

SUMMARY **Assets** $ _____

Minus Liabilities − _____

Net Worth $ _____

at its present value. Check around to find out what similar homes in your area are selling for or have sold for recently, ask a real estate agent for an estimate of current market value, or check Web sites such as http://www.homegain.com or http://www.domania.com. Try to get reliable estimates of the value of any other real estate or business interests you own, too.

The current market value of financial assets such as stocks, bonds, and mutual funds is easy to find in the newspaper, online, or on recent statements from your funds or broker.

You can get a good idea of what your car is worth by consulting a car-price guide, such as the *Kelley Blue*

If you sold all your assets and paid all your debts, what would be left over? That's your net worth.

Book (http://www.kbb.com) or the *N.A.D.A. Official Used Car Guide*, published by the National Automobile Dealers Association (http://www.nadaguides.com). Banks that make auto loans usually have copies of those guides, as do many public libraries, or you can check either online. N.A.D.A.'s Web site also contains guides that will help you put value on a boat, motorcycle, or other vehicle, or you can contact a dealer or check the prices of comparable models in the classified ads.

Ballpark figures will do for the value of household furnishings, appliances, and other personal belongings. It's best to be conservative in your estimates. One conservative approach is to guesstimate that what's inside your home is worth 20 to 30 percent of the value of the home itself. Or make your own item-by-item estimate, then slash it by 50 percent. Use estimated market value (not purchase price) of antiques, furs, jewelry, and stamp or coin collections.

LOOK AT LIABILITIES. Filling out this portion of the form may be painful, but it shouldn't be difficult. Most liabilities are obvious, and whomever you owe probably reminds you of the debt on a regular basis.

Start with current bills—what you owe the doctor and the plumber, this month's phone bill, and credit card charges. Next, list the balance due on every credit card and installment debt. There's a separate line on the form for your car loan and another one for taxes coming due. Your home mortgage is probably your largest single liability, and the year-end statement from the lender should show exactly how much you still owe on it. On other lines, list every debt you can think of because whatever you owe is a liability that diminishes your net worth.

BEHOLD THE BOTTOM LINE. Now it's time to fill in the bottom line. If you sold all your assets and paid all your debts, what would be left over? That's your net worth.

It's probably not what you'd like it to be. It's even possible that it's a negative number, especially if you're young and just took out a big mortgage on a house and a big loan on a car. But don't worry—be happy, because you've just taken the first step toward starting or revising a budget that can show you ways to beef up your assets and trim your liabilities. Before you continue, you need to set some goals.

Why You Must Set Goals

You probably don't expect to attain great wealth in your lifetime. Simple financial security would do, if only you knew what that meant. It's a slippery notion, all right, but it does have a few characteristics you can grab on to.

You need a steady source of income. This comes from your job, or your business if you're self-employed, or investments if you're fortunate and alert. Future income is the bedrock on which financial security is built.

You need financial reserves. Cars break down, household appliances wear out, roofs spring leaks. Kids aspire to college educations, and someday you'll want to retire. These are expenses you have to provide for with savings and investments.

You need protection against financial catastrophes. In a word, this means insurance. You need it in sufficient amounts to cover your life, your health, your ability to earn an income, and your family and your possessions. Without insurance, the best-laid financial plans can be wiped out in an instant.

You need to get further ahead each year. If you stand pat, even modest inflation will grind away at your financial reserves just as surely as if you were spending the money. To stay ahead of the cost of living, you have to be alert for opportunities to make your money grow.

These things don't come to you by accident. You have to go after them, and that means setting some goals.

Choose goals you can get excited about, because that will make you more determined to reach them.

Your Goals, Not Someone Else's

The most important step toward financial security is to translate it into your own terms. What, exactly, are your personal financial goals? If you have trouble sorting them out, try classifying them as either *wants* or *needs*. Go a step further and add long-term or short-term to the description. Now you have some useful labels you can apply to your priorities.

Say you're going to *need* a new car soon. Gathering the money for a down payment without borrowing or dipping into savings would be a short-term need. Let's call it, and other short-term needs such as your daughter's braces or a new winter coat, priority number one.

Longer-term needs, such as contributions to a retirement fund, can get priority two. That vacation in Bermuda next spring is a short-term *want*—making it priority three. The 42-foot sailboat you'd like to own before too many years go by is a long-term want, so it gets a four.

You could shift priorities around, of course, and use lots more numbers. Actual goals and their priorities will vary with your circumstances. The important thing is to give serious thought to your goals and try to anticipate the expenses coming up, whether they're close at hand or several years away.

Choose goals you can get excited about, because that will make you more determined to reach them. "Financial security" sounds good, for instance, but we've already admitted that it's hard to quantify. It needs some skin and bones. Define what it means to you. How about this? "I want to own a million dollars' worth of stocks by the time I'm 50." Or this: "We want to retire to Arizona in ten years with enough money to buy a house near Phoenix and enough income to travel in Europe for a month each year." Now you've got goals you can put a future price on, and that price can be translated into a savings and investment plan that you can start today. Put your goals in writing; that makes for a great motivational tool.

The trouble is, exciting goals and good intentions need cash to back them up. That's where budgeting comes in. It's your best bet for distributing your limited resources among competing goals.

Nitty-Gritty Budgeting

Think of your budget as a planning device, a means of setting and reaching your goals. You project future expenditures (including savings), record them when they're made, and see whether your projections were any good. If they weren't, adjust your planning or your spending, whichever is out of line.

You'll find a suggested budget format on pages 16 and 17. There's space provided for a month's expenditures. Use that format as a model to make your own budget sheets, or make copies of those two pages to give you space for more months.

Use the record of last year's spending that you compiled on page 5 as the basis for the coming year's budget projections. Work only a couple of months ahead at first, until you get the hang of it. Then you can budget further ahead. After a while you'll want to apply the same principles to long-term goal setting by forecasting the growth of your net worth and all the little pieces that compose it. Then you can keep track of the progress you're making by comparing each year's projected growth with the actual results.

Fixed Spending

Some of your projections will be easy: You know what your mortgage or rent payments will be in the months ahead. Same for car payments and the premiums coming due on insurance policies. So why budget for them? Because by recording these and other fixed expenditures as monthly outgo, you can see at a glance how much of your income is committed to current or future expenses. That should stop you from spending it on something else.

Variable Spending

Here you'll keep track of the items over which you have some degree of control. This section is the place

Think of your budget as a planning device, a means of setting and reaching your goals.

One good reason to endure the drudgery of budgeting is that it alerts you to trouble while there's still time to do something about it.

to test your cost-cutting skills. Watch for patterns that may signal trouble. If the "miscellaneous" line keeps growing, for instance, your recordkeeping may be careless.

Plugging the Holes in Your Budget

One good reason to endure the occasional drudgery of budgeting is that it alerts you to trouble while you still have time to do something about it. You're forced to find out why your expenditures are climbing and to take action. If the electric or gas bill is higher because the rates were raised, you'll have to revise your monthly forecasts for that budget item and figure out whether other items need to be cut to pay for it. If rates haven't risen, maybe it's time to discourage the kids from taking such long showers two or three times a day.

Sometimes a budget flashes danger signals that are more difficult to interpret. If you start picking up distress signals, run your budget through these checks:

ARE YOU BUYING TOO MUCH ON CREDIT? Perhaps you got into this fix because you didn't watch what was going on. Examine budget categories where spending overshot allocations, paying particular attention to your credit card statements. The finance charges they generate could be enough to foul up your estimates.

ARE YOU BEHIND THE TIMES? You may be in trouble not because of unnecessary spending but because your necessary spending now costs more. This is a common experience, and people who budget sometimes have trouble coping with it because they estimate spending on the basis of prices in effect at the time the budget is drawn up. You should revise your budget from time to time throughout the year to keep it in touch with reality.

DID YOU CREATE A STRAITJACKET? Consider the couple who thought they were doing fine without a budget of any kind, until their checks suddenly began bouncing all over town. With their two-salary income, they told each other, there was simply no excuse for such embarrassment. So they vowed to budget, and for the first time ever they sat down to list their normal expenses and match them against their normal income.

To their delight, they found that not only was there enough money to go around but also that it would be perfectly realistic to fund a savings program, which they had talked about but never started. They promptly drew up a budget that included a heroic chunk of savings each month, then happily set forth on their road to affluence.

Or so they thought. In their enthusiasm they had been both too ambitious and too rigid. They had tried to shovel too much into savings. They budgeted every penny of the remainder but neglected to allow for the unforeseen expenses that are too petty to budget for but add up nevertheless.

Moral: Allow yourself leeway. Better to budget a bit too much in a few categories (certainly including miscellaneous or contingencies) than to end each month robbing Peter to pay Paul. The purpose of a budget is not to make impossible dreams come true but to make attainable goals come more easily.

ARE YOU DOING SOMEBODY ELSE'S THING? Years ago, the Bureau of Labor Statistics invented a hypothetical urban family of four, and it periodically computed itemized budgets for this family, just to see how much it was costing them to live. Newspapers and magazines faithfully reported changes in this budget and editorial writers clucked sympathetically as costs rose to squeeze this imaginary mom and pop and their imaginary children. But if by wild chance yours happened to be an urban family of four with precisely the same income, it is likely your budget would have looked very little like the BLS version. (And indeed, the agency eventually abandoned this exercise.)

Your budget is unique to you and your family. It embodies private decisions you make about how you will allocate your resources. Behind those decisions are

> **The purpose of a budget is not to make impossible dreams come true but to make attainable goals come more easily.**

your own goals, aspirations, values, hopes, anxieties, lifestyle, commitments, and, to an important degree, even the expectations of people whose expectations you regard as worthy of honoring.

In short, you can't live by somebody else's budget. Yours has to be tailored to your measure—by you.

A BUDGET FOR TODAY AND TOMORROW

Use this format to get on top of your living costs by projecting expenditures in various categories. Then record what you actually spend and see how close your projections came to reality. Do this month-by-month to begin with, and you'll see where you need to plug the leaks in your spending.

INCOME

Take-home pay $ _____

Other (specify)   _____

Total $ _____

FIXED EXPENDITURES	PROJECTED	ACTUAL	(+) OR (-)
Mortgage or rent	$ _____	$ _____	$ _____
Taxes not withheld from pay	_____	_____	_____
Installment and credit card payments	_____	_____	_____
	_____	_____	_____
	_____	_____	_____
	_____	_____	_____
	_____	_____	_____
	_____	_____	_____
Insurance premiums			
Life	_____	_____	_____
Auto	_____	_____	_____
Home	_____	_____	_____
Health	_____	_____	_____
Other	_____	_____	_____
Savings/Investments			
Vacation fund	_____	_____	_____
Emergency fund	_____	_____	_____
Investment fund	_____	_____	_____
Retirement or 401(k)	_____	_____	_____
Other (specify)	_____	_____	_____
Subtotal	$ _____	$ _____	$ _____

Most people approach budgeting by listing first the expenditures about which they feel they have no choice whatsoever. If anything is left over, only then do they consider expenditures they might make from free choice. Budgeting doesn't have to proceed this grimly, however. A few people begin at the other end. First

VARIABLE EXPENDITURES	PROJECTED	ACTUAL	(+) OR (-)
Food and beverages	$	$	$
Fuel and utilities			
Gas or oil			
Electricity			
Telephone			
Water and sewer			
Household operation			
and maintenance			
Automobile			
Gas and oil			
Repairs			
Public transportation			
Clothing			
Mom			
Dad			
Kids			
Pocket money			
Mom			
Dad			
Kids			
Personal care (haircuts, etc.)			
Recreation, entertainment			
Medical and dental			
Charity			
Special expenses			
(tuition, alimony, etc.)			
Miscellaneous			
Subtotal	$	$	$
Plus fixed expenditures	$	$	$
Total	$	$	$

they put down their desired goals, such as "enough money to buy a 36-foot sailboat by 2010." Then they budget to attain those goals before distributing the remainder among items most people would rank as first-order necessities—shelter, food, clothing, and the like.

Granted, this doesn't always work. It takes a strong-minded individual to budget wishes first and needs later. But it can work, which only goes to show how highly personal the whole budgeting process can be.

How to Boost Your Savings

Unless you're expecting a big inheritance sometime in your future, the only way to accumulate a net worth worthy of the label is to make a habit of spending less money than you're taking in. Budgeting, as described in Chapter 1, is a good way to practice this particular fiscal religion. But whether you budget or not, the money that flows through your hands on a regular basis is your key to getting ahead. On a modest income, the difference between halfhearted money management and smart money management can be hundreds of dollars a year, which can be cash in your pocket or cash down the drain. As the years go by, the difference can amount to thousands and thousands of dollars added to your net worth.

How to reach this blessed state? Start with four simple, commonsense principles of smart money management.

1. DON'T SURROUND YOURSELF WITH CASH. Do you keep large amounts of cash around the house instead of putting it in the bank, where it will earn interest, or in an investment plan, where it can grow? Do you often delay depositing checks written to you? Do you neglect to cash traveler's checks after a trip? All these lackadaisical habits deprive you of chances to let your money make more money.

2. DON'T PAY YOUR BILLS EARLY. Paying bills before they are due won't improve your credit standing. It's the persistently late payers who bother the banks and

Excess withholdings could be put to work earning interest, leaving you with even more left over after your taxes are paid.

credit card companies. Prepaying reduces the time your money can be earning interest for you and gains you absolutely nothing in return. (But be sure not to cut it so close that you trigger late penalties that can wipe out the extra interest you earn!)

3. DON'T HAVE MORE TAXES WITHHELD THAN YOU OWE. Many people deliberately have too much taken out of their salaries to avoid a large tax bill in April or to accumulate a refund. Those excess withholdings could be put to work earning interest, leaving you with even more left over after your taxes are paid.

4. GET THE MAX FROM YOUR SAVINGS. This fourth step is the one that the other three have been leading up to. For most people, the difference between depositing a check today and depositing it next week amounts to nickels and dimes in lost interest, and nickels and dimes aren't going to make you rich. The real aim here is to establish good money-management habits. As your income grows, the payoff will grow along with it.

Any plan to maximize your future savings must begin with an up-to-date record of the savings you have now. Use the form on page 23 to list all your savings funds, the institutions where they are held, the names in which the accounts are registered, the rate the money is earning, and any restrictions on when the money can be withdrawn. There are lots of opportunities for squeezing more out of your savings. Following is a guide to the kinds of accounts that will do it, plus some tips on how to use them.

Certificates of Deposit

There are several kinds of savings and investment vehicles commonly referred to as CDs. They range from so-called time-deposit savings certificates—available in modest denominations at banks, savings and loan associations, and credit unions—to negotiable certificates requiring minimum deposits of $100,000 or more.

When you put your money in a CD, you're striking a bargain with the bank: You promise to leave your money with the bank for the term specified on the certificate, which may be as short as three months or as long as five years. In return, the bank pays you a higher rate of interest than it would pay on an account with no such promise, and it probably charges a penalty if you withdraw your money before the certificate has matured. Usually, the longer the term, the higher the rate. Interest rates, penalties, and other terms vary from institution to institution and thus are impossible to generalize about. Shop around and be sure to get a clear explanation of what you'll have to pay if you redeem a CD early.

Another thing to watch for when using a certificate of deposit is the rollover provision. In some cases the certificate will automatically be rolled over (that is, another certificate purchased for you) if you don't notify the institution within a specified number of days before the certificate's maturity. That's fine if you didn't have something else in mind for the money, but irritating if you did because you'll have to pay the premature-withdrawal penalty to get your money out.

You can reduce the risks of a long-term commitment—and take advantage of long-term rates—by staggering, or laddering, maturities, so that some are always coming due in the near future. Then, if you don't need the cash, you can rotate the maturing cer-

---

PAY BILLS OR SOCK IT AWAY?

Q: *I recently got a nice bonus from my job and I want to use it to start an investment account for my daughter's college education, which should begin in about ten years. My wife thinks we should pay off our Visa bill first. It's nearly $3,000, and I do plan to pay it off a little at a time, but I'm itching to get that college plan started. Which is the better move?*

A: Pay off the Visa bill. If your account is typical (see Chapter 3), you're paying about 13% interest on that $3,000, which amounts to around $400 a year. By paying the bill in full, you get to keep a whole year's worth of interest—the equivalent of investing that $3,000 at 13%, guaranteed. That's a return that's hard to beat, especially with absolutely no risk.

tificates back into long or short maturities, depending on rates available at the time.

For example, if you have $2,000 to put in CDs, consider putting $500 each in a three-month, six-month, one-year, and two-year certificate. When the three-month CD matures, roll it over into a six-month certificate. Do the same when the first six-month CD matures, and continue rolling over so that you'll always have a certificate within three months of maturity.

If you want even more protection against getting locked into a low rate or being caught short of ready money, arrange to have the interest from some of the certificates paid out on a quarterly or semiannual basis. That gives you a constant stream of cash for use or reinvestment. You will lose part of the extra return you'd get from compounding, but if rates are volatile, that's a relatively small price to pay for retaining your liquidity. Also, in an emergency you can pledge a certificate as collateral for a loan. Some banks will let you specify the maturity dates for your certificates, so you can time maturities to coincide with your need for the principal.

Interest-Earning Checking Accounts

These don't pay as much interest as certificates of deposits or money-market deposit accounts (see page 25), but they are convenient ways to keep your money earning interest and quickly available at the same time. But interest-earning checking accounts often have strings attached to them that keep modest deposits from sharing in the potential benefits. In fact, the profusion of service charges, minimum balances, fees for checks, and other fine-print items can create what seems to be an impenetrable jungle.

The key to choosing the right account lies in the minimum-balance requirement. If you don't maintain that balance, you'll probably have to pay a service charge, and it can easily exceed what you earn in interest. Suppose, for example, you kept an average balance of $900 in an account on which you got 1 percent interest but which required a $1,000 minimum balance to avoid service charges. You'd earn about $0.75 in monthly interest, but you'd pay the service charge because your balance was under the minimum. If that charge were, say, $5, you'd be $4.25 a month in the hole.

Some banks, credit unions, and savings and loan associations require a lower minimum balance than others and charge smaller service fees, so shopping around can pay off. Credit unions often offer the most attractive terms on their accounts, which they call share-draft accounts.

Sometimes you think you're meeting the minimum-balance requirement but lose out on interest because of the way the institution computes it. Here are the key questions to consider when you're trying to decide whether an interest-earning checking account will pay

WHERE YOU'VE STASHED YOUR SAVINGS

ACCOUNT / INSTITUTION	AMOUNT	WHEN AVAILABLE
Standard savings accounts		
_____	$ _____	_____
_____	_____	_____
_____	_____	_____
Subtotal	$ _____	
Certificates of deposit		
_____	$ _____	_____
_____	_____	_____
_____	_____	_____
Subtotal	$ _____	
U.S. savings bonds		
_____	$ _____	_____
_____	_____	_____
_____	_____	_____
Subtotal	$ _____	
Other (e.g., money-market funds, interest-earning checking)		
_____	$ _____	_____
_____	_____	_____
_____	_____	_____
Subtotal	$ _____	
Total	$ _____	

off for you, or when you're comparing one account with another.

How Is the Minimum Balance Determined?

Some institutions impose a strict minimum-balance requirement all the time. They add up your balance at the end of each day; if it falls below the minimum for even one day in a monthly cycle, you're charged the full service fee. An average-balance requirement gives you more leeway. Your account can drop to zero for days at a time, but as long as you deposit enough to bring the monthly average up to the minimum, you won't have to pay a service charge.

Comparing minimum- and average-balance requirements can be confusing. When shopping around, think of them this way: A typical pattern is for the average monthly balance in your checking account to run about twice your minimum balance. That means an average-balance requirement at one bank that is higher than the minimum-balance requirement at another bank may actually be easier to meet, provided it is less than twice as high.

What Fees Will You Pay?

If your balance dips below the minimum, you may be charged for every check written during the month or at least for those written while your balance was too low. Sometimes check fees aren't charged, no matter how little you have in your account, unless you write more than a specified number of checks (usually 15 to 20).

In addition to monthly service and check fees, you may run into another kind of charge—loss of interest for all or part of the period when your account dips below a certain amount.

How Is Interest Calculated?

Interest-earning checking accounts generally pay interest daily, but there are some exceptions. At credit unions, for instance, dividends that are paid on share-draft accounts may be based on the lowest balance during a dividend period, which can be a month or as long as a quarter. This quirk can dull the interest edge that some credit unions have over banks and savings and loans. But because credit unions often don't set minimum-balance requirements or charge service fees, share-draft accounts can still be a better deal.

You'll get the very best deal on interest if it is figured from day of deposit to day of withdrawal, or on your average daily balance over the period being measured. In either case you get credit for all the money you have in your account, and compounding sweetens the deal even more.

If you're accustomed to maintaining a very low balance, you might be better off with a traditional checking account that pays no interest. Regular checking-account fees are generally set below the fees for interest-earning accounts, so even though you're not earning any interest, you could be better off with the traditional account.

You get the best interest deal when it's figured from day of deposit to day of withdrawal, or on the average daily balance for the period.

Money-Market Deposit Accounts

The main attraction of money-market deposit accounts (MMDAs), which are sometimes called money-market investment accounts or some other variation on the name, is that they usually pay higher interest rates than checking accounts do. The potential drawbacks to these accounts, whatever their name, are that minimum-deposit levels are higher and that transfers from the account—that is, checks or other movements of money—are limited. MMDAs are meant for savings, not for funds to which you need ready and repeated access. Institutions often charge fees if your account falls below minimum-balance requirements. Rates aren't guaranteed; they change along with market rates.

Money-Market Funds

These are mutual funds that invest in very short-term debt instruments issued by corporations, banks, and the U.S. Treasury. They can be excellent cash-management tools, especially when you want to park savings someplace while you ponder longer-term investments. Because they are safe and because the market value of their shares doesn't fluctuate, many people have come to consider money-market funds as a permanent part of their savings plans, as well as a hedge against investment market risks.

Although $1,000 is a common minimum initial investment, some funds are available for less, and virtually all accept smaller amounts for subsequent investments.

Most funds permit you to write checks on your account, although the high minimum for checks—usually $250 or $500—makes money-market funds unsuitable for everyday bill paying. Shares are generally redeemable at any time by mail or telephone, and you can arrange to have the money wired or mailed directly to your bank account. Money-market funds are described in detail in Chapter 25.

Asset-Management Accounts

This type of account, which is offered by brokerage firms and banks, can be a good vehicle for managing your cash if you have a lot of it and feel you can use the other services such accounts deliver.

Merrill Lynch introduced the idea with its Cash Management Account more than two decades ago. Now called the Working Capital Management Account, the minimum initial balance required is $100,000 in stocks, bonds, cash, mutual fund shares, or a combination of the four. WCMA customers get a line of credit, unlimited check-writing privileges on their money-market funds, and several other services. The fee is $300 a year. Similar accounts are available at other full-service and discount brokers, although fees and features vary a bit.

As money-management tools, asset-management accounts are valuable because of the detailed consolidated records you get from their monthly statements and the easy access they provide to several alternative investment instruments. These accounts are described in more detail in Chapter 4.

The Smart Use (and Common Abuse) of Credit

How much debt is too much? It depends. That's not the answer you wanted, perhaps, but it's the only sensible one: It depends on how easily you can repay the money and what you borrowed it for in the first place.

A long-standing rule of thumb holds that monthly payments on debts (not including a home mortgage, which is really more of an investment) shouldn't exceed 20 percent of take-home pay. The closer you get to that 20 percent ceiling, the greater your risk of overindebtedness.

Rules of thumb can be useful, but don't count on this one to keep you out of trouble. It says nothing about your total financial obligations or your level of income. If you take home $4,000 a month and live in a paid-up house, you can more easily afford $800 in monthly credit card bills than if you take home $2,000 and have to shell out $400 on top of the rent. Whatever you make and whatever you owe, you probably have a pretty good idea of whether you're heading for trouble. Too much debt starts flashing these warning signals:

- **You find it more and more difficult** each month to make ends meet.
- **It's taking extraordinary effort** to pay your ordinary expenses. Perhaps you rely heavily on overtime pay or income from moonlighting, just to pay the rent and buy the groceries.
- **You've picked up the habit** of paying only the minimum due on your credit card bills each month, and sometimes you juggle payments, stalling one company to pay another.

If you're having a problem with debt, solving it should go right to the top of your list of financial priorities.

■ **You can't save even small amounts** and don't have enough set aside to get you through such setbacks as a pay cut, an unexpected car repair, or an emergency visit to your parents.

Even if you seem to be getting along fine, you should examine your debt situation occasionally. For instance, you might take a stab at filling out the debt worksheet on the opposite page. Use your checkbook and credit card statements to find information on expenses. Where you have to estimate, be realistic, not optimistic. (If you filled out the cash-flow form on page 5, this form will be easy.)

Pay attention not only to how much you have to pay each month but also to how many months into the future you'll be stuck with those payments. If you quit using credit today, for example, how long would it take to pay off your nonmortgage debts? Six months? A year? Longer?

The worksheet shows you the maximum amount you can afford to pay on debts each month. How close you want to come to that limit is your call. Base it on these considerations: How secure is your income? Can you count on raises every year? How far down the road have payments on today's debts pushed the starting date for an investment program?

Set a debt limit that considers what you can afford today and, just as important, what today's obligations are borrowing from tomorrow. If debt is a problem, solving it should go right to the top of your list of financial priorities.

How to Get Out of Debt

Whatever the elusive "proper" level of debt may be, a lot of people are exceeding it. Despite generally widespread prosperity for the past decade or so, Americans have been going broke in record numbers, filing for personal bankruptcy as never before. If you see such drastic action looming in your future, better to take some steps now before your credit rating is ruined.

SIZING UP YOUR DEBTS

Use this worksheet to set a personal debt limit.

1. Figure your monthly income

Your take-home pay	$ _____	
Spouse's take-home pay	_____	
Other regular income	_____	
A. Total monthly income		$ _____

2. Figure your monthly expenses

Rent or mortgage	$ _____	
Food	_____	
Utilities	_____	
Savings and investments	_____	
Insurance	_____	
Charitable contributions	_____	
Transportation and auto maintenance	_____	
Entertainment	_____	
All other	_____	
B. Total monthly expenses		$ _____

3. Figure your annual expenses

Taxes (not deducted from pay or included in mortgage payment)	$ _____	
Insurance (not paid monthly)	_____	
Medical and dental bills	_____	
School costs	_____	
Major purchases and repairs	_____	
Vacation	_____	
Clothing	_____	
All other	_____	
C. Total annual expenses		$ _____

4. Divide C by 12 to find the amount to set aside monthly to cover these expenses

D. Total to set aside monthly for annual expenses	$ _____
E. Total monthly expenses (B+D)	$ _____

5. Figure your payments on current debts Monthly expenses (credit cards, car loan, etc.)

	MONTHLY PAYMENT	BALANCE	MONTHS LEFT
_____	_____	_____	_____
_____	_____	_____	_____
_____	_____	_____	_____
F. Total payments on current debt		$ _____	
G. Total monthly outlay (E+F)		$ _____	

6. Compare total on line (G) to monthly income (A)

If you know things are going to get worse before they get better, call creditors and spill the beans. They might be willing to stretch out payments.

Roll Your Debts into a Lower-Rate Loan

Perhaps you can reduce your monthly payments by combining your major debts into a longer-term loan at a lower interest rate. This can be an especially rewarding strategy for credit card debt, which clobbers you with the highest interest around. A home-equity loan or a loan from a 401(k) plan at work may make sense. The rate will be lower, and you'll reduce the number of checks you have to write each month. But before you take this step, read the sections about home-equity loans on page 41 and 401(k) loans in Chapter 29.

Switch to a Lower-Rate Credit Card

Credit card offers are everywhere, and card issuers will gladly arrange for you to roll balances on existing cards into a new account with them provided your credit rating is still good (see below). Just make sure that you don't sign up for a low introductory rate that converts to a high rate after only a few months.

Check Your Credit Record

You can get a free credit report if you've been denied credit in the past 60 days. Also, federal law requires the credit-reporting firms to provide free reports to people who are out of work and looking, who are on welfare, or who believe that their credit record is inaccurate because of fraud. And the Fair and Accurate Credit Transactions Act (FACT Act), which became effective in September 2005, provides that all U.S. residents are entitled to an annual free credit report from each of the credit-reporting agencies. For a free report, call 877-322-8228 or order online at http://www.annualcreditreport.com. The credit-reporting agencies are Equifax (800-685-1111; http://www.econsumer.equifax.com), Experian (800-311-4769; http://www.experian.com), and Trans Union (800-888-4213; http://www.transunion.com).

Confess to Your Creditors

If you know things are going to get worse before they get better, call your creditors and spill the beans. Tell them you that can't pay on time but are determined to pay them back. Could they possibly stretch out the payments for you? Some will do it, and some will even waive interest and late fees for a while. If you get such an agreement, follow up with a letter to the company describing the terms you discussed. This protects you later if the company decides to change its mind.

Know Your Rights
See the section on credit rights later in this chapter.

Get Some Help
If things are looking bleak and you can't handle it alone, consider calling the nonprofit National Foundation for Credit Counseling (NFCC) (http://www.debtadvice.org; 800-388-2227), which operates more than 2,000 local offices. The national number will put you in touch with the local office of the Consumer Credit Counseling Service (CCCS), where counselors can help you set up a repayment program and negotiate with your creditors for reduced monthly payments and lower—or even waived—finance charges. The CCCS then helps you set up a budget that calls for you to make one monthly payment to the service, which parcels it out to your creditors. There may be a small fee involved.

Why would creditors agree to such a program? For one thing, half a loaf is better than none: This way they are assured of getting at least some of their money from borrowers who might otherwise pay back nothing. In fact, creditors are so anxious to cooperate that they often pay the CCCS a percentage of the money they collect. This is a next-to-last resort, but you said you were desperate, right?

Declare Bankruptcy
When you can't possibly pay what you owe and informal arrangements with creditors have failed, it might be time to think about declaring bankruptcy. Remember, bankruptcy is a last-ditch solution, and it's not a do-it-yourself proposition; you'll want to hire an attorney with expertise in bankruptcy to help you make important decisions that will affect the outcome. The

Bankruptcy is a last-ditch solution, and it's not a do-it-yourself proposition; hire an attorney with expertise in bankruptcy to help you make important decisions.

A bankruptcy stays in your credit file for seven to ten years. You may be able to qualify for new credit during that time, but not on terms you'll like.

Bankruptcy Abuse Prevention and Consumer Protection Act of 2005 makes declaring bankruptcy more difficult and requires increased paperwork, more stringent limitations, and financial counseling from an approved nonprofit credit counseling service.

What kind for you? Individuals in tough financial straits typically can declare one of three types of bankruptcy: Chapter 7, Chapter 11, or Chapter 13.

In Chapter 7, known as straight bankruptcy, you give up your property to the court, which will divide it among your creditors, and ask the court to erase your debts. (The court can't repossess certain exempt property, which the law deems necessary for your survival. That might include, for example, a certain amount of your equity in a residence or a motor vehicle.)

In order to qualify for Chapter 7 bankruptcy you must pass a "means test" involving an analysis of your income and expenses. If the test results show that your discretionary income is below $100 a month, you can file for Chapter 7. If discretionary income is over $100, you will have to file Chapter 13.

A provision of the new law bars filers who owe more than about $1.2 million from filing under Chapter 13, but allows them into Chapter 11, which is usually meant for businesses. Since Chapter 11 is designed to keep a business going, it allows the debtor to retain income earned after the bankruptcy filing while using only assets he had at the time of filing to pay past debts.

If you find yourself considering filing for bankruptcy, think again. You shouldn't take this step before you have exhausted the options outlined above. A bankruptcy stays in your credit file for seven to ten years. You may be able to qualify for new credit during that time, but not on terms you'll like.

Finding the Best Credit Deals

The best way to stay out of credit trouble is to borrow sparingly. The second-best way is to know what you're talking about and, perhaps even more important, what you're hearing when you do borrow.

When you're shopping for the best credit deal, whether it's a plastic card or a paper mortgage, the only basis of comparison to use is the annual percentage rate (APR). It is figured on the size of the unpaid balance, which shrinks as you pay off the loan. The federal Truth in Lending Act requires that lenders use APR when quoting interest rates, so that you can be sure you're comparing apples with apples. If the rate you're quoted sounds suspiciously low or if the lender quotes you only a monthly dollar payment, make sure to get the APR. If you're still unsure of a rate you're quoted, check it with another lender.

There are different kinds of credit, different sources of credit, and different prices for credit. It pays you, literally, to know the difference. Here are some credit rules of thumb that are worth remembering when you're in the market for a loan.

- **Finance companies charge higher interest rates** than banks, which generally charge higher rates than credit unions.
- **Secured loans**—that is, loans backed by some sort of collateral, which the lender takes if you default—cost less than unsecured loans.
- **Some kinds of collateral provide better security than others.** For example, you'll get a lower rate on a new-car loan than on a used-car loan, and you'll get a lower rate on a first mortgage than on a second mortgage.
- **The longer the term of a loan, the lower the monthly payments**—but the more interest you'll pay before it's over.

Credit à la Card

When discussing the kind of credit that comes with a plastic card, the first distinction to make is between charge cards and credit cards. American Express Green Card and Gold Card and Diners Club Charge Card are charge cards. You are expected to pay their bills in full within a specified

> **There are different kinds of credit, different sources of credit, and different prices for credit. It pays you, literally, to know the difference.**

Pay a credit card bill in full before the grace period runs out, and you get, in effect, a free loan — the closest you'll come to free money.

time period. If you don't, you'll be penalized (more about them later).

Visa, MasterCard, Discover, and other credit cards (including some offered by companies that also issue charge cards) don't necessarily encourage you to pay your bill in full because they profit by charging interest—lots of interest—on the unpaid balance. The smart way to use credit cards is to use them as if they were charge cards: Pay your bill in full each month. Often the card will allow a grace period of 20 to 25 days from the date you're billed before interest begins accruing. If you pay the bill in full before the grace period runs out, you get, in effect, a free loan. Deals like this make some credit cards the closest you'll ever come to free money. And if you make your purchases right after your billing date, you can stretch the term of this free-money period to nearly two months.

Unfortunately, grace periods aren't universally available. Many card issuers start charging interest from the date of a purchase if you carry over a balance. This system is also popular among department stores that issue their own credit cards. Nevertheless, you can still keep the cost of your multipurpose cards under control if you keep an eye on the charges you're paying.

Compare cards on the following features.

ANNUAL FEES. These charges, if any, range from an average of $0 to $20 for the run-of-the-mill Visa or Master-Card, to $0 to $50 or so for a gold card. As the credit card business has grown more competitive, card issuers have shown a willingness to drop the annual fee for customers they'd like to keep. If you think your fee is too high, ask to have it waived. Explain that you've been a good customer and you don't see why you should have to pay a fee when so many cards are available without one. If you have been a good customer, odds are good that the company will drop the fee (and you will have earned back the price of this book).

FEES FOR "FREE RIDERS." Pay your bills on time and you pay no interest, right? Yes, but some card issuers have found a way to sock it to free riders like you, who have the audacity to pay off their balances in full before incurring any interest charges. Some simply levy a different charge, perhaps by nicking you with a small fee each time you use the card. Cardholders who run up interest charges for the month escape the fee, as do cardholders who use the card frequently (generating fees paid by the merchants who accept the card). But if you find yourself with a card like this, look for a different one.

INTEREST RATES. Interest rates are set by the bank or savings and loan that issues your credit card, not by the card company. Issuers have to stay under the interest limits set by the state in which their headquarters are chartered. But that's rarely much comfort because the limits are often 13 to 16 percent, or more. Introductory rates, which may last six months or a year, are often lower.

OTHER FEES AND CHARGES. You will be charged interest on cash advances, a fee for paying late, and a fee for exceeding your credit limit.

PROTECTION AGAINST FRAUD. Plastic credit is pretty safe. If your card or your card number is used fraudulently by someone else, the law limits your liability to $50, and issuing banks often don't make customers pay even that much. If your account is used fraudulently to charge something without actually showing the card—say, if someone orders merchandise over the phone or online—you owe nothing. All this is provided you report the fraud within 60 days of the date of the statement on which it appears.

Finding the Best Credit Card Deal

The great variety of credit card fees can work to your advantage. If you aren't satisfied with the terms your card company is offering, you may be able to find a less expensive plan somewhere else. The way you use your credit card should determine which pricing scheme works out best for you.

> Interest rates are set by the bank or savings and loan that issues your credit card, not by the card company.

KEEP YOUR INTEREST RATE LOW—AND AVOID THOSE FEES

Like a lot of other things in life, credit card rules used to be simpler. But then came rebates, balance transfers, and a wave of penalties for day-late and dollar-over-the-limit transgressions. Today, keeping a low interest rate, avoiding penalties, and making sense of rebate programs takes a rule book worthy of Hoyle. The queries and answers below can help you make the most of the cards you hold and anticipate the aces up the issuer's sleeve.

Q: *I love a good deal. To take advantage of low introductory rates, I've opened and closed a dozen accounts in the past three years. Will that hurt my credit rating?*
A: There's nothing wrong with chasing teaser rates, but it's important to close your old accounts and make sure your credit report reflects that they were "closed by customer." Otherwise you could be denied a loan because you have too much available credit. In addition, some credit card issuers have begun to screen out people who jump from card to card, so you might be turned down for a card at some point. Just in case, favor cards that give you a low rate even after the introductory period is over.

Finally, keep an eye on the fine print. A few issuers have tried to impose account-closing fees, or charge a fee for using a convenience check to transfer your balance.

Q: *My balance includes purchases, cash advances, and balance transfers, each of which carries a different interest rate. The bank applies my payment to the transferred balance* first because it has the lowest interest rate. Is there a way to apply the payment to purchases or cash advances instead?
A: Your bank's policy is common—there's no federal or state law that requires creditors to allocate your payment in any particular manner. The best way around the practice is to transfer your balance to a new card with a low interest rate for balance transfers. Then use a separate, low-rate card for new purchases and cash advances and pay off the card with the higher rate first.

Q: *I signed up for a card with a 7.9% rate, and later I got a solicitation for the same card with a 5.9% rate. Can I get the lower rate?*
A: Ask for it. Because it costs card issuers a lot more to acquire a new customer than to retain an old one, the lower rate is probably yours for the asking.

Q: *I mailed in my credit card payment on time, but the bank says it arrived late. Can I do anything to avoid a late fee and interest?*

DO YOU PAY YOUR BILL IN FULL EVERY MONTH? In this case, you don't care about the APR but still need to find an account that doesn't start charging interest from the date of purchase. Look for the longest grace period you can find.

A: A phone call may be all it takes to remove the charge, especially if you have a clean record. Or you can dispute the fee as a billing error by writing the issuer within 60 days of your statement date. (You may be able to bolster your case by finding out when your check cleared.)

If the bank won't budge, your options aren't great. You can cancel the card and refuse to pay the fee; if it shows up on your credit report, you'll want to add a notation that you dispute the entry. It might be easier to cough up the fee and let it go. But that can make matters worse, as some banks are switching customers who pay late more than once to higher interest rates.

One way to avoid the problem altogether is to use a bill-paying service, such as Quicken (http://www.quicken.com) or CheckFree (http://www.checkfree.com). Most guarantee that your payment will arrive on time if you send instructions four or five business days before the due date.

Q: *I never got my bill this month. Am I stuck if I don't pay on time?*
A: Unfortunately, yes. According to Federal Reserve regulations, banks must send you a statement at least 14 days before your payment is due. But you're still responsible for paying on time, even if the bill doesn't arrive. If you're going to move, give card issuers your new address well ahead of time.

Q: *My card issuer is about to raise my interest rate. Can I ditch the card and pay off the balance over time at the current rate?*
A: Usually, yes. Credit card issuers in several states (including Delaware, where many issuers are based) are required to let you pay off your balance at the old rate as long as you close the account to new charges. Even in states where there is no such law, many card issuers offer the same arrangement. But if you use the card after the new rate takes effect, you will have automatically accepted the new terms.

Q: *I hadn't used my credit card for about a year when my bank suddenly canceled my account. Can a bank do that?*
A: Afraid so. Even if your account is in good standing and you haven't been late with a payment even once, an issuer has the right to rescind your card. Some have even closed accounts on active customers because they incurred no fees or interest charges.

DO YOU CARRY OVER BALANCES? Then you'll be paying interest on interest. Look for the lowest interest-rate-and-fee combination.

Because both Visa and MasterCard are welcome just about anywhere credit cards are used in this coun-

Watch for deals offered by the banks that issue credit cards, and by the bankcards' most serious competitors.

try, acceptability should have nothing to do with which one you choose. Watch for special deals offered by the banks that issue these cards, and by the bankcards' most serious competitors, such as Discover and the general-purpose cards issued by airlines, phone companies, and auto manufacturers. The market is awash with cards that reward customers with frequent-flier miles on selected airlines, or discounts on cars or other major purchases. Since the terms of these deals change so frequently, your own alertness is your best hope for finding offers that reward people with your particular spending pattern.

Credit card deals change frequently. You can keep up by consulting the listings in *Kiplinger's Personal Finance* magazine and other financial publications. For more frequent updates, consult the Kiplinger Web site (http://www.kiplinger.com) or those of Bankrate Inc. (http://www.bankrate.com) or BanxQuote (http://www.banxquote.com).

Travel and Entertainment Cards

Travel and entertainment (T&E) cards, such as those issued by American Express and Diners Club, are charge cards, not credit cards. That means you are expected to pay your bill in full each month, although they may allow you to stretch out payments by establishing a line of credit with an affiliated bank.

Membership fees for T&E cards are higher than for bank-issued cards, and the kinds of service they offer—an annual accounting of charges, traveler's checks, cash in an emergency—are commonly available with bankcards, too, especially gold cards. You may be able to get a bigger credit line with a T&E card, but they're not as widely accepted as, say, Visa or MasterCard. While there may be a resort or a store here and there that accepts these cards and excludes bankcards, you'd have to work hard to find it.

Debit Cards

A debit card appears to work the same way as a credit card: The merchant runs it through a little machine and off you go without any cash actually changing hands. But that's where the similarity ends. When you use a debit card, the amount of your purchase is deducted from your checking account or some other account you have designated. It's useful to think of a debit card as a paperless check that clears immediately, with no grace period, or "float." If you're not paying close attention, you may find yourself carrying a debit card from your bank that you think is a credit card. That mistake usually lasts no longer than the arrival of your first bank statement showing your depleted balance.

The main use for debit cards used to be to get cash from automated teller machines, but devices known as point of sale terminals have been installed in an increasing number of retail outlets. If you offer a debit card for a purchase and your balance shows up as insufficient, the terminal will disallow the transaction unless you have an overdraft credit line (see the discussion below).

Two key facts to remember about debit cards:

1. Although they look like credit cards, they aren't.

2. Safeguards against loss or theft and unauthorized use of your card aren't as strict as they are with credit cards. By law, you're liable for the same $50 as with a credit card, but only if you report an unauthorized transaction within two business days of discovering it. Miss that deadline and you're legally responsible for up to $500. But MasterCard and Visa will waive it entirely in many cases.

Other Lines of Instant Credit

Credit cards are convenient, but with annual fees or higher interest rates, they can also be expensive. There are other sources of "instant" credit, a few of which are available at bargain rates.

Overdraft Protection
This arrangement allows you to write checks for more money than you have in your account. It's convenient in an emergency, and you avoid overdraft charges. In addition, some banks will charge overdrafts to your home-

If you're carrying a debit card you think is a credit card, the mistake usually lasts no longer than the arrival of your bank statement showing your depleted balance.

One potential drawback of overdraft credit lines is that there's often no compulsion to repay them in full right away.

equity line of credit, if you have one (see page 41), thus giving you a source of tax-deductible interest at a pretty low rate. It is one of the easiest sources of credit to use; unfortunately, it is also one of the easiest to misuse.

As with credit cards, interest rates vary among banks. Because checks cost much less to process than loan applications, banks may offer lower rates on overdraft accounts than on personal loans, especially small ones.

Because the interest on overdraft accounts is usually lower than the interest on credit card balances, these accounts can come in handy if you want to pay credit card bills in full but don't have the cash.

You can lose the interest-rate advantage if the bank imposes a transaction fee each time you write a check. Even if the fee sounds small, it can have a significant effect. Suppose your overdraft account carries a 12 percent APR (1 percent per month) and a 50-cent fee for each check. And suppose you write a $100 overdraft check and pay it back one month later. You will have paid a total charge of $1.50 for the month—the same as an APR of 18 percent ($12 \times \$1.50 = \$18$). Whatever interest is charged, you will pay it from the date of the transaction; overdraft lines of credit don't have grace days.

Odds are that your bank will not advance you money in the exact amounts that you request it. Overdraft loans are commonly made only in multiples of $50 or $100. If your bank uses the $100-multiple system, and you write a check that overdraws your account by $210, you'll have to pay interest on a $300 loan. (You will, however, have $90 left in your checking account.)

One potential drawback of overdraft credit lines is that there's often no compulsion to repay them in full right away. Some banks automatically deduct a minimum monthly payment from your checking account, but as with all minimum payments, you don't make much headway. You may find your supposedly revolving line of credit has turned into a permanent debt.

Credit Card Cash Advances

Credit card cash-advance privileges have many of the same advantages and disadvantages of overdraft accounts. Interest rates may be lower than on charges, but as a rule they're assessed from the date of the transaction, with no grace period. And a low interest rate can be, in effect, considerably higher if there's a transaction fee.

Retail Installment Credit

When you buy a big-ticket item such as furniture or a major appliance, you often have the option of paying the retailer in equal installments over a set number of months. This kind of credit may sound convenient, but it can also be expensive.

Before you sign on the dotted line, consider how the retailer's APR stacks up against what you would pay if you got a loan from a credit union, wrote a check on your overdraft account, or used your credit card.

Borrowing with Collateral

Pledging collateral can help you get a bigger loan than you could get on an unsecured basis, or a break on the interest rate. Most lenders want only highly liquid assets as collateral, things that can easily be sold for cash if they must be seized to pay off the loan.

Equity in Your Home

You can tap into your home equity by refinancing your existing first mortgage, by taking out a second mortgage, or by using a home-equity line of credit.

With refinancing you negotiate a new first mortgage, use all or part of the proceeds to pay what's due on the existing loan, and pocket any difference.

If you have a low-interest loan and need to borrow more, though, it doesn't make much sense to refinance the loan. Better to keep it and borrow against your equity via a second mortgage, also called a junior mortgage. A straight second mortgage works just like a regular mortgage (see Chapter 6), although it usually lasts only

> **If you have a low-interest loan and need to borrow more, it doesn't make much sense to refinance the loan. Better to keep it and borrow against your equity.**

SIZING UP HOME-EQUITY LOANS

Knowing the answers to these questions, adapted from a Federal Trade Commission checklist, will help you compare home-equity loans from different lenders. Before you compare, have in mind how much you want to borrow.

	LENDER		
	A	B	C
What size credit line is available?			
What is the length of time for repayment?			
Is there access to loans by check or credit card?			
Is the interest rate fixed? What is it?			
Is the interest rate variable?			
What is the initial rate?			
What is the maximum rate possible?			
How often can the rate be adjusted?			
What index is used?			
What margin, if any, is added to the index?			
Can the loan be converted to a fixed rate?			
What closing costs does the borrower pay:			
Points (percent of line of credit)			
Application fee			
Title search fee			
Appraisal fee			
Lawyer fee			
Other fees			
Is there an annual fee? What is it?			
Are there fees per transaction?			
What are they?			
What are the repayment terms:			
Is the monthly payment fixed?			
How much is it?			
Is the monthly payment variable?			
How much is it to begin with?			
How much is the maximum?			
Do payments cover both principal and interest?			
Are payments interest-only?			
Is there a final balloon payment?			
Can a balloon be refinanced or extended?			
What's the penalty for late payments?			
What are the default provisions?			
Is there a penalty for early repayment?			

5 to 15 years or so rather than 25 or 30 years. These days, most second mortgages come in the form of a home-equity line of credit. Home-equity lines are available from banks, savings and loan associations, and even brokerage firms. They are secured by the equity in your home, meaning the lender will foreclose if you default.

It is sometimes possible to borrow 100 percent of your home's appraised market value, minus what you still owe on the first mortgage, but 80 percent or so is a more typical limit. In many cases, there are no closing costs, but check the fine print for annual fees or other miscellaneous charges.

When you want to use a home-equity credit line, you simply write a check or use a credit card for the amount you want to borrow. Interest generally runs one to three percentage points above the prime rate, adjusted monthly and capped at a certain level above the starting rate. You get five to ten years to repay, at which time you may have to pay off the whole thing. The main advantage of using a home-equity loan is that the interest is tax-deductible as long as the loan doesn't exceed $100,000.

Because a home-equity line of credit is, in effect, a second mortgage on your home, the application process is very similar to that for a mortgage. Use the form on the opposite page to compare the terms of loans you might consider. It shows that the best features of a particular loan aren't always obvious. You may not have to pay closing costs, for instance, but could get clobbered by lenders' fees, third-party fees, and rate increases. You may discover that a low initial rate that makes one loan sound attractive is outweighed by other factors that make another loan a better bet.

Life Insurance Policies

If you have permanent life insurance, when you pay your premium, part of it goes into a cash reserve. You can borrow against the accumulated cash value in your policy. It's quick, easy, and cheap. You can borrow up to 95 percent of the cash value at very good rates. Best of all, there is no set date for repayment of principal; you

Interest is usually tax-deductible on home-equity loans that don't exceed $100,000.

If you borrow against securities to buy more securities, interest is deductible if it doesn't exceed net investment income.

can even skip interest payments and have them added to the balance of the loan. Any balance due at your death will be deducted from the proceeds your beneficiary receives. If you've built up enough cash value, you may be able to withdraw money instead of borrowing it, reducing the cash value and possibly the death benefit. Check with your agent to see whether you can use this option.

Stocks and Bonds

Borrowing from the broker who holds your securities account can be an especially good deal for two reasons. First, rates are comparatively low—usually floating one to three percentage points above the prime rate. Second, if you use the money to buy more securities, you can deduct the interest you pay as an investment expense so long as it doesn't exceed your net investment income. There's no requirement that you use the money to buy more stocks or bonds, but if you don't, the interest falls under the consumer-interest rules and isn't deductible. (Borrowing on stocks to buy more stocks is usually referred to as buying "on margin," and it's used by some investors as a way to load up on stocks they think will rise. It creates "leverage" [see Chapter 26] and it's risky.) If you want a loan to buy more stocks, you can't borrow more than 50 percent of your stock's value.

On loans for other purposes, you might be able to borrow more than 50 percent of value by pledging your stocks as collateral for a loan from a bank. Bank policies could depend on what kind of stock you own. For example, a bank might lend up to 70 percent of the value of stocks traded on the New York Stock Exchange, less for stocks traded on the Nasdaq. The same bank might lend up to 90 percent of the value of Treasury bills.

If you pledge securities, the bank will hold them for the life of the loan and keep an eye on the market. If the value of your stock tumbles, the bank can require additional collateral and might call in the loan (make you pay in full) if you can't provide it. Same goes for the broker, who will issue a "margin call." That could force the sale of your stock at a depressed value.

Other Kinds of Loans

There are several methods of getting a loan without putting up anything as collateral. These loans are made by banks, credit unions, and finance companies and are based on your signature, and perhaps your spouse's, and your promise to repay the debt.

Unsecured Personal Loans

Usually, the top amount that you can get easily and quickly with this type of loan is a few thousand dollars from a bank, perhaps more from some specialized finance companies. Interest rates can run high; repayment periods normally range from 12 to 36 months.

You can arrange to pay back a personal loan in either fixed monthly installments or one flat payment at the end of a set term. There are advantages either way. Lenders usually prefer monthly installments, which enable you to climb slowly and steadily out of debt. On the other hand, if you can count on some future sizable lump-sum income, such as a bonus, you might prefer a single payment. The repayment plan selected may have a bearing on the interest rate you'll be charged.

Because the lender's means of getting its money back is more complicated if you default, the interest rate you pay on an unsecured loan will be higher than for a collateralized loan.

Debt-Consolidation Loans

There is nothing basically wrong with the idea of borrowing money to pay your debts, as long as you realize that consolidating bills doesn't eliminate them. Used wisely, a consolidation loan can get you through a period of income reduction or an emergency that puts a sudden drain on the funds normally available for debt payments. It can be a way to get back on course if you find yourself temporarily overextended. In fact, it might be a more convenient, even cheaper, way to pay off some debts. You could consolidate them into a home-equity loan, for instance, or you could roll several high-rate credit card balances into one lower-rate card.

There is nothing basically wrong with the idea of borrowing money to pay your debts, as long as you realize that consolidating bills doesn't eliminate them.

One reason lenders are leaning on computers to make their decisions: Federal law limits the criteria that can be used to decide who will get credit.

If you must consolidate, figure out precisely how much you need to do the job and borrow that amount—no more, no less. Aim for the lowest possible interest rate on an installment schedule that fits your situation. Don't take on bigger payments just to reduce the term of the loan, or you may end up as harried as before. And avoid interest-only payments that come with a final balloon payment calling for the principal in one lump sum. If you don't have a monthly payment obligation, you may be lulled deeper into debt.

How Lenders Size You Up

In essence, your application is a test, usually scored by a computer, and how high you score depends on how many points you get for your answers to such questions as: How long have you been in the same job? Do you own your home or rent? How many credit cards do you have? Owning a home might be worth 15 points, for example, compared with 5 for renting. If you score enough points on a dozen or so questions, you get the credit; if not, you don't.

The questions that make up the test, and the score needed to pass, often depend on where you live as well as what kind of credit you want and the creditor's experience with previous customers. A computer identifies the characteristics that most clearly distinguish customers who paid their bills as agreed from those who did not, and it assigns point values to specific attributes. It then predicts the creditworthiness of applicants whose answers add up to certain scores.

One reason for the use of computer analysis as a basis for credit decisions is that the growth of credit markets to include nationwide retailers and credit card issuers has made it comparatively rare for a lender to know applicants or their references personally. With the loss of such firsthand information, the methods of winnowing out bad credit risks have grown impersonal.

But there's another reason lenders are leaning on computers to make their decisions. Federal law limits the criteria that can be used to decide who will get credit. The Equal Credit Opportunity Act prohibits discrimination on a number of grounds. A lender can program a computer to consider only legally permissible information and to apply the same standards to all applicants.

This does not mean that all credit-scoring systems use the same criteria. A trait that is valuable in one system may carry little weight in another. A doctor, for example, might win high points for his profession from a bank but very few from a finance company, which might wonder why such a high-income individual would show up at its door.

Although the way you've handled credit in the past—your credit record—is considered by most lenders to be the best predictor of your future performance, it might not be scored. Many creditors check with a credit bureau only if a score falls in a gray area between automatic approval and automatic rejection. When it is considered, a bad credit record—several late payments, for instance—can knock down an otherwise passing grade. A good record might boost your score to the approval level.

If You Are Denied Credit

What if you are denied credit? If a credit report helped tip the scales against you, you must be told the name of the bureau that provided the information so you have an opportunity to find out whether outdated or erroneous data killed the deal. If you're turned down for credit, take the time to find out what the credit bureau is saying about you. The federal Fair Credit Reporting Act arms you with the following weapons:

- **You have the right to receive a copy** of your report at no charge if you've been denied credit within the past 60 days. (You are also entitled to annual free credit reports. See page 30.)
- **You have the right to expect the credit bureau to investigate** any errors that you report, and to recontact the creditor who reported the negative information.

If you're turned down for credit, take the time to find out what the credit bureau is saying about you.

If you find information in your credit record that's wrong, demand that the credit bureau investigate. If it can't verify the item, the information must be dropped from your file.

■ **If the creditor involved confirms the information** but you still think it's wrong, you can add a short statement to your file, telling your side of the story.

What to Do

Start by calling the credit bureau in question and getting your report mailed to you. If you're dealing with a local credit bureau, arrange for an appointment to go over your file.

When you examine your report, you should not see any negative information more than seven years old, unless you have been declared bankrupt. Federal law requires that most unfavorable reports be purged after seven years (ten in the case of bankruptcy) so that past financial problems won't haunt someone for life.

If you find any information in your credit record that's wrong, demand that the credit bureau investigate the report. If it can't verify the accuracy of the item, the information must be dropped from your file. When unfavorable information is accurate, you may be able to minimize its damage by attaching to the report a short statement. If you missed several payments during a period in which you were unemployed or ill, for example, an explanation of the extenuating circumstances might give you a better chance with the next potential creditor who calls up your report.

Assuming your report is changed after your review, either because negative information is dropped or because an explanation is attached, you can have the credit bureau send the revised report to credit grantors who got the original version during the previous six months.

Other Laws That Protect Your Rights

When you apply for and use credit, you should expect a fair deal from the lender. In addition to the Fair Credit Reporting Act, and the Fair and Accurate Credit Transactions Act, three other federal laws protect your rights: the Truth in Lending Act requires the lender to disclose the terms of the deal in a way you can understand; the Equal Credit Opportunity Act prohibits unfair discrimination in the granting of credit; and the Fair Credit Billing Act, which is designed to prevent foul-ups on your bills and help straighten them out when they do occur. You could benefit from detailed knowledge of these laws.

The Truth in Lending Act

Federal truth-in-lending rules require that lenders express the cost of borrowing as the annual percentage rate, or APR. This piece of information, which allows you to compare like quantities, is essential for shopping the cost of loans. The APR and the method of calculating the finance charge must appear prominently on lenders' loan disclosure forms; otherwise, they are not in compliance with truth-in-lending rules.

The Equal Credit Opportunity Act

This law says that you cannot be denied credit because of sex, marital status, age, race, color, religion, national origin, your receipt of public-assistance income, or your exercise of your rights under truth-in-lending and other credit laws. Understand that neither this law nor any other guarantees anyone credit. There are many valid reasons for a creditor to deny credit. But the law does guarantee that your creditworthiness will be evaluated on the same basis as that of all other customers. The law contains a number of special provisions designed to protect women:

- **When evaluating a joint application** by a husband and wife, creditors must consider the wife's income, even if it is from a part-time job, in the same way they consider the husband's in determining the couple's creditworthiness and allowable credit limit.
- **If you want them to,** creditors must count as income any alimony and child-support payments to the extent that they are likely to continue. If these payments are included as part of income on a credit application,

The Equal Credit Opportunity Act contains a number of special provisions designed to protect women.

Creditors must permit a woman to open and maintain credit accounts in her first name and married surname or combined surname, whichever she prefers, regardless of marital status.

then the lender can ask for proof that the income is reliable (copies of court judgments, checks, and the like), and the lender is also entitled to check on the credit record of the ex-spouse if it is available.

- **Creditors must permit a woman** to open and maintain credit accounts in her first name and married surname or combined surname, whichever she prefers, regardless of marital status. For example, if Jane Doe marries Robert Smith and takes his name, she has a right to obtain credit as Jane Smith or Jane Doe Smith. If she keeps her own name, of course, she has the right to obtain credit as Jane Doe.

- **When checking on the history of any kind of account,** joint or separate, used by a woman or her husband, late husband, or former husband, the creditor must take into account any additional information she presents to show that the credit history being considered does not accurately reflect her willingness and ability to repay debts. This protects her from getting poor marks as a result of an unpaid bill that was solely her husband's responsibility, or such things as a creditor's failure to clear the record on an account mix-up.

- **When creditors pass along information** about an account to credit bureaus or other agencies, they must report all information on joint accounts in the names of both spouses if both use the account or are liable for it. This is to ensure that both husband and wife get equal acknowledgment for the credit history.

- **If lenders deny credit or close an account,** the borrowers have the right to know the specific reasons, so they can compare them with anything they might have been told that leads them to believe discrimination was the reason.

- **Creditors must not discourage people** from applying for credit because of their sex or marital status, and they must not consider an applicant's sex or marital status in any credit-scoring systems they have for evaluating creditworthiness.

- **They cannot refuse to grant husband and wife** separate credit accounts if each is creditworthy without relying on the other's income or credit history.

- **Creditors cannot ask about childbearing intentions** or capability, or birth-control practices, whether a woman is applying individually or jointly.
- **They cannot require a cosignature on a loan** or credit account unless the same requirement is imposed on all similarly qualified applicants—that is, others whose income, existing debt obligations, and credit history are comparable.
- **They must not change the conditions** of a credit account or close it solely because of a change in marital status while the borrower is contractually liable for it. However, they can require the borrower to reapply for the credit when the marital status changes, if the credit was initially granted in part because of a spouse's income.
- **They must not ask for information** about a woman's husband unless he will be liable for or will use the credit account or loan, they live in a state with community-property laws, she is relying on alimony provided by him as part of the income listed in credit applications, or she is applying for a student loan.

The Fair Credit Billing Act

The heart of the Fair Credit Billing Act obligates credit card issuers and firms that extend revolving-type credit to do the following:

- **Credit payments to your account** the day the payments are received at the address the company has specified, so that you don't run up finance charges after you've paid the bill.
- **Mail your bill at least** 14 days before payment is due, if your account is the type that gives you a period of time to pay before finance charges are assessed.
- **Send you a detailed explanation** of your rights and remedies under this law twice a year or, if the company prefers, enclose a brief explanation with every bill and send the longer explanation when you ask for it or when you complain about a billing error.
- **Follow certain procedures** in resolving complaints you may make about billing errors. Six common types of situations covered are:

Creditors must not change the conditions of a credit account or close it solely because of a change in marital status while the borrower is contractually liable for it.

While a charge on a bill is in dispute, you don't have to pay the disputed item.

1. *An unauthorized charge on your bill,* for which you received no goods or services, or a charge that is for a wrong amount or a wrong date or is not correctly identified.
2. *A charge or debt for which you want an explanation or clarification.* Example: You need to see the creditor's documentation before paying for an item.
3. *A charge for goods or services that were not delivered to you or were not accepted by you in accordance with your agreement with the seller.* Example: a charge for something that was delivered in the wrong quantity or size.
4. *A failure to properly reflect a payment or credit to your account.*
5. *A computation or accounting mistake.* Example: computing finance or late-payment charges incorrectly.
6. *An additional finance charge or minimum payment due that resulted from the creditor's failure to deliver a bill to your current address.* However, if you moved, you must have notified the creditor of your address change at least ten days before the closing date of the billing cycle.

If you run into any of those problems, here's what the law provides.

You must write to the creditor. Telephoning may not preserve your rights under the law. Include in the letter your name and account number; a description of the error, including an explanation of why you believe it to be an error; the dollar amount involved; and any other information (such as your address, including zip code) that will help identify you or the reason for your complaint or inquiry. You have 60 days from the postmark on the questioned bill to get your letter to the creditor. The creditor must acknowledge your letter within 30 days of receiving it and resolve the matter within 90 days or explain in writing within that time why it considers that no billing error occurred.

While an amount on a bill is in dispute, you needn't pay the disputed item. If you have a checking or savings account and a credit card account at the same bank, and your payments are made automatically, you can stop payment on the disputed amount or have it restored if you notify the card issuer of the error at least three business days before the scheduled billing date.

During the dispute-settlement period the creditor must not harass you. This means it cannot sue you, report you to a credit bureau as delinquent, close your account, deduct money from your other accounts to pay the amount, or otherwise hassle you about the disputed amount. It can, however, continue to include the disputed amount in your bills and levy finance charges against it, as long as it notes on the bill that disputed amounts don't have to be paid until the dispute is settled in the creditor's favor.

Your complaint has to be resolved in one of two ways: If your contention proves right, the creditor must correct the error and subtract any finance charges added as a result of it, then notify you of the correction. If the company turns out to be right, it must show you why the bill is correct. Then you'll have to pay the amount you disputed plus the finance charges added during the dispute. If you don't, the credit card company can start normal collection procedures against you.

Banking Today

Competition is fierce for your day-to-day financial business: savings and checking accounts, loans, investments, even insurance. You could accomplish virtually all of this in one place—one bank or savings and loan, one credit union, or one brokerage firm. But one-stop financial service may not be the smartest choice. Where you take your money should depend on considerations of convenience, costs, services, and safety. You won't always find the best of all four in one place.

Sizing Up Banks and S&Ls

Banks and savings and loan associations (sometimes called savings banks) have different histories and different traditions. But they are virtually indistinguishable from the consumer's point of view, so we'll consider them together. (Having an account at what's called a mutual savings bank makes you part owner of the bank and means you earn dividends instead of interest, but otherwise mutuals operate the same as conventional S&Ls.)

Convenience

It's probably safe to say that most people choose their bank or savings and loan on the basis of location, picking one that's closest to their home or job. Before you do that, however, drop into the branch you're considering to see how it handles its customer traffic during the peak lunch-hour rush, particularly on Fridays. Is there an express line for customers with simple deposits or withdrawals? Is there a single line that moves people

If you work in the city and live in the suburbs, make sure you'll be able to do your banking in either place.

most efficiently to the next available teller? Are there enough tellers? Are there 24-hour automated teller machines? If you work in the city and live in the suburbs, will you be able to do your banking in either place?

Costs

There are two sides to cost, or price. One is the rate the bank pays you on the kinds of accounts you have in mind; the other is the fees it charges you for those accounts. Only by matching one against the other can you know how much you are making—or paying—for doing your business at a particular institution. Shopping around is the only way to discover the best deal.

Some banks discourage small depositors by levying fees on accounts below a certain size or by charging for withdrawals over a certain number within a specified length of time. Even if you are not in the small-saver category, you could find yourself paying fees for services you used to get for free.

COMPARING INTEREST RATES. In comparing the interest you would earn on competing savings accounts and certificates of deposit, remember that your real yield, usually referred to as the effective yield, is determined by how often interest is compounded and how often it is credited to your account. It's easy to understand that if a bank credits your account with interest every day (even if it's only 1/365th of the annual rate), and compounds that interest daily, over the course of a year you will earn more than you would on an account that credits and compounds less frequently.

For example, a 5 percent nominal (stated) annual interest rate actually pays a 5.13 percent effective yield if interest is compounded daily, as shown in the table on the next page. What you gain on compounding, however, can easily be lost to infrequent crediting. If the interest isn't credited to your daily compounded account until the end of the quarter and you withdraw, say, $1,000 five days before the quarter ends, you usually lose all the interest earned on that amount up to that point.

COMPOUNDED RATES OF RETURN

Stated Annual Rate	Effective Annual Rate if Compounded	
	Quarterly	Daily
3%	3.03%	3.05%
4%	4.06	4.08
5%	5.10	5.13
6%	6.14	6.18
7%	7.19	7.25
8%	8.24	8.33

The ideal account is one that pays the highest rate, compounds interest daily (or "continuously," a formula that yields fractionally more), and credits interest daily to the day of withdrawal. Many institutions offer these day-of-deposit-to-day-of-withdrawal accounts.

Compounding practices also affect the yield from certificates of deposit. CDs are commonly advertised with both their nominal and effective yields, so you can spot the differences fairly easily. The more frequent the compounding, the higher the effective yield, as the table above shows.

Services

The variety of services available is limited mostly by the ingenuity of individual bankers and the competitive environment in which the bank operates.

At most banks you can find safe-deposit boxes; bill-payer accounts, which permit you to direct the bank by phone or personal computer to pay certain bills directly from your account; overdraft protection, which will automatically grant you a loan to cover any checks you write that exceed the balance in your checking account (see Chapter 3); direct deposit, through which your paycheck or other regular income, such as a Social Security check, is sent directly to your bank account; automated teller machines, or ATMs, at which you can do most of your banking business, including obtaining cash; and brokerage services, which permit you to buy

An ATM's business day may end earlier than the teller's window closes.

and sell stocks and bonds through your bank at a discount from the rates charged by full-service brokers. Some also have arrangements by which you can purchase insurance on your car, home, or life.

USING AN ATM. Because so much banking is done at ATMs, it's important to know how ATM transactions differ from old-fashioned face time with a teller.

Some nickel-and-dime you to death. Or, more accurately, some nick you for a dollar or two each time you use them. The damage usually occurs at "foreign" ATMs— that is, machines owned by an institution other than the bank at which you have your account. You're probably not going to be deterred by such a fee when you need the cash, but think about it: If you pay a dollar to withdraw $20, you're paying a commission of 5 percent. You'd pay that same dollar to withdraw $100, but it would represent only 1 percent of the transaction. So doesn't it make sense to draw out big amounts every once in a while rather than small amounts every day or two?

For deposits, machines may be slower than tellers. When you deposit a check at your own bank's ATM that's within 50 feet of the bank itself, the money must be available in your account within two business days for a local check and five days for an out-of-town check— same as if you'd handed it to a teller. But if you go around the corner to a foreign ATM where deposits are permitted, the bank gets five days to post the check to your account no matter where it came from. Also, cashier's checks, certified checks, and checks drawn on a Federal Reserve Bank take one day to clear when you hand them to a teller, but two days when you deposit them at an ATM. Finally, remember that an ATM's business day may end earlier than the teller's window closes, and that can also delay your access to funds.

Safety
Most banks, savings and loans, and mutual savings banks are members of the Federal Deposit Insurance

Corporation, a government agency that provides $100,000 of insurance per account. The insurance covers you in case the bank goes broke and can't return your money. Normally, all checking accounts, savings accounts, and CDs owned by one person at the same bank, including all its branches, count toward the $100,000 limit. But you can increase your coverage at the same bank by opening accounts in different categories of ownership.

A married couple, for example, could open individual accounts in each spouse's name plus a joint account in both names and qualify for $300,000 of insurance coverage.

Irrevocable trust accounts also qualify for separate coverage. Totten trust ("pay on death") accounts and revocable living trust accounts qualify if the beneficiary is a spouse, child, or grandchild. But the FDIC's rules concerning trust accounts are very complex. Check with the bank and get its response in writing. For more information on FDIC coverage, ask your bank or S&L for the FDIC publication, *Your Insured Deposit*, or check the FDIC's Web site, http://www.fdic.gov.

The most reliable way to make sure that an account is covered if you find yourself with more than $100,000 at a single institution is to move the excess to another bank.

What if your bank does go broke? As long as it's federally insured and your balance is under $100,000, you won't lose anything except possibly a few days' interest. In most cases a failing institution is merged with a healthy one, with no interruption in business. If an institution is shut down, you may have to wait a few days to get your money.

One thing you should know about savings and loans that makes some of them different from banks: A few states have their own insurance plans for state-chartered savings associations that aren't members of the FDIC. Spectacular collapses of state insurance systems in Ohio and Maryland in the mid-1980s, and in other states before that, should cause you to think long and hard before entrusting your savings to an institution that does not carry federal deposit insurance.

What if your bank goes broke? As long as it's federally insured and your balance is under $100,000, you won't lose anything except possibly a few days' interest.

If you're comfortable in the electronic environment, there's no reason not to do your banking online.

Banking Online

Millions of Americans do their banking from home via modems in their computers. Some gain access to their accounts via their bank's Web site; others use the bank's proprietary software, or some general personal-finance software such as *Quicken* or *Microsoft Money*.

The advantages of online banking are hard to beat: You can check your balance anytime day or night, seeing which checks have cleared and which haven't, whether interest has been credited or fees deducted. You can move money from checking to savings and vice versa. You can designate which bills to pay with which funds and when to pay them. Some banks offer online banking free. Others charge a fee for bill paying, plus perhaps regular checking-account fees.

If you're comfortable in this electronic environment, there's no reason not to do your banking online. Banking services take special measures to safeguard your online transactions by using firewalls and encrypting your account information to prevent hackers from performing unauthorized transactions with your money.

Before you bank online, make sure the bank is legitimate and the deposits are federally insured. Watch out for copycat Web sites that deliberately use a name or Web address similar to a real financial institution. Keep your personal information such as account numbers, PINs, and passwords private.

When you are online conducting a transaction, look for a closed padlock or key icon, which will indicate that your transaction is being encrypted and is secure.

Sizing Up Credit Unions
Convenience

By law, credit union members must have a common bond, such as working for the same employer, living in the same community, or belonging to the same professional association, church, or fraternal group. Even employees of different businesses in the same complex, such as a shopping center, can band together to form credit unions.

Costs

Unlike banks, credit unions are nonprofit organizations. Unconcerned with making a profit, they can often pay more interest on accounts and charge less in fees. They offer a distinct advantage for interest-earning checking accounts, which they call share-draft accounts, because on average they pay more interest and most impose no minimum-balance requirements. On the other side of the equation—rates charged on loans and fees charged on accounts—credit unions usually offer the best deal available. They generally charge less on credit card balances and less for car loans. If you are eligible to join a credit union, you should certainly compare what it has to offer with what's being offered elsewhere.

Services

With some major exceptions, credit unions tend to be on the small side and may not have the resources to offer the kind of services provided by banks and savings and loan associations. Thus they are often not all-purpose financial institutions. Their competitive edge comes chiefly from the rates they pay on savings and checking accounts and the rates they charge for loans.

Safety

The great majority of the nation's credit unions are federally insured by the National Credit Union Administration (NCUA), whose National Credit Union Insurance Fund provides the same coverage that FDIC does for banks and thrifts. But many credit unions carry only private insurance. If a credit union doesn't post a sign at the door or teller's window stating "Insured by the NCUA," ask whether the institution has federal insurance or is applying for it. If the answer is no, take your money elsewhere.

Sizing Up Brokerage Firms
Convenience

Most small towns have a bank or two to call their own, but residents may have to travel to the nearest city to

Unlike banks, credit unions are nonprofit organizations. Unconcerned with making a profit, they can often pay more interest on accounts and charge less in fees.

What makes brokerage houses eligible for consideration as substitutes for banks are the very attractive special accounts many of them have developed.

find a stockbroker. That's a useful reminder that no matter how much banks and brokerage firms have come to resemble each other over the years, they still serve largely different functions. Banks and S&Ls are for savers and borrowers; brokerage firms are for investors. Most brokerage offices are open only during normal business hours on weekdays, when the markets in which they trade are open, although telephone and online transactions are common in the off-hours.

Costs

The brokerage business is divided into two camps: full-service firms, which maintain research departments and issue a constant stream of recommendations for brokers to pass along to their customers, and discount firms, most of which simply take orders to buy and sell, passing along the benefits of their bare-bones approach in lower commissions. Merrill Lynch, Smith Barney, Morgan Stanley, and Prudential are a few well-known full-service houses. Charles Schwab, Fidelity Brokerage, and TD Waterhouse are among the prominent discounters (see Chapter 23). If you want the research services, you should expect to pay for them. But if you have your own sources for making investment decisions, there's no need to pay a brokerage firm for something you don't use. Either way, however, you should shop around. Call a number of firms and ask how much they would charge to perform the trade you have in mind. If you can't get a clear answer, keep looking.

Services

Most services offered by brokerages are designed for investors—that is, for buyers and sellers of stocks, bonds, shares in real estate syndicates, and so forth. Those sorts of transactions are discussed in later chapters.

ASSET-MANAGEMENT ACCOUNTS. What makes brokerage houses eligible for consideration as substitutes for banks are the very attractive special accounts many of them have developed. They are packages of financial services known generically as asset-management accounts (AMAs). Banks, brokerage houses, discount brokers, and even deep-discount brokers are competing to let you write checks, use a debit card, take out loans, pay bills, and trade stocks, bonds, and mutual funds. You receive only one statement each month, summing up all your transactions in one place.

To open an account, you'll generally need between $5,000 and $20,000 in a combination of cash, stocks, bonds, and mutual funds. Specific features, minimums, and fees vary, but these are the plans' chief attractions:

- **A money-market account.** Typically you can choose among a basic, taxable money-market fund, a tax-free fund, a U.S. government securities fund, and some single-state tax-free funds.
- **Automatic "sweep" of funds** into the money-market account. Most brokerages deposit all of your "idle" cash daily into an interest-earning money-market account. Others sweep only when such cash reaches a minimum amount. Idle cash might include dividends from stocks or interest from bonds you own.
- **The ability to write checks** based on the value of assets in your account. No-minimum, no-fee checking is typical. But there are important differences in services. Very few firms return canceled checks monthly. Most send only a list of checks, so if you need actual checks for your records, you must place a special order and pay a per-check fee. Some send substitute canceled checks or small reproductions of the checks.
- **A substantial line of credit.** A margin account lets you borrow against your securities on deposit with that broker. If, for example, you write a check, the brokerage computer will first look for any unswept cash waiting to go into a money-market account. Second, it will take the cash from your money-market fund, and third, it will lend you any cash needed to complete the transaction. So, if you write a $15,000 check against $10,000 in a money-market fund, you'll automatically borrow the extra $5,000. If the value of your underlying securities is insufficient to cover the loan, you could be forced to add to the account or sell part of your portfolio. However, the

To open an account, you'll generally need between $5,000 and $20,000 in a combination of cash, stocks, bonds, and mutual funds.

margin-loan rate is low, perhaps just a point or two above the prime rate.

- **Use of a debit or credit card** for making purchases or obtaining cash. This is usually a Visa or MasterCard debit card. Purchases are debited from your account either as they occur or monthly. Monthly debiting is better for you because of the extra float it provides: That's free money for a while.
- **A monthly statement** showing all transactions plus the current and previous months' account balances.
- **Other services.** Some asset-management accounts include such extras as ATM access, toll-free hotlines to handle questions about your account, increased insurance for your portfolio, bill-paying services, and direct deposit of regular checks, such as paychecks.

Costs range from nothing (at discount broker Charles Schwab) to $300 per year at Merrill Lynch, which includes a Visa gold card. Fidelity charges fees according to services used.

Comparison shop if you're in the market for one of these accounts. Look at different sponsors' required minimum opening amounts, annual fees, commission charges, and margin-loan rates, and see how they handle debit card or credit card transactions. Also check on how long it takes to sweep cash into the money-market fund, and look at how comprehensive and readable monthly statements are. Before you choose an account, study the sponsors' prospectuses and other literature.

Safety

The Securities Investor Protection Corp. (SIPC) is a federally chartered body that provides insurance for brokerage firms' customer accounts up to $500,000 on assets in stocks, bonds, or mutual funds, with a $100,000 limit on cash. Many firms purchase additional private insurance that jacks coverage into the millions. Note that the coverage is for broker insolvency, not market losses on your investments. If your broker does go broke, you'll be covered, although it could take several weeks or months for the SIPC to clear up the accounts.

Your Home

Part 2

Buying a Home

Chapter 5

Homeownership is an enduring part of the American dream, not to mention the American way of life. Better than six out of ten American households own the roof over their heads, and three of the other four aspire to own it. Homeownership is considered a sign of maturity, stability, and financial independence. It can even be the path to some profit.

This chapter will make the case for homeownership, describe the different forms it can take, and suggest ways to make your homebuying experience a happy one. Later chapters will go into the details of getting a mortgage, selling your home, and related topics.

Three Reasons to Own
You Get a Tax Shelter
Unmatched Anywhere Else

It may not be fair to renters, but the tax laws favor homeowners—no question about it. If you rent, you pay the owner's mortgage interest and property taxes as part of your rent, but only the owner gets to deduct them from taxable income. Fortunately, you don't have to be a landlord to claim these write-offs. All you have to do is own the place.

In the early years of a home mortgage, nearly all of your monthly payments go toward fully deductible interest. Take a conventional, 30-year, $100,000 mortgage at a fixed rate of 8 percent. Each year interest and principal payments total $8,805. In the first year $7,970 of that amount—more than 90 percent of it—

is deductible as interest. Even in the 15th year, about 70 percent of your monthly payments would be deductible.

Interest on up to $1 million of mortgage debt is fully deductible. What this is worth to you depends on your tax bracket. In the 25 percent bracket, $1,000 in deductions saves you $250 in taxes. In other words, for each $1,000 of housing payments consisting of interest and property taxes, Uncle Sam pays $250 by reducing your federal income-tax bill by that amount. You save some on top of that by taking the same deductions on your state income-tax return.

WHAT DO YOU WANT IN A HOME?

Price range: _____

Desired neighborhoods:

_____

_____

_____

Desired school districts:

_____

_____

_____

How far are you willing to commute?

_____

Would you prefer:

❏ an older home   ❏ a new home

Architectural style of home:

❏ one-story ❏ two-story ❏ split-level
❏ colonial ❏ contemporary ❏ other:

_____

Are you willing to take on a fixer-upper?

❏ yes   ❏ no

Number of bedrooms you need: _____

Number of bathrooms: _____

Master bedroom suite? ❏ yes ❏ no

Check off the features that you want in a home:

	Very Important	Negotiable
Public transportation nearby	❏	❏
Yard	❏	❏
Eat-in kitchen	❏	❏
Fireplace	❏	❏
Separate dining room	❏	❏
Walk-in closets	❏	❏
Finished basement	❏	❏
Walk-out basement	❏	❏
Garage	❏	❏
Expandability	❏	❏
Located on a cul-de-sac	❏	❏
Plenty of windows and light	❏	❏
Family neighborhood	❏	❏
Close to shopping	❏	❏

Other features you want (list):

_____

_____

_____

When you sell the place, you can make a profit of up to $250,000 ($500,000 for a couple) without owing a dime of tax. There is absolutely no other way to make that kind of money and legally get to keep it all.

Homeowners can also use the equity in their home as a source of tax-sheltered loans. You can borrow against your home—through either a second mortgage or a home-equity line of credit—and deduct all the interest you pay on up to $100,000 of such loans, regardless of how you use the money. (For more information on home-equity loans, see Chapter 3.)

You Get Leverage

Most people buy a home with a little of their own money and a lot of somebody else's. This use of borrowed money means you can profit from price increases on property you haven't paid for yet. That's the "leverage" everybody talks about. The bigger your loan as a proportion of the home's value, the greater your leverage. Say you buy a home for $100,000 with no mortgage and sell it three years later for $110,000. The $10,000 gain represents a 10 percent return on your $100,000 outlay after three years. That's okay, but not great.

Now look at the deal another way: Make a down payment of $20,000 and get a mortgage for the rest. You still make the $10,000 profit, but you've invested only $20,000 to get it. Your return: a spectacular 50 percent (ignoring for the sake of simplicity the cost of the loan, tax angles, commissions, and other costs).

You Get a Hedge against Inflation

People aren't worried much about inflation these days, but what if it were to heat up? What would happen to home prices? Well, let's look to the past for a clue. In the high-inflation period from the mid-1970s to the early 1980s, the cost of living rose about 70 percent. Home prices doubled in the same period. Since then, in a time of generally tame inflation, home values in most of the country have risen a little faster than the inflation rate, providing at least some profit potential, and, in more recent years, some metropolitan areas saw home

When you sell your home, you can make a profit of up to $250,000 ($500,000 for a couple) without owing a dime of tax.

HOW MUCH CAN YOU SPEND FOR HOUSING?

I. Before you can know how big a mortgage payment you can afford, you need to tally your other monthly expenses. Do that on this worksheet. Then subtract the total on line B from the total on line A to see how much you have available for housing (line C).

Monthly Income

Take-home pay (after taxes) $_____

Other income _____

TOTAL $_____ **A**

Monthly Nonhousing Outlays

Food and household
  supplies $_____

Transportation _____

Insurance _____

Health care _____

Clothing and cleaning _____

Education _____

Debt and installment
  payments _____

Recreation and vacation _____

Telephone _____

Personal _____

Taxes
  (not deducted from pay) _____

Savings _____

Charity _____

Other _____

TOTAL $_____ **B**

Amount Available for Housing

Monthly income (A) $_____

– Nonhousing expenses (B) $_____

AMOUNT AVAILABLE $_____ **C**

II. Now, with the figure on line C in mind, plus a firm idea of the size of the down payment you plan to make, you're ready to begin comparing individual homes using the simple worksheet below. Real estate agents or current owners can give you reasonably precise estimates for the expenses listed there. Under "other" you might include any additional cost of commuting to work from that location, or new expenses such as community association fees. If you would reduce any of your current nonhousing expenses by buying a particular home, estimate your savings and subtract that amount from anticipated expenses. Then add up the housing costs and compare line D with line C. If C is larger than D, you've probably found a place you can afford. Chapter 6 describes how the type of mortgage you choose can often be tailored to the resources you have available.

Anticipated Monthly Housing Expenses

Mortgage payment $_____

Insurance _____

Property taxes _____

Utilities _____

Maintenance and repairs _____
(figure at least 1% of the price per year)

Other _____

TOTAL $_____ **D**

prices increase by at least 40 percent. If inflation soars again, homeowners should be well protected against its damage.

How Much Can You Afford?

The question of whether you can afford a home and, if so, how much home has two parts. Any deal you might make depends on how much you can afford as a down payment and how much you can safely shell out for monthly mortgage payments.

You can find the answer to the first part of the question—how much down payment can you muster—in the net-worth statement in Chapter 1. This inventory of your assets and liabilities will point the way to a realistic down payment and even show you where it might come from. Lenders usually want you to put down 10 percent to 20 percent of the purchase price of the property. Although it is possible to get a mortgage with a smaller down payment, if you buy with less than 20 percent down you'll probably be required to reduce the lender's risk by buying private mortgage insurance (PMI). First-year premiums range from about 0.5 percent of the loan amount to 1 percent or so, depending on the size of the loan and the size of your down payment, among other things. As the years go by and your loan balance is paid down, and rising home values boost your equity above 20 percent, you can ask the lender to drop the PMI.

One more point about down payments: If you plan to use a gift of money from family or friends, you'll find that lenders may expect at least a 3 percent cash down payment from your own resources in addition to any funds you receive as a gift.

What Kind of Home Should You Buy?

The best preparation for homebuying is to inventory not just your financial resources but also your likes and dislikes. Start with the general—

The best preparation for home-buying is to inventory not just your financial resources but also your likes and dislikes.

A good-quality home in a good location is probably a better buy than a "perfect" home in a lousy location.

your price range and approximate location—and then move to the specific: neighborhood, age and type of home, quality of nearby schools, and kind of ownership (traditional, condominium, or cooperative).

Most important, focus on the location and quality of the property. Don't go chasing an exact price or a particular feature. Price is negotiable, and a good-quality home in a good location is probably a better buy in the long run than a "perfect" home that has the bad luck to be in a lousy location.

Walking into a real estate office with a list of features you consider necessary in a home and a neighborhood (see page 68) will help guide the agent and save you the time of looking at homes that don't fit your needs.

It wouldn't hurt to draw up a list of dislikes, as well. Think of all the houses and apartments that for one reason or another made a negative impression on you, and try to identify exactly what it was you didn't like. Also consider things that other buyers might not like. Heavy traffic on the street might not bother you, but it will make resale tougher. You might not mind the 28 steep steps up to the front door, but they surely will turn away some potential future buyers.

Starting from Scratch

Buying a home that hasn't been built yet, whether it's being custom-built for you or is part of a new development, takes some special care.

Before you sign any contract, thoroughly check out the builder. You are counting on the builder's reputation; check it with the Better Business Bureau. Make sure the company is a member in good standing of the local builders association.

Next, find a recently completed development the same builder has worked on. Attend a homeowners meeting if you can, or talk to several owners about their dealings with the builder. Ask if they are satisfied with the way complaints have been handled and whether necessary repairs were made in a reasonable amount of time. Would they buy another home from the builder? The answer to that question should carry a lot of weight.

Here are some actions to take before deciding whether to buy a home that's still on the drawing board.

CONCERNING THE DEVELOPMENT:

- **Contact** the city or county planning department to see the master plan filed by your builder.
- **Find out** if other developments are planned for empty land surrounding the property you're considering.
- **Talk to** local school officials to learn about the adequacy of current facilities and any plans for future construction.

CONCERNING THE HOMEOWNERS ASSOCIATION:

- **Get a copy** of the association's rules. You'll have to live with them.
- **Review** the financial statements to see if adequate reserves have been established to maintain existing facilities (such as swimming pools, tennis courts, or a community center) or to build new ones.
- **Find out** how high the association dues are and whether there are limits to the amount they can be raised each year.

CONCERNING YOUR CONTRACT WITH THE BUILDER:

- **Make sure that** all upgrades and features are listed.
- **Include a clause** that allows you to visit the site on several occasions during the construction process (you'll probably have to be accompanied by a builder's representative).
- **Remember** that you don't have to accept the builder's contract as is; negotiating is expected, so do it. A typical deposit is 5 percent, but you may be able to get it lowered. If the market is slow, you should be able to get the builder to throw in some upgrades, but in fast-selling markets don't expect any concessions.
- **Be sure to make** the deal contingent on your ability to get mortgage financing, and ask the builder to provide at least 30 days' notice before closing. Try to get the builder to hold your deposit in escrow (this is common in some areas of the country, but you may have a fight on your hands in other areas).

> **If you're buying a home that hasn't yet been built, make sure that all upgrades and features are listed in the contract.**

Condos and co-ops are legal forms of ownership, not any particular kind of building.

CONCERNING THE CONDITION OF THE HOUSE:
■ **Inspect** everything in the home—try the faucets, flush toilets, turn on the heat and the air-conditioning. If you're not comfortable doing it yourself, hire a home inspector. They normally inspect older homes, but there is no reason they can't inspect a new one.

Buying a Condo or Co-op

Condos and co-ops are legal forms of ownership, not any particular kind of building. In a condominium, the owners of individual dwelling units hold title to their own units and own a proportional interest in the land and common areas of the development. Garden apartments, high-rises, and town houses are the most common forms that condos take, but the category can also include detached houses, beach houses, offices, and warehouses. The common property may belong to the condo developer at first, but eventually it is conveyed to an owners association. Thereafter the development is controlled and operated by directors of the condo owners association, often through a hired manager. Condominiums can be purchased with conventional and government-backed mortgages.

In a cooperative, residents do not hold title to their individual units. Instead they own shares of stock in a corporation that owns the development. They are, in effect, tenants of the corporation entitled to occupancy by virtue of their ownership of stock.

You normally can't get a mortgage to buy a co-op. Instead you get a "share loan," which is similar to a mortgage, except that it is somewhat more expensive and harder to find. In addition to loan payments to the lender, co-op residents make monthly maintenance payments to the cooperative corporation, which pays for the mortgage on the building, real estate taxes, and general upkeep. As a partial owner of the corporation, you can deduct your proportional share of the corporation's mortgage interest and taxes on your income-tax return.

Advantages and Amenities—at a Price

Many condos and co-ops have amenities that few residents could afford on their own—swimming pools, saunas, game rooms, tennis courts, even golf courses. Usually, lawns are mowed, leaves raked, and shrubbery trimmed by hired hands. Condos and co-ops often cost less than detached houses in comparable locations. You have a say in how the development is run. The value of your unit may rise.

All this comes at a price. You are required to pay your share of the cost of all luxuries, and you can't put off paying monthly fees or special assessments the way you can postpone maintenance or repairs on an individual home. You probably have less space than in a detached house. You can't enlarge your unit. You are subject to strict rules adopted by the majority of owners. Certain activities and hobbies, such as gun collecting or amateur radio (with its three-story antennas), may be banned or restricted. Some developments may ban pets.

You're also dependent on directors and professional managers to maintain both reserve funds and the property itself. If they fail to do their jobs, then the building or grounds could deteriorate and you could lose some, or all, of your equity.

Shopping Tips for Condos and Co-ops

Buy the largest unit that you can afford. A town house will have more of a market than a two-bedroom apartment, and a two-bedroom apartment will fare better on resale than a one-bedroom.

Look for a unit that has a special location—proximity to the pool might appeal to young families or a serene park view to an older couple. If something sets your unit apart from others, it will work to your benefit when you want to sell and there are ten other units in your development on the market.

If you are considering an apartment-style condo or co-op, pay close attention to potential problems with reserves and assessments—even though that means wading through detailed records. Insufficient reserves can have wrenching financial consequences if there's

Many condos and co-ops have amenities that few residents could afford on their own. All this comes at a price.

an emergency. Find out before you buy whether the association has accumulated adequate reserves to pay for major repairs and to replace obsolete or worn-out equipment. As buildings age, residents must be prepared for such expenses as replacing the roof, upgrading the electrical system, and installing a new boiler.

Monthly assessments can be expected to rise over time, so look for a record of reasonable increases. Assessments should be large enough to cover routine maintenance and still permit the buildup of reserves. Some condos and co-ops choose to deal with big repair bills by imposing special assessments rather than accumulating cash in a reserve fund. If you buy into a building in which residents have postponed needed work, remember: The repairs lie ahead—at your expense.

What Makes a Good Condo

Generally, the best locations are residential areas that have a good mix of quality apartment buildings and

---

CONDO FACTS

- **Condos historically have not appreciated** as rapidly as single-family homes, but since the late 1990s. they have been appreciating faster than their single-family counterparts.
- **In some cities,** like Chicago and New York, condos seem to be swept up as soon as they come on the market. But in other areas, the market is slower.
- **If you live in an area** of rapid development, you should be aware that if you need to sell your condo, you'll be competing with new units that are springing up around you.
- **Some experts believe** that the condo market will continue to boom as baby boomers age and look for more carefree housing options. Many of those boomers will probably be looking for high-end, luxury condos that most young people can't afford, while the young, first-time home buyers, especially those in high-cost areas, buy entry-level units.
- **After you become an owner,** you'll need insurance on your unit and its contents. The development should have its own insurance. You should also be protected from claims arising from damage you do to others, which could occur if, for example, water from a leak in your kitchen seeped into the apartment below.
- **If you become a director** of the condo or co-op association, you will need liability insurance in case negligence or damage suits are brought against the board.

homes in the middle to upper price range, with rising property values. Make sure that the area provides easy access to public transportation, stores, hospitals, and parks, and that it boasts a highly rated public school system. Check out zoning regulations for the land surrounding the development, and try to visualize the neighborhood in 5, 10, and 15 years. You don't want the wooded view from your living-room window turned into a six-lane highway in five years.

Take note of the vacancy rate and the supply-demand situation in the area. A glut of empty units or a high percentage of renters can affect property values in a general area or in a particular building.

Are rentals necessarily bad? Not if you live in a resort community. But potential buyers in developments with less than a 51 percent owner-occupancy rate will have difficulty getting mortgages, which cuts down the potential market.

Find out who owns the common facilities—the swimming pool, tennis courts, parking areas, and laundry room, for example. If the developer owns these (and leases them to the development), it means that your fees could escalate at his discretion, rather than the condo board's. And check out the facilities themselves to make sure they are adequate for the number of residents.

Walk around the condo grounds and decide if you'll fit in with the other residents. Are you considerably older or younger than most? Perhaps you have young children and most of the residents are single professionals, leaving your kids without playmates.

If you're comfortable with what you've found so far, look into the condo's rules and regulations, which you'll find in the master deed, bylaws, or house rules—all documents that the builder or owner must give you (see pages 80–81 for an explanation of these papers). Strangely enough, too few rules can lead to problems down the road, but you have to be sure you can live with the ones that exist.

Finally, investigate the financial condition of the condo association, which you can learn from examining

Check if you'll fit in with other condo residents. Are you much younger or older? Are there many kids? Is that what you want?

the documents that must be given to potential buyers. What debts does it have and to whom are they owed? Are the reserve funds adequate to handle both routine maintenance and replacement of such expensive items as roofs and furnaces? Is the association quick to impose special assessments to cover emergency needs?

Finding a Good Co-op

Co-op buyers need to ask many of the same questions as prospective condominium buyers: What is the neighborhood like? Will you fit in with the other residents? Are you willing to give up some privacy for the conveniences afforded by co-op living? Can you live with the rules and regulations imposed on the residents? Is the co-op financially sound? How many of the units are rented? Are you allowed to sublet your apartment?

In addition, you'll want to find out about the age and condition of the building; ask to see an engineer-

BUYING INTO A DEVELOPMENT

If It's a New Development

Never buy into an uncompleted condo or co-op project unless you are provided with site drawings, floor plans, maintenance-cost projections, and other descriptive material. Model apartments may be larger than those to be sold. Measure them yourself if you have doubts. Find out whether you have any recourse if the project isn't finished when you're ready to move in.

If It's an Older Development

This is often the safer route because you may be able to obtain an evaluation of the development's construction and can judge the competence and experience of the owners association. You can also talk with residents and walk through the building and grounds to get a feel for atmosphere and general upkeep.

Learn all you can about the building's structure and equipment. Some states require that buyers be given such information in writing. Warranties should be provided in a condo purchase; be sure to ask whether you'll get them on common property as well as on your own unit.

If the building was renovated before it was put on the market, make sure improvements aren't merely cosmetic. Getting an appraisal of the entire development would be too costly for individuals, but if a lender has agreed to finance purchases of units, you may be able to obtain a copy of its appraisal.

ing report on the condition of the property (if one is available). If the co-op building is more than 40 years old, for example, the plumbing system may need to be replaced. How would the co-op board cover the expense? Are there sufficient reserves to pay for it or will owners receive a special assessment?

Cooperative corporations whose shares can be bought using share loans (see page 74) must meet minimum standards for structural soundness, restricted commercial use, and appropriate management. In addition, approved projects must have adequate cash flows and monthly assessments sufficient to meet current operating costs and to build reserve funds.

As a prospective co-op buyer, you may be asked to meet with members of the co-op's board of governors. You could be asked to submit financial records and personal references. But no matter how selective the co-op residents are, federal law and many state statutes prohibit them from rejecting or discouraging prospective buyers on the basis of race, gender, creed, or national origin.

The National Association of Housing Cooperatives, 1707 H. St., NW, Suite 201, Washington, DC 20006 (202-737-0797; http://www.coophousing.org) can provide information on buying into a cooperative.

The National Cooperative Bank, which makes loans to co-op tenant-shareholders, has helpful brochures, *Co-op Financing* and *A Consumer's Guide to Buying a Co-op*. Call the NCB at 800-322-1251, or write to 139 S. High St., Hillsboro, OH 45133. You can also view the publications on NCB's Web site, http://www.ncbhomeloans.com.

Rules and Regulations

Before you purchase either a condo or co-op, it's important that you understand the rules and regulations that will be imposed upon you and other residents by the condo or co-op association. Study them carefully because they are legally binding.

State or local law usually requires that the seller supply you with all the documentation you need to be fully informed. Once you sign the purchase contract,

Find out about the age and condition of the co-op building; ask to see an engineering report on the condition of the property.

you've explicitly and contractually agreed to abide by the community's rules.

WHAT IF YOU DON'T LIKE ONE OF THE RULES? Let's say that you want to hang a wreath on your door year-round or even just during the holidays, but your

---

CONDOS AND CO-OPS: A GUIDE TO THE DOCUMENTS

Condo and co-op buyers face a pile of often incomprehensible documents. Read each one slowly enough to digest it, and refuse to be rushed into a decision. You'll find the answers to many of your questions about the development or corporation in these documents.

CONDO DOCUMENTS
Sales contract or purchase agreement

This is similar to other real estate contracts, but the differences are important. Check for conditions under which you could back out of the deal, such as your inability to get mortgage money. If the contract doesn't give you the right to withdraw within a specified period, don't sign until you have studied it and the other papers with legal assistance. For a new community, there should be assurances that it will be completed as promised, and you should have the right to make an inspection prior to settlement. It would be advantageous to you to have your deposit placed in an escrow account, preferably one that pays interest.

Master deed

Also called an Enabling Declaration, Plan of Condominium Ownership, or Declaration of Condominium, this is the most important instrument. When recorded, it legally establishes the project as a condominium or co-op. It also, among other things, authorizes residents to form an operating association and describes individual units and commonly owned areas.

Bylaws

These spell out the association's authority and responsibilities, authorize the making of a budget and the collection of various charges, and prescribe parliamentary procedures. They may empower the association to hire professional managers or may contain other special provisions. The bylaws may also set forth insurance requirements and authorize the imposition of liens or fines against owners who fail to pay monthly charges.

House rules

They state what owners can and can't do. Any restrictions on pets, children, decorations, use of facilities, and such will be found here. The rules may be incorporated in the bylaws or set out in a separate document.

Other papers

Look for a copy of the operating budget, a schedule of current and proposed assessments, a financial statement on the owners

condo association won't allow it. Start by asking your governing board for an exception. If you're rejected, consider proposing a change to the association's rule. This will probably require a vote by all owners of the association, but if others feel the same way you do, you may have success.

association, any leases or contracts, a plat (a drawing of the project and your unit), and an engineer's report if one was done. One of the financial documents should show how much money has been reserved for unforeseen and major projected outlays, an important consideration. A few states require developers to give each potential buyer a prospectus that details all the important facts about the offering. Read it carefully; information that may be buried in small print or obscured by legalese in the other papers may be more readily understandable in the prospectus.

CO-OP DOCUMENTS
Articles of incorporation
The corporation's purpose, powers, and obligations are described in this document, which will vary according to state law.

Audited financial statements
Get statements for at least the past year, which can be used to check on reserves, maintenance records, income sources, and other pertinent facts.

Bylaws
Just as in a condo, these lay out the duties and responsibilities of the development's shareholders, officers, and directors.

Shares, stock, or membership certificate
You'll receive these as proof of ownership in the corporation.

Proprietary lease or occupancy agreement
This specifies the number of shares allocated to your unit (the more expensive the unit, the larger your share of ownership in the corporation) and spells out the terms under which you occupy the apartment. It also obligates you to pay your share of the corporation's expenses, including real estate taxes, operating costs, and debt. Rules on using your unit, subleasing, and maintenance are also in the agreement.

Recognition agreement
This sets out the rights of the share-loan lender, and the corporation's responsibilities and obligations to the lender. A cooperative may have recognition agreements with more than one lender.

Security agreement or share loan
In this document, the share-loan borrower (that's you) assigns the lease or occupancy agreement and pledges his or her stock, shares, or membership certificate to the lender in return for a loan.

A buyer wants the most house for the money; a seller wants the most money for the house. A good agent can guide events toward a mutually beneficial conclusion.

WHAT IF YOU JUST IGNORE THE RULE? The board could impose a financial penalty, bill you for the cost of returning something to its original condition, sue you, or even force you out of your unit.

WHAT IF YOU BELIEVE THE BOARD ISN'T ACTING IN THE BEST INTERESTS OF THE OWNERS? You'll need to have good documentation to back up your complaint, or you could find yourself facing a libel suit. If you're not sure what's going on or feel that board members aren't acting in your best interests, try either getting yourself elected to the board (which will allow you to learn firsthand what the board is doing) or getting the "problem" directors removed from the board.

Check your documents for information on the proper way to handle the removal of a board member. It would be a good idea, however, to first discuss your complaints with board members and to hear their side of things. Let them know that you're keeping tabs on them and that you expect them to fulfill their obligations. They may change their tune and save you the trouble of trying to have them removed.

How to Get Your Money's Worth from a Real Estate Agent

A buyer wants the most house for the money; a seller wants the most money for the house. A good real estate agent can guide events toward a mutually beneficial conclusion. A bad one can make an already stressful situation worse.

What can you reasonably expect an agent to do for you? Do you really need one? How much should you pay? What recourse do you have if something goes wrong?

It's helpful to learn the lingo first. Agent is the commonly used term for a salesperson who is licensed to work for a real estate broker. A broker is licensed to conduct a real estate business and to negotiate transactions for a fee. Both may properly be called agents because they act as agents for clients. Some brokers and agents may be called Realtors. Realtors (note the capital "R"—it's a trade name) and Realtor-Associates (who work for a Realtor) are members of the National Association of Realtors, a trade and lobbying organization.

Whom the Agent Works for

Unwary homebuyers may innocently divulge their strategies to the wrong real estate agent. If you are working with anyone other than a buyer's broker, such disclosure is a big mistake because the agent works for the seller and may be obliged to report on your conversation.

A seller's agent can help you with information about market conditions, neighborhoods, schools, public facilities, tax rates, zoning laws, proposed roads and construction, and other essentials for evaluating your purchase. No agent can know everything about a property, but an honest one will tell you about problems he or she is aware of. And an agent could be held accountable for providing wrong information on something he or she ought to know about. (A buyer could also sue an owner who conceals known defects.)

Does a buyer really need an agent? Almost certainly. As a house hunter on your own, you're at a disadvantage. Unless you are thoroughly familiar with a given area, you'll miss an agent's knowledge and resources. And while you can now get online access to the computerized Multiple Listing Service (MLS) yourself, you'll still need to go through the agent to see the house and make the purchase.

Buyer's Brokers

The conflict of interest created by an agent's need to represent both the buyer and seller but being paid by the seller has led to the creation of buyer's brokers. When you hire a buyer's broker, you enter into a "single agency" relationship—the broker is hired by you and represents only you, having no allegiance to the seller.

There are several ways that a buyer's agent representing you can be paid: by the hour, with a flat fee, or, most commonly, from part of the sales commis-

The conflict of interest created by an agent's need to represent both the buyer and seller but being paid by the seller has led to the creation of buyer's brokers.

Because the buyer's broker represents you alone, not the seller, and preferably works for a flat fee, any conflict of interest is eliminated.

sion, the same way other real estate agents are paid. The sales commission is split between the listing broker and the broker of the buyer's agent. The difference is that the contract states that the buyer's agent's portion of the commission is paid "on behalf of the buyer" and comes from the proceeds of the transaction. There is no need for the buyer to incur any additional costs for the agent's services.

There are some obvious advantages to dealing with a buyer's broker. You needn't fear discussing your buying strategy with your agent or asking for advice on your opening offer. Because the agent represents you alone, not the seller, and preferably works for a flat fee, any conflict of interest is eliminated. The buyer's broker is free to negotiate the best possible price and terms for you.

To find a buyer's broker in your area, ask your local Board of Realtors or large real estate firms for referrals, or contact one of the following:

- **The Buyer's Agent Inc.,** 5705 Stage Road, Suite 199, Bartlett, TN 38134 (800-766-8728; http://www.forbuyers.com) is a franchise operating in most states. It represents buyers on a fee or commission basis.

- **The National Association of Exclusive Buyer Agents,** NAEBA Referral Service Corp., 541 S. Orlando Ave., Suite 300, Maitland, FL 32751 (800-986-2322; http://www.naeba.com) is a consumer-advocacy and professional training organization that can provide information on the role of an exclusive buyer's agent as well as names of agents in your area.

Dual Agency

A real estate agent who serves both the buyer and the seller, acting only as an intermediary, is known as a dual agent. The dual agent can't advise you on negotiating tactics, nor can he pass along confidential information to the other party. Compensation for a dual agent is based on commission—so once again there is incentive to get the highest possible price.

Some real estate firms appoint different agents to represent the buyer and seller, some represent only the seller on properties they list and only the buyer on properties listed by other firms, and some allow agents to represent both.

What's best for you? If you're familiar with the real estate market and are comfortable negotiating on your own behalf, then a dual agent will be fine. On the other hand, if you want some help from an agent or advice on tactics, your best bet is hiring a buyer's broker to represent you.

Get a Home Inspection

When drawing up an offer on your dream home, be sure you make the contract contingent on a professional home inspection, satisfactory to you. Such a clause provides you with an "out" in case the inspection uncovers a serious problem with the house that you didn't see.

A thorough home inspection covers the structural integrity of the house, the roof, siding, and other exterior features, interior walls and doors, kitchens and bathrooms, the electrical system, heating and air-conditioning systems, and the plumbing. If the home has a swimming pool, tennis court, well, or septic system, you'll need to arrange for a separate inspection.

How to Find a Good Home Inspector

Begin by asking friends and associates for referrals. Consider inspectors recommended by your real estate agent, but make sure the inspectors don't work for the agent or for a contractor looking to drum up repair jobs. Ask to see a couple of completed inspection reports. Look for an inspector who writes up thorough reports on current problems as well as problems you may encounter in the future. You don't want an inspector whose idea of a report is just preprinted forms with checked-off boxes.

Try to find an inspector who is a member of the American Society of Home Inspectors (ASHI), 932 Lee St., Suite 101, Des Plaines, IL 60016 (800-743-2744; http://www.ashi.org). This group sets the standards for

Make your contract contingent on a professional home inspection. You'll have an "out" in case the inspection uncovers a serious problem.

the industry—requiring its members to pass a series of exams, perform 250 fee-paid inspections meeting ASHI standards, and complete 60 hours of continuing education every three years. The National Institute of Building Inspectors (NIBI), 424 Vosseller Ave., Bound Brook, NJ 08805 (888-281-6424; http://www .nibi.com), founded by the HouseMaster of America Home Inspection Service (a franchise business), trains its inspectors according to the standards set by ASHI

IMPORTANT TAX ANGLES OF HOMEOWNERSHIP

Uncle Sam is a silent but generous partner in homeownership. First he subsidizes your mortgage payments, then he deliberately overlooks part or all of the profits you make when you sell. But this generosity has a price, and a misstep on your part can have expensive consequences. Following are some answers to the kinds of questions that come up when people buy and sell homes—and while they own them.

DEDUCTING MORTGAGE INTEREST

Q: *Is there a limit on the amount of interest a homeowner can deduct?*
A: All the interest on debt you take on to build or buy a principal residence and second residence is deductible on loans totaling up to $1 million. The $1-million ceiling on this so-called acquisition debt includes money you borrow to renovate your home.

Q: *What are the rules for deducting interest on home-equity loans?*
A: Interest on home-equity loans is deductible up to $100,000, except in a few cases, including if the money is used to invest in tax-exempt bonds or single-premium life insurance or if you are subject to the alternative minimum tax (AMT).

Q: *We have completely paid off the mortgage on our home, which is now worth $200,000.*

We want to take out a new mortgage to renovate the kitchen and add a small wing to the house for guests. The estimated cost will be $110,000. In addition, we intend to borrow $10,000 for a car. Because I'll be borrowing more than $100,000, will the extra $20,000 debt be nondeductible?
A: Interest on the entire loan is deductible. Because you have no other mortgage on the property, the $110,000 borrowed for renovations is considered acquisition debt, subject to the $1-million ceiling. The $10,000 for the car qualifies as home-equity debt and counts against the $100,000 limit.

Q: *We refinanced our mortgage and were told we wouldn't be able to deduct all the points we paid. Somehow we're supposed to write it off a little at a time. Will the proper amount be included in the interest the bank reports we paid each year, or is there a special way to figure it out?*

and requires its inspectors to carry liability insurance and meet certain continuing-education requirements. Contact either organization for a list of inspectors in your area.

GO ALONG FOR THE INSPECTION. Accompany the inspector as he tours the home. Expect this to take about two to three hours—and take advantage of the excellent opportunity to ask questions about both existing

---

A: It's an extra deduction and you have to figure it out yourself. The IRS considers points paid to refinance a mortgage to be prepaid interest and says they must be deducted proportionately over the life of the loan. If you paid $3,000 in points on a 15-year mortgage, for example, $200 would be deductible each year. If you refinanced around midyear and made six payments, your first-year deduction would be $100. Don't include the amount as part of the mortgage-interest deduction. Claim it on the indicated line of Schedule A.

Q: *We recently inherited some money, enough to pay off the mortgage on our home. If we do so, we'll be stuck with a prepayment penalty. Would it be deductible?*
A: Yes. Prepayment penalties are treated as interest and may be deducted in the year paid.

DEDUCT COMMISSIONS?
Q: *We sold our home for $125,000, and the real estate commission took $7,500 of it. Can we deduct this charge on our taxes?*
A: Sorry, but no.

TAX-FREE PROFITS
Q: *Is the law that allows tax-free profit when you sell homes as good as it sounds?*
A: Yes, it is as good as it sounds. The law allows single sellers filing an individual return to earn up to $250,000 in profit on a principal residence and not owe a penny of tax. For couples filing a joint return, the figure is a generous $500,000. There is no age requirement to meet, and you can invoke this break again and again, as long as you don't use it more than once in a two-year period. To qualify, you must have lived in the home for at least two of the five years leading up to the sale. (If the home was a rental property acquired in a tax-free exchange, you must own it for five years before selling.)

A catch to be aware of if you have an office at home: Any portion of your house that qualifies for home-office tax deductions doesn't qualify for the tax-free profit. In such a case, you might want to stop claiming home-office deductions for at least two of the five years leading up to the sale. That would allow the entire home to qualify as your principal residence.

and potential problems, and to get estimates on repair costs. If the inspector finds serious problems, you can get out of the contract. If the inspector uncovers less serious problems, try to get the owner to pay for the repairs or adjust your original offer to reflect the cost of repairs.

How to Be a Mortgage Maven

The mantra for mortgage shopping is simple: Focus on the loan, not the lender. Concern yourself with interest rates, points, processing costs, and other variables that affect the cost of the loan. Don't worry much about where the lender is located—your mortgage will be sold once or twice before you're done, anyway. Study the pros and cons of fixed-rate and adjustable-rate borrowing. Learn the lingo so you can ask the questions that lead you to the best deal. This chapter will help you.

What It Takes to Get a Mortgage

Before you can worry about comparing mortgages, you need to worry about qualifying in the first place. How will lenders evaluate your application?

The answer is pretty much the same wherever you live. Lenders want to play by the rules set by Fannie Mae (the Federal National Mortgage Association), or Freddie Mac (the Federal Home Loan Mortgage Corp.). These government-sponsored organizations buy up mortgages from lenders, repackage them as securities, and then resell them to investors (see Chapter 24).

By selling their mortgages to Fannie Mae or Freddie Mac, lenders convert their loans to cash, with which they can make more loans. Fannie and Freddie insist that the mortgages they buy meet certain standards, which lenders are anxious to meet. If they don't, they risk being unable to sell their loans and thus replenish their supply of lendable cash.

Debt ratios are only guidelines, and 30 to 40 percent of the loans that Fannie Mae buys exceed them.

Fannie Mae measures your borrowing power by matching your projected housing expenses to your household income. Principal and interest payments, property taxes, and homeowners insurance—what lenders refer to as PITI—should total no more than 28 percent of your gross monthly income. And that monthly house payment plus other debts with ten or more monthly payments still outstanding (that could include automobile or student loans) should total no more than 36 percent of your gross income.

Gross income is what you and your spouse earn before taxes for work that you have been doing for a year or longer. Income from the extra job you took a few weeks before applying for the loan doesn't count. Other income—such as bonuses, commissions, and overtime pay—must be averaged over two years to be considered wages. You can count alimony and child-support payments as income if the payments will continue for at least three years from the date of your loan application.

Not all loans get the straight 28/36 treatment. To qualify for certain adjustable-rate mortgages (ARMs), you'll be expected to meet stricter requirements for the first year's payments because they are typically lower than second and subsequent years' payments. Loans with low down payments also draw tougher scrutiny. On the other hand, a down payment of 20 percent or more may earn you a 33/38 ratio instead of 28/36. FHA and VA mortgages also get higher ratios because they are backed by the federal government.

Debt ratios are only guidelines, and 30 to 40 percent of the loans Fannie Mae buys exceed the guidelines because other factors can tip the scales. It counts in your favor if you have a good credit history, make a substantial down payment, possess liquid assets equal to at least three months of home payments, or have in the past paid a large proportion of your income for rent or toward a mortgage.

The worksheet on page 70 will help you assess your home-buying potential. If you anticipate sizable financial obligations, your employment outlook is uncertain, your down-payment fund is low, your family is likely to grow, or you'll need money for improvements or furnishings, prudence suggests spending less per month than the calculations indicate you can afford.

With some idea of how you'll be judged by lenders, you're ready to go shopping for a mortgage. But first you've got to know the language of these loans.

Loan Lingo: Interest and Points

Lenders charge for mortgages two ways: with interest and with "points." You pay interest for the life of the loan, but you pay the points up front. They may be called a loan discount fee or a loan origination fee. Other mortgage-related charges nickel-and-dime you in several ways, as we'll see later, but interest and points constitute your biggest mortgage burdens.

One point equals 1 percent of the loan amount. Because a point is prepaid interest, it raises the effective interest rate of the loan. Look at it this way: If you borrow $100,000 and pay two points, or $2,000, to get the loan, the lender has actually laid out only $98,000. But you'll have to pay back the full $100,000 face value of the loan, plus interest. In effect, you've given the lender a discount off the face amount of the mortgage. Thus points are sometimes referred to as a discount fee. Just remember that the discount goes to the lender, not to you.

One point is roughly equivalent to an additional one-eighth of one percentage point (0.125 percent) on the interest rate of a 30-year fixed-rate mortgage. Thus a 6 percent, 30-year fixed-rate mortgage with no points is about equivalent to a 5 percent loan with eight points. Of course, lenders never charge that many points on a loan. After all, how many borrowers could afford to pay so much additional cash on top of their down payment? Not many. So instead of insisting on so much cash up front, lenders bump up the stated interest rate on the loan. That 5 percent mortgage with eight points becomes, in the marketplace, a 5.5 percent mortgage with four points, or a 5.625 percent mortgage with three points, or a 5.875 percent mortgage with

Lenders charge for mortgages two ways: with interest and with "points." You pay interest for the life of the loan, but you pay the points up front.

The money you save with a lower rate (and lower monthly payments) could add up to more than you paid in points for the lower rate.

one point. In the end, these are all the same; the only difference is when you pay the money.

Which is better, a lower-rate loan with several points or a higher-rate loan with no points? The answer depends on how long you'll be paying on the loan. Over time, the money you save with a lower rate (and thus lower monthly payments) will amount to more than you shelled out in points to get the lower rate. In general, the longer you'll be in the home, the better off you'll be paying more points up front to get the lower rate for the long term. A three-step calculation can help you choose the best combination of rates and points:

■ **First,** estimate the number of years you'll be paying on the loan.
■ **Second,** divide the years into the number of points.
■ **Third,** add that to the interest rate and compare with other offers.

Say, for example, that you expect to be paying on the mortgage for five years. One lender offers a 6 percent loan with three points, another offers a 6.25 percent loan with two points, and a third offers a 6.375 percent loan with 1.5 points. Which is the best deal?

Over one year, those three points boost the effective rate of the 6 percent loan up to 9 percent (three points added to 6 percent). The 6.25 percent loan with two points works out to 8.25 percent, and the 6.375 percent loan with 1.5 points translates to 7.875 percent. But over five years, as you'll see in the table on the opposite page, the loan with the lowest interest rate is the best deal even with those additional points. And the longer the loan runs, the bigger the advantage of the loan with the lowest rate. The table also shows the effective rate over 30 years.

Points go with the territory in the mortgage business, so you'll have to live with them (although sometimes you can shave them through negotiation). The way to compare different loans at different interest rates with different numbers of points tacked on to them is to get from each lender the annual percentage rate (APR) of the loans you're considering. The APR takes points and other incidentals into account. But in weighing whether

HOW POINTS RAISE THE RATE			
Stated Rate	**Points**	**Effective rate Over five years**	**Over 30 years**
6%	3	6.6%	6.38%
6.25	2	6.65	6.50
6.375	1.5	6.675	6.56

to pay more points to get a lower-rate loan, don't forget to consider how long you'll be paying on the loan.

Loan Lingo: The Different Kinds of Mortgages

Mortgages come in lots of flavors. The standard fixed-rate variety—with its preset, life-of-the-mortgage, monthly payments covering principal repayment and interest—offers the peace of mind that comes with a predictable monthly check-writing exercise. But if interest rates fall, the holder of a fixed-rate mortgage is stuck with the higher rate unless he or she refinances.

On the other hand, if rates rise, it's the lender who's stuck. Who wants to be holding a vault full of 7 percent mortgages when rates are at 10 percent? In fact, the reluctance of lenders to make fixed-rate mortgage loans in a climate of rising interest rates in the late 1970s led to the creation of the adjustable-rate mortgage (ARM). With an ARM, the interest rate you pay rises and falls with other interest rates throughout the economy, thus passing the risk of rising rates from the lender to the borrower. In exchange, you get a lower rate to begin with.

Which kind of mortgage do you want? Let's take a closer look at these two major types and their various incarnations.

30-Year Fixed-Rate Loans

This is the most familiar mortgage. The interest rate—and your monthly payments—remains the same for the life of the loan.

The higher monthly payments on a 15-year mortgage can be burdensome, especially for first-time buyers.

Shorter-Term Fixed-Rate Loans

Fifteen- and 20-year fixed-rate loans have become popular for home buyers who can afford the higher monthly payments. The loan is paid off faster than with a 30-year loan, and interest rates are usually one-half to one percentage point lower. A 15-year loan lets you own your home free and clear in half the time and for less than half the total interest cost of a 30-year fixed-rate loan. But when it comes to calculating the monthly payments, the slightly lower interest rate isn't enough to cancel the effect of the shorter repayment period. The higher monthly payments can be burdensome, especially for first-time buyers. On a 15-year, $100,000 mortgage at 7 percent, the monthly payments are $899—about $200 more than for a 30-year, 7.5 percent mortgage for the same amount.

Adjustable-Rate Mortgages

The interest rate on an ARM changes periodically, in sync with an index selected by the lender. The adjustment interval may be every six months, or once a year, or once every three, five, or seven years. At adjustment time (or, more accurately, on the calculation date, which will be a month or so before the actual adjustment date), the lender looks at the index rate and slaps on a margin—typically two to three percentage points—to come up with the new rate.

Interest rates being paid on one-, three- and five-year Treasury securities are commonly used as ARM indexes. The Federal Housing Finance Board's National Average Contract Mortgage Rate, often called the FHB Series of Closed Loans, is also popular with lenders. The Federal COFI (Cost of Funds Index) and the Eleventh District COFI are used by lenders throughout the country even though the latter is based on interest rates in California, Arizona, and Nevada.

Some indexes are more volatile than others, and the COFIs are generally the least volatile. They are listed in the business pages of major newspapers, or you can follow them—and other common rates—by calling the Yield and Commitment Information Hotline sponsored by Fannie Mae (800-752-7020 or online at http://www.fanniemae.com).

Find out which index will be used in any ARM you are considering. It is impossible to predict which index will move most in your favor. When rates decline, you want to benefit as quickly as possible. One-year Treasury securities will do that for you. When rates rise, you'd be better off with a slower-moving index, such as five-year Treasuries.

Most ARMs have limits, or caps, on rate changes. When interest rates are rising rapidly, caps protect you from huge jumps in your monthly payments. Most ARMs have both periodic ceilings (limiting the increase from one adjustment period to the next) and lifetime ceilings (limiting the overall interest-rate increase over the term of the loan). Limits of two percentage points on annual increases, with a lifetime cap of six points, are typical. Caps work the other way, too. If rates plunge between adjustments, the limits protect the lender from drastic drops in the payments you have to make.

ARMs with *payment* caps rather than *rate* caps limit your monthly payment increase at the time of each adjustment, typically to a certain percentage of the previous payment. They can create negative amortization when rising interest rates would dictate payments higher than the cap permits. The difference in such cases is added to the loan principal, and as a result your indebtedness can actually grow while you think you're paying off the loan. ARMs with payment caps are rarely offered today and should be avoided.

Convertible ARMs

Some ARMs can be converted to fixed-rate loans. You might want the right to convert in the future—say, after two or three years—if you expect rates will be lower then. If the cost is the same, you should always pick a convertible ARM over a nonconvertible one. But costs usually aren't the same. You'll have to pay a conversion fee and probably a slightly higher rate to start,

Most ARMs have limits, or caps, on rate changes. When interest rates are rising rapidly, caps protect you from huge jumps in your monthly payments.

CHECKLIST FOR COMPARING ARMs

After you've obtained preapproval for the amount of money you can borrow, use this worksheet to assess different lenders' adjustable-rate mortgage (ARM) offerings. Make yourself a copy for each lender.

Lender's name_____

Telephone number _____

Down payment required _____%
Beginning interest rate (APR) _____%
Points _____%
Beginning payment $_____
Lifetime cap on interest rate _____%
Periodic cap on the interest rate? ❑ yes ❑ no
 What is the cap? _____%
How often can payment be adjusted? _____
Is there a cap on payment? ❑ yes ❑ no
What is the cap? _____%
Does loan permit negative amortization? ❑ yes ❑ no
 How much negative amortization is allowed
 relative to the original loan amount? _____
 For example, can mortgage balance grow to
 105% of original loan, 110%, and so on?
Loan is tied to which index?
❑ *1-year Treasury securities*   ❑ *3-year Treasury securities*
❑ *5-year Treasury securities*   ❑ *Other:_____*
❑ *Federal Housing Board's National Average Contract Rate*
 series for closed loans
Number of adjustments loan calls for_____
 First adjustment occurs_____ months/years
 Second adjustment occurs_____ months/years
 Third adjustment occurs_____ months/years
Can loan be converted to a fixed-rate? ❑ yes ❑ no
 Under what circumstances?_____
 Cost of conversion option $_____
Can loan be prepaid in whole or in part at anytime without penalty?
  ❑ yes ❑ no
 If yes, what are the conditions?_____
Is loan assumable by a qualified buyer? ❑ yes ❑ no

for example. That makes a convertible ARM a good idea only if you are convinced that rates will be lower in the future (as might be the case if you are getting the mortgage during an unusual period of high inflation, for example) and you plan to stay in the same place long enough to benefit from a conversion.

Two-Step Mortgages

These are usually five- and seven-year variations on the ARM, often called 5/25 and 7/23 mortgages. They are amortized over 30 years, with a fixed rate for the first phase and a one-time adjustment to the current market rate after five or seven years. Because they start as much as a full percentage point below the going rate on 30-year fixed loans, two-steps are a sure thing for buyers who know they're going to sell before the adjustment hits.

The 10/1 mortgage is a variation on the two-step idea that turns the theme around: You start with a rate that's fixed for ten years, and then the loan automatically converts to a one-year ARM. Its attraction is a slightly lower initial rate than you could get on a 30-year fixed-rate loan, which makes the 10/1 an appealing package for borrowers who are pretty certain they will sell and pay off the loan within ten years.

Biweekly Mortgages

You make your mortgage payment every other week instead of monthly, which speeds up repayment to about 18 to 20 years and reduces total interest costs. You might be better off and have more flexibility by having a 30-year fixed loan and making additional prepayments as you can afford to do so. Or you could invest the extra amount a biweekly mortgage would require.

FHA Loans

The Federal Housing Administration insures a wide variety of mortgages. FHA insurance was conceived as a way to assist low-income homebuyers by encouraging lenders to make loans to them, and the debt-to-

Rather than taking out a biweekly mortgage, consider having a 30-year fixed loan and making additional prepayments as you can afford to do so.

HOW ARM PAYMENTS COULD GO UP OR DOWN

Say you have a $100,000 one-year adjustable-rate mortgage (ARM) with an initial rate of 4%, an annual cap of two percentage points, and a lifetime cap of five percentage points. Here's what the monthly payment would be on a fully amortized loan if payments were adjusted up every year to the maximum and then remained at that level for the life of the loan:

Year	Rate	Years of Amortization	Monthly Payment	Principal Balance at End of Period
1	4 %	30	$ 477.42	$ 98,238.85
2	6	29	596.32	96,942.11
3	8	28	723.92	95,975.45
4	9	27	790.00	95,097.70
5–30	9	26	790.00	—

And this is what the monthly payments would be if interest rates on a $100,000, 7½% ARM dropped one-half percentage point every year for five years:

Year	Rate	Years of Amortization	Monthly Payment	Principal Balance at End of Period
1	7½ %	30	$ 699.21	$ 99,078.15
2	7	29	665.93	97,987.84
3	6½	28	634.00	96,711.39
4	6	27	603.46	95,232.24
5	5½	26	574.39	93,534.91
6–30	5	25	546.80	—

income ratios are more generous than they are for other loans. Still, even high-income buyers can get FHA loans. The maximum loan amount varies somewhat from one geographic area to another, depending on local housing prices. The FHA insures both fixed-rate loans and ARMs.

Because FHA loans are insured by a federal agency, they are practically risk-free to lenders and should carry an interest rate a bit below the going market rate. Down payments can be 5 percent or less for buyers who will live in their homes themselves. The buyer must pay the cost of FHA insurance, which has recently been

1.5 percent. It is collected at the time of settlement, but you can increase the size of your mortgage to cover the cost and roll it into your monthly payment.

Veterans' Loans

The Department of Veterans Affairs protects lenders against losses by guaranteeing mortgages taken out by eligible veterans. The primary advantage of such a mortgage is that no down payment is required unless a veteran is obtaining a loan with a graduated-payment feature or the loan amount requested is more than the agency thinks the property is worth. The VA guarantees conventional 30-year mortgages, as well as graduated-payment mortgages, growing-equity mortgages, and other types of loans.

In the past, mortgage rates were set by the VA. Rates are now set by lenders, not by the government. The VA permits veterans to pay points but not to finance them in their loans. The VA collects from the buyer a one-time funding fee of 2 percent of the loan amount at settlement. This pays for the guarantee and will be reduced a bit if you make a down payment.

It's important to understand that the VA does not guarantee the entire mortgage. For example, in 2005, it guaranteed no more than about $89,912 on loans over $144,000. Since lenders generally insist that the guarantee, plus your down payment, cover at least 25 percent of the loan amount, as a practical matter, VA loans maxed out at about $359,650 in 2005.

You can find out whether you qualify for a VA loan by calling or writing the nearest VA office. For general information, call 800-827-1000 for recorded messages describing the program, or visit the VA Web site at http://www.homeloans.va.gov. From the home page, click on "Information on the Home Loan Program," then on "Pamphlets on the VA Home Loan Program" to download VA pamphlets 26-4 and 26-91-1, which cover this topic in detail.

For specific information about eligibility, you will have to supply your military service number, Social Security number, birth date, date of entry into the ser-

> **It's important to understand that the VA does not guarantee the entire mortgage.**

Call a number of lenders. Ask for the interest rate and the points, and how the size of the down payment might affect the rate you'll pay.

vice, date and place of separation, name of the unit you were with when discharged, and type of discharge.

Serious Mortgage Shopping

Begin your search for a mortgage with your real estate agent, who can provide you with a list of potential lenders from the broker's computerized loan origination (CLO) system. These lists don't necessarily cover everything, though, so you need to do some checking on your own. Begin by finding out the rates at your own bank, and then pick up the Yellow Pages and start calling independent mortgage companies, savings institutions, commercial banks, and any credit unions to which you belong.

Simply ask for the current rate on the kind of loan you want—30-year fixed, ARM, and so forth. Ask for the interest rate and the points, and how the size of the down payment might affect the rate. (Mortgage brokers can be helpful because they represent several different lenders. You pay for their service, so make sure you ask for the effective rate to you, net of the broker's fees.)

You can tell from the table on page 102 what your monthly payment would be for different interest rates. (Be aware, however, that the table shows the payment for interest and principal only. Property taxes and insurance are extra and will vary according to the price of the house you're considering and where it is located.) And the worksheet on page 70 should help you determine how much you can afford. In about half an hour on the phone, you can do a pretty good job of surveying the lenders in your area. In some cities, the real estate sections of the newspaper do a lot of the work for you by publishing a list of lenders and their rates, usually once a week. The listing should tell you the name and phone number of the mortgage reporting service that compiled the data. Call that number for a more complete list. There may be a small charge.

But don't stop there. Mortgage lending is a national business these days, so you can conduct a national search for the best rate. The fastest way to do it is on-line. If you don't have access to the Internet, ask your broker to help or make a trip to a computer-equipped friend's house or a large public library. The following sites can be especially helpful. Each carries up-to-date listings of lenders and rates, as well as general mortgage information, calculators, and other helpful tools for mortgage shoppers.

HSH Associates (http://www.hsh.com). Provides mortgage rates, averages by city and state, calculators, and links to lenders.

HomePath (http://www.fanniemae.com/homebuyers/homepath). Sponsored by Fannie Mae, this site lists mortgage lenders in all areas, and provides general information on home and mortgage shopping.

Interest.com (http://mortgages.interest.com). Lists rates from the nation's largest mortgage lenders and brokers and allows online mortgage applications.

Kiplinger.com (http://www.kiplinger.com). Click on "Your Finances," then on "Yields and Rates" for help in comparing mortgages. This links to the BankRate Inc. Web site (http://www.bankrate.com), which follows competitive rates in all 50 states and Washington, D.C., with credit news and helpful calculators.

When you've selected a lender, find out how long the advertised or quoted rate remains effective. Some lenders guarantee the rate for 45 days or 60 days, but others offer no guarantee. If rates have been rising and experts predict that they will hold or continue to rise for the foreseeable future, consider locking in the rate with a loan commitment letter. In addition to including your name and the lender's name, the letter should specify the interest rate, any points and rate-lock fees, the date the rate was locked, and how many days it will be locked. The lock-in guarantees you the rate quoted at the time of application for a specific

> **Mortgage lending is a national business these days, so you can conduct a national search for the best rate. The fastest way to do it is online.**

HOW MUCH WILL THE PAYMENTS BE?

This table shows the monthly payment required per $1,000 of mortgage amount at various interest rates for three common mortgage terms. The numbers shown include principal and interest only; insurance and property taxes would be additional. To determine the monthly payment for a mortgage you're considering, multiply the appropriate amount in the table by the number of thousands of dollars involved. Example: $120,000 at 6.25% for 30 years would be 120 x 6.16, or $739.20 per month for principal and interest.

Interest Rate	15 Years	20 Years	30 Years
4.00 %	7.40	6.06	4.77
4.25	7.52	6.19	4.92
4.50	7.65	6.33	5.07
4.75	7.78	6.46	5.22
5.00	7.91	6.60	5.37
5.25	8.04	6.74	5.52
5.50	8.17	6.88	5.68
5.75	8.30	7.02	5.84
6.00	8.44	7.17	6.00
6.25	8.58	7.31	6.16
6.50	8.72	7.46	6.33
6.75	8.85	7.61	6.49
7.00	8.99	7.76	6.66
7.25	9.13	7.91	6.83
7.50	9.28	8.06	7.00
7.75	9.42	8.21	7.17
8.00	9.56	8.37	7.34
8.25	9.71	8.53	7.52
8.50	9.85	8.68	7.69
8.75	10.00	8.84	7.87
9.00	10.15	9.00	8.05
9.25	10.30	9.16	8.23
9.50	10.45	9.33	8.41
9.75	10.60	9.49	8.60
10.00	10.75	9.66	8.78
10.25	10.90	9.82	8.97
10.50	11.06	9.99	9.15
10.75	11.21	10.16	9.34
11.00	11.37	10.33	9.53
11.25	11.53	10.50	9.72
11.50	11.69	10.67	9.91
11.75	11.85	10.84	10.10
12.00	12.01	11.02	10.29

period of time, in exchange for a fee. The longer the lock-in period, the higher the fee you'll have to pay.

Creative Financing for Difficult Markets

When the housing markets are slow, buyers and sellers often turn to creative financing—unusual loan arrangements that most would shun in ordinary times—to strike deals. Because of their complexity and because so much is at stake, these agreements should be drawn up by a lawyer familiar with the tax and legal ramifications of such deals.

Seller Carryback Mortgage

The seller accepts a mortgage from the buyer for part of the purchase price. Seller carrybacks, also known as take-backs, often bridge the gap between the price of the property and the combined amounts of the down payment and first mortgage. They can be attractive to sellers who don't need the entire proceeds from the sale right away and to buyers trying to work out a contract with terms they can handle.

The seller's interest is protected by a lien on the property that is subordinate to the primary lender's lien—a second mortgage. If the buyer defaults and a foreclosure results, the second mortgage holder will get reimbursed only after the first mortgage holder gets its money. If the foreclosure doesn't yield as much as the original sale price, the second mortgage holder could lose money on the deal.

Payments on seller carrybacks may be figured as though the loan would be paid back over a 20- or 30-year period, but the loans are often due in full (with a balloon payment) 3 to 10 years after the sale. That means the buyer will probably have to sell or refinance.

Seller Financing

In this deal, the seller agrees to finance part of the buyer's down payment through a second mortgage,

These complex and high-stakes agreements should be drawn up by a lawyer familiar with their tax and legal ramifications.

In a typical shared-equity arrangement, the home-buyer is paired with an investor—frequently a parent, relative, or friend.

usually of three to five years. The primary mortgage lender should be told of such an arrangement because the payments on the second mortgage may affect the buyer's ability to meet payments on the first.

Equity Sharing

In a typical shared-equity arrangement, the home-buyer is paired with an investor—frequently a parent, relative, or friend—who supplies all or part of the down payment, plus all or part of the monthly mortgage payment. In return, the investor owns a proportionate share of the home. The other buyer occupies the property, pays part of the mortgage, and pays rent to the investor on the investor's share of the property. The investor reports the rent as income and deducts his or her ownership cost as an investment expense for a rental property. The owner-occupant takes normal homeownership deductions for his or her share of the property. At some future point, when the property is sold or refinanced, the investor gets back the down-payment money plus a share of any appreciation that has taken place. The owner-occupant may buy out the investor and stay put or sell and use the proceeds for a down payment on another home.

Shared-equity arrangements can run into trouble if the parties disagree over when to sell, how much to sell for, or how to treat the value of improvements made by the owner-occupant. A shared-equity arrangement should address such issues in the agreement—for instance, by specifying that an appraiser will arbitrate disputes over what is a fair price.

Buy-Down

A buy-down is a mortgage that carries a below-market interest rate because the seller of the home has paid the lender a fee to make such a loan. When new homes are hard to sell, builders are sometimes willing to subsidize buyers this way. The low-interest feature usually lasts two or three years, then is adjusted to the market level or some other preset rate. The cost of a buy-down may or may not be passed on to you in the form of a higher home price. Make sure you measure the trade-offs and read the fine print.

Balloon Loan

In a balloon-payment contract, the borrower agrees to make a lump-sum payment of the loan balance at the end of a certain period, typically two to ten years. In the meantime, periodic payments are set up as though the loan were going to run for much longer. Some require only interest payments until the date the loan is due. This arrangement keeps current payments down and gives the borrower an opportunity to sell the property or refinance the loan before the balloon comes due.

Balloon-payment contracts can be useful, but they can also be dangerous. Before you sign such a loan, be sure you know exactly when the balloon payment will be due, how large it will be, and whether an escape clause exists if for some reason you can't come up with the money.

A lender, especially if it is an individual, will want to schedule the balloon payment to coincide with his or her future financial needs. But for the borrower, the further away the due date the better. Seven years should be long enough to ensure an opportunity to sell or refinance before the balloon falls due.

Should You Refinance Your Mortgage?

A popular rule of thumb says you should consider refinancing your mortgage—that is, swapping the old one for a new one at a lower rate—if you can cut the old rate by two percentage points or more. That's generally a solid guideline, but like all rules of thumb, it's not entirely reliable. If you're carrying a jumbo mortgage, for instance, or if you plan to stay put for many years, refinancing could be worthwhile with a smaller differential—say, one percentage point. The situation gets even more complicated when you compare fixed rates with ARMs or want to switch to a shorter-term loan.

A popular rule of thumb says to consider refinancing if you can cut your old rate by two percentage points or more. Like all rules of thumb, it's not entirely reliable.

Unlike points for the original mortgage, points for refinancing must be deducted on a pro-rata basis over the life of the loan.

Refinancing isn't free: You'll have to pay a lump sum up front, perhaps several thousand dollars, in exchange for those lower monthly payments. The key in any case is how long it will take you to pay yourself back. The worksheet on the opposite page shows you how to figure that out.

What If You Have an ARM?

If you have an adjustable-rate mortgage and plan to stay in your house for years to come, it could make sense to lock in a fixed rate. You won't necessarily save a lot of money compared with the ARM you're trading in, but you get the peace of mind of knowing you won't lose if rates rise. If you plan to sell within two or three years, stick with the ARM you've got. It could take several years to pay off the cost of refinancing via lower monthly payments, and in the meantime your annual adjustments will keep you within shouting distance of current rates anyway.

SHOULD YOU SWAP AN OLD ARM FOR A NEW ONE? First-year "teaser" rates make it tempting, but remember, after the first year, your interest rate would hover at about the level it would have been on your old ARM, assuming the index and the margin are the same. You come out ahead only if your first-year savings exceed the cost of refinancing. That's possible but unlikely.

Tax Facts for Refinancers

When you're refinancing just the balance of your mortgage, interest on the entire amount you borrow is tax-deductible. If you borrow additional money, the interest on up to $100,000 extra is also deductible, as home-equity debt.

Unlike points for the original mortgage, points for refinancing must be deducted on a pro-rata basis over the life of the loan, whether you pay them in cash or add them to the loan. For a 30-year loan, for instance, you deduct 1/30th of the total paid each year. Exception: If you use the funds for home improvements,

REFINANCING: HOW MUCH WOULD IT SAVE?

This worksheet lets you figure out how long it would take to break even after the expenses of refinancing, and what your savings would be thereafter. The example is based on a fixed-rate $200,000 mortgage at 7% for 30 years, refinanced at 5.5% for 30 years.

	OUR EXAMPLE	YOUR LOAN
The Cost of Refinancing		
1. Points	$2,000	$_____
2. Application fee	125	_____
3. Title search and insurance	500	_____
4. Inspections	200	_____
5. Survey	150	_____
6. Lender's underwriting fee	400	_____
7. Credit report	50	_____
8. Appraisal	300	_____
9. Lawyer fees	400	_____
10. Recording fees	50	_____
11. Transfer taxes	1,000	_____
12. Other fees	0	_____
Total Cost of Refinancing	**$5,175**	$_____
The Payback		
1. Current monthly payment (P&I)	$1,331	$_____
2. Subtract new monthly payment (P&I) (30-year fixed-rate at 5.5%)	−1,136	−_____
3. Pretax savings per month	195	_____
4. Multiply tax rate (e.g., 25%) by savings and subtract result	−49	−_____
5. After-tax savings per month	$146	$_____
Number of Months to Break Even Divide monthly savings ($146) into total cost of refinancing ($5,175)	**35**	_____

the interest is considered to be paid on home-equity debt, and points are deductible in the year paid.

You can keep money in your pocket by folding the closing costs into the loan. This also has the effect of adding normally nondeductible charges, such as for an appraisal, to the amount on which you pay tax-deductible interest.

Where to Look for the Loan

Check first with your current lender to see whether it offers lower rates to its customers. To compare fixed-rate loans, look at the annual percentage rate, even though it has limitations. The APR assumes you'll hold the loan to maturity, for instance. Some lenders include the application fee in calculating the APR, while others do not. Ask for the rate apart from the fees, and note which fees are nonrefundable.

Refinancing usually takes more equity than buying a house. Some lenders won't lend more than 75 percent of a home's value if you're borrowing more money than you owe on the existing mortgage. Some will let you borrow more than the value of the house, which is a bad idea for two reasons: First, you can't deduct interest on any portion of the loan that exceeds the value of the house; and second, why would you want to stick your neck out that far?

Selling Your Home

Chapter 7

Most people selling a home are buying another one at the same time. This creates an interesting dilemma: Should you sell the old place first, thus ensuring that you'll have the money to afford a new house, but taking the chance that someone else will come along and buy the house you want while you're waiting for your old one to sell? Or should you go ahead and put a contract on a new place before you sell the old one, thus taking the chance that when the time comes to settle you won't have the money to close the deal?

The obvious way out of such a predicament is to write a contract making the purchase of the new place contingent on your sale of the old one. But contingency contracts tilt the deal in favor of the buyer, and in this case you're also a seller. Contingencies work best in sluggish markets, when a seller has no other offer and no prospect of another offer in the immediate future. Otherwise, why take your home off the market for 30 to 60 days for what amounts to a definite maybe?

Clearly, selling first makes you a more attractive buyer. But selling means you've agreed to move out of the old place on a particular date, and the closer you get to that date, the greater the pressure to find a new place to buy (or rent). After all, you have to live somewhere.

One thing you can do is try to get your buyers to agree on a settlement date that's more distant than usual—perhaps 90 days away rather than the 30 or 45 days commonly written into a purchase contract. You

Most sellers list their homes with an agent, for whose services they pay 6 percent or so of the sales price. That's thousands of dollars; you'll want to be sure you get your money's worth.

could also ask the buyers to consider renting the place back to you for a short time after closing. You'll have to offer enough rent to cover the new owners' mortgage, taxes, and insurance, plus a security deposit to reassure them about possible damage to the property while you're living there.

If you choose to buy before you sell and can't get a contingency contract, you may have trouble qualifying for the mortgage. What the lender sees is someone who might have to make payments on two houses at once, not to mention come up with a down payment on the new one before selling the old one.

You might be able to use a home-equity line of credit on the old house to get the cash for a down payment on the new one. In that case, the lender sees someone at risk of owing payments on three loans: the mortgage on the old house, the mortgage on the new house, and the equity loan on the old house. Unless you've got a hefty income to draw on, you probably won't get the new mortgage.

Hiring a Real Estate Agent

The overwhelming majority of sellers—about 85 percent—list their homes with an agent, for whose services they pay 6 percent or so of the sales price. That's thousands of dollars, and you'll want to be sure you get your money's worth.

Start with a clear understanding of the labels. An agent is the commonly used term for a salesperson who is licensed to work for a real estate broker. A broker is licensed to run a real estate business and negotiate transactions for a fee. A broker can also be called an agent. Some brokers and agents are also Realtors, which they always spell with a capital "R" because it is a trade name. It signifies membership in the National Association of Realtors, a trade and lobbying organization that offers training for members and holds them to a code of ethics. Your broker should have access to the Multiple Listing Service (MLS), a data bank of homes for sale consulted by other agents with potential buyers.

Some Realtors will list the initials "GRI" after their names. That stands for Graduate, Realtor Institute, which requires at least 90 hours of study. A handful can call themselves CRS, or Certified Residential Specialists. Those initials signify lots of experience and extra hours of study.

Start your search for an agent by getting references from satisfied customers. Ask friends and neighbors (and former neighbors) whether they would recommend an agent they have used in the past. Look for names on "For Sale" signs around the neighborhood because you want an agent who is active in your area. Stop by their open houses and see how they conduct themselves. Then call two or three who impress you and invite them to make a listing presentation—that is, ask them to compete for the listing by showing you how they would market your house.

Each agent should be willing to supply copies of actual ads and brochures he or she has used to sell homes like yours. Ask how many homes in your price range each has sold in the past year. Ask how many ads will run for your home and in which publications. Finally, get names of recent clients and call them to see if they were satisfied with the agent's performance.

Start your search for an agent by getting references from satisfied customers. Ask friends and neighbors (and former neighbors).

How to List Your Home

When you've made your choice of agents, you'll have to decide how the property should be listed. The following are the principal ways:

Exclusive Right to Sell

This arrangement, the most widely used, provides that a commission will be owed to the listing broker no matter who sells the property. Because the broker is sure to benefit from this agreement, you should get the best possible service.

Exclusive Agency

This is similar, except no commission is owed if you sell the property yourself. If you sign an agreement

WHAT AN AGENT SHOULD DO FOR SELLERS

Draw up a full description of the property, plus information about tax and utility rates, the neighborhood, and nearby facilities, such as parks, schools, and public transportation.

Brief you on things you can do to make the place as appealing as possible, such as painting, making repairs, tidying up the yard, and seeing that appliances are working.

Help set the price. You should be provided with "comparables,"or "comps" (recent selling prices and current asking prices of similar properties).

Act as a marketing coordinator. Your agent should market your property to other real estate agents and the public using contacts, referrals, Internet Web sites, and the Multiple Listing Service.

Prepare forms for prospective buyers giving detailed information about the property and terms of sale.

"Sit" on the property—that is, be there or have another agent there to receive prospects, at least one afternoon a week, and hold your open house on specified Saturdays or Sundays.

Be available to show the property during regular business hours and some evenings and weekends.

Know where mortgage money can be obtained and provide prospects with information about rates and other terms.

Screen prospective buyers to find out whether they're financially able to make the purchase.

Promptly present you with all offers to purchase and advise you of any problems with them.

Assist in the settlement of the transaction as your representative. (Also should have a lawyer because real estate agents aren't supposed to give legal advice.)

like this, you are in effect competing with your own listing agent, who, because there may be no commission at all, has somewhat less incentive to work hard on your listing.

Open Listing

With this agreement, you can list your property with several brokers at the same time. You agree to pay a commission to the first agent to produce an acceptable buyer—typically half the standard 6 percent or 7 percent. This type of listing is used by sellers who want to do most of the selling work themselves but want the cooperation of agents in finding buyers. No commission is owed if the owner makes the sale.

What the Agreement Covers

A listing agreement is a legally enforceable contract. It sets forth the kind of listing and other specifics, including a description of the property, the price, the terms of sale, and the fee or commission.

Contracts often run from three to six months. Make the duration as short as possible. You can extend a listing beyond its original life, so don't lock yourself into an initial contract that binds you for too long. Some contracts provide for an automatic extension of the listing period. If you encounter such a provision, have it changed. Your agreement with the broker, like the commission itself, is negotiable.

Some agreements provide that the commission will be payable when a purchaser is produced who is ready, willing, and able to buy on the terms provided, whether or not settlement occurs. That means that if your agent produces a willing buyer, you could be obliged to pay a commission even if you change your mind about selling or are unable to sell for some reason during the listing period. Have any such provision stricken, or choose a different agent.

What If You Have a Grievance?

If the broker doesn't resolve it to your satisfaction, take it up with the state real estate commission and, if the company is a member, the local Board of Realtors.

Selling without an Agent

I f you have a knack for marketing, are well organized, and have a lot of time, you may want to sell your home without an agent. About 15 percent of sellers moving up to a better home successfully sell the old one by themselves. About half as many try to sell it themselves but wind up listing with an agent.

> **You can extend a listing, so don't lock yourself into an initial contract that binds you for too long.**

Married couples filing a joint return can keep, tax-free, up to $500,000 in profit from the sale of their primary residence. Singles can keep up to $250,000.

The obvious attraction of a FSBO—short for "for sale by owner" and usually pronounced "fizzbo"—is that it saves you several thousand dollars. You can pocket the money, or you can share the savings with the buyer in the form of a lower price, which makes your home more competitive in the marketplace.

There's an in-between approach to the broker question, and that's to list your home with a discount broker. Discounters charge a smaller commission in exchange for your willingness to do some of the work. It can be a good solution if you have the time and want to save the money. Shop for a discount broker the same way you'd shop for a full-service broker.

Tax Angles for Home Sellers

Married couples filing a joint return can keep, tax-free, up to $500,000 in profit from the sale of their primary residence. Singles can keep up to $250,000 in profit tax-free. To qualify, you need to have owned and lived in the house for at least two of the five years leading up to the sale. You can cash in on this tax break once every two years, unless you acquired the home through a tax-free exchange. Then you must own the home for five years before you sell.

You should still keep track of your home's cost basis, which is the cash you have invested in your home, in case you ever need to figure depreciation deductions for a home office or for a room you've rented out. Those portions of the house don't qualify for the tax-free gains. Keep invoices for any major home improvements you make over the years, too. The costs add to your basis and cut capital-gains tax if your profit exceeds the tax-free amount when you sell.

One tax break you *won't* get: When you sell your home, you can't take a tax deduction for points you agree to pay on the buyer's behalf.

Rent to Your Heart's Content

Chapter 8

Despite the grand attractions of homeownership, most of us start our adult lives as renters. Some of us even choose to remain renters, and why not? A strong case can be made for the renter's life.

YOU GET MORE SPACE FOR THE MONEY. This isn't always true, but usually you can rent an apartment or even a house for less than the monthly cost of owning it, not to mention the down payment, the cost of painting it, planting shrubbery, fixing the driveway, and on and on.

YOU'VE GOT MORE FREEDOM. When it's time to leave, you just leave, with no encumbering financial investment to worry about, no waiting to sell, no agonizing over all those decisions described in Chapter 7. Compared with a homeowner, you are footloose and fancy-free.

YOU CAN ADJUST MORE EASILY TO CHANGE. If your fortunes improve, you can move to a bigger place or a more desirable neighborhood. If you hit a run of bad financial luck, it's easier to scale down your lifestyle. If you marry, or add a child to the family, you can move more easily than a homeowner.

YOU WORRY LESS ABOUT PROPERTY VALUES. Renters deny this, but it's true. If the neighborhood declines, the worst that can happen is that you have to wait until your lease expires in order to move. The owner, meanwhile, may be facing financial disaster.

Renters aren't entirely free of financial cares. They want to be sure they get a decent lease. And they need insurance to protect their belongings from harm.

YOU HAVE MORE MONEY FOR OTHER THINGS. There's a reason Home Depot got so big. Not only must home-owners spend to maintain their properties, they also have an almost irresistible itch to improve it. They buy ladders and lumber, toolsheds and table saws, fencing and fireplace screens. They add on, upgrade, and re-seed. Meanwhile, their renter neighbors are calling the landlord to fix the plumbing while they're planning their vacation in Cancun and boosting their contributions to their 401(k) plans. (Okay, that last one may be exaggerated a bit, but you get the idea: A good argument can be made for renting.)

Still, renters aren't entirely free of financial cares. While owners fret over zoning changes, property values, and other matters of interest to the landed gentry, renters have a few worries of their own. They want to be sure they get a decent lease. And, though they don't own the walls that surround them, they do own the stuff surrounded by those walls: the TV and stereo, the clothes and the furniture. They need insurance to protect that stuff from harm.

A Lease You Can Live With

Unless you're a lawyer, you can't be expected to understand everything in a lease. Luckily, the dangers said to be lurking there are often overblown. The lease offered by an individual land-lord may be an off-the-shelf form from the local stationery store or, if an agent is involved, a standard-issue form approved by the local Board of Realtors. Big management companies will have their own leases. Either way, the document will favor the land-lord. It will favor the landlord in its raw form, and it will favor the landlord when you've finished negotiating over it. Still, if you know what to expect, perhaps you can get a clause or two to lean your way as a tenant.

Most of a lease is boilerplate. It describes the property, lists the name of the tenant and landlord, and specifies what the rent will be and when and where it is

> ## KEEP AN INVENTORY
>
> If damage is done to your home, you'll want to be in a position to assess your losses. It's easy if you make a good inventory of your home and belongings. The best method is to photograph or videotape them; use close-ups to highlight items of particular value, making a slow sweep of each room, closet, and storage area. Keep the videotape and receipts for high-ticket items in a safe-deposit box away from home; also enclose a list of each item with either its actual cash value or the current replacement value, depending on your type of policy.

to be paid, plus penalties for paying it late. It states the size of the security deposit, how it will be held, and under what circumstances you will get it back. There's an important section that states how long the lease will run (usually a year) and what happens when it expires (usually the tenant can stay on until either party gives 30 days' written notice of a need to vacate the place). All this is standard, but you should check to make sure the lease says what you think it says. Check also for information on the following:

- **Do you get storage space?** Laundry-room privileges? Use of a party room?
- **Can you take in a roommate?** What if you get married?
- **Will the landlord pay you interest** on your security deposit? In some jurisdictions this is required. If not, you may be able to get it just for the asking.
- **Can you keep a pet?** If so, what kind? The lease may require additional rent or a higher security deposit.
- **Who is responsible for utilities?**
- **Can you assign the lease** to someone else or sublet the property? The landlord will probably want to approve anyone to whom you sublet or assign, if such actions are permitted at all.
- **Under what circumstances may the landlord enter** and inspect the property? He or she will have this right, but the right-to-entry clause typically requires 24 to 48 hours' notice to the tenant.

When it comes to paying for losses, policies make a distinction between cash-value coverage and replacement-cost coverage. You want the latter.

■ **If something breaks or malfunctions,** who is responsible for fixing it?

Get Renters Insurance

Renters insurance provides protection for such items as your stereo, TV, personal computer, jewelry, and bike if they're stolen by a burglar or damaged by fire, smoke, explosion, lightning, windstorm, or sudden water damage from a plumbing problem. Renters insurance also provides liability coverage in case someone is hurt in your home and chooses to sue you.

Renters insurance costs a couple of hundred dollars a year for an average level of coverage. Consider it a must. The standard form is what an agent will call Homeowners 4, even though it is designed expressly for renters. It covers your personal property against loss or damage up to the level specified in the policy, plus $100,000 of liability. You get a little coverage for medical payments for others, too, which might come in handy if, say, a friend agrees to help you hang a ceiling lamp, falls off the ladder, and breaks his arm.

If you have expensive antiques or jewelry, or a valuable collection of any kind, ask the insurance agent about a personal-property endorsement to cover them. (No matter what the "value" of your possessions, it's a good idea to make a record of what you have, so you won't have to rely on memory in case of a catastrophe. If you can, walk through the house with a camera or videocamera, carefully scanning each room. Take out valuables and photograph them separately. Finally, put the photos or film in a safe place—a fireproof safe in the house or a safe-deposit box at the bank.)

When it comes to paying for losses, policies make a distinction between cash-value coverage and replacement-cost coverage. You want the latter. In case of a loss, it pays you what it would cost to replace the lost item with a new one. To appreciate the value of this, estimate the current cash value of your three-year-old computer, your five-year-old television set, or your nine-year-old stereo. Not much. That's why you want replacement-cost coverage, not cash-value.

If you rent an apartment with friends, you may run into an unusual insurance problem that affects renters. Say a woman and her two housemates wanted insurance policies to cover individual belongings. Each approached her own auto insurer in the expectation of getting a better price for coverage by carrying multiple policies with the same company. That usually works, but in this case each woman was told that she couldn't get renters insurance unless the other two renters were already insured. That made no sense to them and saved nobody any money. If you run into this problem, consider moving your auto insurance to a company that will cover you on both fronts without involving your roommates.

When the Landlord Won't Fix It

In most states, the law says that landlords provide an implied warranty of habitability, which means that the house or apartment they offer is suitable for living in and that it complies with state and local housing, building, health, and safety codes. As a tenant, you can expect heat, hot water, lights, plumbing, door locks, toilets, and other essentials to work and be maintained properly.

If your home is not made habitable, you may withhold your rent, pay rent into escrow, ask for a reduction in rent, or deduct the cost of repairing the item from your rent (depending on your state and local laws). If things really look bleak, you might also be able to terminate your lease or sue the landlord. If you see trouble coming, put everything in writing, keep copies, and don't go too far down this path without the advice of a lawyer.

> **If your home is not made habitable, you may withhold your rent, pay rent into escrow, ask for a reduction in rent, or deduct the cost of repairing the item from your rent.**

Owning a Vacation Home

Chapter 9

There are lots of good reasons to want a vacation home, and hardly any of them are financial. There are psychological reasons, emotional reasons, family reasons. These kinds of reasons tend to push financial considerations into the background. But the financial side can't be overlooked. Is a vacation home an investment or is it an indulgence? Should you consider it a moneymaking proposition or just admit that you bought it because, well, you wanted it? Often it's a little bit of each. Either way, you're spending money—a lot of it. And if you're counting on rent receipts from other vacationers to help underwrite the cost, the choices you make when you buy carry extra weight.

As with any real estate, location counts more than any other single factor. The best vacation properties offer something special—a view of the ocean, a mountain vista, a dock on a lake. For maximum appeal to potential renters or future buyers, look for a place within three hours' drive of a major metropolitan area. Longer distances or difficult roads make weekend trips a pain, and that limits your market. A wonderful new cabin on a remote beach that can be reached only by four-wheel-drive vehicles appeals to a few renters and buyers. A creaky, aging cottage in an easily accessible area near restaurants and year-round activities appeals to a lot more. By the same token, a condo apartment development complete with pool, tennis courts, and beach has more appeal than the same development without such amenities. The difference, of course, is reflected in the price tag.

Mortgage interest on a second home is deductible on as much as $1 million in principal for both homes combined.

Buying the Place

Vacation-home buyers often make down payments of 20 to 50 percent. Some even pay cash if they're buying a less expensive cabin or condo. Where do they get the money? A home-equity credit line drawn on their primary residence is a favorite source (see Chapter 3). Mortgage interest on a second home is deductible on as much as $1 million in principal for both homes combined.

Higher interest rates used to be the rule for mortgages on second homes, because lenders considered them a greater risk than loans on primary residences. But these days you should be able to find a second-home mortgage at first-home rates. (Exception: If you'll be counting on rent receipts to help pay the mortgage, the rates will probably be higher.) Use the mortgage-hunting tools described in Chapter 6. The bad news is that, burdened though you may be with two mortgages (or three, counting the home-equity line), lenders will expect you to stay within the debt-to-income limits dictated by Fannie Mae and Freddie Mac. Your total debt payments, including all mortgages, can't exceed 36 percent of your gross income. The good news is that if you plan to rent the place out, you can count some of that assumed rent as income when calculating the ratio. The lender will tell you what's an acceptable assumption.

Renting It Out

About one fourth of vacation homes are rented to other people for part of the year, and the appeal of different kinds of properties varies with the seasons. Naturally, Christmas and New Year's are the peak rental times at mountain ski resorts. Beach homes in the South do best in the winter months. Further north, beach and mountain resorts are popular mostly in the summer.

For tax purposes, vacation homes are subject to what's called the 14-day or 10 percent rule. You can rent your place for up to 14 days a year and pocket the rental income without having to declare it on your tax return. If you rent out the house for more than 14 days a year, you are considered a landlord by the Internal Revenue Service and you must report the income. But you also qualify to deduct certain expenses.

The way you divide the time between personal use and rental use of the place determines your status in the eyes of the IRS. If your own personal use amounts to more than 14 days a year, or more than 10 percent of the number of days the home is rented out, whichever is longer, the house is considered your personal residence. If you use it for fewer than 14 days (or less than 10 percent of the time it is rented to others), it's considered a rental property.

The difference determines how much you get to deduct. If you meet the less-than-14-day-or-10 percent test, you can write off all the usual expenses associated with owning a rental property. (For a description of these, see Chapter 26). If you rent the house half the time, for instance, half of your mortgage interest, property taxes, utilities, insurance costs, and repair expenses are deductible against rental income. (The other half of your interest and property taxes would still be deductible against your other income because it's a second home.) You also get to deduct depreciation for the 50 percent of the house that's considered rental property. And you can write off 100 percent of the cost of advertising for tenants or other expenses directly related to renting. If your personal use exceeds the 14-day-or-10 percent limit, you can deduct expenses only up to the amount of your rental income.

Note that "personal use" is broadly defined by the IRS. It covers you or any member of your family, including your spouse, children, siblings, parents, grandparents, and grandchildren. Any day you rent the place to anyone for less than fair market value counts as a personal day. Trading your place for a stay at some other place counts, too, as does any time you donate your property for charitable use.

Vacation-home owners considering retiring to their second home for a while after selling their first home get a double tax break: Make it your permanent resi-

"Personal use" covers you or any member of your family, from your spouse to your grandparents and grandchildren.

With time-span ownership, you can sell your time-share, give it away, or leave it to your loved ones in your will. It's all yours.

dence for at least two of the five years before you sell and you qualify for up to $500,000 of tax-free profit ($250,000 if you're single) on the sale, just as you did on your first home. If you don't convert your vacation home to your principal residence, you'll owe tax on any profit from the sale. If you have owned the place for more than 18 months, the profit is a long-term capital gain and is taxed at a rate of 20 percent, except for the profit created by depreciation deductions you claimed as a landlord. (Remember that depreciation lowers your cost basis in the property, thus increasing any profit when you sell.) Depreciation recapture, as this portion of the gain is called, is taxed at 25 percent.

Suppose all these deductions result in a loss for the year? If your adjusted gross income is less than $100,000, you can deduct up to $25,000 of rental losses. As your income rises to $150,000, this loss allowance gradually disappears. But don't lose faith: If your income is over the limit, you don't lose the deduction entirely. You add up the losses year by year and hold them in reserve. When you sell the home, you add all these unrealized losses to your cost basis, which has the effect of reducing any profit on the sale, and thus any tax you might owe on the profit.

You also must actively manage the property to qualify for the current deduction. Active management isn't strictly defined, but you're probably safe if you make key decisions, such as approving tenants, rental terms, and repairs.

Should You Buy a Timeshare?

When you find a resort you like, you might be tempted by a good sales pitch to purchase a time-share unit (or its younger cousin, the fractional interest) so you can return there year after year.

Timeshares are usually sold in weeklong chunks. Fractional units are sold as quarter-shares (13 weeks), fifth-shares (10 weeks), and tenth-shares (5 weeks). So, for example, if you bought a fifth-share in a resort, you would be entitled to use the property for ten weeks, spread throughout the year (each year, the sequence shifts forward a week, so each fractional owner gets a chance at the best seasons.) You can buy a timeshare for as little as $5,000 or so and a fractional unit starting at about $25,000, so these deals have appeal if your budget won't support a vacation home all your own.

Ownership is usually in the form of tenancy in common with the other owners (also called time-span ownership) or in the form of interval ownership. So what, exactly, do you own? With time-span ownership, you own an undivided interest in the property based on the number of weeks you purchased. You can sell your timeshare, give it away, or leave it to your loved ones in your will. It's all yours. Interval ownership, on the other hand, lasts for a specified number of years, typically, the expected life span of the building. When those years are up, you and the other interval owners become tenants in common, with your percentage of ownership determined by the number of weeks you own.

In general, the value of fractional shares seems to have appreciated better than that of timeshares, but marketing costs often eat deeply into anticipated profits.

One form of timesharing, called a club membership, vacation license, or vacation lease, comes with no ownership rights. The key words are right there: club, license, lease. All these things have finite lives. You can use the property as long as you're a member, or as long as the lease lasts, but ownership stays in the hands of the developer. You have a nice place to go on vacation, prepaid, but the fact is, you own nothing.

Before You Buy

Ask for a copy of the contract, maintenance-fee schedule, disclosure statement, and customer references. Take these papers home and study them carefully, looking for satisfactory answers to the following questions:

- **Has the developer set aside an adequate cash reserve** for maintenance and repairs?
- **What are your annual maintenance fees** and how much can they rise each year?

> **One form of timesharing, called a club membership, vacation license, or vacation lease, comes with no ownership rights. You have a nice place to go on vacation, but you own nothing.**

Unlike other vacation homes, financing for timeshares is usually available only through the developer or by getting a personal loan.

- **Can you be assessed for major repairs**—that is, ordered to pay a share?
- **What happens if the developer sells out?** Make sure the contract contains a "nondisturbance clause" that allows you to stay in the unit even if the resort is sold to another developer.
- **Is the unit listed** with one of the time-share exchange services, or will you have to take care of that yourself (see the discussion below)?
- **Can you resell your timeshare** at any time you want or are there restrictions? Must you use the developer to resell?

Before you buy a new timeshare, be sure to check out the resale market in the same area. Prices are likely to be half what the original owner paid. But remember: Although a resale timeshare may cost less than a new unit, its value is likely to languish after you buy because that's the nature of timeshares. But at least you won't have paid too much!

The price you pay to get in is just the beginning of the cost of your time-share adventure. Count on paying several hundred dollars a year in maintenance fees. If you want to exchange your unit for time at other places around the world, you'll pay between $80 and $90 or so in annual dues to an exchange company, plus an exchange fee of about $120 to $190 each time you swap.

You certainly should visit the resort in person, maybe renting for a few days before deciding whether to buy. Then check the local classified ads and resale brokers, plus the online bulletin boards, to see what else is available. The Timeshare User's Group (http://www.tug2.net) offers reviews and numerical ratings of time-share resorts, posted by people who have visited them. You can also find individual listings of time-shares for sale by exploring through a search engine such as Google, Yahoo!, or Excite.

Unlike other vacation homes, financing for time-shares is usually available only through the developer or by getting a personal loan. Home-equity loans can be useful for this (see Chapter 3). Otherwise, expect to put at least 10 percent down and pay off the balance over a period of 5 to 10 years. Interest is deductible if the loan is secured by ownership in a property.

Exchanging to Get Out of the Rut

When timeshares first got started, owning one meant you were stuck with spending the same week at the same resort year after year. Since the 1970s, though, exchange networks have grown to encompass thousands of resorts around the world. More recently, networks such as those run by Disney, Hilton, and Marriott allow you to trade your time-share rights for lodging at other resorts they own.

Most timeshare owners happily pay $80 to $90 a year to belong to an exchange company such as Interval International (http://www.resortdeveloper.com; 800-622-1861) or Resort Condominiums International (http://www.rci.com; 800-338-7777). Each publishes an annual directory of member timeshares, with photos and a brief description of amenities.

Your timeshare's value on the exchange market will determine where else you might be able to go for a swap. If you want to receive a week skiing in Aspen for your beach condo in Myrtle Beach, then you'll need to own a prime week at an upscale resort there. You'll be able to exchange only for properties that are no more valuable than your own.

Selling a Timeshare (Alas!)

Expect to get no more than half of what you originally paid. That's the sad experience of many time-share sellers. Here are some savvy strategies for selling:

ONLINE: The Timeshare User's Group (http://www.tug2.net) carries classified ads on the Internet, as do several other organizations.

AT AUCTION: Time-share auctions are held regularly by Second Market Timeshare Resales (http://www

> **Expect to get no more than half of what you originally paid when you sell your timeshare.**

.2ndmarkettimeshares.com; 800-826-4670), based in Virginia, and TRI West (http://www.triwest-timeshare .com; 800-423-6377), based in California. Either company will supply scheduling information when you call. At an auction, you might make a quick, low-priced sale—say, at 25 percent of your original cost before the company's fees.

THE OLD-FASHIONED WAY: Real estate firms and national time-share resellers sometimes succeed, but their fees are higher than for a conventional real estate deal. (For instance, Chilson & Associates International Real Estate Co. charges a 20 percent commission on the sale of timeshares.) Check for resale programs run by your own timeshare managers (but again, watch out for high fees). Or try the do-it-yourself approach: Put up "For Sale" notices on public bulletin boards and take out classified ads in newspapers. You can also try to sell your timeshare on eBay.

Homeowners Insurance

Chapter 10

Homeowners insurance is one of those financial facts of life that just kind of happens to you. When you buy a home, the mortgage lender will insist on insurance coverage, so you get an agent's name, call up, and buy a policy. Odds are the premiums are even paid from the same lender-controlled escrow account that pays your property tax. Out of sight, out of mind. You don't give homeowners insurance much thought—unless you try to file a claim and get into a squabble with the company.

The danger here is that insuring your home year after year becomes so routine that you fall prey to three potentially costly errors:

- **Assuming that all homeowners policies are alike.** Actually, policies come in several varieties, and different companies' versions of those varieties differ.
- **Taking it for granted that your insurance company charges about the same premium as others.** Prices, in fact, can differ by astonishingly large margins.
- **Failing to update your coverage periodically.** Even if your policy protects against inflation, the value of your home may outpace it; and as you accumulate more possessions, you may find your personal property dangerously underinsured.

To make sure you have the right protection for your property, review the basic aspects of homeowners policies described in this chapter. They're important to know for another reason, too. Homeowners coverage extends over many areas, some of which seem so unrelated to your house that you may have overlooked submitting claims for losses you didn't realize were covered.

The basic characteristics of the major types of homeowners policies are summarized on the table on pages 136 and 137. The descriptions are based on standard forms used by insurance companies and the most common amounts of coverage. Each policy type is identified in the table by number (HO-2 and so on) and, in parentheses, by the name often used in the insurance business. One or the other designation should appear somewhere on your policy, although details will differ. Homeowners policies combine two kinds of insurance.

Coverage for the House and Contents

This part of the policy pays you mainly for losses to the house and related property. And, perhaps much to your surprise, it also may entitle you to other things, such as reimbursement for additional living expenses or loss of rental income incurred when you or someone renting part of your house has to move temporarily because of damage to the living quarters.

The coverage on losses other than the house itself are generally figured as a percentage of the coverage on the house. For instance, with HO-2 and HO-3, your personal property is automatically insured for 50 percent of the house amount. (More coverage is available on many policies—see the discussion of "replacement cost" for household contents later in this chapter.) That 50 percent is in addition to the insurance on the structure, not part of it. With renters and condominium policies, the coverage depends on how much personal-property insurance you buy.

You can increase some coverages without raising the amount on the structure by paying an additional premium. The special limits of liability that are listed in the table represent the maximum paid for specific items. To get more coverage, you could insure them separately. You can also get additional insurance for a number of items or situations that get limited coverage in a standard policy: off-premises theft; coins, stamps, silverware, and guns; business losses; and household help.

Liability Coverage

If your dog bites the mail carrier, or the neighbor's car is crushed by bricks falling from your crumbling chimney, this part of the policy has got you covered—up to a point. Comprehensive personal liability covers damage to property of others and medical payments to others for injuries or damage caused by you or by an accident around your home. Personal-liability coverage kicks in when you are considered legally liable for an injury. It would even pay for legal bills if necessary. To get coverage for medical payments for others, you aren't required to be legally responsible for the injury. You would be covered, for instance, if a visitor tripped over a gap in your front walk and broke an ankle, or if you accidentally beaned someone on the golf course. A typical policy limits personal-liability coverage to $100,000 and medical payments to others to $1,000 per person. You can see that the coverage, though comforting, isn't exactly overwhelming.

Liability coverage typically extends to the policyholder and to family members who live in the house.

How Policies Differ

There are homeowners policies for houses, for condo and co-op apartments, even for renters (see Chapter 8). The major forms of house policies, called HO-2 and HO-3, offer similar protection on most points. The crucial differences lie in the number of perils your home and property are insured against.

Covered Perils

A homeowners policy will normally compensate you for losses to the building and personal property only if the damage is caused by a peril named in the policy. Other parts of the policy may not apply unless an insured peril produces the loss. For example, all policies

Comprehensive personal liability covers damage to property of others and medical payments to others for injuries or damage caused by you or by an accident around your home.

pay for emergency repairs to protect the house after an accident, but only on the condition that the damage to the house resulted from an insured peril. This isn't a major worry, because the named perils are pretty comprehensive, but ignorance of your policy can lead to disappointments. No homeowners policy covers damage from floods, for instance. You have to buy that separately (see page 140).

Not all the policies that insure against a particular peril necessarily provide the same degree of protection, so you have to ask the agent to walk you through the coverage. The HO-3's all-risk coverage on the structure may also include items inside the home; features like wall-to-wall carpet and a built-in dishwasher add value to the house and are often considered part of the structure rather than personal property (as in the HO-2).

If you're considering the HO-3, check whether the risks you are concerned about are covered. The standard HO-3, for instance, won't pay for damage caused by settling, a problem that often concerns homeowners. It also excludes damage from such perils as earthquakes and war (although damage from "civil commotion," such as a riot, is covered). You should buy earthquake insurance if you live in a high-risk area, especially if yours is an older, masonry home or you have much equity invested in it. For this coverage, you have to buy a special add-on, called an endorsement.

When you're looking for a policy to cover items such as pictures, antiques, furs, and musical instruments, you might do better by buying additional insurance in the form of riders than by purchasing a homeowners policy with more blanket coverage. The upscale package policies now offered by many companies may provide more coverage than you need, although their prices have gotten increasingly competitive in recent years.

Payback and the 80 Percent Rule

Insurance companies compute payments for homeowners policy losses in two ways. One, called replacement cost, covers what it would cost to rebuild your home if it were totally destroyed or to replace items in it. The other, called actual cash value, takes deprecia-tion into account and pays only the market value of the loss. Thus, your three-year-old television that cost $500 new might be worth only $200 in a cash-value policy. A replacement-cost policy would reimburse you for the cost of a comparable new set.

Because homes are rarely completely destroyed, it's possible to save a little on your premiums by insuring the place for less than it would cost to rebuild the whole thing. As long as the face amount of your policy equals at least 80 percent of the insurance company's estimated cost to rebuild (excluding land, which isn't covered), you are fully covered for complete or partial losses—up to the policy's limits. If you have an $80,000 policy on a home the company estimates will cost $100,000 to re-build and you suffer $10,000 in damage from a kitchen fire, you will be reimbursed for the full $10,000, minus your deductible. If the house burns to the ground and it costs $100,000 to rebuild, your coverage will stop at $80,000.

But insuring for less than full replacement value can be a false economy because of the way insurance compa-nies compensate for partial losses. Say you buy coverage for 80 percent of the home's value but as prices for labor and building materials rise, that same amount would cover only 70 percent of the cost of rebuilding. That's seven-eighths of 80 percent, so for that $10,000 fire, you would get seven-eighths of $10,000 ($8,750) or the actual cash value (replacement cost of appliances and so forth, minus depreciation based on the age of your old appliances).

Even if you insured your home for 100 percent re-placement value a few years ago, you may need to brush the cobwebs off your policy. A policy feature called in-flation guard protects you by automatically raising your policy limits in step with rising prices. Insurance agents have access to cost-index figures you can use to help update the replacement value. When you com-pute the required amount of insurance, remember to eliminate the estimated value of the land, excavations, foundation, underground pipes, and similar building components not likely to be damaged.

Because homes are rarely completely destroyed, it's possible to save a little on premiums by insuring the place for less than it would cost to rebuild the whole thing. But that could be a false economy.

Insurers have developed special policies for older homes that may be entitled to lower insurance limits based on their market value.

Replacement-Cost Guarantee

Most major insurers offer a replacement-cost endorsement that will cover costs of rebuilding or replacing your home in case of a total loss, even if the expense exceeds the amount of coverage you carry. This is a feature worth considering if residential construction costs in your area have outpaced inflation in recent years. A typical replacement guarantee comes as part of a 100 percent coverage policy and requires you to accept a yearly inflation adjustment and notify the insurer of any additions that alter the value by more than $5,000.

REPLACEMENT-COST COVERAGE FOR CONTENTS. Many companies sell an endorsement that extends replacement-cost coverage to the contents of the place. For an additional premium, some companies will increase the total for personal property from 50 percent of the insurance on the house to 75 percent. Endorsements typically exclude fine arts, antiques, and other items that are expected to appreciate. They also limit payments for other items to a maximum of four times the cash value.

Insurance for Older Homes

Good as it may be for ordinary homes, the replacement-cost system presents problems for old houses that might cost more to restore to their original condition than to replace using modern materials. Take an old house with a market value of $100,000. It's made with plaster walls and nine-foot ceilings, hand-carved crown molding, and so many other nice features that it would cost $160,000 to rebuild. But if you insure this $100,000 home for 80 percent of its $160,000 replacement cost, or $128,000, the house is overinsured.

That's why insurers have developed special policies for older homes that may be entitled to lower insurance limits based on their market value. Some companies sell them subject to different conditions, and some don't sell them at all. The plans take three forms:

- **A homeowners policy that pays for repairs** with less costly and more pedestrian modern materials instead of those originally employed (a parquet floor, for instance, replaced by carpeting over a plywood base). These repair-cost policies generally cost less than other homeowners policies because they cover less.

- **A policy that pays the actual cash value of the loss.** This amount might be interpreted by the company as the current market value of the structure, or its replacement cost minus depreciation.

- **An endorsement—or policy addition—that allows you** to insure for less than 80 percent of the replacement cost of your structure without giving up your right to replacement cost for partial losses. But for furniture, appliances, awnings, outdoor equipment, clothing, and other personal property, the company usually need not pay more than the cash value. If your couch goes up in flames, its value is adjusted for wear and tear.

Take time to get price quotes from several insurers. You may discover some surprising variations in rates.

Finding the Best Deal

Take time to get price quotes from several insurers. You may discover some surprising variations in rates. Differences of 100 percent for comparable coverage in the same area aren't unheard of. You can't survey all the companies selling insurance in your area, but contacting a few might produce considerable savings.

There's enough uniformity among the companies' policies that you can use their standard forms to compare premiums. Companies sometimes modify the standard provisions, but it's not always easy to tell whether the changes broaden or narrow your protection, so compare carefully.

You're usually entitled to a lower rate for a brick home than for a frame structure. Also, you might qualify for a discount if your house is new or only a few years old, or if you have installed smoke alarms or antitheft devices.

Be sure to take advantage of differences in deductibles. The base deductible is around $250. Consider raising yours further still; many companies will reduce premiums in return for not covering the small losses. However, discount plans are not as common for homeowners insurance as they are for auto policies.

(continued on page 138)

A GUIDE TO HOMEOWNERS POLICIES

These are the principal features of standard homeowners policies. The policies of some companies differ in a few respects. Policy conditions may also vary according to state requirements. You can usually increase coverage for some items by paying an additional premium.

	HO-2 (Broad Form)	HO-3 (Special Form)
Perils covered (see key below)	items 1–16	all perils, except those specifically excluded, on buildings
Covered item or loss	**Amount and limits of coverage**	
House and attached structures	based on structure's replacement value	based on structure's replacement value
Detached structures	10% of insurance on house	10% of insurance on house
Trees, shrubs, plants	5% of insurance on house; $500 maximum per item	5% of insurance on house $500 maximum per item
Personal property	50% of insurance on house; 10% for property normally kept at another residence or $1,000, whichever is greater	50% of insurance on house; 10% for property normally kept at another residence or $1,000, whichever is greater
Loss of use, additional living expense; loss of rental unit, uninhabitable	20% of insurance on house	20% of insurance on house
Special limits on liability	money, banknotes, bullion, gold other than goldware, silver other valuable papers, deeds, manuscripts, passports, tickets and stamps, and outboard motors—$1,000; trailer not used with boats— stones—$1,000; theft of silverware, goldware, and pewterware—	
Credit card loss, forgery, counterfeit money, electronic fund transfer	$500	$500
Comprehensive personal liability	$100,000	$100,000
Damage to property of others	$500	$500
Medical payments	$1,000 per person	$1,000 per person

Key to Perils Covered: 1. fire, lightning 2. windstorm, hail 3. explosion 4. riots or civil commotion 5. damage by aircraft 9. theft 10. volcanic eruption 11. falling objects 12. weight of ice, snow, sleet 13. leakage or overflow of water or steam from a of appliance for heating water 15. freezing of plumbing, heating, and air-conditioning systems and domestic appliances 16. damage

The special limits of liability refer to the maximum amounts the policy pays for the types of property listed. Usually jewelry, furs, boats, and other items subject to special limits must be insured separately if you want more coverage.

HO-4 (Contents Only)	HO-6 (Co-op or Condo)	HO-8 (Limited Coverage)
1–16	1–16	1–10

Amount and limits of coverage

no coverage	$1,000 on owner's additions and alterations to unit	based on structure's market value
no coverage	no coverage	10% of insurance on house
10% of amount of personal-property insurance, $500 maximum per item	10% of amount of personal-property insurance, $500 maximum per item	5% of insurance on house, $25 maximum per item
based on value of property; 10% of that amount for property normally kept at another residence or $1,000, whichever is greater	based on value of property; 10% of that amount for property normally kept at another residence or $1,000, whichever is greater	50% of insurance on house; 5% for property normally kept at another residence or $1,000, whichever is greater
20% of personal-property insurance	40% of personal-property insurance	10% of insurance on house
than silverware, platinum, coins, and medals—$200; securities, etc.—$1,000; boats including their trailers, furnishings, equipment, $1,000; theft of jewelry, watches, furs, precious and semiprecious $2,500; theft of firearms—$2,000		theft on premises limited to $1,000; no coverage for theft of items (named at left) off premises
$500	$500	$500
$100,000	$100,000	$100,000
$500	$500	$500
$1,000 per person	$1,000 per person	$1,000 per person

6. damage by vehicles not owned or operated by people covered by policy 7. damage from smoke 8. vandalism, malicious mischief plumbing, heating, or air-conditioning system 14. bursting, cracking, burning, or bulging of a steam- or hot-water heating system or to electrical appliances, devices, fixtures, and wiring from short circuits or other generated currents

Record what you've got in your house so you won't have to rely on memory in case of theft, fire, or some other catastrophe.

If the agent computes the replacement cost of the house on the basis of its square footage, be sure to check the figures before you agree to the resulting premium.

Take Inventory

It's a good idea to record what you've got in your house so you won't have to rely on memory in case of theft, fire, or some other catastrophe. Better yet, walk through the house with a camera or a video camera, carefully scanning each room, plus the garage and outside of the house and yard. Take out the silver and other valuables and photograph them separately. Put the film or videocassette in a safe place—a fireproof safe in the house or a safe-deposit box at the bank.

Making a Claim

Notify your agent or broker of damages as soon as possible. If your losses are covered, he or she will probably arrange to have an adjuster inspect the damages and estimate the repair cost. You will not be charged a fee if you use your insurance company's adjuster.

If damage from a fire, windstorm, or other natural disaster is extensive, you may want to have a public adjuster represent you in filing your claim. Public insurance adjusters are listed in the telephone book. They usually charge a fee of up to 15 percent of the total value of your settlement.

If you're considering using a public adjuster, ask your agent, a lawyer, or friends or associates for recommendations and check his or her qualifications with your state insurance department (see box on page 178). Don't use individuals who go door-to-door after a major disaster unless you can check qualifications.

Don't make any permanent repairs before the insurance adjuster arrives. The company can legally refuse to reimburse you for repairs made prior to inspection.

You don't necessarily have to defer to the insurance company if your claim is refused; policies often allow for varying interpretations. One insurance company adjuster might consider your request for expenses to have someone thaw out frozen pipes an uninsured maintenance cost; another would consider it an insurable peril. Ask for a second opinion, and be persistent.

Don't sign a final settlement agreement if you're dissatisfied with the terms. Accept partial payment to make necessary repairs, as long as the insurer formally acknowledges that it is only a partial payment. If you can't negotiate a settlement, file a written complaint with the company. If that yields no results, you could either enter into arbitration with the company or contact your state's insurance department, which often acts as a referee in such disputes. You can locate your state's insurance regulator on many Web sites, including http://www.kiplinger.com/basics/managing/insurance/regulator.htm, by calling the National Association of Insurance Commissioners (NAIC) at 816-842-3600, or by going to the NAIC Web site at http://www.naic .org, where you will find a map of the country with links to each state's insurance department. Only after you've exhausted those avenues should you consider filing a suit against the company.

> **When you buy a house, the lender will require you to purchase insurance on the title. If you want to protect yourself as well, you'll have to purchase owner's title insurance.**

Other Types of Home-Related Insurance

Title Insurance

When you buy a house, the mortgage lender will require you to purchase insurance on the title. This protects the lender's lien on the property against a defect in the title, or a lien or some other encumbrance that you didn't know about when you bought the place. If you want to protect yourself as well, you'll have to purchase an owner's title-insurance policy.

There is an important difference between the lender's policy and yours. The lender is protected to the extent of the mortgage, which declines as time goes by. You want protection for the price of the house, which includes your down payment. If you suffer a loss,

An umbrella policy picks up where your existing liability coverage leaves off and protects you to whatever limit you choose— typically $1 million.

then your title-insurance company is on the hook, not you. Most title-insurance policies follow the same general format. You are protected against loss or damage from forgery, misrepresentations of identity, age, or other matters that could affect the legality of the ownership documents, and liens recorded in the public record that may come to light after the deal is closed.

Some title-insurance companies offer special reissue rates on policies for homes changing owners. If you're buying, find out whether the current owner has title insurance and whether the company offers a reissue rate.

Flood Insurance

The federal government is the main underwriter of flood insurance, but most homeowners insurance agents can sell you a federal policy. The average cost is about $360 per year for $100,000 of coverage, with a ceiling of $250,000 on the structure and $100,000 on the contents, if you are in a zone with low to moderate risk of flooding. You can get details from the Federal Emergency Management Agency (on the Internet, go to http://www.fema.gov; or call FEMA at 888-356-6329 for information and referrals to agents).

If you live in an area that is not covered by a government flood program, check with your insurance agent or local government to ask about local flood programs. If this fails, you may have to ask your agent to help you buy flood insurance from Lloyds of London.

Umbrella Liability Insurance

Homeowners and auto insurance can provide pretty good protection, but in light of the millions of dollars that sometimes constitute the settlements in personal-liability cases, a policy that stops at $300,000 or $500,000 may strike you as inadequate. Suppose someone sued you for a million?

Fortunately, you can buy extended personal-liability coverage in the form of what's called an umbrella policy. It picks up where your existing coverage leaves off and protects you to whatever limit you choose—typically $1 million. A typical umbrella policy covers accidents involving your home, motor vehicles, boat, and other property, as well as the cost of defending yourself against charges of slander and libel (provided, in the last two cases, that you're not a professional writer and thus considered more at risk of being sued for libel).

Umbrella coverage costs less than you might expect because it works largely on an "excess" basis, meaning it pays for claims not completely covered by your other policies and doesn't kick in until that coverage is exhausted. For $1 million worth of coverage you can expect to pay between $175 and $250 per year, more if you're insuring more than one house, car, or driver, or if you own a recreational vehicle.

If you're considering buying such coverage, check with a few of the leading property insurers. Rates and conditions differ significantly; some umbrellas are bigger than others. Make sure you know what's excluded, particularly for business or professional liability. Finally, take into account not only the cost of the premiums but also any extra premiums needed to raise your underlying insurance to the umbrella policy's required limits.

Your Car

Part 3

Controlling the Cost of Your Car

Chapter 11

Here's the single most reliable way to save money on cars: Keep your clunker and drive it till it drops. A decently cared-for vehicle should still be running long after the odometer has clocked 100,000 miles. Keep driving it and you save money not only because you don't have to make payments on a new car, but also because insurance premiums are lower, and in some states, so are registration fees. Personal-property taxes are also lower in states that base them on the market value of the vehicle.

Unfortunately, at some point the statute of limitations runs out on this particular money-saving tip. The more the car is in the shop, and the wider the oil slick grows on your usual parking spot, the more you may think seriously about replacing the old chariot with something nicer. Meanwhile, the money you save by not buying a new car tends to be eaten up by the growing cost of keeping the old one on the road.

The question is: Where's the tipping point? When does it become counterproductive to keep laying out cash for old-car repairs instead of new-car payments? To put it another way, how long does it take for the higher cost of purchasing a new car to be justified by the growing cost of maintaining the old one?

Longer than you think. Runzheimer International, a management consulting firm that specializes in measuring travel and living costs, runs this sort of calculation on a regular basis. Recently it compared ownership costs of a brand-new car against a similar four-year-old car. Both were sensible sedans. The new car was assumed to cost $23,663, financed over four years at 6 percent.

WHY OLDER IS CHEAPER

	Old Car	New Car
Mileage at end of four years	120,000	60,000
Total car payments	$ 0	$18,272
Gas and oil	6,380	6,380
License, registration, taxes	1,939	2,758
Insurance	3,858	4,333
Repairs, maintenance, tires	4,040	3,120
Resale value at end	2,793	7,219
Total expenses	**$16,217**	**$34,863**
(minus resale value)	−2,793	−7,219
Total costs	**$13,424**	**$27,644**
Difference		+$14,220

Source: Runzheimer International

The old car was worth $8,708 and was assumed to be traded in as the down payment on the new one. The old car has 60,000 miles on it, both cars are driven 15,000 miles per year, and both get 21 miles to the gallon of regular unleaded gas. The box above shows how four years with car payments and low maintenance costs matched up against four years without car payments but higher maintenance costs.

The actual numbers are less important than the overriding message: Those loan payments stack the deck against a new car. You could encounter much higher repair costs than assumed and still come out ahead by keeping the old one. If you're confronting this question, you can use the format above to run estimated numbers and see how they come out. Better yet, don't bother. In the absence of a gigantic repair bill—you need a new engine, for example—an old car is almost always cheaper to own than a new one. You can close the gap a bit with a couple of strategies.

Pay cash. This will reduce your total expense by eliminating the interest on the loan, but to make a fair comparison you'd also have to take into account what else you might have done with that money and the interest you might have earned if you hadn't spent it on a car. This balancing act is described later in the chapter.

Pay a lower interest rate. A lower rate helps. But if you eliminated all the interest in the example above, the old car would still be about $12,157 cheaper to own than the new one over the four-year period.

Buy a used car. This is probably your best bet to close the gap completely. The problem is that, unless it is a certified used vehicle (see below), a used car doesn't come with a new-car warranty, so you take on the same risks of unanticipated high repair bills that you already have with the car you've got. "Certified used" or "certified pre-owned" used cars are often two- or three-year-old previously leased cars. They're offered by local dealers and feature warranties that extend beyond the initial "when new" coverage. According to *Edmund's Car Buying Guide*'s definition, a "certified used" vehicle has a warranty that is backed by the original vehicle manufacturer. Twenty-nine makers have certified pre-owned programs. Terms differ, but a true certified pre-owned program will include at least a 100-point inspection of the car. Most programs:

- **include only vehicles under five years old;**
- **have mileage limits under 100,000;**
- **use only vehicles that have had no major body work from prior accidents;**
- **"refurbish" the vehicle after a multistep inspection (75 to 305 inspection points); and**
- **provide an extended warranty.**

Additionally, some programs offer:

- **consumer cash incentives;**
- **low interest rates;**
- **lease programs; and**
- **an exchange policy.**

Certified pre-owned cars are usually more expensive than other used cars. But the benefits may outweigh the cost—for many buyers, the peace of mind

> **Certified pre-owned cars are usually more expensive than other used cars. But the benefits may outweigh the cost.**

Most of us don't base car-buying decisions on detailed accounting of the costs. Comfort, style, image, safety, convenience, and reliability are the forces motivating us.

alone is enough to justify the extra money. You can search for certified cars on the Internet at car-buying sites such as those listed in the box on page 151.

But let's face it: When all is said and done, most of us don't base decisions on such a detailed accounting of the costs. Comfort, style, image, safety, convenience, and reliability—these are the forces motivating the vast majority of Americans who decide to buy a new car. So be it. The important thing is to choose the right car and to get the best possible deal.

If you're considering a used car, watch out that you don't buy a "clone," a stolen car that has counterfeit documents that match those of a legitimate vehicle. It's best to avoid buying a car curbside, from a parking lot, or through classified ads (see the box on page 155).

Choosing the Right Car

Take some time to consider your choices before you stick a toe in a showroom. Magazine racks are stuffed with new-car guides. Buy more than one to get different perspectives and read about the models that interest you. Use the worksheet on the opposite page to sketch out what you want. Show it to the salesperson when you go to the showroom. You might not be able to get every option you want on the car you want, and you may decide that some options aren't worth the added cost. But this list will get you started.

Getting a Good Deal

Once you've decided on a particular make and model, the fun part of buying a new car is over for a while. Now it's time to get down to the business of finding the best possible deal. It will take some work and some hard bargaining. (If you'd like to opt out of the bargaining part, skip right to the section on car-shopping services. If you want to do the haggling yourself, the following are some recommendations for organizing your campaign.)

Set a Target Price

As every car shopper since Fred Flintstone knows, the sticker price on a car is just a suggestion, a place to start. With a few exceptions—the Saturn being the best known—the actual transaction price is set by bargaining, and the better you bargain, the better the price

---

WHAT DO YOU WANT IN A CAR?

Vehicle type:_____

(Sedan, minivan, sport utility, etc.)

Passenger capacity:_____ **Towing capacity:**_____

CHECK THOSE DESIRED

Storage needs:

_____ large trunk

_____ roof rack

Fuel efficiency:

_____ important

_____ not important

Drive Preference:

_____ rear-wheel

_____ front-wheel

_____ four-wheel

_____ all-wheel

Safety Features:

_____ air bags, front

_____ air bags, side

_____ antilock brakes

_____ antitheft devices

_____ extra bumper protection

_____ child safety seats

Interior upholstery:

_____ cloth

_____ leather

_____ vinyl

Other options desired:

_____ adjustable steering column

_____ air-conditioning

_____ AM/FM radio

_____ AM/FM with cassette player

_____ AM/FM with compact disc

_____ automatic transmission

_____ cruise control

_____ full-size spare tire

_____ power brakes

_____ power locks

_____ power seats

_____ power steering

_____ rear-window defogger

_____ remote-control mirrors

_____ sunroof/moonroof

Other options desired (list):

_____

_____

_____

_____

_____

_____

It helps to have a target price in mind right from the start: a price that gives you a good deal and lets the salesperson make a living.

you'll get. It helps to have a target price in mind right from the start: a price that gives you a good deal and lets the salesperson make a living.

A number of publications can help you set a target price. Every year the December issue of *Kiplinger's Personal Finance* magazine lists hundreds of new models, with sticker price, dealer cost, and target price for each. You can also find information on sticker and dealer cost at http://www.kiplinger.com. Log on, go to "Spending," and you'll find "Cars" listed. Other guides are also available. The important thing you're looking for at this point is complete pricing information on all the models you're considering. Your target price will be somewhere between the sticker price and the dealer cost, but keep in mind that you may pay more or less depending on the demand for the car or truck you want. Large dealerships are often in a better position to bargain because they get volume discounts from the auto manufacturer.

Consider a Twin

You can sometimes find a way to save by comparing similar cars built by different divisions of the same manufacturer. For example, in recent years the Mercury Montego and Ford Five Hundred shared the same body structure, and the GMC Sierra and Chevrolet Silverado have shared the same underpinnings, but prices have been $1,000 to $2,000 or so apart. The 2005 Toyota Matrix and Pontiac Vibe were built on the same platform, but the Toyota was priced about $1,500 less.

So-called "twinned" cars aren't easy to spot, and it would be misleading to suggest that the less expensive car has all the goodies of the more expensive one. When you compare twins, ask yourself: Does the extra money buy more performance and durability, or simply a nameplate?

Shop Late in the Month

Many leasing and rebate programs are set on a monthly basis, and are based on dealers making volume sales.

Also, dealers must finance the inventory on the lot, and if they can sell cars by the end of the month, they'll save on financing charges. Add to this the fact that most car salespeople have monthly goals or quotas, and you'll find that the last few days of the month can be a good time to buy.

Check Inventories

A rising inventory of cars is worrisome to a dealer, but helpful to a buyer in quest of that particular model. Inventories are measured in terms of "days' supply." When dealers have more cars than they can reasonably expect to sell within 60 days, it's generally considered a

---

SHOP ONLINE FOR A CAR

The Internet is a good place to get the latest on prices and options, and other information about both new and used cars. Many sites include a calculator to help you determine loan payments or compare the financing of buying or leasing. Here are a few sites to try:

Microsoft's Carpoint (http://carpoint.msn.com) has information on options, safety, and fuel economy, as well as video tours of car interiors.

Kelley Blue Book (www.kbb.com) provides dealer invoice prices for cars and their options.

Edmund's (www.edmunds.com) provides dealer invoice prices and holdback rates on most cars. (Holdbacks are manufacturers' discounts, which dealers receive after they sell a certain number of cars.)

Intellichoice (www.intellichoice.com) lists the best manufacturers' deals available.

AutoSite (www.autosite.com) also has a calculator to work out lease payments.

LeaseSource (www.leasesource.com) contains a wealth of information about leases, including residual values of cars,

which are hard to come by. (The residual value of a leased car is the estimated value of the car at the end of the lease.)

Carfax (www.carfax.com) offers a free "lemon check" (and powers the same tool for several other auto sites), but it makes its money selling detailed title histories for $19.95. (You can check up on more than one car for $24.99.) By entering the car's vehicle identification number, Carfax can tell you if the car was ever titled as salvage, was rebuilt or reconstructed, was flood-damaged, or had its odometer rolled back.

In addition, nearly every car and truck manufacturer has a Web site that may offer exact specifications for cars, lists of available options, and financing and leasing information.

If you can get a rebate for buying the car you want, it's probably better to use the rebate to cut the price of the car rather than taking the cash.

buyer's market. You can check inventory in *Automotive News,* a weekly industry publication that is available on some newsstands, in large public libraries, and online (http://www.autonews.com).

Look for Incentives

When inventories get high, car manufacturers may begin offering rebates, low-cost financing, and subsidized leases. You can find an up-to-date list of incentives in *CarDeals,* a semimonthly publication that typically cites more than 200 deals. It's available from the nonprofit Center for the Study of Services, 733 15th Street., NW, Suite 820, Washington, DC 20005 (http://www.checkbook.org; 800-213-7283; $7.00 per issue). *Automotive News* also publishes the latest rebates each week, and on the Internet rebates and incentives are listed at http://www.edmunds.com, a Web site sponsored by the company that publishes the Edmund's car-buying guides.

Most dealer incentive programs expire around the end of the month, another good reason to shop then. In an incentive program that's based on volume, a dealer can make thousands of extra dollars by selling one more car at the end of the program, even if the sale involves minimal profit.

If you can get a rebate for buying the car you want, it's probably better to use the rebate to cut the price of the car rather than taking the cash. In some states, that will reduce the sales tax on the deal. If you can choose between a rebate and a cut-rate loan, the loan is likely to be the better choice if the car costs more than $20,000. See the box on the opposite page for Web sites with calculators that can help you determine the better deal.

Hire Some Help

If you're not confident about your bargaining skills— or if you simply don't like to haggle—you may want to turn to a car-buying service. CarBargains is an example of this sort of service. For a $190 fee, CarBargains (http://www.checkbook.org; 800-213-7283), run by the

---

GREAT RATE OR FAT REBATE?

Here are two online calculators that will tell you which is the better deal.

Kiplinger.com At http://www.kiplinger.com, click on "Spending" and select "Cars." Under "Car Tools," click on "Which is better: a rebate or special dealer financing?" Fill in the information to determine the better deal.

Bankrate.com. Go to http://www.bankrate.com and click on "Auto." Under "Related Calculators," click on "Great rebate vs. low interest rate." Fill in the information about your loan and rebate options for the best deal.

Center for the Study of Services, in Washington, D.C., will do the legwork for you, getting competitive bids for the car you want from at least five dealers in your area. CarBargains is sometimes able to get lower prices than other car-buying services partly because it receives no money from dealers and thus is working only for you. Dealers pay fees to some other services for the privilege of being the sole dealer the service uses in the area. This really shouldn't matter to you if you get a good deal.

Join a Club

You can join a new-car buying program offered by warehouse clubs such as Costco or Sam's Club and by affinity groups such as credit unions and the American Automobile Association (AAA). If you belong to one of these groups and there's a participating dealer that carries the car you want, you can use the group program to get a discount off the sticker price without haggling. But a shrewd buyer can often beat these prices by a few hundred dollars (or by a lot more if any dealer incentives are in effect).

Club buying programs are typically free to shoppers, but the participating dealers pay the service either a flat advertising fee or a commission on every sale the service steers their way. Because these programs usually work with only one dealer per car line per geographic

The factory pays dealers to prepare new vehicles; if you pay a dealer-prep charge, the dealer gets paid twice.

area, there's no competition. So while the price you get may be a good one, it may not be the best price that's available in your area.

Don't Win the Battle and Lose the War

Be careful not to lose the money you've saved negotiating a good price when you get to the finance and insurance (F&I) office. Here you may confront the offer of a car loan, plus such charges as document preparation, processing, dealer prep, and national advertising fees. Dealers look to these extras as their chance to win back some of the concessions they made on the price. In addition to the fees mentioned above, the profits in F&I come from extended warranties, credit life insurance, undercoating, fabric protection, rustproofing, and other extras.

Car dealerships put their best salespeople in the F&I departments, so remember the Scout's slogan and be prepared. Here's what to know when presented with such extras.

FINANCING PACKAGES. Often you can find the best loan at the dealership, but in order to evaluate what you're being offered, you'll need to do your homework before heading into the showroom. Call local banks, savings and loans, and credit unions for their lowest rates. Be prepared to get your own financing if you don't like the dealer's deal. If you announce your intention to pay cash, don't be dissuaded if an F&I closer presents a computer printout showing that borrowing would be cheaper than paying cash. It would not be cheaper. Customers with marginal credit ratings should be especially wary. You should expect to pay higher rates, but not as high as some dealerships charge.

DOCUMENT PREP AND OTHER FEES. Dealers are paid by the factory to prepare new vehicles, so if you pay a dealer-prep charge, the dealer gets paid twice. And national advertising is a normal business expense for manufacturers, so it shouldn't be listed on the invoice or added to your final bill by the dealer. (In many states

BEWARE OF THE CLONES

The practice known as vehicle cloning involves the criminal changing the identity of a stolen car to match that of a legitimately registered vehicle, meaning that even with a data check the vehicle appears to be legitimate.

The criminals copy a vehicle identification number (VIN) from a legally owned and documented car parked in a lot or car dealership and use the number to create one or more counterfeit VIN tags. They then steal a similar car and replace that car's VIN tag with the counterfeit one. The thieves also create counterfeit ownership documents.

The National Insurance Crime Bureau, a not-for-profit organization that deals with insurance fraud and theft solutions, offers these tips to help you avoid becoming a vehicle clone-crime victim.

- **Check out the vehicle's VIN** with appropriate government agencies and your state bureau of motor vehicles.
- **Analyze the ownership pattern** for any new or late-model vehicle with no lien holder.
- **Have a private company conduct a vehicle history search.**
- **Trust your instincts:** If a used vehicle deal sounds too good to be true, walk away.

it's illegal for manufacturers to charge dealers for national advertising.)

An invoice charge listed as "local dealer advertising/marketing association" usually represents an actual charge incurred by the dealer to pay for group advertising. The factory invoice has a box for this item, and the dealer enters the amount, which is typically 1 to 2 percent of the invoice price. Dealers consider this to be a legitimate part of their "invoice cost," so if you're being offered a deal that's at or below invoice, you'll probably have to pay it. But if the deal is for a significant amount over invoice, consider this charge to be part of the dealer's gross profit and negotiate accordingly.

Also, beware of expensive last-minute extras such as paint sealant, fabric protection, undercoating, rustproofing, and extended warranties.

EXTENDED SERVICE WARRANTIES. Don't go for these unless you purchase a car with a lot of electronic or computerized gadgets on board. Most extended service warranties never pay out as much as they cost, which gives you some idea of how often they are needed by

Don't buy rustproofing, ever. Today's cars are usually warranted by the factory against rust.

buyers for serious, expensive repairs. If you do decide on the warranty, review the contract carefully to make sure you aren't paying extra for something already covered by the standard manufacturer's factory warranty.

You don't have to buy an extended warranty the day you buy the car. Most carmakers give you 12 months or 12,000 miles, which should be ample time to see how reliable your car is.

CREDIT LIFE INSURANCE. This may be the most expensive way in the world to buy life insurance. Unless your health is so bad that you have no other way of protecting your loved ones from debts you leave behind, don't buy credit life. Turn to Chapter 19 for help in choosing a better policy for a lot less money.

RUSTPROOFING. Don't buy it, ever. Today's cars are usually warranted by the factory against rust. In fact, the process of rustproofing an already-built car is quite tricky and could be botched, which could lead to more rust and even void the factory warranty.

FABRIC PROTECTION AND PAINT SEALANT. These also aren't worth the additional money. Fabric guard can actually stain the fabric and, of course, the factory warranty won't cover any damage that results from this process. You would be better off buying a can of Scotchgard-type spray and applying it yourself. And rather than paying extra for paint sealant, just wax your car from time to time. That should protect it well enough.

The Lure of a Lease

Three things to know about leasing: First, if you like a new car every two or three years and the thought of never-ending car payments doesn't bother you much, then leasing may be a good choice for you. Second, if you plan to purchase your car at the end of the lease, then you'd be better off skipping the lease and buying the car to begin with. Third, to get the best deal on a lease, just as with a purchase, you're going

(continued on page 160)

GETTING A FAIR DEAL ON A LEASE

Monthly payments are less on a lease than if you buy the car but, heck, you're not buying the car. Don't let the allure of lower payments sucker you into paying more than you have to. So what's a fair payment?

This "calculator," prepared with the help of Cedric Rashad, a leasing consultant in Atlanta, will show you. Here's what you need to know to use it:

CAPITALIZED COST. This is the cost of the car written into the lease. Start with your target price or a dealer's quote, and add title and registration fees and other costs, such as taxes or insurance, that will be rolled into the lease.

CAPITALIZED-COST REDUCTION. The total of your down payment, the cash value of your trade-in, and any rebates or discounts.

RESIDUAL. The estimated value of the car at the end of the lease. Ask the dealer for this figure or check LeaseSource (see box on page 151). The residual is expressed as a percentage; you can convert it to dollars by multiplying it by the manufacturer's suggested retail price. Manufacturers sometimes subsidize a lease by inflating the residual so you pay for less depreciation.

MONEY FACTOR. This represents the cost of financing the car. It is the equivalent of an interest rate divided by 24. So if the finance charge is 9%, the money factor would be 0.00375 (0.09/24). Automakers sometimes cut the money factor to subsidize a lease. Ask the dealer for the money factor.

SALES TAX. In some states, this tax is charged in full at the beginning of the lease; in others, it's added to each payment. Ask how it works where you live.

Figuring the Lease Payment:
DEPRECIATION
    A. Gross capitalized cost (cap cost) $ _____
    B. Cap-cost reduction   _____
    C. Net cap cost (A - B)   _____
    D. Residual   _____
    E. Depreciation (C - D)   _____
    F. Lease term (in months)   _____
1. Monthly Depreciation (E ÷ F) $ _____
FINANCE CHARGE
    G. Finance base (C + D)   _____
    H. Money factor   _____
2. Monthly Finance Charge (G x H) $ _____
SALES TAX
3. Monthly Sales Tax $ _____
ESTIMATED LEASE PAYMENT (1 + 2 + 3) $ _____

WHAT YOU MUST BE TOLD ABOUT A LEASE

The Federal Trade Commission requires leasing companies to disclose the terms of any consumer car lease in a way that potential customers can understand. Here's an example of what you must be told before you sign. The car in this case has a selling price of $30,000 and the customer is trading in a car worth $4,000.

1. AMOUNT DUE AT LEASE SIGNING $ 5,799.88

ITEMIZATION OF AMOUNT DUE AT LEASE SIGNING

Capitalized cost reduction	5,000.00
First monthly payment	381.44
Refundable security deposit	381.44
Title fees	12.00
Registration fees	25.00
TOTAL	$ 5,799.88

HOW THE AMOUNT DUE AT LEASE SIGNING WILL BE PAID

Net trade-in allowance	$ 4,000
Rebates and noncash credits	0
Amount to be paid in cash	1,799.88
TOTAL	$ 5,799.88

2. MONTHLY PAYMENTS

Your first monthly payment of $ 381.44 is due on Jan. 1, followed by payments of $ 381.44 due on the 1st of each month.

The total of your monthly payments is: $ 13,731.84

Your monthly payment is determined as shown below:

Gross capitalized cost. The agreed-upon value of the vehicle ($ 30,000) and any items you pay over the lease term (such as service contracts, insurance) and any outstanding prior loan or lease balance   30,000

Capitalized cost reduction. The amount of any net trade-in allowance, rebate, noncash credit, or cash you pay that reduces the gross capitalized cost   − 5,000

Adjusted capitalized cost. The amount used in calculating your base monthly payment   = 25,000

Residual value. The value of the vehicle at the end of the lease used in calculating your base monthly payment

− 13,000

Depreciation and any amortized amounts. The amount charged for the vehicle's decline in value through normal use and for other items paid over the lease term

= 12,000

Rent charge. The amount charged in addition to the depreciation and any amortized amounts (also called the "interest.")

+ 1,300

Total of base monthly payments. The depreciation and any amortized amounts plus the rent charge

= $ 13,300

Lease term (months)

÷ 36

Base monthly payment

= 369.44

Monthly sales/use tax

+ 12.00

TOTAL MONTHLY PAYMENT

= 381.44

3. OTHER CHARGES (not part of your monthly payment)

Disposition fee (if you do not purchase the vehicle)

$ none

Annual tax

333.00

Total

333.00

4. TOTAL OF PAYMENTS

(the amount you will have paid by the end of the lease)

$ 14,064.84

EARLY TERMINATION: You may have to pay a substantial charge if you end this lease early. The charge may be up to several thousand dollars. The actual charge will depend on when the lease is terminated. The earlier you end the lease, the greater this charge is likely to be.

EXCESSIVE WEAR AND USE. You may be charged for excessive wear based on our standards for normal use (and for mileage in excess of 12,000 miles per year at the rate of $.025 per mile).

PURCHASE OPTION AT END OF LEASE TERM. You have an option to purchase the vehicle at the end of the lease term for $ n/a (and a purchase option fee of $ n/a).

OTHER IMPORTANT TERMS. See your lease documents for additional information on early termination, purchase options and maintenance responsibilities, warranties, late and default charges, insurance, and any security interest, if applicable.

The reason you pay a lower (or no) down payment and monthly payment on a lease is simple: You're paying only for the anticipated depreciation over the term of the lease.

to have to be ready to bargain a bit. And the arcane language of leasing can make the deal harder to judge.

What Goes Into a Lease

The chief lures of a lease are the low or nonexistent down payment, followed by lower monthly payments than you'd have to make if you bought the same car. The reason for this dual blessing is simple: You're paying only for the anticipated depreciation of the car over the term of the lease—typically two or three years. Thus your payments need to cover only a portion of the car's value.

Take, for example, a nice, new Pontiac Grand Prix, selling for about $25,200. In two years it is expected to depreciate by about 46 percent of its value, or $11,600. If you lease the car for two years, the dealer will place your payments at a level high enough to cover that $11,600 of depreciation (plus a little profit), plus the cost of the money the dealer borrows to pay for the car in the meantime (plus a little profit), plus charges for this and that, with a little profit tacked on to them, too.

Fortunately, you've got an ally in your effort to sort all this out. The Federal Trade Commission requires that every lease contract disclose the information you need to figure out what you're getting into. It must clearly show:

- **the "capitalized cost"** of the vehicle, which is essentially its selling price;
- **any down payment** you'll have to make;
- **registration fees;**
- **trade-in allowances or rebates** built into the deal;
- **interest and other charges;**
- **the exact size of the monthly payment** (including taxes and insurance);
- **the residual value of the car,** meaning its anticipated value at the end of the leasing period;
- **any extra charges or penalties** levied during or at the end of the lease.

The monthly finance charge, which is one important element of the lease subject to negotiation, can sometimes be difficult to interpret. If the dealer uses an interest factor or money factor instead of the interest rate, simply multiply the factor by 24 and you'll have an approximate estimate of the interest rate involved. A factor of .0038, for example, is equivalent to an interest rate of 9.1 percent.

Finally, the dealer adds sales tax to the depreciation and interest charges to arrive at your lease payment. Make sure when you are comparing leases from one dealer to another that monthly lease payments all include the sales taxes.

How to Negotiate a Lease

The lower the price of the car, the lower your lease payments. That seems obvious, but many people who set out to lease don't realize that they should bargain just as hard on the price of the car as they would if they were buying it. The leasing contract will refer to the "capitalized cost" of the vehicle. That means price, so set a target price as described in the buying section of this chapter. Some new-car guides, including Kiplinger's, provide invoice prices and suggest target prices. Some also give expected resale values after two and four years, which can be especially helpful in anticipating the residual value of the vehicle you want to lease. Arm yourself with these figures before you start bargaining and you'll have a better idea whether you have much leeway to negotiate a residual value more favorable to you. Remember, what you want is the lowest possible capitalized cost and the highest possible residual value. As a leaser, you're paying the difference.

Other things being equal, the best car to lease is the one that retains more of its value over the term of the lease. If two cars cost the same, you'll pay less to lease the one that depreciates less. This makes luxury cars, which tend to retain more of their value than economy cars, attractive candidates for leasing.

Should you make a down payment? Not if you can avoid it. Though putting more money down will lower your monthly lease payment, why pay the money up

Other things being equal, the best car to lease is the one that retains more of its value over the term of the lease.

If you think you're likely to exceed the mileage allowance, negotiate for additional miles up front.

front when one of the chief attractions of a lease is that it keeps your up-front outlay to a minimum?

Can you get a better deal if you wait until the end of the model year? This often works for buyers because dealers want to clear off their lots to make room for the new models. But when you're leasing, you're looking for the most favorable relationship between the cost of the car and its residual value. (Low cost, high residual, remember?) And a car that leaves the lot at the end of the model year is likely to depreciate faster than a car that begins its leased life at the beginning of the year. As soon as the new cars hit the showroom, you're driving last year's model.

The best leasing deals are usually offered by auto manufacturers that are trying to move a particular model. They can lower the cost of the lease by either reducing the cost of the car or offering a low financing rate. You'll see lots of great deals advertised in newspapers and on television, but remember that the terms you see there apply only to the specific model being advertised. As with everything else, it pays to shop around.

Traps to Watch For

Check the lease terms for a "capitalized cost reduction" fee. This is simply another way of asking for a down payment.

Watch out for excess-mileage charges. Dealers want to maximize the resale value of the car when the lease is up, so they limit the number of miles you can drive each year without paying extra. Some leases allow 15,000 miles, but more manufacturers are trimming the allowance to only 10,000 or 12,000 miles per year. If you think you're likely to exceed the allowance, then negotiate for additional miles up front. This can save you a few cents per mile over the end-of-lease mileage charge.

Don't take a longer lease term than you want in a misguided attempt to lower the monthly payments. If you need to get out of the lease before its term is up, you will almost certainly have to pay a steep charge for early termination. Exactly how steep will be spelled out in the contract.

Insuring Your Car

Chapter 12

Accidents happen. In cars, they happen nearly 100,000 times a day, and insurance can be the only thing standing between you and financial catastrophe. The policy describing this protection isn't what you'd call interesting reading. But if you want to know what you are entitled to for your insurance premiums, your policy constitutes the best single source of information.

This chapter opens with explanations of the major parts of a typical policy. The goal is to help you find your way through the thick language still so common there. Later in the chapter, you'll find suggestions for getting the best possible deal on your coverage.

Liability Coverage: In Case You're at Fault

This part of the policy protects you if you (or another person driving your car with your permission) injure or kill someone or damage property.

Assume an accident for which you are clearly responsible: You run a red light, strike another car, and injure the driver. Your liability coverage obliges the company to defend you—in court, if necessary—and pay claims to the other driver for vehicle damage and bodily injuries, including medical and hospital costs, rehabilitation, nursing care, and possibly lost income and money for pain and suffering. (The liability section of your policy does not compensate you for damage to your own car or any injuries to you. They are covered by other parts of the policy.)

Insurance companies use a shorthand to describe their liability coverage, and even if you understand the lingo, it might not be immediately apparent how much coverage you carry.

Now assume that you're involved in a collision at an intersection with no witnesses or evidence to pin the blame on either driver. Again, under your liability coverage, your insurer agrees to defend you against most proceedings the other driver may take against you.

The company limits its liability payments to the policy limits, or the amount of coverage you select. You can be held personally accountable for any excess.

Liability coverage is mandatory in nearly all states (the others have financial-responsibility laws that can be met by purchasing this coverage). But state requirements are modest—typically $20,000 to $30,000 for bodily injury suffered by one person in an accident, $50,000 for all people hurt in the same accident, and up to $25,000 for property damage resulting from that accident. Alaska and Maine, which have the toughest requirements, dictate $50,000 of coverage for one person's injuries, $100,000 for all those hurt in the same accident, and $25,000 for property damage.

How Much Coverage Do You Have?

Insurance companies use a shorthand to describe their liability coverage, and even if you understand the lingo, it might not be immediately apparent how much coverage you carry. The Alaska policy described above, for instance, might be listed as 50/100/25. The first figure refers to the coverage (in thousands of dollars) for injury to one person, the second number is the limit for injuries to all people in the same accident, and the third figure is the coverage for property damage in the same accident. Some companies issue single-limit policies, with one liability limit that applies to total payments arising from the same accident, regardless of the number of people injured or the amount of property damaged. In Canada, single-limit policies are the rule.

If the company incurs legal expenses to defend you in a lawsuit, those expenses don't count toward the liability limits. Nor do payments you receive under the policy for bail bonds and earnings lost while attending hearings and trials at the company's request. However, many policies free the company from any obligation to continue your legal defense for sums above the amount it has to pay.

How Much Coverage You Need

You should carry as much liability coverage as you can comfortably afford because damage claims today are sometimes settled for millions. State minimums don't come close to covering the cost of a serious accident. You should carry bodily-injury coverage of at least $100,000 per person, and $300,000 per accident, and property-damage coverage of $50,000, or a minimum of $300,000 on a single-limit policy. Raising your limits isn't expensive: $300,000 in coverage costs 20 percent more than $100,000, on average. The more coverage you buy, the less you have to pay per $1,000 of coverage. Ask your agent for precise figures. If your net worth is more than $300,000, investigate raising your liability coverage further through an umbrella policy (see Chapter 10).

> **Carry as much liability coverage as you can comfortably afford. State minimums don't come close to covering the cost of a serious accident.**

Crash Protection

Collision insurance pays for damage to your car, not the other guy's, and it's optional. After all, you can sue someone you think is to blame for damages to your car. So why buy collision insurance, unless you have to (for instance, if you are financing a car)? For a number of reasons:

- **You may be the world's most careful driver,** but it is still possible that you will cause an accident or be held responsible for one. In that case you can't collect for damage to your car from the other driver. Collision coverage will pay for the damage, even if an accident is your fault.
- **You may think an accident is the other driver's fault,** but he may disagree, casting you both into lengthy legal proceedings. With collision coverage, your company can repair the car and take over your claim against the other driver (a procedure known as subrogation). Your company is ethically, but not legally, bound to fight for enough money to pay you back part or all of the deductible.

The amount of collision coverage your policy provides, and its cost, will depend on your car and its value.

- **You could get into an accident** in which the other driver is clearly at fault but has no liability insurance. Suing could be pointless. As you will see later in this chapter, the auto policy's uninsured (or underinsured) motorist coverage does not necessarily pay for damage to your car in this situation. Collision does.
- **Suppose you smash your car into a tree** or a telephone pole. There's no one to sue. Collision will pay for the damage to your car.

The amount of collision coverage your policy provides, and its cost, will depend on your car and its value. Premiums are much higher for vehicles that are expensive, accident-prone, easily damaged, frequently stolen, or hard to repair. Those that score well for safety and durability often cost much less to insure. How much you will be paid for an accident depends on the nature and extent of the damage, whether new or refurbished parts are used, and other factors.

However, you should be aware of one special restriction: The company is obligated to pay only up to the car's cash value. That means the market value of the car before the accident, minus the salvage value of the damaged vehicle.

For example, say your car was worth $4,000 before the accident and $500 for salvage afterward. The company does not have to pay more than $3,500 in repairs. If the repairs would exceed that amount, the company can take the damaged car and give you the $4,000.

The cutoff for declaring a car to be totaled is usually somewhere around 75 to 80 percent of the car's retail value, though it may be the cost of repairs plus the car's salvage value. If your car was in the kind of condition that would make it worth more than others of its kind, you'll have a fight on your hands to get what you think it's worth. You don't have to accept the claims adjuster's first settlement offer. Counter with an amount you think is fair. If that fails, take your case to a senior adjuster at the company. Bring your agent in as an ally. Ultimately, you can seek help from your state insurance commissioner, take your case to arbitration, or even file a lawsuit. As your battle gets more and more expensive, you may decide to settle for a somewhat better offer than you got to begin with.

For an extra premium, some insurers will offer replacement-cost coverage for new or recent-vintage cars under the collision (and/or comprehensive) part of a policy. This coverage provides for the full cost of replacing a new or similar car—not just its cash value before the accident—as long as the insurer considers the car not repairable.

Many companies extend their collision coverage to rental cars (provided they are not being used for business). If you are covered, you can turn down the costly collision-damage waiver that car-rental agents sell. Check with your insurance agent to find out whether your policy covers rental cars. There are other economical ways to get insurance on rental cars. If you're a member of an auto club, such as AAA, you can get collision protection covering damage to rental cars above a certain amount. Some credit cards provide similar coverage when you charge a rental to them.

Medical Payments: Coverage You May Not Need

If you have coverage for medical payments on your car policy, you and your family members are entitled to reimbursement of medical costs resulting from auto accidents while in your car or someone else's car, or if you're injured by a car while walking or bicycling, regardless of who is at fault. Your guests qualify if they are injured in your car. Medical-payments coverage is typically $1,000 to $10,000 for each person protected by your policy. It would cost you relatively little to raise the coverage to a higher amount.

The company will reimburse a wide range of expenses, from eyeglasses to funeral costs, subject to varying conditions. One policy may pay medical expenses only for the first year after an accident, another for the first three years afterward, and still another up to five years, provided you buy more than a stipulated amount

Many companies extend their collision coverage to rental cars. If you are covered, you can turn down the costly collision-damage waiver that car-rental agents sell.

If you are hit by an under- or uninsured driver, this coverage protects you while you're in your car, walking, or, in some policies, bicycling.

of protection. Payments may be reduced by any amount that you receive or are entitled to receive from other parts of the policy or from other sources. In certain situations the company may pay only expenses that exceed the compensation obtainable from other insurance.

Before you consider additional medical coverage, check to see if it would duplicate coverage you already have under other medical policies, especially comprehensive, high-limit health insurance.

Protection against Uninsured and Underinsured Drivers

Despite laws requiring auto insurance in practically every state, a lot of people are driving without any—or without enough—liability insurance. The uninsured/underinsured motorist section of your policy protects you if you or family members who live with you are hurt by one of those drivers while you're in your car, walking, or, in some policies, bicycling. Your guests also qualify if they are hurt while in your car. This coverage also applies when you are struck and injured by a hit-and-run driver and, in some cases, by a driver insured by a company that becomes insolvent.

In order for this coverage to kick in, the other driver has to be declared at fault. In most states, when blame is in doubt or the amount payable is contested, you and your insurer have to submit your differences to arbitration. This kind of insurance usually covers only costs arising from bodily injuries. In states in which property damages are included, claims may be reduced by a deductible.

Generally, companies are obligated to pay claims up to the minimum amount fixed by your state for liability insurance. But often you can purchase higher limits for an additional premium. Most states require insurance companies to offer uninsured or underinsured coverage; some companies combine them. If your company offers them separately, buy both.

Comprehensive Coverage

A combination of liability, collision, medical payments, and uninsured/underinsured motorist insurance would seem to take care of all conceivable risks. Yet none of that insurance would necessarily cover losses to your vehicle from these hazards: theft of the car or some of its contents, collision with an animal, glass breakage, falling objects, fire, explosion, earthquake, windstorm, hail, water, flood, malicious mischief, vandalism, or riots. Comprehensive insurance, which is optional, will cover those losses, usually up to the car's cash value and sometimes subject to a deductible.

In some areas, if you keep your car in a garage or off-street parking area or if the car has a good anti-theft device—for instance, one that prevents the car from being started—you can get a reduction in your comprehensive-coverage premium.

Comprehensive coverage also entitles you to some compensation for renting a car if yours is stolen. Check your policy to see how much the policy would pay per day and for how long; different companies pay different amounts, subject to state requirements.

No-Fault Insurance

Liability insurance is your main financial defense against catastrophic damage you might cause to others or their property. But it's not always clear who's to blame for an accident, and proving fault, when it is possible, can entail delays and expensive legal action. Meanwhile, the victims may not get paid.

Enter no-fault insurance, an attempt to take the fault out of liability. The idea is to have accident victims' medical expenses paid by their own insurance companies, regardless of who is to blame for the accident, thereby eliminating the costs and delays of legal actions.

No states currently function under a pure no-fault system. Instead, 12 "no-fault" states have adopted a modified no-fault system. Some of those states have

No-fault insurance is an attempt to take the fault out of liability.

**The means
by which
companies
sort out good
risks from bad
aren't always
obvious. The
price you pay
is determined
by a complex
process that
begins before
you apply for
a policy.**

adopted "add-on" plans that increase the benefits you can obtain from your own insurance company but do not restrict your right to pursue a liability claim. No-fault laws vary greatly, but they do tend to have some elements in common.

- **Your insurance company pays you and others** covered by your policy for medical bills, lost wages, the cost of hiring people to do household tasks you are unable to perform as a result of injuries, and funeral expenses up to specified limits.
- **No-fault plans don't pay for property damage.** This is covered by other parts of the policy.
- **No-fault plans usually don't pay for pain and suffering.** For that you have to be able to sue someone.
- **You usually can't sue others** until expenses of the type covered by the no-fault insurance exceed a certain level. By the same token, you are immune to suits by others until their costs exceed that limit.

To protect themselves against fault-based suits permitted under no-fault regulations, drivers in some states must also buy traditional liability insurance. But liability payments may be reduced by compensation received under the no-fault provisions. Add-on no-fault plans generally provide benefits similar to, but less generous than, the pure no-fault programs, and the injured person has the right to sue for pain and suffering.

How Your Rate Is Set

If you have a lot of accidents or get a lot of tickets for moving violations, you're going to pay more for auto insurance. Everyone knows that. But the means by which companies sort out the good risks from the bad aren't always so obvious. The price you pay is determined by a complex process that begins long before you apply for a policy. When you apply, you are screened by a company underwriter who decides whether the company wants to insure you and, if so, in what general category to place you.

Who Are You?

The insurance company starts with a set of base premiums for each of the coverages that make up its standard policy. Those base rates are set to cover a particular customer: an adult male with a standard car used only for pleasure. Everyone else pays more or less, depending on the company's evaluation of his or her relative risk potential.

In effect, you are assigned to a group defined according to characteristics that are believed to predict the group's chances of creating insurance losses. Although classification plans differ, the companies employ for the most part these basic criteria: age, sex, marital status, accidents and traffic violations, the number of cars being insured, the models, use of the cars (pleasure, commuting, business, farm), mileage expected, whether a young driver has taken a driver-education course, and whether he or she is entitled to a good-student discount. Some even take your credit record into account.

Each characteristic is assigned a numerical weight based on its tendency to increase or reduce the probability of loss. All the factors that apply to you are combined to fix your position on the company's premium scale. A ranking of 100 indicates that you pay 100 percent of the base premium. With a 90 ranking you pay 90 percent of the base, which means you are getting a 10 percent discount. If you're pegged at 225, you are charged 225 percent of the base.

Despite a few attempts at simplification, risk classification systems have tended to become more complex over the years. Michigan's insurance bureau once estimated that the possible combinations of rating factors in some plans exceeded the number of people insured.

Where Do You Live?

Each company periodically computes the premium income it needs in each state in which it operates. It wants enough money to pay for claims and expenses, and a margin for profits and contingencies. The total state premium is then allocated among the various ter-

> In effect, you are assigned to a group defined according to characteristics that are believed to predict the group's chances of creating insurance losses.

Auto premiums have long since reached big-ticket status, so it pays to look for opportunities to keep your costs down and still have enough protection.

ritories into which the state is divided for rating purposes. The boundaries are supposed to demarcate areas with significantly different loss records.

The exact relationships vary from one state to another, but according to one study, people in central neighborhoods of small metropolitan areas (100,000 to 400,000 population) generally pay less than the state average; their counterparts in big cities (over one million) pay substantially more. Small-city suburbanites are charged less than the state average; big-city suburbanites are charged somewhat more.

Are You a Good Driver?

A company may separate drivers into three underwriting categories: preferred, standard, and nonstandard. Its rates for preferred applicants generally run 15 percent lower than standard rates. Nonstandard policyholders are charged anywhere from 35 to 75 percent more than standard rates, depending on the number of accidents they've been involved in and, in many cases, the number of traffic violations.

If you're considered a high-risk driver, you might be rejected and eventually forced into a state-assigned risk plan that requires a regular insurance company to give you protection—at a price that may be at least 50 percent more than other drivers are charged. Alternatively, one of the regular companies might shunt you into a subsidiary company that specializes in high-risk drivers. Those "substandard" insurers, as they are known in the business, also charge higher premiums.

Getting a Good Deal

Auto-insurance premiums have long since reached big-ticket status, so it pays to look for opportunities to keep your costs down and still have enough protection.

Do Some Homework

Posing as ordinary buyers, investigators with the Pennsylvania Insurance Department once visited 186 insurance agencies in three cities. Of the 92 Philadelphia agents contacted, fewer than 30 percent volunteered information on discounts and deductibles that could have reduced premiums 20 to 40 percent.

The lesson: Arm yourself with as much information as you can before you start calling companies. You'll find that some kinds of information are easier to get than others. It is fairly easy to solicit cost, coverage, and deductible information from auto insurers; it's much more difficult to find out their financial stability and service record—things you'd be interested in knowing if, for example, you get a good cost quote from a company you're not familiar with. You can check out stability in *Best's Insurance Reports: Property-Casualty* at your local library; insurers with the top two ratings can be considered solid. (You can also ask an agent how A.M. Best, the rating service that publishes the above guide, rates his or her company.)

Also contact your state insurance office; many of them keep track of consumer complaints and will share the results if they're asked. You'll find a list of phone numbers in the box on page 178. Finally, read through your policy carefully so that you're sure of the kind and amount of protection you have.

Compare the Premiums

Survey after survey confirms that auto-insurance companies often charge greatly different premiums for the same coverage. In New York, Pennsylvania, and elsewhere, premiums have been shown to vary sometimes by more than 100 percent. A recent shopping trip by the Arizona Department of Insurance found six-month premiums for a 48-year-old Phoenix man driving a late-model car ranged from about $650 at one company to more than $1,900 at another company, with others scattered somewhere in between.

Rates may not vary as wildly in your area, but the odds are you will discover substantial differences if you take the time to get premium quotes from a number of companies. Begin with a market leader, such as State Farm or Allstate. Then use that quote as a mea-

Surveys show that auto-insurance companies often charge greatly different premiums for the same coverage.

DISCOUNTS TO ASK FOR

1. Multicar and multipolicy. It often pays to insure your home and all of your family's vehicles with the same company. Families with teenagers at home who drive their own cars can usually save 15% to 20% by insuring all the vehicles and drivers on one policy. (New drivers seeking individual policies, on the other hand, are frequently referred to state-run "assigned-risk plans," which have high premiums.)

You can have the company assign drivers to particular cars your family owns. The rate will go down if your insurer assigns your highest-risk family member (the youngest, newest, or most accident-prone driver) to the family's oldest, least valuable car.

2. Antitheft devices. This discount applies to comprehensive coverage only. Not all car alarms and security devices are equal in the eyes of insurance companies, so check with your insurer before you have an antitheft system installed.

3. Safety features. Some insurance companies give discounts for safety features, such as air bags. Don't expect a windfall, however. Discounts will reduce your payments by only $8 to $10.

A few states require insurers to offer discounts for antilock brakes. But in other states some companies have stopped giving these discounts because they say antilock brakes have not reduced claims.

4. Carpooling. Commuting mileage drives up your insurance premium more than non-commuting mileage. All ten of the leading insurers polled by the Insurance Information Institute offered a 15% to 20% discount to commuters sharing driving responsibilities in car pools so they don't drive their cars to work every day. You can also save by using public transportation.

5. Good driver. If you avoid accidents and traffic violations through safe, sensible driving, you'll be rewarded handsomely with lower rates. Good-driver discounts range from 10% to 20% of the total premium. You may also get a discount if you or another family member complete a defensive driving course, or if your teenage son or daughter completes high-school driver's education.

6. Nonsmoker. If you or a family member quit smoking, it could lower your car insurance premium as well as your homeowners and life insurance premiums.

7. Good student. If you have a teenage driver, you may be eligible for a discount of 5% to 25% if he or she gets good grades at school.

8. College student. Alert your insurance company when a son or daughter goes away to college, whether he or she takes along a car or not.

sure against which to judge identical coverage at other companies. Many state insurance offices distribute auto-insurance pricing guides, but the categories they use may not match yours. Your best bet is to use such a guide to identify your state's most cost-effective insurers. Then get price quotes from a handful and you'll have a truly comparative guide. Use the phone numbers in the box on page 178.

Manage Your Teenagers' Driving

Young drivers pay much more than most others because, as a group, they have more accidents. Rates will drop several notches when they reach age 25 or marry. But meanwhile, if possible, avoid letting them become the principal driver of a car, which pushes up the premium even more. Most companies give good-student discounts to young drivers—commonly 5 to 25 percent off for a consistent B average—because statistically, good students are superior drivers. Young drivers can also get discounts for completing an approved driver-training course. The parents of students who spend part of the year at a school more than 100 or 150 miles away from home (and the family car) may also get a break.

Drive Carefully Yourself

Discounts are common for safe-driving records: Some companies give 5 percent off for drivers with three years of a clear record, raising the discount to 10 percent for drivers with six or more accident- and violation-free years. Depending on which company insures you and where you live, you may even get a discount if you're a nonsmoker, a woman who is a household's only driver, a senior citizen, or a member of a certain profession (such as law or medicine) that is statistically less accident-prone. All ten of the leading insurers polled by the Insurance Information Institute offered a 15 to 20 percent discount to commuters sharing driving responsibilities in car pools, meaning they don't drive their cars to work every day. When comparing policies, consider discounts but don't fixate on them. A discount may very well be offset by a higher premium to begin with.

Check Your Car's Rating

Insurers charge more for cars with high claims rates, no matter how good the driving record of the owner.

When comparing policies, consider discounts but don't fixate on them. A discount may very well be offset by a higher premium.

INSURANCE WORKSHEET

VEHICLES YOU PLAN TO INSURE	VEHICLE 1	VEHICLE 2
Vehicle identification number (VIN)	_____	_____
Annual mileage	_____	_____
Commuting mileage	_____	_____

FAMILY MEMBERS YOU PLAN TO INSURE

Name	Birthdate	Driver's license number
_____	_____	_____
_____	_____	_____
_____	_____	_____
_____	_____	_____

HOW PREMIUMS COMPARE

	CURRENT PREMIUM		1ST COMPANY PREMIUM		2ND COMPANY PREMIUM		3RD COMPANY PREMIUM	
	Vehicle 1	Vehicle 2	Vehicle 1	Vehicle 2	Vehicle 1	Vehicle 2	Vehicle 1	Vehicle 2
Liability								
$100,000 per person bodily injury	____	____	____	____	____	____	____	____
$300,000 per accident bodily injury	____	____	____	____	____	____	____	____
$50,000 per accident property damage	____	____	____	____	____	____	____	____
No-fault/ personal injury protection*								
$ _____	____	____	____	____	____	____	____	____

*Check with your state's department of insurance for state-mandated minimums.

Some charge less for collision and comprehensive coverage on models that score well for safety and durability, but add surcharges for others. A surcharge or a discount isn't a judgment of a car's quality. The rate variations reflect repair costs, accident frequency, theft losses, and other factors.

Before you buy your next car, it might pay to check on such differentials. The Insurance Services Office

	CURRENT PREMIUM		1ST COMPANY PREMIUM		2ND COMPANY PREMIUM		3RD COMPANY PREMIUM	
	Vehicle 1	Vehicle 2	Vehicle 1	Vehicle 2	Vehicle 1	Vehicle 2	Vehicle 1	Vehicle 2
Medical payments (in states without no-fault coverage)								
$2,000	____	____	____	____	____	____	____	____
Uninsured/ underinsured motorist								
$100,000 per person bodily injury	____	____	____	____	____	____	____	____
$300,000 per accident bodily injury	____	____	____	____	____	____	____	____
Collision								
no deductible	____	____	____	____	____	____	____	____
$250 deductible	____	____	____	____	____	____	____	____
$500 deductible	____	____	____	____	____	____	____	____
Comprehensive								
no deductible	____	____	____	____	____	____	____	____
$250 deductible	____	____	____	____	____	____	____	____
$500 deductible	____	____	____	____	____	____	____	____
Discounts								
_____	____	____	____	____	____	____	____	____
_____	____	____	____	____	____	____	____	____
Subtotal	____	____	____	____	____	____	____	____
TOTAL	$___	$___	$___	$___	$___	$___	$___	$___

provides a rating service used by hundreds of insurance companies, and your agent should be able to tell you the new car's rating. Or get free loss data on more than 300 makes and models online or by requesting the *Injury, Collision & Theft Losses by Make and Model* from the Insurance Institute for Highway Safety, Communications Dept., 1005 N. Glebe Road, Arlington, VA 22201 (http://www.hwysafety.org; 703-247-1500). Loss data

INSURANCE SHOPPING GUIDES

Your state insurance department may publish a guide that shows what insurers charge for different policies in various parts of your state.

Alabama	334-269-3550	Missouri	573-751-4126
Alaska	907-269-7900	Montana	406-444-2040
Arizona	602-912-8444	Nebraska	402-471-2201
Arkansas	800-852-5494	Nevada	775-687-4270
California	213-897-8921	New Hampshire	603-271-2261
Colorado	303-894-7499	New Jersey	609-292-5360
Connecticut	860-297-3900	New Mexico	505-827-4601
Delaware	302-739-4251	New York	202-480-6400
District of Columbia	202-727-8000	North Carolina	919-733-3058
Florida	800-342-2762	North Dakota	701-328-2440
Georgia	800-656-2298	Ohio	614-644-2658
Hawaii	808-586-2790	Oklahoma	800-522-0071
Idaho	208-334-4250	Oregon	503-947-7980
Illinois	217-782-4515	Pennsylvania	717-783-0442
Indiana	317-232-2385	South Carolina	803-737-6160
Iowa	877-955-1212	South Dakota	605-773-4104
Kansas	800-432-2484	Tennessee	615-741-2241
Kentucky	800-595-6053	Texas	800-578-4677
Louisiana	225-342-5423	Utah	801-538-3800
Maine	207-624-8475	Vermont	802-828-3301
Maryland	410-468-2090	Virginia	804-371-9694
Massachusetts	617-521-7301	Washington	360-725-7100
Michigan	517-335-3167	West Virginia	304-558-3354
Minnesota	651-297-7161	Wisconsin	608-267-1233
Mississippi	601-359-3569	Wyoming	307-777-7401

Source: Insurance Information Institute

do not necessarily translate into discounts, but they do show which vehicles are most likely to qualify.

Consider Raising Your Deductibles

It might make sense to choose the highest deductible you can afford to pay without seriously disrupting your finances. The idea is to pay for affordable damage yourself and let insurance kick in for bigger losses.

Whatever your situation, you can save something by accepting a larger deductible and thus transferring part of the risk from the company to yourself. It's not an ideal solution, but it's one of the few cost-cutting opportunities that are readily available. By increasing your deductible from $100 to $1,000, you might be able to shave as much as 25 percent from your annual premium (if you're financing the car, your lender might insist you limit the deductible to $500). But be realistic. You can still save 10 percent or more if you increase your deductible from $250 to $500. Keep the deductible at a level you can afford.

Reduce the Coverage on an Old Car

You could consider dropping comprehensive and collision coverage on an old car to reduce your insurance costs fast. That would expose you to additional risk, but remember that the insurance company won't pay more to fix a car than it's worth. Each year's depreciation therefore diminishes the maximum claim you can make against your collision coverage. If your car is five or more years old, depending on its value, you may be better off dropping both collision and comprehensive coverage and banking the savings. Estimate your car's value by studying the classified ads or by consulting used-car price guides, and consider how much protection you're really buying for your collision and comprehensive premium.

Insure All Cars with the Same Company

You get a break for the second and successive cars covered by the same policy, so it's usually more economical to put all your cars on one policy. Similarly, consider using the same company for other policies. Some insurers offer discounts of up to 10 percent if you cover both your car and your home with them.

Don't Pay by Installments

The company tacks an extra amount on to your premium when you pay in monthly or quarterly installments. If you can afford it, pay your premium in a lump sum.

> **You get a break for the second and successive cars covered by the same policy, so it's usually more economical to put all your cars on one policy.**

If you're dealing with your own company, look for support for your position in the policy.

How to Make Sure You Get Paid

There are millions of accidents every year, maybe 90 percent of them covered by insurance. When claims are filed, the companies usually settle them reasonably well. Still, state insurance departments receive a steady stream of complaints, and many states have felt the need to adopt rules on unfair claims practices.

If you have trouble settling an accident claim quickly—whether it's with your own or the other driver's company—your best strategy depends on the issue in dispute, the circumstances of the accident, and other factors. Here are several pointers that may prove useful.

Know Your Policy and Your Rights

If you're dealing with your own company, look for support for your position in the policy, which constitutes a legal agreement between you and the company and spells out its obligations to you. When you're seeking compensation from another company, your agent should have an idea of what you can reasonably demand.

Take Names

Companies range from the large to the colossal. The largest cover millions of cars and employ thousands of claims workers. To avoid getting lost among the thousands of claims the company is processing each day, record the names and telephone numbers of people you contact, take notes on important conversations (don't forget the dates), and make copies of letters and other material affecting your claim.

Don't Sweat the Small Stuff

Rarely has a government agency offered such sage counsel as in this excerpt from the automobile insurance guide of the Washington State Insurance Department:

"Unfortunately, no one can ever be fully compensated for all the trouble and expense that an accident causes. A certain amount of running around is often unavoidable, and petty frustrations sometimes result. Accepting these difficulties is sometimes the only solution, and knowing this in advance may help make a bad situation bearable."

You needn't, however, submit gladly to unfair treatment. Anticipating an accident's inevitable inconveniences helps channel your anger into purposeful action.

BE ASSERTIVE. Quietly tell the company representative how you feel and what you need, without using derogatory terms that will only harden his or her opposition. If you want a new bumper and the adjuster insists on a used one, state—don't argue—your position: "My bumper was in good condition before the accident. I feel I'm entitled to a new one. I need my car. How can we settle this matter?"

The adjuster is hardly likely to concede immediately. Continue asserting your position calmly and firmly, and throw the burden of finding a solution on the adjuster. If he or she won't budge, ask to speak to the supervisor and resume presenting your interests. It may be a transparent tactic, but assertive behavior can work where blustering and name-calling won't.

DON'T RUSH TO SETTLE. Sometimes a troublesome claim against another driver can be settled by what's called subrogation. Your company pays the claim and then goes after the other driver's company for reimbursement. It's a convenient alternative when the company insuring the driver you believe caused the accident balks at settling, because you get some money sooner. But subrogation has a few potential drawbacks.

- **Your company reduces its payment** by your deductible. If it succeeds in settling the case with the other insurer, you may be refunded only part of your deductible, depending on the sum recovered and the expenses incurred.
- **If your company loses its case,** it might declare you liable for the accident and make you subject to a premium surcharge.

It may be a transparent tactic, but assertive behavior can work where blustering and name-calling won't.

A majority of states have adopted a model law that specifically prohibits several unfair claims practices by insurance companies.

■ **You may not be entitled to car-rental expenses** when the claim is covered by your company, as you might be when you take action against the other company.

Explore these possibilities with the agent before you turn over the claim to your company. If you have a strong case against the other driver, it may be better to push the claim with his or her company before you try subrogation.

COMPLAIN TO THE STATE. Very few states have complete authority to order an insurance company to pay a disputed claim or increase the settlement. Still, state insurance regulators do have influence. Most state insurance departments respond to complaints and contact the insurance company about them. Moreover, a majority of states have adopted a model law that specifically prohibits several unfair claims practices by companies, including the following. If you find yourself confronting any of these situations, you probably have a friend in the state insurance office.

■ **The company fails to acknowledge and act promptly** on communications about insured claims.

■ **The company fails to provide** a reasonable explanation of policy conditions or laws under which a claim is denied or a compromise offer is made.

■ **The company delays settlement of one part of a claim** in order to influence settlement of another (for instance, the company resists paying car damages to pressure you into settling on bodily injury costs).

■ **The company doesn't try to make prompt,** fair, and equitable settlement even though liability has become clear.

■ **The company forces you to start legal action** by making an unreasonably low settlement offer.

Your state insurance department may have someone designated to handle consumer complaints. If not, write to the insurance commissioner. Keep a copy of the letter and any important material you enclose. You can locate your state's insurance regulator on many

Web sites, including http://www.kiplinger.com/basics/ managing/insurance/regulator.htm or by calling the National Association of Insurance Commissioners (NAIC) at 816-842-3600 or checking their Web Site at http://www.naic.com.

CONSIDER HIRING A LAWYER. If you're injured in an accident, you might want to hire a lawyer, even if only for guidance. The decision depends on the extent of the injury and the type of claim.

Lawyers usually charge a percentage of the recovered amount in personal-injury cases. The standard contingency fee is 30 to 40 percent, but you might also have to pay court costs if the case goes to trial. Few cases go that far.

Find a lawyer experienced in injury claims. If you can't find one through personal contacts, call a legal referral service. It may be listed in the Yellow Pages.

The available evidence indicates that lawyers obtain larger settlements for their clients than claimants get on their own. But a study made by insurance companies suggests that the net payment after fees may be less in some cases than unrepresented claimants receive.

CONSIDER PAYING FOR THE DAMAGE YOURSELF. This seems to defeat the purpose for which you bought insurance. But by facing facts as they are, not as they should be, you may find that it costs less in the long run to cover a small loss yourself.

Most insurance companies use demerit rating plans that raise premiums when you violate certain traffic laws or cause an accident that results in physical injuries or damage over a certain amount—say, $400. At the time of purchase, some companies assess you penalty points for each incident during the preceding three years, and impose further points for accidents and traffic violations occurring while the policy is in force. Everyone who regularly drives your car counts, so you will be surcharged even if your spouse or teenager is responsible. Generally, each point sticks on your record for three years.

> If you're injured in an accident, you might want to hire a lawyer, even if only for guidance. The decision depends on the extent of injury and type of claim.

Tell your company promptly about an accident involving another car or person, even if you have no plan to file a claim.

The premium increases that result from this system vary. Just one demerit point might be enough for a 30 percent hike in the base premium for the collision and liability coverages in your policy. Two points could lead to a doubling of the premium.

All this can pose some interesting dilemmas. Say that you scrape the side of your car against a post in a parking lot and the repairs come to $325. If you have a $100 deductible, the company will pay you $225. But if you have already received payment for other small claims, you can be charged with a point that will hike the premium for the next three years by considerably more than $225. You might be better off paying the $225 yourself and saving your points for a big claim.

You're on shakier ground, though, when the accident involves another car or person and you could be considered responsible. You can still try to pay for the damage yourself, but you should tell your company promptly about the accident, even if damages are minor and you have no plan to file a claim. The other person might accept your check but come back several weeks or months later with a claim for hidden damages or personal injuries. You would then be forced to refer the case to the insurance company, which, although obliged to pay justified claims against you and defend against unjustified ones, might be reluctant to accept liability. It could argue that you failed to observe the policy clause requiring prompt reporting of accidents. Whether it would actually refuse the case would depend on company policy, state law, and the circumstances. Conceivably, it might take a tough position if the delay resulted in the loss of key evidence. Thus, you might add to your problems by paying a claim.

After you've been a policyholder for a while, ask your agent for a copy of the company's demerit rating provisions. If the figures suggest that it may be advantageous to pay for small losses yourself, you might also consider raising the deductible on your collision policy. That way you will at least save something on the premium.

Your Money and Your Life

Part 4

The Money Side of Marrying

The psychology of money changes dramatically when you get married. For one thing, you've got to pay closer attention to what you're doing. You've embarked on a financial pas de deux in which each partner needs to be able to anticipate the moves of the other. A serious misstep by either can bring both of you crashing down in an embarrassing heap. This chapter will explore ways to keep you twirling away like Fred and Ginger.

Frank talk about money is difficult for many couples, but it's an absolute necessity to get your marriage off to a good start and keep it on a sound footing. (If you're already married, you may have learned this the hard way.) Facing the financial facts of life together will pay off in the long run.

What to Know Before You Marry

Each of you needs to lay out for the other what you earn, what investments or savings you have, and what debts you're paying. List the assets and liabilities that you'll bring into the marriage. (A lawyer might advise you to make a signed and dated copy of this document and keep it in a safe place because it could be useful in case of divorce some day. Whether you want to look at your brand-new marriage that way is up to you.) If one of you has significant debts, now is the time to devise a realistic plan for paying them off as soon as possible so they don't put a strain on your future plans.

Each spouse should have credit cards in his or her name, even though one account with two cards might work fine. Each of you needs to establish your own credit history.

Choose a Family Accountant

In the process of figuring out what the balance sheet will look like after the merger, you'll gain some insight into the question of who should be the family accountant. Odds are that one of you is better organized than the other or more disciplined or simply better equipped by way of knowledge and experience to handle the details of household money management. That's the one who should keep the books at first. After six months or so, it's a good idea for the other to take over for a while, so both of you know where the money is going.

Joint Accounts or Separate?

You have to decide whether to set up a joint checking account or maintain your own accounts. Joint accounts can work well if at least one of you is a top-notch bookkeeper. But many couples have trouble keeping track of checks and ATM receipts when both partners are drawing on the same account.

If you decide to create two family accountants by opening separate accounts, make sure each of you gets responsibility for some aspect of the family's finances—one of you pays the mortgage, for instance, and the other pays the electric and telephone bills. Separate accounts can help keep the peace between spouses who are on opposite ends of the money-management spectrum. Neither has to account to the other for minor expenditures or sloppy checkbook management.

Still, you're supposed to be in this partnership together, so you can't go your separate financial ways entirely. One solution is to open a joint account to cover household expenses and keep your separate accounts for personal spending. Each contributes an agreed-upon amount to the joint account. This means that one of you will have two checking accounts to keep track of, but for many couples this has been a workable compromise.

Checking accounts are one thing, credit cards are another. It's a good idea for each spouse to have credit cards issued in his or her name, even though one account with two cards might work fine. Each of you needs to establish your own credit history. But here, too, a joint account might be useful for household purchases. Set a limit for using all cards without consulting each other—for example, you could say that any purchase over a certain amount requires that both be involved in the decision.

You will also need to decide in whose name you'll own major assets like cars, savings accounts, and investments. The discussion of joint ownership later in this chapter looks at the advantages and disadvantages of listing all your assets in both names.

Set Some Goals

Separately, make a list of your short-term, intermediate, and long-term goals, guided by the goal-setting techniques described in Chapter 1. Decide what you'd like to buy (a new suit? a bicycle?) or save for over the next year. Then do the same for a three- to five-year horizon (a home? a new car? a week in Cancun?). Take into account nonfinancial goals with financial consequences (do you hope to have children?). Now think about long-term goals (saving for retirement or college tuition? considering buying a vacation home?).

Compare lists. Then discuss your priorities and devise a realistic financial plan both of you can support.

Review Your Insurance

MEDICAL COVERAGE. Review the health plans available to each of you through your employers and carefully compare the benefits and costs of each. There's no marriage penalty here: You may even discover that the premium for you as a couple is lower than your combined premiums as two singles. If one plan offers better coverage for a lower cost, you'll naturally want to switch to that plan. But before you do, find out how you or your spouse can get back into the plan you're leaving. You may change your mind as circumstances change, or your spouse may lose his or her job. Will you have to wait until there is an open enrollment period? Will preexisting conditions be covered?

> Separately, make a list of your goals. Compare lists. Then discuss your priorities and devise a realistic financial plan both of you can support.

Disability insurance is perhaps more important than life insurance in the early stages of your marriage.

If you plan to have children, examine each medical plan with children in mind. Compare maternity coverage. If you know ahead of time that one of you will stay home to care for children, then obviously you'll want to keep your coverage in the plan of the spouse who will continue working. (See Chapter 20 for more information on medical insurance.)

LIFE INSURANCE. If both of you will continue working and you don't have children or a large mortgage, you don't need a lot of life insurance unless one of you makes considerably more money than the other. In that case, the spouse with the big income might want to buy enough insurance so that the surviving spouse can continue to live in the style to which you're about to become accustomed. The lower-income spouse can get by with less insurance. If only one of you will continue to work or you plan to start a family right away, then be sure that you have enough coverage to allow for the support of your family if either of you should die. See Chapter 19 for more on figuring how much life insurance you need.

DISABILITY INSURANCE. This is perhaps more important than life insurance in the early stages of your marriage. Temporary or permanent disability is statistically more likely to strike than an early death, and disability, in addition to making it difficult or impossible to earn an income, can entail major medical and other expenses. Each of you should have disability coverage that replaces two-thirds of your current income. Chapter 20 tells you how to find it.

AUTO INSURANCE. If you have two cars, you can probably save money by insuring both vehicles with the same company. See Chapter 12 for help with car insurance.

Start a Savings Plan
First, build an emergency fund. A good goal would be to set aside three to six months' worth of living expenses in case one of you loses your job, you suddenly need a new furnace or a new roof, or some other major expense hits when you're least expecting it.

With your emergency fund tucked safely in interest-bearing bank certificates of deposit (or in a money-market fund, which is almost as safe and usually pays more interest), you're ready to start an investment plan, modest though it may be. Start with whatever you can afford and don't make the mistake of waiting around until you can afford to set aside big money each month. Just $75 a month stashed in a mutual fund earning 8 percent will grow to $13,720 in ten years. See Chapter 22 for help in designing an investment plan that suits your income and goals.

Don't Worry about the Marriage Tax Penalty—at Least for Now

After years of fanatical rhetoric, Congress finally did something about the marriage penalty—the way the law worked so that millions of married couples paid more tax on their combined income on a joint tax return than they would have if they were single and reported their separate incomes on individual returns. The relief from this marriage penalty is in effect through 2010, unless Congress decides to extend it or make it permanent.

The standard deduction amount for married couples has been increased to twice as much as the standard deduction for single people. The value of that change depends on your tax bracket. The bigger standard deduction simplifies life for many taxpayers who have been itemizing. If the larger standard deduction is more than the total of their itemized deductions, they can skip that paperwork.

This change helps married couples whose incomes fall in the 15 percent bracket, whether they itemize or not. In 2005, the amount of income taxed in the 15 percent bracket equaled twice the amount of the income that fell in the 15 percent bracket for individual filers.

For higher-income taxpayers filing jointly—those who had some of their income taxed in the 25 percent bracket and higher—this relief went only part way because these higher brackets were not expanded to be twice the size of their single-return counterparts.

Relief from the marriage penalty is in effect through 2010, unless Congress decides to extend it or make it permanent.

The beginning of your life together seems an indecorous time to be thinking of the end of your lives, but marriage is one of those life events that calls for will writing.

We should really put the word penalty in quotation marks because this change applies to—and will cut the tax bill of—all married couples, including the millions who already enjoy a marriage bonus: When one partner in a marriage makes considerably more than the other, the couple actually pays less together than they would if they were single filing individually.

Write Two Wills

The beginning of your life together seems an indecorous time to be thinking of the end of your lives, but marriage is one of those life events that calls for will writing. In addition to a new spouse, you've just acquired a new legal status. State law tends to protect surviving spouses, but you can do a better job of it with a will. Make your wishes clear regarding any real estate, bank and brokerage accounts, cars, jewelry, valuable art, insurance policies, or other assets you may own.

Sort Out Your Papers

Find a place to keep all your important documents so either of you can get to them quickly in an emergency. This means birth certificates, your marriage license, wills, insurance policies, and a list of names and phone numbers for such people as your accountant, lawyer, insurance agent, and broker. You can keep originals in a safe-deposit box at a bank, but be sure to keep copies at home in a safe place both of you can find. Kiplinger's CD, *Your Family Records Organizer* ($14.95, http://www.kiplinger.com/organizer), offers a series of forms on which you can list where you keep all of your important materials and list key contacts.

Prenuptial Agreements

Prenuptial agreements are legal documents that describe the division of a couple's property and assets should they divorce or otherwise part company. The agreement documents the assets each party brings to the marriage and describes how these assets and any acquired during the marriage will be divided if there's a divorce, separation, or annulment.

Prenups aren't what you'd call romantic, but their use is spreading. We tend to think of them as an invention of the 1970s, when the prenups of wealthy celebrities made headlines. But prenuptial agreements have been around for a long time—in fact, they can be traced back to the ancient Romans. Today, approximately 5 percent of married couples have prenups—a significant increase over the 1 percent of marriages blessed with prenups 20 years ago.

Prenups aren't what you'd call romantic, but their use is spreading.

Who Needs a Prenup?

In most relationships, a prenuptial agreement probably isn't worth the expense or the emotional turmoil it will create. But there are cases in which you might want to consider drawing one up:

■ **You earn a high salary** and have significant assets that you want to protect.

■ **You have your own business.**

■ **You want to be sure** that your children from a previous marriage will be taken care of after your death. Even if your children are grown and independent, you probably want to know that they will inherit part, if not all, of your assets and property after your death.

■ **Your partner is paying child support** for children from a previous marriage. If your marriage fails, you want to be sure that your assets aren't used for those payments.

■ **You have agreed to pay** for the professional education of your soon-to-be spouse and want to be assured that you will benefit from the income he or she will receive in the future.

On the other side of the question, you may be offered a prenup that you shouldn't sign. Women, for instance, are often the ones who leave the workforce to raise children or care for ailing parents, and thus are financially vulnerable in a divorce. You should be wary of any agreement that:

■ **offers you a poor settlement** because you are starting the marriage with little money or assets of your own;

■ **doesn't offer you some income** if the marriage ends;

Joint ownership is sometimes called a mini estate plan. Although it offers some protection, it is no substitute for a will.

■ **doesn't have a time limit** so that the agreement basically disappears after the marriage has survived a certain length of time—say, five years;
■ **you feel pressured to sign.**

In such cases, you are probably better off not signing the agreement and clearing up these concerns before you enter into marriage.

Whatever the issues, don't attempt a prenup without two lawyers—one for each of you. You want one well versed in family and contract law who has had considerable experience in this specialized area. If the agreement is contested later on and one of you didn't have a lawyer, the court may be persuaded by the other that the agreement was not negotiated in good faith.

Considering Joint Ownership

Joint ownership is the traditional way for husbands and wives to hold property. It's a nice symbol of economic togetherness. And it's sometimes overrated.

Joint ownership is actually shorthand for two ways of owning property: joint tenancy with the right of survivorship, and tenancy by the entirety. Although they differ in some respects and about half the states don't recognize the entirety variety, both forms of joint ownership provide a survivorship feature that's especially attractive to married couples. When one joint owner dies, the other automatically becomes sole owner of the property. The property bypasses probate, avoiding delays and usually trimming the costs of that final accounting process. In some states joint ownership can also ease the inheritance-tax bite, and such property may be exempt from seizure by creditors of the deceased.

Possible Problems with Joint Ownership

Those advantages, buttressed by some imagined benefits that don't actually exist, help explain the appeal of joint ownership. Offsetting the advantages are a few potential problems.

For one thing, control of jointly held property is sometimes muddled. Depending on what's involved, one spouse may be able to dispose of it without the other's knowledge (as is generally the case with the entire balance of a joint checking or savings account). Or each partner may be hamstrung, unable to sell the property without the other's consent (a situation that can apply to a home or to stocks and bonds).

Another potential problem of joint ownership is that it is often seen as a substitute for a will. Sometimes it is even called the poor man's will or a mini estate plan, because it guarantees that the surviving spouse will get the property when the other dies.

Although joint ownership offers some protection, it is no substitute for a will. For one thing, if the surviving owner later dies without a will, the property will be divvied up according to the state's scheme of who should get what.

Also, joint ownership can dilute the power of a will to parcel out assets as you wish because jointly owned property can't be controlled by a will. Say, for example, that you and your spouse buy a mountain cottage. If you take title as joint owners and you die first, your share disappears and your spouse automatically becomes sole owner. That may be what you want, or it could mean unintentionally disinheriting someone else, such as a child. Taking joint title makes the decision: Your fellow owner gets the property if you die first.

(It is possible to co-own property without being joint owners. If you take title as tenants in common, which has no right of survivorship, your will controls what happens to your share of the property.)

Finally, many people make the mistake of assuming that jointly owned property escapes estate taxes just as it avoids probate. It doesn't. Half will be subject to tax when the first owner dies.

Who Should Own What?

Today's ownership decisions should be made with an eye on the future. There can be clear advantages to joint ownership, and in many circumstances they easily

Many people make the mistake of assuming that jointly owned property escapes estate taxes just as it avoids probate. It doesn't. Half will be subject to tax when the first owner dies.

Your best course may be a careful mix of joint and individual ownership, depending on the property that's involved.

outweigh the potential drawbacks. A lawyer well versed in federal estate and local property laws can help you make the right choice. You may decide that the best course for you and your spouse is a careful mix of joint and individual ownership, depending on the property involved.

YOUR HOME. The survivorship feature of joint ownership may be especially appealing here. Talk with your lawyer about other options, though, especially if your estate is large. If you own a vacation home in another state, owning it jointly with right of survivorship keeps it out of probate in both that state and your home state when the first owner dies.

SAVINGS AND CHECKING ACCOUNTS. Joint accounts are convenient, but with some types of accounts in some states, part or all of the balance may be frozen by the bank at the death of either owner. Since that could strap the survivor at a difficult time, you may want to have individual accounts, too. Ask your banker about local rules.

LIFE INSURANCE. If you own a policy on your own life, the proceeds will be included in your estate regardless of who receives them. It might be advisable for each mate to own the policies on the other's life. This keeps the proceeds out of the estate of the insured. It also means that the insured gives up the right to change the beneficiary and borrow against the policy's cash value. Check with your lawyer or insurance agent for details.

STOCKS AND BONDS. Joint ownership could restrict flexibility in managing investments because both signatures are needed to buy or sell.

YOUR CAR. There's not much advantage to joint ownership, and there's one drawback: The assets of both owners could be vulnerable to a suit for damages.

SAFE-DEPOSIT BOX. Pitfalls exist here, too. Check local law. A jointly owned box may be sealed upon the death of either owner until authorities have a chance to take inventory.

SPECIAL RULES FOR COMMUNITY-PROPERTY STATES. Community-property states—Arizona, California, Idaho, Louisiana, Nevada, New Mexico, Texas, Washington, and Wisconsin—add a special twist to the ownership question. In these nine states, salaries and assets acquired during marriage are generally considered community property, which means they are owned 50-50 by each spouse. This can be an important protection (or irritant, depending on your point of view) in case of divorce. In case of death, community property doesn't carry the right of survivorship, so the surviving spouse does not automatically assume full ownership. The deceased partner's half is disposed of by will or the state's rules for people who die without a will, and only that part is included in the estate for tax purposes.

Community-property states usually permit couples to set up other types of ownership, either separate or joint. Check on local laws that apply to your circumstances. If you move to a community-property state from another state, or vice versa, be sure to review ownership arrangements and estate plans.

When Seniors Tie the Knot

Marriage is for the young and the young at heart. But older folks who head down the aisle may find financial heartache if they fail to anticipate the effects on their pensions, Social Security benefits, health care, estate planning, and taxes.

Pensions

If you're a surviving spouse, you won't lose your survivor's pension benefit because you remarry. Also, if you are the named beneficiary on a company-sponsored

> Older folks who head down the aisle may find financial heartache if they fail to anticipate the effects on their pensions, Social Security benefits, health care, estate planning, and taxes.

If you choose not to marry, consider appointing your partner as your health care agent or proxy.

401(k) or other retirement plan, you won't jeopardize this inheritance by remarrying.

However, you do need to be concerned if your deceased spouse retired from the military or the federal government. You can forfeit pension benefits if you remarry before the age of 57. After 57, you're free and clear. There are also some police and firefighter benefits that are cut off at any age if you remarry, so check on the conditions before you proceed with your plans.

Social Security Benefits

If you are a widow or widower age 60 or older, you can remarry and still collect benefits on your deceased spouse's record. You get to choose the greatest of: 1) your deceased spouse's full benefit, 2) 50 percent of your new spouse's benefit, or 3) your own benefit based on your own work history. If you remarry before age 60, you lose your deceased spouse's benefit. But if your second spouse also dies, then you are entitled to either deceased spouse's full benefit or to your own benefit, whichever is greater.

Health Care

It is not illegal for an employer to deny health care coverage to a surviving spouse who remarries. This can be a costly turn of events, because you may not be able to find coverage elsewhere (particularly if you have a preexisting condition). If you find coverage, it could be outrageously expensive. This sort of dilemma has caused a growing number of seniors to decide to live together without getting married.

If you choose not to marry, consider appointing your partner as your health care agent or proxy. If illness or an accident renders you unable to make your own health care decisions, medical professionals will want to consult your next of kin (no matter how far away they may live) if your partner hasn't been named as your agent.

The possibility of crippling long-term-care costs, such as nursing-home bills, is another issue confronting people who marry later in life. Long-term-care insurance for each of you (see Chapter 20) could ease your minds.

Estate Planning

In a late-in-life marriage, it is particularly important to have a plan for the division of each partner's estate. A carefully drawn will or a living trust can ensure that your wishes are carried out. The older you are, the more important it is for you to have a good will that can withstand challenges by disgruntled relatives with their own ideas about how your estate should be divided. In particular, you need to make clear what you want your children and your partner to receive. Chapter 30 contains some estate-planning guidance.

Taxes

The marriage penalty can really slam older couples. It's a one-two punch: First they get pushed into a higher bracket, and then their combined incomes can easily be high enough to cause their Social Security benefits to be taxed. Single people can have up to $25,000 in provisional income (which is adjusted gross income plus tax-exempt interest plus 50 percent of Social Security benefits) before some of their Social Security benefits are taxed. A married couple, however, doesn't get twice the allowance. They are allowed a combined provisional income of only $32,000 before the tax kicks in.

There's not much you can do to avoid this nasty little trick, but you may be able to limit its impact. If part of your income is from an IRA distribution, for instance, perhaps you can postpone some of it so that you pass the threshold only every other year. If you sell stocks or bonds to supplement your income, try to time the sales for years in which your income has already passed into taxable territory, and reduce sales in years in which you have a chance to stay under the threshold.

As mentioned earlier in this chapter, the relief from the marriage penalty lasts through 2010.

> The older you are, the more important it is for you to have a good will that can withstand challenges by disgruntled relatives.

The Dollar Side of Divorce

In the short run, divorce is an emotionally wrenching experience for all involved. In the long run, it can sow the seeds of financial disaster if one spouse lets the other dominate the process. Divorce is rarely fair. This chapter can help you make it less unfair.

One of the most important things you can do to prepare for a divorce is to gather information. This is particularly important if you have deferred the financial decisions to your spouse, or if you think your spouse has withheld information regarding debts or assets from you. Collect all the information you can find on your spouse's bank accounts, mutual fund and brokerage accounts, pension plans and retirement funds, insurance policies, and any other financial asset, such as real estate.

Start with papers you might find around your house or apartment. Examine your spouse's payroll stubs for deductions for any savings and retirement accounts, such as pension plans or 401(k)s. Get credit reports for both you and your spouse (see page 30 for phone numbers). Hunt up copies of state and federal income-tax returns from the past several years and make your own copies. Your lawyer will want to see them.

In a divorce proceeding, reliable financial information is crucial. What you can do with it will depend on the laws governing divorce in your state.

Community-Property States

The community-property states—Arizona, California, Idaho, Louisiana, Nevada, New Mexico, Texas, Washington, and Wisconsin—consider any assets acquired

Future pension payments, stock options, profit-sharing plans, and other deferred benefits count as divisible assets.

during your marriage to be owned equally by husband and wife, and they will be split 50-50 in divorce. Money or other assets you or your spouse brought into the marriage are not considered community property.

Non-Community-Property States

In the remaining states, so-called equitable-distribution laws govern the division of a couple's assets. Some states divide only assets acquired during the marriage, while others consider everything available for divvying up. But marital assets aren't necessarily divided equally. State law may consider the length of the marriage, the age of the partners, skills possessed by each partner, assets contributed by each, and the ages of any children. In some states the distribution laws take on a punitive aspect by considering which partner seems most at fault for the breakup.

Future pension payments, stock options, profit-sharing plans, and other deferred benefits also count as divisible assets. Because women are more likely than men to take time off from careers to care for children or aging parents, their retirement income often depends on pension benefits earned by the husband. Federal law governing pensions and deferred-income plans provides some protection here. A covered worker can't cut a spouse out of a share in such plans without the spouse's written consent. Both men and women could benefit from reading *Your Pension Rights at Divorce: What Women Need to Know*, available for $24.95 from the Pension Rights Center, 1140 19th St., NW, Suite 602, Washington, DC 20036; 202-296-3776.

Angles on Alimony

No matter where you live, alimony isn't what it used to be. These days it's usually in the form of "rehabilitative" alimony, which provides financial support to an ex-spouse for a limited time, usually two to five years. Courts may grant alimony for long enough to allow a woman to return to school for a degree or other training, for instance.

In some states, spouses who worked early in the relationship to pay for the other's professional education (for example, law or medical school) can claim a portion of the earnings that have resulted from that education.

Most states typically don't consider marital fault when they award alimony, although each state is different. Alimony is ordered by a court on the basis of one spouse's need or entitlement and the other spouse's ability to pay. In some states, the reason for dissolving the marriage can affect alimony, that is, the court may limit the amount the "guilty" party receives. But courts usually will not order the "guilty" party to pay more.

Under the Bankruptcy Acts of 1994 and 2005, a debtor cannot include in a bankruptcy alimony (or child support) owed to an ex-spouse.

Child Support

Every state relies on a standardized formula to determine a minimum level of child-support payments. Courts can award more if they choose. Federal law requires states to review child-support agreements from time to time and adjust them for inflation or changes in parents' income.

Because child-support payments usually end when the child reaches 18, it's a good idea to write an agreement making clear who will pay for the child's college education.

If you are to receive child-support payments, insist that the paying spouse purchase a life insurance policy covering the term of the payments, naming you as the owner and beneficiary of the policy. If premium payments are missed, you'll be notified. Your ex-partner will also be unable to change the beneficiary without your agreement.

Staying Out of Court

Many divorcing couples use professional mediation to avoid the lengthy, humiliating, and expensive process of dragging their divorce through

Because child-support payments usually end when the child reaches 18, it's a good idea to write an agreement making clear who will pay for the child's college education.

Not all divorces can be handled by mediation, but it can be a less expensive and faster way to reach an agreement.

the courts. Not all divorces can be handled by mediation—if you're kicking and screaming your way out of the marriage or your spouse is sinking her teeth into your jugular vein, you may not be able to check your anger and resentment at the door and get yourself in the mood to negotiate. But in many cases mediation can be a less expensive and much faster way to arrive at an agreement.

The mediator's role is to guide you through the process, not to make decisions for you. Still, before signing a property settlement, you might want to have it reviewed by a lawyer to make sure you haven't overlooked something.

Members of the Association for Conflict Resolution Family Section, 1015 18th St., N.W., Suite 1150, Washington, DC 20036 (202-464-9700) who are approved mediators, have had at least 60 hours of mediation training as well as 250 hours of experience, and they must meet continuing-education requirements. Additional requirements for mediators vary from state to state.

Do It Yourself?

Do-it-yourself divorce kits are available in many states. Use them for guidance, but don't attempt a divorce on your own. If your situation is simple and you're both eager to settle your differences and get on with your lives, then you can quickly arrive at an agreement in mediation or through your lawyers. Do-it-yourself divorces should be reviewed by an expert before they are finalized.

Your Kids and Your Money

A family money-management plan with any hope of success will have to include the kids—which is easier said than done. You can teach your four-year-old to close the front door, but you can't expect him to understand that you don't want to pay for air-conditioning the whole neighborhood. A teenager, on the other hand, should understand that and more.

Raising Money-Smart Kids

Lessons in financial responsibility must take into account a child's age and level of maturity, but there are general guidelines you can follow.

Give Your Child an Allowance

Most child specialists agree that the best way for kids to learn about handling money is to have some to handle. An allowance is a teaching tool through which a child begins to learn about living within his or her means.

How big an allowance is reasonable? When should it be started and how often should it be given? The answers depend largely on the child and will be discussed later. For now, note this rule: Every allowance should include some money the child can spend however he or she wants. If every cent is earmarked for lunches, bus fares, and the like, the child gets no experience in choosing among spending alternatives. Another rule: Don't come to the rescue every time your youngster runs out of money. The allowance should be realistic and determined by mutual agreement. If the child

Don't give kids the idea that money can be used to buy love or to buy your way out of a jam.

consistently spends fast and needs more, either the allowance is too small or spending habits are sloppy. Find the cause and act accordingly.

Be Careful about Using Money to Reward or Punish

Giving bonuses for good grades or withholding part of an allowance for misbehavior may be an effective way to teach a youngster about an economic system based on monetary rewards, but many child specialists fear it puts family relationships on the wrong footing. Such actions mix love with money, and in young minds the two concepts can become confused. A better approach is to reward good behavior by showing pride and affection, and to punish wrongdoing with some penalty that fits the crime.

But this is America, after all, where money speaks, and the experts are divided on this question. Janet Bodnar, *Kiplinger's Personal Finance* deputy editor, addresses the issue in *Raising Money Smart Kids* (Dearborn Trade Publishing, $17.95; http://www.kiplinger.com/books):

> "Using money as an incentive can be appropriate if you give small amounts under the right circumstances. For example, reward your kids after the fact for behaving well at the supermarket instead of promising them money ahead of time if they don't throw a tantrum. It may seem like splitting hairs, but the former is more of a reward, while the latter is an out-and-out bribe."

What about payment for good grades? Bodnar:

> "Some parents are appalled by the idea, but others are quite willing to fork over the cash, on the theory that school is a child's primary employment and he or she ought to be rewarded for doing good work (especially if that child is forgoing a part-time job in favor of full-time studying). One mother compromised by agreeing to pay her son $5 for each A on his report

card, on the condition that the money be put into his college savings account."

The bigger lesson here, according to child specialists: Don't give kids the idea that money can be used to buy love or to buy your way out of a jam. Paying older kids for doing extra jobs around the house is fine, as long as they realize they also have regular family responsibilities that they should not expect to be paid for.

Set a Good Example

Your attitudes toward money, the way you handle it and discuss it, make an impression on your children just as surely as your attitudes toward religion and other personal matters. If you speak longingly of the neighbor's new car or television set, if you spend impulsively, if you often quarrel about money with your spouse, the children will notice. Your behavior reveals the place money has in your life. It's unrealistic to expect your children to develop an attitude toward money that's more mature than your own.

Teaching the Value of Money

Those are general guidelines. The problems parents face are usually more specific. What can you do to encourage financial responsibility in children of various ages, and how much can you expect of a child?

What Preschoolers Can Learn

Three- and four-year-olds aren't too young to start learning about money. At least they can be shown that money is something you exchange for something else. You might want to give your child a few coins to spend on a piece of candy or fruit at the store. This will demonstrate the use of money, even though the relative merits of different purchases are still beyond the child's comprehension.

Giving an allowance probably doesn't make sense at this age because children's concept of time isn't devel-

Three- and four-year-olds aren't too young to start learning about money. At least they can be shown that money is something you exchange for something else.

Most kids are ready for a regular allowance when they start school. A weekly schedule is probably best. The amount depends on what you expect the child to buy.

oped enough to grasp the idea of receiving a regular income. Besides, you know what they'd spend it on!

Nevertheless, there are a few specific money-related exercises that can benefit a preschooler. As your child learns to count, you can demonstrate the relationship between pennies and nickels, then dimes and quarters. Also, children like to play store with play money, acting as salesclerks or customers. It's a good way for them to learn the role of money.

Situations that don't seem to be connected with money at all may be the most important influences. If preschoolers are encouraged to share things, to take care of their toys and pick up after themselves, their sense of responsibility will be reflected in the attitudes they develop about money. Psychologists generally agree that a person's attitude toward money is really an extension of attitudes toward other things. Thus, if children feel secure at home, and are given freedom to explore their environment within reasonable limits—in short, given a healthy, happy start in life—then they are off on the right foot where money is concerned, too.

Elementary-School Age: Start Good Habits

Most kids are ready for a regular allowance when they start school. A weekly schedule is probably best. The amount depends on what you expect the child to buy. If he or she has to pay for lunch and bus fare, then the allowance must be bigger than if you paid those expenses yourself. Either way, remember the rule that kids need free money, to spend or save as they see fit. Handing out exact change for lunch doesn't teach children much if they merely convey the money from your hands to the hands of a cafeteria cashier. Deciding what to do with an extra dollar each week is a more valuable experience than just carting lunch money to school.

You have to be the judge of how much allowance your child can manage. Start small, then gradually increase responsibility for lunches and other expenses as the child matures.

With a little extra money at their disposal, kids in the elementary grades become serious shoppers. Help them learn to compare quality and prices of similar items. Allow them to make small choices on their own, such as gifts for friends or toys for themselves. As they mature, give them more say in buying clothes for school and play, pointing out why one purchase may be a better buy than another because of quality, appropriateness, or price. This will equip them for making intelligent choices.

Allowing kids to do their own shopping means you have to expect some mistakes—a cheap toy that breaks the first day, or too much candy, or clothes that don't fit. Let your child make mistakes like that. Then do your best to make it a learning experience, not simply an occasion to say "I told you so."

Including older elementary-school kids in a few family financial discussions is a good way to demonstrate the kinds of choices adults face. They needn't be in on every detail, but some financial decisions present natural opportunities for including the kids. For example, the cost of a family vacation depends largely on where you go. Would the kids rather spend one week at the beach or two weeks in the mountains? Or say you're thinking of buying a dog. Even though a pedigreed animal may not be under consideration, you can point out how much more one would cost than a dog from the pound. Including the kids in discussions of this type shows them how the relative costs of things affect buying decisions.

This is also a good age for children to begin learning to save money on their own. The simplest way is for you to open savings accounts in their names. In fact, your child can open an account and have full control over deposits and withdrawals if he or she has reached the age of "competence." This is a subjective standard that depends on state law and the policy of each financial institution. It's almost always required that the child be able to write his or her name.

If you would prefer to have some supervision over your child's account, work out an arrangement with the financial institution whereby you'll have to countersign any of your child's withdrawal slips. For an account in the name of a very young child, you, as parent

Kids needn't be in on every detail, but sometimes certain decisions present natural opportunities for including them.

If you wait until the teen years to give your child money-management experience, you've waited too long. Your influence is waning.

or guardian, can make deposits and withdrawals on the child's behalf until he or she is able to act alone.

Some banks charge stiff service fees for small accounts but may make an exception for minors' accounts. If not, the service fees can be high enough not only to wipe out the interest earned each month but also to eat into the principal. That's a valuable lesson to learn, but not one that most young children are ready for.

One institution set up especially to cater to children is the Young Americans Bank, 3550 E. First Ave., Denver, CO 80206 (http://www.theyoungamericans.org; 303-321-2265). It offers savings accounts, checking accounts, even credit cards and loans, to customers under age 22. Parents of children younger than 18 have to become joint owners of the accounts. For your child to withdraw money from the account, both of you have to agree to it, or you can sign a release allowing your child to make withdrawals on his or her own.

But don't be tempted to use such an account as a tax shelter for yourself. If you're in control of an account and you use it for your own benefit, then in the eyes of the IRS you are responsible for paying taxes on the interest income.

Teenagers: Make Allowances

If you wait until the teen years to give your child money-management experience, you've waited too long. Your influence is waning.

The allowance is very important at this stage of life—it is the teenager's ticket to independence. It can now be paid monthly to encourage long-range planning, and it should cover most daily expenses as well as discretionary income. Discuss your teenagers' expenses with them and arrive at a mutually agreeable figure. Then stick to that amount, giving it periodic reviews. Make the payments on time, without having to be reminded.

If a teenager takes a job to earn extra money, fine. This adds to the all-important feeling of independence. In general, you shouldn't penalize initiative by reducing the allowance, unless financial circumstances leave you no choice. Still, there may come a time when the important issue is how much money a teenager really needs. If your son is earning $100 a week mowing lawns, for instance, he doesn't need another $10 or $20 from you. If your daughter babysits once in a while for an extra $30 or $40 a month, you will probably want to subsidize her earnings with an allowance.

Teens should understand that certain responsibilities accompany their growing income. They need to become savers as well as spenders.

You can't always force teenagers to save, but they should be familiar enough with the family's financial circumstances to know whether they will have to pay for all or part of college themselves, or whether you can help with a car plus the expenses of gasoline, repairs, and insurance. Teenagers' savings should be kept in banks, credit unions, or savings and loan associations, not piggy banks. Introduce your youngsters to the services of financial institutions and let them see the advantages.

Teenagers should participate regularly in family financial discussions. They still needn't know every detail, such as total family income or the size of the mortgage, but they should know what pressures are on the budget. Seeing how dramatically the car-insurance premiums shot up when they became eligible to drive might encourage them to drive carefully. Participating in the decision to fix up the old car instead of buying a new one can be a valuable lesson in the importance of taking care of things. And purchases that involve them directly—a lawn mower they will use, for instance—provide opportunities for comparison shopping.

A few cautions about including kids in family financial affairs: First, don't expect them to shoulder the weight of a financial crisis. Second, don't make them feel guilty about costing you money. Show them how mom and dad cost money, too. Dad's golf clubs, mom's new computer—everybody incurs expenses and nobody should get the idea he or she is a burden. If financial setbacks make cutting some expenditures necessary, deciding where to trim the family budget can be an educational exercise.

Don't make kids feel guilty about costing money. Show them how mom and dad cost money, too.

Use your child's Social Security number as the tax identification number for any account you open to ensure the interest will be taxed at the child's rate.

Eventually your kids will be on their own, worrying about how to teach their kids the financial facts of life. Between now and then, you can't teach them everything they need to know. But with your guidance they will learn how to use money properly. Your job is to see that they get easy lessons when they're young and don't have to learn the hard way later.

Kids Owe Taxes, Too

For any account you open for your child, use the child's Social Security number as the tax identification number. This will ensure that the interest will be taxed to the child at the child's rate. The first $800 of unearned income (interest and dividends, for example) is tax-free to children. The next $800 is taxed at the child's rate—presumably 10 percent, which is the lowest tax bracket. Unearned income over $1,600 is taxed in his or her own bracket. (This rule creates the so-called kiddie tax, which was enacted to discourage parents from shifting assets to young children in order to reduce their own tax burden. The $800 and $1,600 thresholds were in effect for 2005. They may rise as the years go by.)

The kiddie tax doesn't eliminate entirely the advantage of shifting some assets to a child's name. After all, it takes a pretty big pile of money to generate $1,600 in interest or dividends in a single year. At a bank-CD level of interest—say, 3.3 percent—the child would need $48,485 in the account to reach the threshold. At 5 percent, $32,000 would be safe from the kiddie tax. And remember that as your dependent, a child gets an $800 standard deduction, which can make half of that interest entirely free of tax.

Ways to Give Money to Children

If you have the wherewithal to start your children off with a bang, it's useful to know that you can give as much as $11,000 a year to each child (indeed, to as many individuals as you want) without any tax consequences to you. For you and your spouse, that makes possible total annual gifts of $22,000 to your children, grandchildren, stepchildren, or anyone else. (If you give more than that to an individual, you may incur a gift tax, which is explained in Chapter 30.)

Using Custodial Accounts

A good vehicle for such a gift to a child is a custodial account opened under the Uniform Transfer to Minors Act (UTMA), which has been adopted by every state except South Carolina and Vermont. These two states still use the Uniform Gifts to Minors Act (UGMA). Your gift doesn't have to be cash. Both UTMA and UGMA accounts can hold cash, stocks, bonds, and mutual funds, but only UTMA accounts allow for the transfer of real estate, life insurance, pensions, and other property.

To open one of these accounts, simply tell a bank, brokerage, or mutual fund company that you want to do it. You'll get a standard form to fill out. An adult must be appointed to act as the custodian of the account—this could be you, your spouse, or a trusted friend or relative.

Here's what else you need to know about custodial accounts:

■ **The custodian has the power** to invest and withdraw funds for the benefit of the child, but the money can't be used to pay for items considered support obligations of the parents. (Private school and college tuition don't count as ordinary support, but in a few recent divorce cases, payment of college costs was ruled to be the financial obligation of the parents. Check with your lawyer before using the funds to pay for college.) Any income used for the child's support could be counted as taxable income to the parents.

■ **Income earned by the account** will be taxed at the child's rate. This is one of the chief reasons for creating such an account in the first place.

■ **Once the child reaches the age of majority**—usually 18 or 21 but it can be extended up to 25 for this purpose in Alaska, California, Nevada, Oregon, Pennsylvania,

> **Once the child reaches the age of majority— usually 18 or 21 but 25 for this purpose in several states—he or she gets the money in the account.**

Setting up a trust is a way to leave money to your children while controlling how it is to be invested, spent, and distributed to them.

and Tennessee—he or she gets the money in the account. If you set up the account with college in mind but the grown child would rather finance the travels of his rock band, there's nothing you can do about it.

- **Your gift is irrevocable.** You can't legally take it back under any circumstances, even if you run into financial difficulty.
- **The gift may haunt your estate.** If you are both donor and custodian, and you die before the child reaches majority, your gift would be considered part of your estate for federal tax purposes. This is an argument for appointing someone other than yourself as custodian.

Putting Your Trust in Trusts

Setting up a trust is a way to leave money to your children while controlling how it is to be invested, spent, and distributed to them. Testamentary trusts take effect upon your death and can be changed or withdrawn while you're still alive. A revocable living trust is in effect while you're alive.

The purpose of a trust is usually to transfer the ownership of property in order to reduce the tax on it but maintain control in the meantime. You choose the trustee and specify what happens to the money placed in the trust. Unlike in custodial accounts, money held in trust needn't be transferred to the beneficiary at any specific age. You can choose to turn over all of it when your child reaches age 21. Or you can specify that the trust pays out a third of its assets to the beneficiary when she reaches 25, another third at age 30, and the last third at age 35. You can even use the trust to establish a retirement nest egg for the child that she can't touch until she is, say, 55.

Trusts are really tools of estate planning rather than gift giving. They are described in more detail in Chapter 30.

Paying the
Price of College

Chapter 16

Colleges and universities occupy a favored place in the American economy. Normally a steadily rising price for a product or service attracts a fresh supply of it to the marketplace, and the competition serves to discourage the price increases. But in the marketplace of higher education, the supply stays about the same. Result: Prices rise higher and higher and there's nothing anybody can do about it.

Perhaps that's oversimplified. Perhaps one day one of your children will write a doctoral thesis that does a better job of explaining this phenomenon. First, though, you've got to get them through school, and that's going to take money—lots of money.

As you contemplate the magnitude of the task, take some comfort in the knowledge that millions of parents pay only part of their kids' college costs. The rest is covered by money that students save or earn, and by scholarships, grants, and loans, many of them subsidized by the government. But most government aid programs are based on financial need, and the money available to fund them runs out long before everyone's needs are met. If college is just around the corner, jump to the sections later in this chapter that describe ways to improve your chances of getting some of that aid.

If college is still some years away, your best strategy is to assume you'll qualify for no aid and start salting away the dollars you'll need. How many dollars is that? Well, colleges, like cars, clothes, and other modern necessities, don't all cost the same. Community colleges and many state colleges and university systems might even be described as bargains. A recent survey of 1,679

215

institutions by the College Board reported that annual tuition at state universities averaged more than $5,000, while most private schools charged more than $20,000. Annual tuition at community colleges ran about $2,000. Room, board, books, travel, and so forth can add several thousand dollars.

Those are today's costs. They'll be higher in the years ahead. The table below shows what increases of 5 percent per year will do to the cost of four years of college with current annual costs of $40,000 (high), $30,000 (medium), and $15,000 (low) over the next 18 years.

How can you possibly pay bills like that? Well, maybe you can't, but before you give up, consider how much of the cost you may be able to accumulate in the time you have available to do it.

WHAT COLLEGE WILL COST

This table will help you figure out the total cost of college, given projected increases of 7% annually during the college years.

If your child begins school in two years, for instance, add the annual cost of years two through five to get an estimate of the four-year cost. If she is an infant, add years 18 through 21.

Use the $40,000 starting point if you have your eye on an elite private institu-
tion, the $15,000 starting point for in-state costs at public schools, and the $30,000 starting point if you're not sure.

If you're starting early, bear in mind that the further out you go, the tougher it is to predict how quickly college costs will rise. As the years pass, you'll want to look into how much college costs are really rising and adjust your planning accordingly.

Today	1 Year	2 Years	3 Years	4 Years	5 Years	6 Years	7 Years
$40,000	$42,800	$45,796	$49,002	$52,432	$56,102	$60,029	$64,231
30,000	32,100	34,347	36,751	39,324	42,077	45,022	48,173
15,000	16,050	17,174	18,376	19,662	21,038	22,511	24,087

Today	8 Years	9 Years	10 Years	11 Years	12 Years	13 Years	14 Years
40,000	68,727	73,538	78,686	84,194	90,088	96,394	103,141
30,000	51,546	55,154	59,015	63,146	67,566	72,295	77,356
15,000	25,773	27,577	29,507	31,573	33,783	36,148	38,678

Today	15 Years	16 Years	17 Years	18 Years	19 Years	20 Years	21 Years
40,000	110,361	118,087	126,353	135,197	144,661	154,787	165,622
30,000	82,771	88,565	94,764	101,398	108,496	116,091	124,217
15,000	41,385	44,282	47,382	50,699	54,248	58,045	62,108

The table on page 218 shows how much you'd have to set aside each month in order to accumulate $10,000 over various periods of time assuming various rates of return. (These are after-tax rates, but the effect of taxes may be negligible if you use one or more of the tax-favored investment vehicles described later.)

Read down the left-hand column until you come to the number of years you have left before college starts. Then read across to the number that lines up under the percentage figure that you think represents a reasonable rate of return. If you're going to accumulate the money in your checking account (not the recommended way to save) choose 2 percent as your rate. If you're wedded to bank certificates of deposit and U.S. savings bonds, choose 4 percent. If you don't know what rate to assume but are willing to follow some conservative suggestions you'll find in the investment chapters of this book, choose 10 percent.

Let's say you've got ten years to go and hope to earn 10 percent. Those columns intersect at $48, meaning you'll have to devote $48 a month to your college investment plan in order to come up with $10,000 in ten years. If $50,000 is your goal, you'll have to set aside five times as much, or $240 a month. If that's more than you can afford, then adjust your goals. If you can afford more, go for it.

There are a few twists and turns to consider when you plan an investment strategy to accumulate a college nest egg.

Where to Stash Your College Cash

The kinds of investments that can help you accumulate a college nest egg are the same that can help with other investment goals. They are described in detail in the investment chapters of this book. But because you need a plan designed specifically to pay for college education, there are a few twists and turns to take into account.

Any plan you set up should be easy and economical to fund on a regular basis. Stocks with dividend reinvestment plans, for example, are ideal if they also permit you to make additional purchases on a regular basis for a small fee or no fee (see Chapter 23). Mutual funds with high front-end loads would be unsuitable if you have to pay the load each time you add to your holdings. By the same token, no-load funds are ideally suited for a college investment plan (see Chapter 25).

Your college portfolio should contain a diversified mix of investments. If you have at least eight to ten years to go, stocks or stock-oriented mutual funds should form the core because stocks historically have paid the highest returns over long periods. As you get within four years of the student's first year at college, sell enough of the stocks or stock-oriented funds to pay for freshman year. Put the proceeds where you may

HOW MUCH DO YOU NEED TO SAVE?

Use this table to determine how much you need to save per month for each $10,000 of college expenses.

Years	3%	4%	5%	6%	7%	8%	9%	10%	11%	12%
1	$820	$815	$811	$807	$802	$798	$794	$789	$785	$781
2	404	400	395	391	387	383	379	375	371	367
3	265	261	257	253	249	245	241	237	234	230
4	196	192	188	184	180	176	173	169	165	162
5	154	150	146	143	139	135	132	128	125	121
6	127	123	119	115	112	108	104	101	98	95
7	107	103	99	96	92	89	85	82	79	76
8	92	88	85	81	78	74	71	68	65	62
9	81	77	73	70	66	63	60	57	54	51
10	71	68	64	61	57	54	51	48	46	43
11	64	60	57	53	50	47	44	42	39	36
12	58	54	51	47	44	41	39	36	33	31
13	52	49	45	42	39	36	34	31	29	27
14	48	44	41	38	35	32	30	27	25	23
15	44	41	37	34	31	29	26	24	22	20
16	41	37	34	31	28	26	23	21	19	17
17	38	34	31	28	25	23	21	19	17	15
18	35	32	29	26	23	21	19	17	15	13
19	33	29	26	24	21	19	17	15	13	11
20	30	27	24	22	19	17	15	13	12	10
21	29	25	22	20	17	15	13	12	10	8

earn less but can be certain that the money will be there when you need it—a money-market fund, for instance. Leave the rest of the investment fund in stocks and repeat the exercise as you draw within four years of the sophomore year of college, and so forth.

See the investment chapters for specific investment suggestions suitable for a wide range of goals. Following are some instruments especially suited for college savings plans.

State-Sponsored College Savings Plans

State-sponsored college savings plans (also known as 529 plans) come in two varieties, and the differences are important. *Prepaid-tuition plans* guarantee participants that if they pay the price of tuition today—in a lump sum or in monthly installments—the state will cover the cost of tuition at state colleges and universities when their child is ready to attend years from now. *College savings plans* are, in effect, state-sponsored investment accounts. Money is invested by the state, and participants share in the earnings of the account.

Both kinds of plans offer significant tax advantages. Thanks to tax reform changes that took effect in 2002. (State taxation varies, so check your state's plan.) Although we think it unlikely, parents of younger children should be aware that this tax-free status could change in 2011 when the provisions of the 2001 tax reform come to an end unless the tax-free provisions are extended or made permanent.

Beyond that, the plans are quite different. As a practical matter, prepaid-tuition plans pay a rate of return equal to the inflation rate at public colleges and universities in your state. That can be attractive when tuition inflation is running at 10 percent or so. It's a lot less appealing when the rate is 5 percent. The main attraction here is the guarantee that college bills will be covered.

The rate of return on college savings plans will depend on how good a job the state's money managers

> **State-sponsored college savings plans (also known as 529 plans) come in two varieties, and the differences are important.**

COLLEGE SAVINGS AND PREPAID-TUITION PLANS

Many states offer both college savings and prepaid-tuition plans, and some have several plans to choose from. This list is a sampling. For more information, check http://www.savingforcollege.com.

STATE	PLAN	TELEPHONE	STATE	PLAN	TELEPHONE
Alabama	P	800-252-7228	Missouri	S	888-414-6678
Alabama	S	800-252-7228	Montana	S	800-888-2723
Alaska	S	800-369-3641	Nebraska	S	888-993-3746
Arizona	S	800-888-2723	Nevada	P	888-477-2667
Arkansas	S	887-615-4116	Nevada	S	800-587-7305
California	S	887-728-4338	New Hampshire	S	800-544-1722
Colorado	P	800-478-5651	New Jersey	S	877-465-2378
Colorado	S	800-448-2424	New Mexico	P	800-337-5268
Connecticut	S	888-799-2438	New Mexico	S	877-337-5268
Delaware	S	800-544-1650	New York	S	877-697-2837
District of Columbia	S	800-987-4859	North Carolina	S	800-600-3453
Florida	P	800-552-4723	North Dakota	S	866-728-3529
Florida	S	800-552-4723	Ohio	S	800-233-6734
Georgia	S	877-424-4377	Oklahoma	S	877-654-7284
Hawaii	S	866-529-3343	Oregon	S	866-772-8464
Idaho	S	866-433-2533	Pennsylvania	P	800-440-4000
Illinois	P	877-877-3724	Rhode Island	S	888-324-5057
Illinois	S	877-432-7444	South Carolina	P	888-772-4723
Indiana	S	866-400-7526	South Carolina	S	888-244-5674
Iowa	S	888-672-9116	South Dakota	S	866-529-7462
Kansas	S	800-579-2203	Tennessee	P	888-486-2378
Kentucky	P	888-919-5278	Tennessee	S	888-486-2378
Kentucky	S	877-598-7878	Texas	P	800-445-4723
Louisiana	S	800-259-5625	Texas	S	800-445-4723
Maine	S	877-463-9843	Utah	S	800-418-2551
Maryland	P	800-463-4723	Vermont	S	800-637-5860
Maryland	S	888-463-4723	Virginia	P	888-567-0540
Massachusetts	P	800-449-6332	Virginia	S	800-471-4120
Massachusetts	S	800-544-2776	Washington	P	877-438-8848
Michigan	P	800-638-4543	West Virginia	P	866-574-3542
Michigan	S	877-861-6377	West Virginia	S	866-574-3542
Minnesota	S	877-338-4646	Wisconsin	S	888-338-3789
Mississippi	P	800-987-4450	Wyoming	S	877-529-2655
Mississippi	S	800-486-3670	**KEY: P**= prepaid plan **S**= savings plan		

do with the funds they have to invest. There is usually no guarantee, meaning you could actually lose money.

You can shop around for the best plan, because all 50 states and the District of Columbia offer plans that are open to any U.S. resident. Before you decide whether to commit your child's college fund to such a plan, examine the prospectus with the following questions in mind.

What if your child decides to attend a private college or an out-of-state college? Money in a college savings plan can be used at any accredited college in the country. Prepaid-tuition plans are sometimes less flexible. You may pay a penalty for using the money at a school not covered by the plan.

What if your child decides not to go to college? Both kinds of plans will generally transfer the account to a sister or a brother with no penalty, but if the money is not used to pay for college at all, you'll pay a price. The usual penalty is 10 percent of earnings, although it is sometimes higher with prepaid plans.

What is the effect of the account on your child's eligibility for financial aid? The money in a prepaid-tuition plan

> **All 50 states and the District of Columbia offer plans that are open to any U.S. resident.**

THE INDEPENDENT 529 PLAN ALTERNATIVE

The Independent 529 plan lets you pay tomorrow's tuition (or part of it) at today's prices for more than 240 private colleges. (See www.independent529plan.com for the list of participating colleges.) Basically, the money you invest represents a percentage (possibly 100%) of a school's current tuition. For example, say you prepay $10,000 today to cover one year of tuition and current tuition at the school your child ultimately attends is $20,000. Your $10,000 investment is 50% of that current tuition, so you'll be covered for 50% of the future tuition once your child starts college. If current tuition is $30,000, your $10,000 investment represents one-third of the total tuition, and you'll be responsible for coming up with the remaining two-thirds tuition in the future.

If your child doesn't go to a participating school, you get your money back, but the annual return is capped at just 2%. If you worry that your child won't attend one of the schools on the list, you might be better off investing in a traditional 529 state college savings plan.

Their predictable payout makes zeros ideal for a conservative college-savings plan because the maturities can be timed to coincide with the year college bills come due.

reduces your calculated need dollar for dollar. College savings plans, on the other hand, are counted just like any other investment, meaning your need will be reduced by 5.6 percent of the balance if included in your assets.

Zero-Coupon Bonds

Zeros get their name from the fact that they pay no interest at all until maturity. This lack of income along the way means that zeros must sell at a huge discount from face value in order to attract any investors, and the further away the maturity date, the bigger the discount must be. A $1,000 zero-coupon bond yielding 3.8 percent and maturing in 5 years would sell for $819. A 3.8 percent zero maturing in 10 years would go for a bit under $700. The same bond maturing in 15 years would sell for about $565.

This sort of predictable payout makes zeros ideal for a conservative college-savings plan because the maturities can be timed to coincide with the year college bills come due. On top of that, zero-coupon Treasury bonds (see Chapter 24) come with no risk of default.

There is a catch, however. Even though zeros pay no interest each year, at tax time you have to act as if they do. As the "phantom" interest accrues year by year, you must pay income tax on it. This heads off a big tax bill at maturity, but it's a pain in the neck to pay tax today on income you won't see for years. Zero-coupon municipal bonds, which pay tax-free interest (see Chapter 24), are the surest way around this annoyance. In addition, there may be a way to take advantage of the so-called kiddie tax to minimize the damage from a taxable zero.

The kiddie tax is a provision of the law that says children under the age of 14 must pay tax at their parents' rate on any "unearned" income—such as interest, dividends, or capital gains—to the extent that it exceeds a certain level, currently $1,600. A child's first $800 of income is tax-free. The next $800 is taxed at the child's rate. Any investment income above $1,600 is taxed at the parent's rate. (These thresholds may change with inflation.)

Assume that the child's rate is 10 percent, which is the lowest tax bracket, and the parent's rate is 25 percent. Clearly you have much to gain by shoveling the maximum amount of interest into the child's bracket. And, in fact, the way the IRS says zero-coupon bond interest must be reported works to your advantage.

Say that you or the child's grandparents or all of you together buy your newborn a $10,000 zero paying 4.3 percent and maturing in 18 years. You pay $4,612 for it. The interest earned by the bond each year isn't 1/18th of the $5,388 difference between the purchase price and the maturity price. Because of compounding, the interest is lower in the early years than it is in the later years. In the first year, $4,612 earning 4.3 percent compounded semiannually earns about $200. That gets added to your principal, so that in the second year the bond pays 4.3 percent of $4,812, or $209. The third year you'd earn $218, and so forth.

As you can see, your child can earn a lot of interest before he or she incurs any tax at all. Because of the accelerating nature of the interest payments, a large part of the taxable buildup will occur after the child turns 14 and is taxed on all income at his or her own rate, probably 10 percent. Chapter 15 describes how to set up a custodial account for your child that will accomplish such a feat.

U.S. Savings Bonds

Savings bonds that you use to pay college bills for your kids offer some tax advantages that help to compensate for the rather puny interest they pay. The interest can be entirely tax-free under certain circumstances. First, the bonds must be purchased in the parents' names. Bonds purchased in your child's name don't qualify for the tax-free feature. Second, you must be at least 24 years old at the time of purchase. Third, you must use the bond interest to pay tuition or fees. You can't use the money for room and board, books, transportation, or other personal expenses.

There is a catch that prevents some parents from benefiting from Uncle Sam's limited largess. At the time

Savings bonds that you use to pay college bills for your kids offer some tax advantages that help to compensate for the rather puny interest they pay.

If you meet the income tests, you can put up to $2,000 a year into a Coverdell ESA (education savings account) for any child under age 18.

you redeem the bonds, what's called your "modified adjusted gross income" can't exceed $91,850 if you're married or $61,200 if you're single. (Modified adjusted gross income includes the interest on the bonds.) Above those levels, the allowance is phased out gradually until it disappears completely at incomes exceeding $121,850 for married couples and $76,200 for single parents. (These figures were for 2005. They will be adjusted to keep pace with inflation.) For more on savings bonds, see Chapter 24.

Coverdell ESAs

If you meet the income tests, you can put up to $2,000 a year into a Coverdell ESA (education savings account) for any child under age 18. You can't deduct the contribution, but your account grows tax-deferred, and if you use withdrawals to pay college expenses, they are completely tax-free.

You're eligible to make the full $2,000 contribution if your adjusted gross income is less than $190,000 on a joint return or $95,000 on a single return. You can make partial contributions with AGI up to $220,000 and $110,000, respectively. The income limits apply to whoever funds the account, which doesn't have to be the student's parent.

Be aware that the Coverdell ESA account could be considered the child's asset under financial-aid formulas, which would reduce the amount of financial aid you might receive.

The Roth Alternative

If you can afford to save more than the $2,000 annual maximum for the Coverdell ESA, consider putting additional funds in a Roth IRA, where your contributions might serve a double purpose. The Roth allows you to take out your contributions at any time, tax- and penalty-free, so you can tap those contributions for college expenses if you need to or let them ride for retirement if you don't.

Here's how: A husband and wife can each contribute up to $4,000 annually to a Roth. (The contribution will increase to $5,000 for 2008.) Say the couple starts out on this path with a newborn. They could accumulate $174,000 in contributions over 18 years. That sum could then be tapped for college bills or left to continue growing for retirement. The earnings on those contributions (another $208,000 in a pair of fully funded accounts that grow at 8 percent per year) could be withdrawn penalty-free if used to pay college bills (but tax would still be due if the parents are under age 59½). Or earnings could continue to grow inside the accounts and be withdrawn tax-free by the couple when they retire. You'll find more on Roth IRAs in Chapter 29.

When College Bills Are Due

Most Americans need some serious help with college bills, and Congress has devised a couple of significant programs of college tax credits to provide that help.

HOPE SCHOLARSHIP CREDIT. This is the more valuable of the two. It permits you to subtract from your tax bill 100 percent of the first $1,000 you pay for tuition and fees (but not room and board) and 50 percent of the next $1,000. The credit applies only to the first two years of college, but you can claim it for as many of your children as qualify.

LIFETIME LEARNING CREDIT. This takes up where the Hope credits leave off. The Lifetime Learning credit is 20 percent of the first $10,000 of higher-education costs, for a maximum credit of $2,000 per year. You simply lop the qualifying amount off your tax bill. It can be used after freshman and sophomore years and you can even use it for yourself if you return to school. But you may claim only one Lifetime Learning credit per year, regardless of how many students in your household qualify for it.

If your adjusted gross income exceeds $43,000 on an individual return or $87,000 on a joint return, you begin to lose your eligibility for the Hope and Lifetime

The Hope Scholarship permits you to subtract from your tax bill 100 percent of the first $1,000 you pay for tuition and fees and 50 percent of the next $1,000.

Although the feds don't count home equity when estimating family contribution, many private colleges do.

Learning credits. Eligibility disappears completely at $53,000 and $107,000, respectively, where the phase-out zones end. Within the zones, you qualify for a partial credit.

Careful timing of your tuition payments can maximize the benefit. Say, for instance, that your child's final college semester begins in January. If you pay the bill in late December, you'd have no qualifying payments in the following year. Postponing the payments until January buys you an extra Lifetime Learning credit worth as much as $2,000.

Getting Financial Aid

The quest for financial aid begins with a form: The FAFSA (Free Application for Federal Student Aid) will determine your fate at most public schools and even some private colleges. Colleges that offer their own sources of aid may also require a PROFILE form, which asks for additional data. Both forms are available from your child's high school guidance office or the college's financial-aid office. You can also get them for a fee online at http://www.fafsa.ed.gov.

The FAFSA demands detailed information on your income and assets as well as your child's. Forms must be filed in January or February of your child's senior year in high school. The government processes your data and generates your "expected family contribution" to college costs. In other words, based on what you put on the form (plus some corroborating paperwork), the government decides what you can afford to pay. It's probably more than you think it should be.

Armed with this official assessment, the college will assemble your financial-aid package. But you're not finished yet. Although the feds don't count home equity and money in retirement accounts when calculating your estimated family contribution, many private colleges do, and they'll adjust your contribution accordingly. A financial-aid officer may also make adjustments for private-school tuition for younger siblings, unusually high medical expenses, or a recent job loss.

You can expect your notification of financial aid in the spring—usually following on the heels of college acceptance letters. Most aid packages are a combination of grants, scholarships, and loans, with a growing emphasis on loans in recent years.

Protecting Your Assets

The process seems cut-and-dried, but there are a few perfectly legal moves you can make to minimize your income and assets, and thus maximize your chances for aid. FAFSA measures your income and assets beginning in January of your child's junior year in high school, and ending in the fall of her junior year in college. Therein lies the key to your campaign. Before January of your child's junior year in high school:

- **Try to get bonuses paid early**—perhaps your employer will issue you a check on December 31 of your child's junior year in high school instead of January 1.
- **If you're going to sell stocks or mutual funds** or any other appreciated property to pay for college, complete the sale before the magic date so the profits won't boost your income during the crucial years.

More income- and asset-reducing ideas include:

- **Postpone IRA distributions** until after the financial-aid years. IRAs don't count as an asset, but the withdrawals will count as income.
- **If you own your business,** consider purchasing business equipment during the financial-aid years. You can deduct up to $105,000 (in 2005) in the year you purchase the equipment, which will serve to lower your business income.
- **Don't overwithhold from your paycheck** for state and local taxes. Any refund will have to be reported on your federal income-tax return and will boost your income the following year.
- **If you were planning to purchase a computer** or new car, do it before sending in your FAFSA form. You might also consider spending money in a custodial account for your child's college computer or a car

> There are a few perfectly legal moves you can make to minimize your income and assets, and thus maximize your chances for aid.

If grandparents (or other relatives) are going to contribute to the college bills, ask them to pay the college directly, rather than giving you the money.

for the college years if these are expenses you would have incurred anyway.

■ **If grandparents (or other relatives)** are going to contribute to the college bills, ask them to pay the college directly, rather than giving you the money. FAFSA doesn't request information about contributions from family members. (However, the PROFILE aid form does ask for that information and will factor it into your expected family contribution.)

Sources of Aid

Financial-aid packages are typically made up of grants, loans, and perhaps a job for the student. Most of this money comes from the federal government, and from the school's own resources. The only way to discover what's available is to apply for it. You can get information about school-based programs from the schools and information about federal programs from high school guidance counselors, college financial-aid officers, or from the Federal Student Aid Information Center (800-433-3243). Here's a rundown of major sources of federal assistance.

Pell Grants

These go to the neediest students—more than five million of them in the 2004–2005 school year, ranging up to about $4,000 but often a lot less. The size of Pell grants is difficult to predict because funding is usually such a battleground in Congress. To qualify your child for a Pell grant, your FAFSA must show a big shortfall between the cost of college and the amount your family can afford to pay.

Federal Loan Programs

STAFFORD LOANS. These low-interest loans go to students, not parents, and may be subsidized or unsubsidized, depending on the applicant's assessed need. With a subsidized Stafford, the federal government pays the interest while the student is in college and for six months afterward. With an unsubsidized Stafford, the borrower can defer payments on principal and interest until after graduation, but the government won't pick up the tab.

Stafford loans are guaranteed by the federal government and usually made by banks, although some come directly from the government itself, through the school. They can be as much as $2,625 for freshmen, $3,500 for sophomores, and $5,500 per year for juniors and seniors. Independent students and graduate students can borrow more. Interest rates are adjusted annually to equal the rate on a 91-day Treasury bill plus 2.3 percentage points, capped at 8.25 percent. Borrowers pay a 4 percent loan fee up front, which is deducted from the loan amount. Ten years is the usual payback period.

PERKINS LOANS. Perkins loans come through the financial-aid offices and are limited to students with significant financial needs. They carry a superlow interest rate of only 5 percent, and payments are deferred until nine months after graduation. Certain jobs after graduation could also result in the cancellation of some or all of the debt. For example, if your child becomes a teacher in a low-income area, a law enforcement officer, or a Peace Corps volunteer, the government might repay the loans for him. The borrowing limit is usually about $4,000 per year, although the school has the option of setting a higher limit.

PLUS LOANS (FOR MOM AND DAD). Unlike Perkins and Stafford loans, these loans are made directly to parents. Though you must have a good credit history to qualify, you can borrow just about whatever you need to meet college expenses. (The name is an acronym for the original name of the program, which was Parent Loans to Undergraduate Students.) The interest rate is the 91-day Treasury-bill rate plus 3.1 percentage points, but it can't go any higher than 9 percent. Repayment begins 60 days after the lender pays the school, but you can opt to pay only interest while your child is attending college. Lenders include banks, credit unions, and other financial institutions, as well as some colleges.

> **You can opt to pay only interest on PLUS loans while your child is attending college.**

STUDENT LOANS AT A GLANCE

The 10- to 30-year repayment term reflects the extended payment options discussed in this chapter, but 10 years is the standard term.

TYPE	BORROWER	INTEREST RATE	FEES	TERM
Federal loans				
Stafford	student	91-day T-bill + 2.3 points	4%	10–30 years*
Perkins Loan	student	5%	none	10 years
PLUS Loan	parent	91-day T-bill + 3.1 points	4%	10–30 years*
Private loans				
Nellie Mae Excel	parent	prime plus 2.25 points	7%	4–20 years
Sallie Mae Signature Loan	student	prime plus 0 to 3 points	0% to 6%	up to 20 years
TERI Alternative Loan	parent or student	prime plus 1.5 points	0% to 6.5%	up to 20 years

Private Loan Sources

You could borrow money for college from noncollege-related sources. Chapter 3 describes the ins and outs of home-equity loans, life-insurance loans, and other sources. Here are some nongovernment sources of loans designed especially for the parents facing college bills.

NELLIE MAE'S EXCEL LOANS. Through Excel, you can borrow the money you need to cover the cost of college, less any financial aid you've been awarded. The annual interest rate is the prime rate plus 2.25 percentage points. To qualify, you need a clean credit report for the past two years, and your debt payments (including your mortgage and the Excel loan) cannot exceed 50 percent of your gross monthly income. There's an up-front fee of 7 percent, which goes into an insurance fund to cover defaults. (For information, contact Nellie Mae at 800-367-8848 or at http://www.nelliemae.com.) Nellie Mae, based in Braintree, Massachusetts, also makes Stafford and PLUS loans.

SALLIE MAE. Sallie Mae, the Student Loan Marketing Association, offers what it calls Signature Loans for up to the full cost of college, minus any financial aid you have received. The interest rate is variable, based on the 91-day Treasury bill rate plus 0 to 3 percentage points (depending on the creditworthiness of the borrower and whether there is a coborrower). A 0 to 6 percent up-front fee (depending on the same variables) is subtracted from the proceeds you receive. If your child has a Stafford loan with a lender participating in the Signature Loan program, all your loans can be consolidated into one account, and you may qualify for discounts if you make payments on time. (Call Sallie Mae at 888-272-5543 for a brochure or visit its Web site at http://www.salliemae.com.)

THE EDUCATION RESOURCES INSTITUTE (TERI). TERI offers loans through banks for the full cost of college, less any amount you're awarded for financial aid. You must qualify for the loan and meet the same qualifications as for a Nellie Mae loan. Rates are prime plus 1.5 percentage points. You'll be charged a 0 to 6.5 percent origination fee, which can be added to your loan balance. For information call 800-255-8374 or visit its Web site at http://www.teri.org.

IN QUEST OF THE ELUSIVE SCHOLARSHIP. For help in finding a privately sponsored scholarship, talk with your high school guidance officer and college financial-aid officers to get ideas and applications. You should also spend an afternoon at the library looking through the scholarship guides. Information is, of course, also available on the Internet. Try the College Board's Web site at http://www.collegeboard.com or fastWeb at http://fastweb.monster.com. Other good sources of scholarship information include your employer, professional associations, unions, local civic groups, state agencies, religious groups, and advocacy organizations for ethnic groups or people with disabilities. You'll find a sampling of major scholarships beginning on the following page.

SCHOLARSHIPS OF BROAD INTEREST

Here's a sampling of major scholarships in various areas awarded nationwide with high dollar prizes.

ACADEMICS & LEADERSHIP
Coca-Cola Scholars Foundation Inc.
Awards: 250 awards from $4,000 to $20,000 per year
Criteria: Character, personal merit, leadership in school and community, academic achievement
Deadline: October 31
Contact: High school counselor or www.coca-colascholars.org

Educational Communications Scholarship Foundation
Awards: 127 awards from $1,000 to $6,000 per year
Criteria: Grades, SAT/ACT test scores, and school and community activities
Deadline: May 15
Contact: Educational Communications Scholarship Foundation, 1701 Directors Blvd., Austin, TX 78744 or www.ecsf.org

Elks National Foundation Most Valuable Student Award
Awards: 500 four-year scholarships, from $1,000 to $15,000 per year
Criteria: Scholarship, leadership, and financial need.
Deadline: Mid-January
Contact: Local Elks Club will provide state association address or www.elks.org

Sam Walton Community Scholarship
Awards: Two scholarships of $1,000 from each community with a participating Wal-Mart store
Criteria: High school records, SAT or ACT scores, financial need, school involvement, and must be a U.S. citizen.
Deadline: February 1
Contact: High school counselor or www.walmartfoundation.org/scholarships

William Randolph Hearst Foundation U.S. Senate Youth Program
Awards: 104 $5,000 college scholarships for high school juniors and seniors who hold elected student office and who pledge to study government or a related field. Winners participate in an all-expenses-paid trip to the Senate Youth Program's Washington Week.
Criteria: Must be nominated by high school principal. Awards based on merit and community service, and must hold an elected school office.
Deadline: Varies by state; usually early fall
Contact: Guidance counselor, state-level education administrators, or U.S. Senate Youth Program, William Randolph Hearst Foundation, 90 New Montgomery St., #1212, San Francisco, CA 94105 (800-841-7048 or www.ussenateyouth.org)

THE ARTS
Annual Glenn Miller Scholarship Competition

Awards: Four $1,000 to $2,400 awards for instrumentalists and vocalists who "intend to make music a central part of their future life." Winners perform at the Glenn Miller Festival Stage show.

Criteria: Applicants send a screening tape and statement of musical intention. Finalists audition live.

Deadline: March 15

Contact: Glenn Miller Scholarship Committee, 107 E. Main St., Clarinda, IA 51632; 717-542-2461

National Foundation for Advancement in the Arts/Arts Recognition and Talent Search

Awards: Hundreds of cash awards from $100 to $10,000

Criteria: Students submit examples of their work on videotape, audiotape, slides, or in writing. Those accepted compete in dance, music, theater, visual arts, writing, photography, and voice.

Deadline: Early deadline is June 1; regular deadline is October 1.

Contact: Arts Recognition & Talent Search NFAA, 444 Brickell Ave., P-14, Miami, FL 33131 (800-970-2787; www.nfaa.org)

ATHLETICS
Western Golf Association/Chick Evans Caddy Scholarship

Awards: 200 full-tuition and housing scholarships, renewable for up to four years

Criteria: Outstanding character, integrity, leadership, financial need, top 25% in class, and two years as an outstanding caddy

Deadline: September 30 of senior year

Contact: Sponsoring golf club or Scholarship Committee, Western Golf Association/Evans Scholars Foundation, 1 Briar Rd., Golf, IL 60029; (847-724-4600; www.westerngolfassociation.com)

Women's Western Golf Foundation

Awards: 18 to 21 $2,000 annual scholarships, renewable for four years, for high school senior girls with involvement in golf (skill isn't a criterion)

Criteria: High academic achievement, financial need, and excellence of character

Deadline: April 5; preliminary application form due March 1

Contact: Send SASE to Mrs. Richard Willis, Director of Scholarships, 393 Ramsay Rd., Deerfield, IL 60015 (847-945-0451; www.wwga.org)

BUSINESS
Distributive Education Clubs of America (DECA) Scholarship Awards

Awards: More than 20 scholarships of $1,000 each for students planning to major in management, marketing, marketing education, or entrepreneurship

Criteria: Must be an active member of DECA and rank in top third of class. Selection based on merit, club participation and accomplishments, leadership, responsibility, and character.

(continued on the next page)

SCHOLARSHIPS, SCHOLARSHIPS, SCHOLARSHIPS *(continued)*

Deadline: Second Monday of March; must first meet state deadline, usually January or February
Contact: DECA, 1908 Association Dr., Reston, VA 20191 (703-860-5000 or www.deca.org)

Karla Scherer Foundation Scholarship Program

Awards: Varying number of scholarship awards and amounts, depending on available funds and number of applicants, for women who are accepted into the Master of Arts in the Humanities at the University of Chicago
Criteria: Applicant must send a statement that includes her particular area of interest and detailed description of her career path.
Deadline: March 1; SASE required
Contact: Karla Scherer Foundation, 737 N. Michigan Ave., Suite 2330, Chicago, IL 60611 (www.comnet.org/kschererf)

ETHNICITY
National Italian American Foundation

Awards: Varying number of scholarships, from $2,500 to $10,000, for Italian American students or students of any ethnic background who are majoring or minoring in Italian language or Italian studies
Criteria: Need, academics, field of study interest, and career objectives. Applications are available online and must be submitted electronically at www.niaf.org/scholarships.
Deadline: April 30
Contact: Send e-mail to scholarships@niaf.org, or write to the National Italian American Foundation, 1860 19th St., NW, Washington, DC 20009

United Negro College Fund

Awards: More than 400 awards ranging from $500 to full tuition at 38 member colleges and universities, mostly historically black schools. $20 million in scholarships awarded each year.
Criteria: Students are considered without regard to race, creed, color, or ethnic origin. Must take SAT and file for financial aid.
Deadline: Varies
Contact: Send SASE to Program Services, 8260 Willow Oaks Corp. Dr., P.O. Box 10444, Fairfax, VA 22031-4511 (www.uncf.org)

MILITARY AFFILIATION
AMVETS National Scholarships

Awards: Undetermined number of $4,000 awards ($1,000 per year) to high school seniors and veterans. Seniors who are members of the Junior ROTC are also eligible for one $1,000 scholarship.
Criteria: Membership in AMVETS, or have one parent or grandparent who is a member (or deceased parent or grandparent who would have been eligible). Academic achievement and financial need.
Deadline: April 15
Contact: Send an SASE to AMVETS National Headquarters, 4647 Forbes Blvd., Lanham, MD 20706, or download an application (www.amvets.org)

PUBLIC SPEAKING
American Legion National High School Oratorical Contest

Awards: Three national winners ($14,000 to $18,000), 50 state and four foreign division winners ($1,500 each), and six national semifinalists ($1,500 each)

Criteria: Excellence in addressing topic on U.S. constitution; contest open to all high school students.

Deadline: State deadlines January 1

Contact: Local American Legion post (www.legion.org) or high school guidance counselor

SCIENCE AND ENGINEERING
Intel Science Talent Search

Awards: Ten awards of $20,000 to $100,000, 30 awards of $5,000

Criteria: Research report, teacher recommendations, high school records, SAT scores

Deadline: Mid-November (call for date)

Contact: Science Service Inc., 1719 N St., NW, Washington, DC 20036 (202-785-2255 or www.sciserv.org)

General Electric Corp./Society of Women Engineers

Awards: $1,000 to $5,000 scholarships available for freshman women entering engineering

Criteria: High school record (minimum 3.5 GPA), teacher recommendation, character reference, essay on why applicant would like to be an engineer. Must be a U.S. citizen.

Deadline: May 15

Contact: Society of Women Engineers, 230 E. Ohio St., Suite 400, Chicago, IL 60611-3265 (312-596-5223 or www.swe.org)

TEACHING
Horace Mann Scholarships

Awards: One $15,000 scholarship, one $10,000 scholarship, and 10 $2,500 scholarships for high school seniors who are dependents of public or private school employees

Criteria: Academics, written essay, activities

Deadline: March 15

Contact: P.O. Box 20490, Springfield, IL 62708 (www.horacemann.com)

WRITING/JOURNALISM
Veterans of Foreign Wars of the U.S. Annual Voice of Democracy Contest

Awards: Awards totaling more than $145,000. Top scholarship is $25,000.

Criteria: Contestants write and tape-record essays on a patriotic theme. Essays are judged in local, state, and national competitions.

Deadline: November 1

Contact: High school principals or teachers can get official entry forms from local VFW posts (www.vfw.org).

Funeral Finances

Plan your own funeral? Hah. Most of us not only avoid talking about it, we manage to avoid thinking about it. Even writers of personal-finance books get a little queasy at the thought. But ignoring the subject can add untimely financial shocks to the lives of those we leave behind. Counting cemetery fees, a funeral these days can easily cost more than $10,000, on average, and you're definitely the above-average type, right? Do you really want your grieving loved ones to be forced to confront financial decisions of that magnitude within a day or two of your demise?

It's easier said than done, but a little thinking ahead about the kind of arrangements you'd like and talking it over with your family will head off a lot of distress when the time comes. Family discussions are particularly important if you have any special instructions. If you've signed an organ-donor card, for instance, your family needs to know about it.

Put It in Writing

For openers, create a file in a folder or on your computer. Put in it a list of the people you'd want notified of your death. Record the location of your important documents: insurance records and policies, pension plans, investments, and trusts. Note the location of the keys to any safe-deposit boxes or other important places. Include the names, addresses, and phone numbers of your lawyer, broker, accountant, and financial planner, along with the relevant account numbers.

If you're inclined to pay for your funeral in advance, make sure you're being guaranteed the services you specify at the contracted price.

Consider including personal information that can be used for writing your obituary. Memorial societies (see the box on page 243) and funeral homes offer planning forms for this purpose. They can be useful, but you might want to add some personal notes to this one-size-fits-all approach.

When you've done all this, record any specific instructions you have regarding burial, cremation, or organ donation. Make copies of the entire file and hand them out to your spouse, to other appropriate family members, and perhaps to the attorney who drew up your will. (If you want to spare them the stress of contemplating the details of your disposal before your demise, put everything in an envelope marked "To be opened in the event of my death.") Why hand out this information when you could just tuck it away in your safe-deposit box or attach it to your will? Others have done that and their loved ones always discover the documents—but often after the funeral.

Pay Now, Die Later?

It is possible, if you are so inclined, to choose the funeral home long before you need it, and even to pay for all or part of the home's services years in advance. So-called preneed plans, sold by funeral homes, allow you to arrange for the type of services and casket you want and pay now with a lump sum or through installments. The home either puts your money in a trust fund with the payout triggered by your death, or buys an insurance policy naming itself as the beneficiary.

If you're inclined to choose this route, make sure you're being guaranteed the services you specify at the contracted price. Some contracts call for additional payments for "final expense funding." That means that if the funeral home's charges increase between the time you sign up and the time you sign off, somebody will have to pay the difference. Also consider these questions:

■ **What if you change your mind?** Can you get all or part of your money back?

- **Will your money earn interest?** If so, how much? Who gets it?
- **If there is an insurance policy involved,** is there a waiting period before it takes effect? How long?
- **What happens when prices increase?** Are increases covered by the plan or will your family have to pay extra?
- **Does your health affect** the terms of the plan?
- **What happens if the funeral home** goes out of business? Is your plan taken over by another funeral home? If so, which one?
- **What happens if you move?** Can the plan be transferred to another funeral home in a different state?
- **If there's money left over** after your funeral, will your heirs get it, or does the home keep it?

You could set up your own burial "trust fund" through your bank or credit union; it's not as complicated as it sounds.

A Better Way to Pay Ahead

Aprepaid plan like the ones described in the previous section can be a convenient and reassuring way to spare your family some measure of emotional stress when the time comes: The big decisions about your funeral will have been made, the money paid, and that will be that. Still, from a strictly financial point of view, you can do better.

For example, you could simply buy a life insurance policy with the proceeds earmarked for funeral expenses, although the relatively low level of coverage it would take to pay for a funeral doesn't translate to the most economical level of insurance premiums.

You could even set up your own burial "trust fund," which isn't as complicated as it sounds. You do it at a bank or credit union through what's often called a Totten trust. Now, a Totten isn't actually a trust. It's a regular bank account with a designated "pay on death" inheritor. When you open the account, you name a relative or friend (or even the funeral home) as beneficiary. You put in the money and collect the interest. You can close the account any time you want, transfer the balance to a different bank, or change the beneficiary. When you die, the beneficiary collects the account balance and pays for the funeral.

If you want a simple burial or cremation, pick a home with a low up-front fee. If you want an elaborate one, look at the cost of the whole package.

When the Funeral Is Now

L et's face it: Most people don't plan their own funerals. The planning gets compressed into a few days by those they leave behind, who aren't in a frame of mind to go shopping around for the lowest possible price. And because it's not something most people do very often, few would know what to do, anyway. As a result, we fall back on familiar choices: the "Catholic" funeral home, or the "Polish" funeral home, or, if we've been in one place long enough, the place our family has always used. This could serve you perfectly well, but you can't go wrong by being a knowledgeable buyer of funeral services.

How much should a funeral cost? We can cite national averages but no rules of thumb. Some funeral homes are busy all the time, others aren't. It seems reasonable to expect that the busier homes would cost less because they can spread their fixed costs over a larger number of funerals. By the same token, the trend to national chains of funeral homes should be creating economies of scale in purchasing and management structure that should benefit consumers.

Not so. Because so few people shop around for the best deal, funeral homes have little incentive to offer it. As you venture out into the marketplace, here's what you can expect.

THE PROFESSIONAL SERVICE FEE. It can range from as little as $695 to as much as nearly $3,000, and you have to pay it—it's "nondeclinable." Some are higher than others, but the important thing to remember is that your total cost will be this fee plus the cost of the other services that are described on the following pages. Some mortuaries set a high nondeclinable charge and comparatively low fees for other services. Others set a lower fixed fee but make it up with higher charges for the individual products and services you select. Here's the rule to remember: If you want a simple burial or cremation, choose the home with a low up-front fee. That way you won't subsidize services you don't use. If you want a more elaborate funeral, you'll have to look at the cost of the whole package before judging the up-front fee.

THE CASKET. You're not looking forward to spending time in a casket showroom, but this is where a lot of your money will be spent or saved. An 18-gauge-steel casket, a common choice, costs an average of about $2,300. A 20-gauge casket, which is lighter weight, sells for a lot less. Most people tend to buy a middle-priced casket—a habit that funeral homes can exploit through the price range they choose to display. In addition, industry critics charge, some homes attempt to "vulgarize" their lower-priced selections by ordering them in ugly colors for the showroom.

Because markups of 300 percent over the wholesale price aren't uncommon, it pays to look around a bit. If you've got the time and the inclination, here's how to save serious money.

Order your casket from a third party. For instance, Direct Casket (800-732-2753; http://www.directcasket .com;) in Huntington Station, New York, will deliver a casket to any funeral home in the country within 24 hours and sells directly to the public, at a substantial savings. For example, you can buy a 20-gauge steel casket for $795 to $1,395. A simple pine box, traditional for Jewish funerals, costs $395 to $995. Top-of-the-line models made of cherry or solid bronze cost $3,395 to $4,295, compared with $5,000 to $10,000 in the funeral home showrooms. You can order a casket for overnight delivery, and by law a funeral home must accept it without charging any kind of handling fee.

THE HIGH COST OF A FUNERAL

AVERAGE CHARGES

Professional service fee	$ 1,500
Embalming	500
Dressing and cosmetology	300
Visitation	400
Funeral-home ceremony	500
Transfer of remains to funeral home	250
Hearse and driver	200
Flower van and driver	100
18-gauge-steel casket	2,330
Memorial cards	30
Burial vault	1,000
Single cemetery plot	1,500
Grave marker	700
Other cemetery expenses (such as digging the grave)	1,000
TOTAL	**$ 10,310**

Sources: Funeral-home costs for a traditional adult funeral are based on numbers from the Funeral Help Program (FHP), 1236 Ginger Crescent, Virginia Beach, VA 23453; 877-427-0220; www.funeral-help.com. The FHP aims to help people make more educated decisions on funerals.

You're entitled to receive a price list disclosing the professional service fee and charges for all other services.

Don't pay extra for a "protective sealer" casket, which keeps out water, air, and insects. The seal adds $500 to $800 to the cost and does nothing to protect the body.

OTHER COSTS

Embalming. This procedure is usually mandatory for open-casket viewing, when it may be accompanied by charges for hairdressing and cosmetics. Otherwise, embalming isn't generally required unless the body is going to be transported across state lines. A typical embalming charge is about $500.

The funeral service. If the ceremony is at the funeral home, you'll be charged for use of the chapel and any necessary staff. Thus, it's usually less expensive to have the funeral service at a church rather than a funeral-home chapel.

Transfer of the remains. This is the fee for picking up the body and taking it to the funeral home, and it typically runs about $250.

Hearse and driver. Count on at least $200.

Forwarding fees. These come into play if someone dies a long distance from where the burial will be. In this case, you'll be dealing with two funeral homes—one on each end of the journey. The first home charges a "forwarding" fee, for embalming and transportation. Average fee: $1,100. The mortuary that handles the funeral will charge its usual fees.

Cremation. One in five Americans chooses cremation instead of burial. Because cremations can be so much simpler, they tend to cost a lot less, as little as $600 to $1,400. This isn't necessarily good for the funeral business, which would like you to spend a lot more. Thus, you'll be offered elaborate and expensive urns, even cremation jewelry, such as a pendant that holds the ashes of a loved one. Be careful or before you know it, you'll be spending almost as much as you would for a traditional burial service.

You can get a reading on funeral-home prices in your area from one of the more than 150 memorial societies in the U.S. and Canada. Many regularly survey local funeral-home prices and distribute the results. Some even negotiate discounted prices with certain funeral homes. (See the box at the bottom of this page.) If you contact a funeral home directly, you're entitled to receive a general price list disclosing the professional service fee and charges for all services provided.

The Cost of Burial

For a realistic idea of what a funeral costs, you must include burial fees that will vary depending on the type of burial—in-ground burial, interment in a lawn crypt, or entombment in a mausoleum. Here's a sample of some of the costs.

THE PLOT. The cost ranges from little or nothing in a community or church cemetery to from $1,000 to $3,000 at a for-profit cemetery.

BENEFITS OF MEMORIAL SOCIETY MEMBERSHIP

To check funeral-home prices in your area, contact a memorial society. Many regularly survey local prices and make the information available. Memorial societies also offer educational materials to help members make informed decisions about funeral planning, and some will put you in touch with local funeral homes that have agreed to provide society members with services at a discount.

Membership costs between $10 and $30 and is transferable to any other society that belongs to the more than 150-member Funeral Consumers Alliance (FCA). New members get a funeral prearrangement form you can use to inform your family of your wishes regarding your funeral. Societies also can provide forms for preparing living wills and durable powers of attorney.

The national offices of the FCA keep track of current legislation and funeral issues of concern to consumers in both state and federal governments.

To find a memorial society in your area, contact Funeral Consumers Alliance, 33 Patchen Road, South Burlington, VT 05403 (800-765-0107), or check its Web site at http://www.funerals.org for access to educational material and membership data.

Losing your spouse creates enough emotional turmoil without adding financial distress. Don't make any financial decisions for a while.

DIGGING THE GRAVE. To open and close the grave, you'll pay from $350 to $1,500, although you could spend much more depending on the time and day. A burial between 9 AM and 3 PM on weekdays is the cheapest. Burial after 3 PM could cost twice as much, and a weekend funeral could cost three times the weekday morning rate.

REINFORCING THE GRAVE. Most cemeteries require a concrete vault or grave liner to prevent the ground from settling. You may have no choice about this, but you needn't buy an expensive one. It does nothing for your loved one, and no one will see it. A simple concrete grave liner, at about $500 to $800, will do.

THE HEADSTONE. The cost is between $700 and $1,000, but it's possible to spend a lot more. If you're determined to get a first-class funeral, spend the money on the headstone, rather than on the casket. For the best price, buy the stone directly from the monument company.

CRYPT IN MAUSOLEUM (SINGLE). The cost is from $2,500 for an outside space (crypts in the outer wall rather than inside the mausoleum building) and up. Savings come primarily from what you won't have to buy—plot, sealer, burial vault, headstone, and grave opening and closing fees.

Finances after the Funeral

Losing your spouse creates enough emotional turmoil without adding financial distress. Don't make any financial decisions for a while. You don't even have to decide what to do with any insurance money right away. Your insurer can hold it in an interest-bearing account until you want it. While you're waiting for grief to subside, look into Social Security and other benefits to which you might be entitled.

When you get the life insurance benefits, be sure to set aside enough to get yourself through the first

year, including any major expenditures you can anticipate, before making any long-term investment decisions. Take time to become accustomed to your new
pattern of income and expenses. You'll know fairly
quickly what you can expect to receive from Social Security and your spouse's pension, but it will take
longer to assess how much income you'll need from
employment or investments. Resist the temptation to
make expensive purchases until you've lived for a
while with your new pattern of income and expenses.

Social Security

If your spouse was entitled to receive Social Security
benefits, then you might be entitled to a survivor's benefit. In addition, spouses and dependent minors can receive a $255 death benefit from the Social Security
Administration. That sounds laughably small compared
with the cost of a funeral, but there's no reason to turn
it down. Eligibility depends on age. Call Social Security
(800-772-1213) or visit its Web site (http://www.ssa.gov)
for information about survivor's benefits of all kinds
and to have application forms sent to you. For more information on Social Security in general, see Chapter 29.

Veterans Benefits

Anyone on active military duty at the time of death, or
who has served in the armed forces during his or her
lifetime, may be eligible for burial in one of the national
cemeteries—at the expense of the federal government.

There are 120 national cemeteries in the country,
though not all states have one. A number are nearly
full and are closed to new casket burials, although ac-
commodations for cremated ashes may be possible. For
more information on the death benefits available and a
copy of *Federal Benefits for Veterans and Dependents*, go to
the Department of Veterans Affairs' Web site at http://
www.cem.va.gov. To reach the regional Veterans office in your area, call 800-827-1000.

If your spouse was entitled to receive Social Security benefits, then you might be entitled to a survivor's benefit.

The Money Squeeze of Aging Parents

Are you among the growing number of Americans who count themselves reluctant members of Generation S? The "S" stands for Sandwich, and to qualify you must be feeling sandwiched between the financial demands of raising children and the growing financial needs of your aging parents—to say nothing of your own financial needs. "Squeezed" might be a better word for it.

People over age 85 are the fastest-growing segment of the population, and the squeezed generation is growing with them. With rising life expectancies, millions of middle-aged adults will be pushed into S-hood. It won't be easy to cope, but there are some things you can do.

Do They Need Your Help?

Aging parents are often the first to notice that they could use some help tending to their finances. Sometimes their children notice the telltale signs: bills that go unpaid, confusion about financial and other matters where there used to be alertness, growing anxiety about medical and other expenses. You may have to act like a detective to get to the bottom of the problem and gather the information you need to help them. Where to begin? Start with the basics.

Income and Assets

Find out as much as you can about their sources of income, their assets, and their debts. What would they like to do in the years ahead? Would they like to stay where they are, move to a retirement community, or

To avoid forcing wrenching choices on their adult children, parents should have a living will, a durable power of attorney, and some form of health care proxy.

move closer to where you live? Do they have enough income to do what they want to do? Are they making the most of their assets, or might they benefit from a visit to a financial planner who could suggest ways to deploy their resources to better advantage?

Important Documents

Find out where they keep their important documents, such as wills, insurance policies, pension and Social Security records, and tax returns. Suggest that they review their wills with a lawyer if they haven't done so within the past five years or if they have moved from one state to another since the document was drawn up. Make sure each knows where to find these records in an emergency. Ask for copies to keep yourself. Kiplinger's *Your Family Records Organizer*, available as a CD-ROM or in print ($14.95 for either or $20 for both at http://www.kiplinger.com/organizer or 800-280-7165) offers an easy-to-use series of forms on which you or your parents can record where all important documents are kept and how to reach key advisors.

Insurance Coverage

The older we get, the more important medical insurance becomes. Your parents should be covered by a Medigap policy, which picks up the deductible and payments not reimbursed by Medicare. (See Chapter 20.)

Long-term-care insurance should also be considered, because Medicare generally won't pay nursing-home bills or the cost of in-home nursing care. If paying the premiums for a long-term-care policy would put a strain on your parents' finances, then forget it. See Chapter 20 for guidelines on who should buy this coverage and who shouldn't.

What If They Become Incapacitated?

Coping with a stroke or other catastrophic illness is difficult enough, but being forced to make life-or-death decisions for a parent when you don't know his or her wishes can haunt you forever. Would your mother want to be kept alive on a respirator? Should you let the doctors insert a feeding tube?

To avoid forcing such wrenching choices on their adult children, parents should visit a lawyer and draw up three documents: a living will, a durable power of attorney, and some form of health care proxy. These give them an opportunity to clarify their choices and appoint someone they trust to make those choices for them when they no longer can.

You should consider drawing up your own set of these documents at the same time.

> **A health care proxy grants the person you appoint the power to make health care decisions if you can't.**

The Importance of a Living Will

A living will spells out a person's wishes regarding the use of feeding tubes, intravenous fluids, mechanical ventilation (being placed on a respirator), resuscitation (including CPR), antibiotics, and other procedures that might be used to prolong life in the event of a terminal illness or accident.

Laws vary by state. You can get state-specific documents for doing this on your own free of charge from The National Hospice and Palliative Care Organization (NHPCO), 1700 Diagonal Road, Suite 625, Alexandria, VA 22314 (800-658-8898 or 703-837-1500, or from its Web site http://www.nhpco.org). To be sure of what you're doing, have a lawyer review the documents.

Because there are religious and moral implications in any life-or-death decision, it's a good idea to discuss the provisions of a living will within the family and with any physicians involved. In addition, be sure that the doctors agree to be guided by the document and that the hospitals in which the doctors practice will honor it. Most states allow doctors to follow the instructions in a living will, but they are not legally obligated to do so.

Health Care Proxy

A health care proxy should accompany a living will. It grants the person you appoint the power to make health care decisions if you can't. This

A durable power of attorney delegates to someone you choose the authority to make legal, financial, and medical decisions on your behalf.

includes choosing or dismissing doctors, consenting to surgery, and representing your wishes regarding life-support options. All states recognize these proxies. (Alabama does not allow designated agents to withhold or withdraw life support if the patient is pregnant.)

Durable Power of Attorney

A durable power of attorney delegates to someone you choose the authority to make legal, financial, and medical decisions on your behalf. It usually becomes effective as soon as it's signed, although there are two variations on that. A limited power of attorney grants a designated "attorney-in-fact" the power to make only certain decisions on your behalf—to pay bills from your checking account, for example. A springing durable power of attorney, recognized in many states, does not take effect until you are declared incompetent to make such decisions yourself. You (or your parent) might consider the springing type if serious surgery looms, for instance. In your power of attorney, you can name the doctor or doctors allowed to declare you incompetent, or you can direct the attorney-in-fact to name them.

Get a lawyer to draw up your durable power of attorney. Make separate ones for finances and health care. Sign several originals because some banks, hospitals, and brokerage houses want to have an original on file. You should also spread copies of the document around, making sure that family members, doctors, and financial advisors are aware of what it says. Anyone who lives in more than one state—wintering in Florida, for instance, and summering in Maine—should make sure to have powers of attorney that conform to both states' laws. Elderly people who travel should take a copy with them.

What if you change your mind? A durable power of attorney can be revoked at any time as long as you are mentally competent. Simply put the revocation in writing, have it witnessed and notarized, and give copies to all parties concerned.

Where Will They Live?

Most older Americans don't want to move. Fortunately, the growth of home services for the elderly has made aging in place possible for those who can afford it. For those who can't, or think they can't, some creative financial thinking could help to make the difference.

If your parents' mortgage is paid off but they are still straining to make ends meet, they might consider a reverse mortgage or a sale-leaseback to ease their financial burden.

Reverse Mortgage: The Bank Pays You

A reverse mortgage can allow a homeowner to borrow against a portion of the equity in the home without having to pay back any principal or interest until the home is sold, possibly after the owner's death. Borrowers can take the money as a monthly income stream, a lump sum, or even a line of credit to be tapped as needed. Borrowing limits are based on life expectancy and the amount of equity recognized by the lender.

Once hard to find, reverse mortgages, now available in all 50 states, the District of Columbia, and Puerto Rico, come in many shapes and sizes and can be adapted to suit almost anybody's needs. There's more information on them in Chapter 29.

Sale-Leaseback: You Become the Landlord

Sale-leasebacks typically involve parent and child, though an outsider can also be part of the deal. Say you're the adult child looking for a way to help your parents stay in their home. You buy the home directly from them (they act as the lender, taking back a mortgage), then you lease it back to them. Your down payment gives them an immediate infusion of cash and your mortgage payments provide a monthly income. In turn, your parents write you a check each month for the rent. Any difference between the mortgage payment they get and the rent they pay can be additional income for them. Here's how it works:

If your parents' mortgage is paid off but they are still straining to make ends meet, they might consider a reverse mortgage or a sale-leaseback.

Independent-living communities offer healthy seniors a sense of security in addition to some basic services.

Suppose your parents' home is worth $250,000. You make a down payment of $50,000. Your parents make a mortgage loan to you for the difference of $200,000 at, say, a 5.5 percent interest rate over 30 years. Your monthly mortgage payment to your parents would be $1,136. In exchange, you get an investment and a tax shelter. Because it's a rental property, you can deduct the interest, taxes, insurance, maintenance, and depreciation on the property. Rather than exchanging checks with your parents, you can deduct their rent from the principal and interest payments you make to them. Be sure to keep accurate records of your transactions, though. In order to qualify for the tax deductions, the sale price, the mortgage interest rate, and the rent must be set at a fair market value.

Should They Move In?

Don't be surprised if your aging, widowed mother doesn't want to move in with you. According to surveys, most seniors would rather move into a facility that offers some assistance than move in with a relative or friend. Message: They don't want to be a burden.

To allay that feeling, perhaps your parents would want to pay rent. Consider the idea if your parents suggest it. If you don't need the money, put it in your child's college savings fund or suggest that they establish such a fund. If you do need the money, why not let them help pay their way?

All of this depends on how well you get along. If you and your parents communicate honestly and share a sense of mutual respect and love, then the arrangement could work just fine. It's the only option in many families. If it won't work in yours, and you or your parents have the wherewithal to consider alternatives, read on.

Options for Elderly Housing
Option 1: Independent Living

Independent-living communities offer healthy seniors a sense of security in addition to some basic services. Often enclosed by walls or fences, such communities usually offer a variety of housing choices, including single-family homes, patio homes, cottages, and apartments. Residents generally lead active lives and need little or no assistance, although they may choose to pay for services such as housekeeping, meals, alarm systems, and a nurse or health clinic on-site.

There are hundreds, perhaps thousands, of such retirement communities around the country, ranging from luxurious developments that are built around golf courses or marinas to modest communities offering manufactured housing that caters to less affluent retirees. Some healthy retirees love them because they're surrounded by people their own age. Other retirees loathe the idea for the same reason.

Option 2: Assisted Living

Assisted-living facilities provide round-the-clock assistance for residents who can't manage completely on their own. Some may need help bathing or dressing, making meals, paying bills, or performing other basic daily activities. These facilities generally have a nurse on duty during the day. Medical emergencies are dealt with the same way they would be at home: Somebody calls an ambulance. Done right, the great appeal of the assisted-living idea is its dedication to preserving residents' autonomy. Residents live in apartments or rooms, either alone or with another resident.

Assisted living offers companionship and security, as well as transportation for shopping, social outings, and appointments with doctors, dentists, and so forth. Residents can use physicians associated with the facility or keep their own.

Residents typically pay on a month-to-month basis, but some facilities require residents to sign a lease for one year, at the end of which either party may choose not to renew. Assisted-living homes aren't nursing homes, and they aren't inclined to retain residents who need more care than they can deliver (although some do have special facilities for Alzheimer's sufferers). Find out what the discharge rules are and how much

Assisted-living facilities provide round-the-clock assistance for residents who can't manage completely on their own.

notice you are entitled to if the facility decides not to renew the lease. In turn, find out how much notice you must give if your mom or dad is unhappy there and wants to move out.

WHAT THEY COST. Costs vary from region to region, with metropolitan areas being more expensive, and depend on the type of amenities chosen. Typical charges run from about $2,500 to $3,000 a month,

---

RESOURCES FOR AGING PARENTS

GENERAL RESOURCES AND SUPPORT
BenefitsCheckUp

(www.benefitscheckup.org) is a free nationwide service provided by the National Council on Aging that includes a database of about 1,000 federal and state programs available to help older people. After a person fills in responses to an online questionnaire that does not require personal information such as name, address, or Social Security number—just a zip code to pinpoint benefits that are available in a specific geographic area—BenefitsCheckUp produces a list of programs for which the inquirer most likely qualifies, including phone numbers, addresses, and Web sites, if available. It also provides step-by-step advice on how to apply for benefits.

CAREGIVER SURVIVAL RESOURCES
Two membership organizations that provide information, referrals, and support to caregivers are:
■ **National Family Caregivers Association,** 10400 Connecticut Ave., Suite 500, Kensington, MD 20895–3944; 800-896-3650; www.nfcacares.org; and

■ **Children of Aging Parents**
P.O. Box 167, Richboro, PA 18954; www.caps4caregivers.org.

HIRING A CAREGIVER
■ **Eldercare Locator** (800-677-1116; www.eldercare.gov) is a nationwide database carrying lists of local providers of care and services for the elderly. This is particularly helpful when trying to handle matters from a distance.

■ **The Joint Commission on Accreditation of Health Care Organizations** (630-792-5800; www.jcaho.org) accredits home health agencies and publishes free reports on them.

■ **Members of the National Association of Professional Geriatric Care Managers** (1604 N. Country Club Rd., Tucson, AZ 85716; 520-881-8008; www.caremanager.org) can assess your parent's situation, recommend a plan of care, and monitor paid caregivers.

CHOOSING OUTSIDE CARE
■ **American Association of Homes and Services for the Aging** (2519 Connecti-

according to the Assisted Living Federation of America (www.alfa.org). Check to see what services are included in the basic monthly fee, and then get a list of other services offered and how much they cost. If the resident needs a service that's not on the list, find out if you can get it there and, if so, for how much.

Find out what happens if your parent has to be hospitalized or moved into a nursing home for rehabilitation for several weeks or months. How long will the

cut Ave., NW, Washington, DC 20008-1520; 202-783-2242; www.aahsa.org)

■ **Assisted Living Federation of America** (11200 Waples Mill Rd., Suite 150, Fairfax, VA 22030; 703-691-8100; www.alfa.org) has a free pamphlet on picking an assisted-living facility.

INSURANCE

■ **The Eldercare Locator** (previous page) can help you locate insurance counseling.

■ Send 65 cents to the **National Association of Insurance Commissioners** (NAIC Publications, 2301 McGee St., Kansas City, MO 64108-2662; 816-842-3600; www.naic.org) for a copy of *A Shopper's Guide to Long Term Care Insurance.*

■ Call or check the Web site for **Medicare** (800-638-6833; www.medicare.gov) for answers to basic questions regarding benefits and services.

■ **Medicare Rights Center** (1460 Broadway, New York, NY 10036; 212-869-3850; www.medicarerights.org) publishes a series of Medicare-related leaflets and brochures; write for a price list, or check the Web site and order online.

■ **The National Council on Aging** (300 D St., NW, Suite 801, Washington, DC 20024; 202-479-1200) offers *Planning for Long-Term Care,* Item No. SC100 ($14.95), which covers planning, insurance coverage for long-term-care, and various levels of available care, such as assisted living and nursing-home care. To order, call 800-373-4906, or check their Web site at www.ncoa.org.

FINANCIAL AND LEGAL HELP

■ **National Academy of Elder Law Attorneys** (1604 N. Country Club Rd., Tucson, AZ 85716–3102; 520-881-4005; www.naela.org) provides referrals to its members.

■ There is no need to have a living will drawn up by a lawyer. State-specific documents for writing a living will and designating a health care power of attorney are available free of charge from **The National Hospice and Palliative Care Organization** (1700 Diagonal Rd., Suite 625, Alexandria, VA 22314; 800-658-8898 or 703-837-1500; www.nhpco.org).

If your parents have a long-term-care insurance policy, check to see if it covers any of the costs of assisted living.

unit be held? Will you have to continue paying while the resident is away?

If your parents have a long-term-care insurance policy, check to see if it covers any of the costs of assisted living. Some newer policies cover a portion of the costs. Medicaid won't cover the costs, and Medicare will cover only medical bills, not room and board. If a resident needs considerable assistance, the cost of assisted living can actually exceed that of a nursing home.

FINDING A FACILITY. Contact the local Area Agency on Aging (it's in the phone book as part of the local-government listings). Ask for a list of assisted-living homes in the area. Or look at the Retirement Living Information Center at http://www.retirementliving.com, where you can search by state. Then get ready to make some visits, and be prepared to see a wide range of places. Assisted-living homes aren't regulated by the federal government, and rules vary from state to state, so standards are all over the map. Once you have shortened the list to a few facilities, visit each one again and look at the following factors:

- **Location.** Is it near a grocery store, doctors, pharmacies, shops, and other places your mom or dad might want to walk to?
- **Safety.** Is it adequately equipped with fire-safety equipment, emergency call buttons, handrails in bathrooms, wide hallways and doors to accommodate wheelchairs and walkers? Are the public areas and apartments clean? Are windows fixed so that they can't be raised high enough for a resident to fall out? Is an attendant on duty 24 hours a day?
- **Residents' opinions.** Talk to as many residents as you can to get their thoughts on the facility. You want to find out if the residents are treated well and their concerns handled by management. Is there a resident group that addresses problems in the facility?
- **Activities.** Does the facility offer engaging activities or provide transportation for residents interested in pursuing outside activities or volunteering in the community?

■ **Layout and amenities.** Are the units well designed and the common areas attractive and well cared for? Look at the specific unit that your parent will be renting. If your mother enjoys cooking, for example, and there is no kitchen in the unit, then it may not be a good match for your mom.

Option 3: Continuing Care

Continuing-care retirement communities, or CCRCs, offer a range of living options. Residents start in the in-dependent-living portion. They hope to stay there, but if the infirmities of age get the better of them, they have the right to move into an assisted-living facility and, if necessary, a skilled-nursing home in the same development.

Of particular concern for couples who enter a CCRC together is how it handles a situation in which one spouse requires some care and the other doesn't. Will they move one into the assisted-living facility and leave the other in the independent housing? Or will the facility allow someone to provide the services in the independent-living area? Who makes the final decision about when it's time to move into the assisted-living area? If the couple is forced to split up, or residents and families are not involved in the decision-making process, then consider another facility. Dissatisfaction over these issues is the main reason people leave CCRCs.

A RANGE OF FEES. Along with the range of housing, there is a range of fees at such facilities.

Entry fees. Most continuing-care facilities require a con-tract and charge an entry fee. In some cases it's refund-able—either fully or partially—and some states require that refunds be available for long enough to give resi-dents a chance to see if they can adjust. There may be a penalty, however.

Monthly service fees. All CCRCs charge a monthly ser-vice fee, which covers the costs of the unit, services such as housekeeping and gardening, meals, and some

In continuing-care communities, residents start in the independent-living portion and can move to assisted living or even a skilled-nursing home if they need to later.

Buying into a continuing-care community is a lot like buying into a condominium. You want to be sure the facility has adequate reserves to cover expenses.

level of health care. Some contracts cover only the unit and certain services, while health care and other needs are paid for on a fee-for-service basis. Residents can usually contract for one of three types of monthly fees:

- **Extensive agreements** (sometimes called life-care agreements) cover all needs, including housing, services, and unlimited medical care. In effect, residents prepay for services they may or may not need in the future. In return, the monthly fee stays the same except for inflation adjustments and increases in operating costs.
- **Modified plans** cover the costs of housing, services, and a predetermined level of long-term nursing care. Under this plan, residents might be entitled to, say, 60 days of skilled-nursing care if needed.
- **The fee-for-service agreement** charges a monthly fee that covers housing and services. Residents pay for assisted living and skilled-nursing care on an as-needed basis. This gets you the lowest monthly fee, in return for assuming the risk of higher medical costs if you need such services.

OWNERSHIP PLANS. At some facilities you can buy your residence or a "membership" in the CCRC, then contract separately for the service and health care portion. Some offer mortgages, so purchasers can write off the interest. An issue to explore in arrangements like this (in addition to the up-front cost) is what happens if you want to sell or if you die while still an owner. Does the facility get a percentage of the sale price?

Buying into a CCRC this way is a lot like buying into a condominium. You want to be sure the facility has adequate reserves to maintain the buildings and grounds, to cover salaries, and to pay for unexpected repairs and maintenance items. Owners and managers should be experienced in the development and operation of a CCRC.

Most states have laws governing the operation of CCRCs. The Commission on Accreditation of Rehabilitation Facilities reviews rehabilitation, employment, child and family, and aging services (including CCRCs, assisted-living residences, and adult day care services) that voluntarily submit to the process and accredits those that meet its standards. To find out if they have accredited CCRCs or assisted-living facilities in your state, call 888-281-6531 or search its Web site at http://www.carf.org.

The Continuing Care Retirement Community: A Guidebook for Consumers is available for $20 (order #CC001) from the American Association of Homes and Services for the Aging by phone (202-783-2241) or from its Web site (http://www.aahsa.org). The guidebook explains CCRCs and tells consumers how to compare one CCRC with another. It includes a checklist of amenities and services designed for consumers to take with them as they visit communities and refer to as they make their decisions.

Option 4: Nursing Homes

Nobody wants to go to a nursing home, and people send loved ones there only as a last resort. Be prepared for a wrenching experience.

A skilled-nursing facility provides a high degree of care with a registered nurse on staff 24 hours a day and doctors and clergy on call. If a resident needs tube feeding or a respirator, then she'll probably need the care offered by a skilled-nursing facility.

If, on the other hand, someone needs special medicines or therapy but not round-the-clock care, then an intermediate-care facility may be sufficient. Although registered nurses are on staff, they may not be available 24 hours a day.

Some nursing homes offer a combination of care levels, with separate wings for skilled-nursing and intermediate care.

FINDING A GOOD NURSING HOME. For names of nursing homes in your area, contact your state's Area Agency on Aging, as well as the Eldercare Locator (800-677-1116; http://www.n4a.org). Doctors with elderly patients and anyone who has a relative or friend in a nursing home can provide you with invaluable information about the process.

> **Nobody wants to go to a nursing home, and people send loved ones there only as a last resort. Be prepared for a wrenching experience.**

If you provide most of a parent's support, you can deduct some of the cost on your tax return, provided the parent qualifies as your dependent.

Some homes will not accept Medicaid residents or have only a limited number of beds designated for Medicaid patients. The expense of a nursing home—$5,000 to $8,000 a month is not unusual—is such that many residents must fall back on Medicaid eventually.

Try to make at least two visits to each facility you're considering—one planned and one unannounced. Consider making the unannounced visit in the evening, when the staff is smaller and management is usually off duty. This will give you a sense of how the staff operates when management isn't looking over their shoulders.

What should you look for? Check the cleanliness of both the public areas and the residents' rooms and bathrooms. Check the condition of furnishings, carpeting, plumbing—is it out-of-date or worn out? And also take note of the interaction between staff and residents.

When you visit during the day, are residents dressed? Are they involved in some activity or are they just parked by the nurses' station in wheelchairs? Get a list of the activities for the next month to see if there is a good variety. If you have time, try to attend one or two of them to see if residents are encouraged to participate.

A nursing-home resident must have an advocate acting on his or her behalf. If there are problems with treatment or your parent complains of abuse, a family member needs to step in and work with the staff to resolve the problem.

When Your Parents Need You

Your parents may reach a point when they're unable to live alone without financial assistance from you. Some of the expenses you incur to help support your parents may generate tax benefits.

If you provide most of a parent's support, you can deduct some of the cost on your tax return, provided the parent qualifies as your dependent. That means their taxable income must not exceed a certain amount ($3,200 in 2005 and adjusted annually for inflation) and you must pay for more than half of the parent's living expenses. If you also pay for medical expenses, you can add the cost to the amount you paid for the rest of the family and deduct the amount that exceeds 7.5 percent of your adjusted gross income.

You may qualify for a further tax break if you pay for someone to come into your home and care for your parent or if he or she attends one of the growing number of adult day care centers. You can claim a federal tax credit of up to $1,050, depending on your income and how much you spent on care during the year. To qualify for this credit, you must pay for over half of your parent's expenses, but there is no limit to the income your parent can earn. You claim it on Form 2441, available with instructions from the IRS at 800-829-3676, or on the Internet at http://www.irs.gov.

An employer's flexible-spending, or set-aside, account might be another way to recoup some of the costs of caring for your parents. These accounts allow you to pay for dependent care with up to $5,000 of pretax dollars. Your employer deducts the money from your paycheck before taxes are applied, then as you submit vouchers for qualified dependent care expenses, you get your money back. There's a catch: You decide how much to put into the account at the beginning of the year; whatever you haven't spent by year-end you lose.

You must choose between the tax credit and the flexible-spending account; you can't use both. Generally, however, if you spend more than $2,400 and you are in the 25 percent tax bracket or above, the flexible-spending account is the better deal.

If you share the costs of caring for your parent with your siblings and together you contribute more than half of your parent's total support, then one of you can claim a dependency deduction, provided the income test is met. Each sibling must pay for more than 10 percent of the parent's support, and each must sign IRS Form 2120 (Multiple Support Declaration), which you submit with your 1040.

Helping at a Distance

The angst of adult children trying to care for elderly parents far away has become so common that a new profession has blossomed to help them.

An employer's flexible spending account might be a way to recoup some of the costs of caring for dependent parents.

Geriatric-care managers are usually former nurses or social workers. They visit the parent's home to assess the needs, then determine ways to meet those needs locally. They follow up to make sure their clients are getting the care and to monitor changes in their condition.

According to the National Association of Geriatric-Care Managers, you can expect to pay between $300 and $800 for an initial assessment and $50 to $150 per hour thereafter, depending on the services offered. Several states have also started assessment and case-management programs to meet this growing need. Call your local Area Agency on Aging for referrals to geriatric-care managers in your area. You can get the number of your local aging agency from the Eldercare Locator (800-677-1116; http://www.eldercare.gov).

Protecting Your Life and Health

Buying the Right Life Insurance

Chapter 19

First, a word about insurance in general. You need insurance for two reasons: first, to protect you and your family from the consequences of a financial loss—affecting your health, your car, your home, your belongings, or your life—and second, to make good on your obligations to others who might suffer injury or loss for which you are responsible.

What you get for your money is a promise to pay if the event you hope never happens does happen. In most cases, if the dreaded event doesn't happen, about the only tangible thing you have to show for your money is the policy document itself and maybe a card you carry in your wallet. You may also have a stack of canceled checks, a reminder of what a big-ticket item insurance can be. Homeowners and car insurance are covered earlier in the book; now it's time to move on to life and health insurance—and to describe some insurance policies you don't need.

What Have You Got?

An insurance policy is a legal contract, with specific meanings attached to certain words. Those words spell out your rights and obligations as well as those of the insurance company. Unless your policy expressly calls for the payment of a certain benefit upon the occurrence of a certain event, you probably won't be paid, no matter what a salesperson or other representative may have told you. If the fine print takes away what the big print appears to bestow, that's your tough luck. What's more, the marketplace is constantly

Your need for life insurance changes with the stages of your life.

in flux, characterized by increasingly complex policies, changes in coverage, wildly varying rates, confusing discounts. A lot of smart people work for insurance companies, and they are always thinking up new policies with new twists. As mind-numbing as it sounds, there's really only one way to know what's in your policies: Read them, each and every one, new or renewal, from front to back, with a dictionary at your elbow and perhaps the phone numbers of your agents at hand. Understand what's behind the policy titles, which are only occasionally informative. What would you know from their titles about life insurance policies named Contender, Vision, Preference, or Optimiser 100? Some insurance companies have undertaken laudable campaigns to make their policies more understandable. But don't get your hopes up: There's still a long way to go.

When Should You Buy Life Insurance?

Your need for life insurance changes with the stages of your life, starting with no need when you're young, progressing to greater and greater need as you take on more and more responsibility, and finally beginning to diminish as you grow older. Consider these situations:

When You're Single

Sad though your death would be, it would quite probably create financial hardship for no one. Any honest financial assessment of your situation would have to conclude that you have little or no need for life insurance. An argument could be made that you should buy a policy now while you're young and rates are low. And if someone—a parent, say—depends on you for financial support, then by all means consider life insurance. But consider the interest you could earn by saving and investing your money instead of spending it on insurance premiums. Still, if somebody—a parent, a grandparent—wants to buy you a policy now to lock in low rates for later in your life, accept it gratefully.

Love and Marriage

A few years have gone by and now you're half of a married couple with no children. Together you earn $80,000 a year, each contributing about equally. The death of either of you would not be financially catastrophic; the other could presumably survive on his or her own income. Still, it could be a strain. Perhaps the survivor couldn't afford the mortgage or rent payments on a single income, or maybe you have big credit card debts. Also, there would be funeral costs. Each of you should probably buy a modest amount of life insurance to protect the other.

Married with Children

More time passes. Now you're half of a couple living in a one-income household. You have two young children. This is the classic high-need situation. Four people are dependent on one breadwinner for their total support, so insurance on that life is vital. And if the nonearning spouse should die, the other would have to pay for child care—a very expensive proposition that argues for insurance on both lives. This same high-need situation exists for dual-income households with children, for single parents, and for anyone caring for elderly parents who have limited resources of their own.

You're Your Own Boss

Married or single, if you own your own business, life insurance offers an excellent safety net to protect that business from taxes when you die. And a life insurance policy can serve as a great equalizer if you're giving the business to one child who's been active in the business but want to be fair to your other children who haven't. Name those children as beneficiaries who will receive payment equivalent to the business's worth.

The Golden Years

Now you're retired. The kids have grown and are making it on their own. You have a pension and considerable assets that can be used to generate a good income after you die. In circumstances like this, you

Married with children living is the classic time for needing life insurance.

Deciding whether you need life insurance is pretty easy. Figuring out how much you need is not easy at all.

clearly don't need as much life insurance as you once did. Still, life insurance can come in handy for estate planning, a subject we'll get to later on.

How Much Do You Need?

Deciding whether you need life insurance is pretty easy. Figuring out how much you need is not easy at all. Many people just pluck some figure out of the air that seems reasonable and settle on that. Some lean on an old rule of thumb that says you need four to five times your annual income. That's better, but in this day and age you really should approach the problem more scientifically. You can arrive at a reasonable estimate of your life insurance needs without getting too technical, and the worksheet on the next page will help you do it.

The first step is to estimate the income your dependents would need to maintain their standard of living if you were to die tomorrow. Then subtract from that figure the income they could expect to receive in Social Security survivor's benefits (to get the form you need to estimate that, call the Social Security Administration at 800-772-1213 or visit the agency's Web site at http://www.ssa.gov). Next subtract the salaries your dependents now earn or could earn, the value of investments, and other income sources. The difference is the amount of income your life insurance should provide.

You have to make a number of assumptions in the course of this exercise—complex assumptions that scare many people away from the task. For instance:

■ **What will inflation be in the future?** Unless you've got some special insight into this question, assume that it will average 4 percent.

■ **Will the family be able to live on the earnings** generated by the proceeds of the policy, or should they expect to gradually use up the capital as well? The answer to this depends a great deal on how much money is involved. If the policy will pay half a million dollars and there are other sources of income, then you can reasonably expect that the beneficiaries could use the earnings and leave the principal pretty much alone. On the other hand, if the policy pays $100,000, then the family will need considerable additional assets if the principal is to remain intact.

■ **What rate of interest** can you safely assume the money will earn? For a conservative after-tax return based on historical norms, you should assume 8 percent.

■ **Will your spouse take a job** if he or she doesn't have one now? Will that require a period of training? How much can your spouse realistically be expected to earn? The answers will depend on your own situa-

---

FIGURING YOUR LIFE INSURANCE NEEDS

A. Survivors' Annual Expenses

Annual expenditures from cash-flow worksheet
(see Chapter 1, page 5)   _____

Minus your own living expenses   – _____

A. Total annual expenses $ _____

B. Survivors' Annual Income

Anticipated salaries   _____

Interest from savings   _____

Investment dividends   _____

Rents received   _____

Annuity income   _____

Social Security benefits   _____

Veterans benefits   _____

Payments from pension plan   _____

Income from trusts   _____

Other income   + _____

B. Total annual income available $ _____

C. Annual Income Needed from Additional Insurance

Annual expenses minus annual
income (A minus B)   _____

Minus annual benefits from
existing life insurance policies   – _____

Annual income needed from additional insurance $ _____

Keep in mind: the purchasing power of the insurance you buy today will be eroded by inflation as the years go by.

tion, of course. It is impossible to anticipate everything, but it's wise to make reasonable guesses about what sorts of choices the surviving spouse might confront and provide as much breathing room as you can afford.

You can see what makes this task so difficult. Insurance companies will make the financial assumptions for you, using computerized programs developed for the purpose. These can be helpful, but many of the decisions described above are too important to turn over completely to the company trying to sell you the policy.

Eventually you will have to pick some total insurance figure that seems a reasonable compromise between what you'd like to have and what you can afford, using the companies' estimates for reference. Keep in mind that the purchasing power of the insurance you buy today will be eroded by inflation as the years go by. Remember the inflation assumption you made above and refer to the inflation table on page 483 to get an idea of the effect of that on your coverage five or ten years down the road.

The Life Insurance Menu

L ife insurance companies are brilliant at devising new kinds of policies. But try to remember that whatever the name on the policy—universal life, variable life, Irresistible Life, Irreplaceable Life, The Champion, The Solution—all are in fact variations on the two basic kinds of coverage: term insurance and cash-value insurance (also called permanent or whole life).

Term Insurance

This is as simple as life insurance gets and is the easiest to understand. You insure your life for a certain amount of money for a fixed period of time—one year, five years, or more—and pay an annual premium based on your age and the amount of coverage you're buying. There's nothing fancy about term insurance. It has no savings or investment features built into the rates, making it the purest form of life insurance around and thus the cheapest for a given amount of coverage.

ANNUAL-RENEWABLE TERM. You buy a series of one-year policies and the insurance company guarantees you the right to renew the coverage each year without having to undergo an additional medical exam. Your premium rises with each new policy year.

GUARANTEED-LEVEL TERM. This is the most common form of insurance sold today. Instead of rising each year, premiums start out a little higher but stay level for 5, 10, 15, or even 20 years or more. At the end of the period, you have usually paid less than you would have under an annual-renewable term policy. Insurance companies developed guaranteed-level term policies to discourage customers from hopping from one company to another each year at policy renewal time, chasing the lowest rates.

DECLINING, DECREASING, OR REDUCING TERM. The amount of coverage gradually declines according to a fixed schedule over 10, 15, 20, or more years. Mortgage insurance policies, which pay the loan balance when the policyholder dies, are a common form of decreasing term.

CONVERTIBLE TERM. For a higher premium than regular term, a convertible policy can be rolled into a whole life, or cash-value policy, without your having to meet medical standards at the time of conversion. Most companies offer policies that are both convertible and renewable up to specified ages or for fixed periods.

Whole-Life Insurance

This is commonly called cash-value or permanent insurance. In its basic form, it charges you the same premium for as long as you keep the policy. Because the premium remains level as you grow older, it must be

Whatever the name on the policy, all are in fact variations on the two basic kinds of coverage: term and cash-value insurance.

Why give extra money to the insurance company when you could buy term insurance and invest the difference?

set to exceed the company's cost of insuring your life during the early years. The extra premium and the interest it earns go into a reserve fund. Part of the fund is used to pay the agent's commission and the company's administrative costs. The rest gets credited to your account, where it earns interest. After a couple of years your reserve begins to build, tax-free, creating a "cash value" that you can draw on in a number of ways.

You can get at your accumulated cash value by borrowing against it while the policy stays in force; by directing the company to use it to purchase a paid-up insurance policy of some amount; by directing the company to use it to pay your premiums; or by surrendering the policy and taking the money. When you die, if the policy is still in force, the company pays your beneficiary the policy's face amount (less any loan balance), not the face amount plus cash value.

Insurance companies offer a wondrous array of cash-value policies, ranging from the standard, no-frills kind (sometimes called straight or ordinary life) to specially designed contracts in which the premiums or face amounts change according to a set schedule, investment results, or some other factor.

Even though some of the excess premiums charged by whole-life insurance policies in their early years may eventually find their way into your pocket via the cash-value buildup, the question remains: Why give all that extra money to the insurance company when you could simply buy term insurance and invest the difference yourself? This is the great debate of the ages in the insurance industry.

The Case for Term

The fundamental purpose of life insurance is to provide dependents with the financial support they would lose if you died. If you're straining to buy enough insurance to accomplish that goal, then term is what you should buy. Dollar for dollar, term gives you the most protection for your money. Period.

Beyond that important truth, the arguments for term are the arguments against whole life. True, the cash value in a whole-life policy could add to your financial resources as the years pass, but as mentioned above, you can get your hands on the cash usually only by surrendering the policy (thereby terminating your coverage) or by borrowing some of it (although some policies permit cash withdrawals within certain limits). Borrowing keeps the policy in force, but any unpaid loan balance will be deducted from the face amount if you die. To restore the full face amount of the policy, you'll have to repay the loan, plus interest.

How expensive are these loans? Some companies charge variable rates so that the interest they collect reflects the current market. Others reduce dividends to reflect the amount of the cash value encumbered by the policyholder's loan, an approach called direct recognition. Under direct recognition, in effect, the more you borrow the less your policy earns. Either of these approaches can make policy loans more expensive than they appear. In any case, you can leave your options open by starting with a term policy that you can convert to whole-life coverage.

The Case for Whole Life

All this is not to say that whole-life insurance doesn't have a lot going for it. Premiums don't rise as you get older, and you don't have to worry about renewing the coverage every year or every few years. Whole-life policies stay in force up to age 100. (If you live that long, the policy will pay you off.) They may be participating (in other words, pay dividends) or nonparticipating (pay no dividends).

One of the strongest arguments for whole life is that the cash value in the policy builds up tax-free, which substantially boosts the compounding power of your earnings. If you have maxed out on 401(k) plans, individual retirement accounts, and other tax-sheltered savings and investment plans, then cash-value insurance provides another option. It's entirely possible that a

You can borrow against the cash value of a whole-life policy without having to pay the money back.

Flexibility is a universal life policy's primary appeal. You can raise or lower the face amount with no need to rewrite the policy.

$250,000 policy bought at age 35 could accumulate a cash surrender value of $100,000 by the time you reach age 65—a nice addition to your retirement nest egg if you decide you don't need the insurance anymore.

Meanwhile, you can turn in your policy any time after the first several years and collect the cash value, no questions asked. The proceeds are tax-free to the extent that the cash value doesn't exceed the premiums you've paid. Or, as described above, you can borrow against the cash value and leave the policy in force, with no requirement that you pay the money back (although you will owe interest on the loan, and if you die with a loan outstanding, it will be deducted from the face amount paid to your beneficiaries). It's safe to say that cash-value life insurance has financed many a college education, even though there may have been better ways to do it (see Chapter 16).

Variations on Whole Life

The creativity of life insurance companies seems boundless, and they have managed to find ways to make whole-life policies increasingly attractive—and increasingly complex. The major variations are universal life and variable life.

Universal Life Insurance

Flexibility is universal's primary appeal. You can raise or lower the face amount with no need to rewrite the policy. You can, within limits, designate how much of your premium you want used for insurance and how much for investments. You can vary the premium payments. And, as with regular whole-life policies, you build up a cash value as the years go by.

Universal life offers yields on the cash-value portion that may be higher than those on basic whole-life policies. Guaranteed rates of return are disclosed in advance, and although they are generally low—4 percent or so—it's possible to earn considerably more, depending on the company's own investment results.

The company calculates its own rate of return for universal policies each year or ties it to some financial index, such as the Treasury-bill rate. You get annual reports showing the amount of insurance protection you've got, the cash value of the policy, costs of the insurance, company fees, the amounts credited to savings from premium payments, and the rates of return on the cash value.

PICKING THE BEST UNIVERSAL POLICY. Universal life is a complex form of insurance requiring special vigilance as you compare policies.

Compare the sales fees. They vary quite a lot and are imposed in different ways. There may be a lump-sum deduction of several hundred dollars from the first-year premiums, plus deductions from future premiums. You can reduce such loads by buying so-called low-load life insurance.

Find out how the rate of return is calculated and how long the initial rate is guaranteed. Check the projected cash value at the end of the first year and compare it with the first year's premium. Bear in mind that the advertised rates are paid on the money that's left after commissions, administrative expenses, and the cost of insurance are deducted. The ads often don't make that clear. Moreover, some companies have paid less than advertised rates until premiums reached a certain threshold, such as $1,000.

Size up the surrender charges. They can make canceling the policy especially expensive in its early years.

If a company sells more than one universal-life policy, compare them carefully. Many companies sell two generic types. In one the death benefit is limited to the policy's face amount until the cash value has built up considerably over a couple of decades or so, at which time the cash value begins to be added to the death benefit. In the other option, the cash value is added to the face amount right from the start and the death benefit rises gradually as the years go by. The latter policy will carry higher premiums.

Variable life lets you invest part of your cash value in stocks and other securities, through mutual funds run by the insurance company.

Variable-Life Insurance

Variable life lets you invest part of your cash value in stocks and other securities, through mutual funds run by the insurance company. With a variable-life policy, both the death benefit and the cash value depend on the performance of the investments you choose, which can go down as well as up. There is no guaranteed minimum interest rate for the cash value, as there is with a straight universal-life policy.

You decide how much of your net premium—that is, the amount left after commissions and other expenses are paid—will be invested in different areas: stocks, bonds, and short-term money-market instruments. (Policyholders' investment funds are segregated from the insurance company's general accounts so that they reflect the actual experience of the investments chosen.) Because you decide where your money is invested and bear the risk of those investments, variable life is considered a security and is the only kind of life insurance sold by prospectus.

NO GUARANTEED CASH VALUE. A minimum death benefit—the policy's face amount—is guaranteed, but your cash value is not. If your investments perform poorly over a long time, it's possible your policy could end up with a cash value smaller than what you would have achieved with a traditional whole-life policy. A poorly performing policy would represent an extremely expensive form of life insurance if you died after paying premiums for many years. On the other hand, good performance in the investment account could increase the death benefit above the guaranteed level or create a substantial cash value.

Details of variable-life policies are spelled out in their prospectuses, which you can get from the agent or the company. This is a complex product, so read the prospectus carefully. The first year's premium is largely consumed by one-time administrative costs and the agent's commission. Thus, it takes several years to accumulate significant cash values even if the investment portion of the policy does well. Also, a variable-life policy must be watched closely after you buy it. It will be up to you to change your investments to get the best return.

Variable Universal Life

This is essentially a variable-life policy with a wider range of investment options and the added flexibility of being able to raise or lower your premiums and direct as much as you wish into the investment account, where it grows tax-free until you take it out. You can pump thousands of dollars a year into a VUL policy, directing most of it to the investment account. If money gets tight, you can throttle back, even stop paying premiums entirely, if there's enough cash value in the policy to cover them.

Like universal life, VUL offers flexibility. Like variable life, it offers no guarantees. If your investments perform poorly, you take the hit, not the insurance company. As with whole-life products, a big chunk of your premium goes for a variety of fees and charges, especially in the first year. It may take a decade or more for the cash value to exceed the premiums you've paid. As life insurance, VUL is expensive; its main attraction lies in the tax-deferred buildup in the investment accounts.

You are a candidate for this kind of policy only if you meet the following conditions:

- **you need life insurance;**
- **you have a tolerance for investment risk;**
- **you are in a high tax bracket** and have maxed out on other tax-deferred investment opportunities such as 401(k)s and IRAs;
- **you can wait at least ten years** before you borrow from the policy (to give cash value time to build up); and
- **you plan to leave the policy in force** for the rest of your life.

If you don't meet all those tests, choose some other kind of life insurance.

Like universal life, variable universal life offers flexibility. Like variable life, it offers no guarantees. If your investments perform poorly, you take the hit.

Even if term would have been a better buy to begin with, the equation changes after the whole-life policy has been in force for a while.

The Itch to Switch

Suppose you've had a whole-life policy for a few years and are approached by a sales rep who says you'd be better off if you dropped it, switched to a term policy with lower premiums for the same coverage, and invested your savings in a good mutual fund. Cash value, he says, is trash value. Buy term and invest the difference. Should you listen? Maybe, but as attractive as the idea may sound, this decision is not a no-brainer. You need to take several "ifs" into account before you decide.

Even if term would have been a better buy to begin with, the equation changes after the whole-life policy has been in force for a while. The first year's premium was probably eaten up entirely by the agent's commission and the company's expenses, so you earned no cash value then. In the early years the value grows very slowly, reaching significant levels only after a decade or so. And if you abandon the policy too soon, you get smacked with surrender charges that take a chunk out of whatever cash value does exist.

In other words, you'd be bailing out after paying all those heavy expenses, just as the policy was about to start generating all that tax-sheltered income you signed up for in the first place.

As a rule of thumb, the earlier you dump a whole-life policy, the better your chance of coming out ahead by switching to term and investing the difference. If you have held the policy for ten or more years, odds are good that you'd be better off hanging on to it and supplementing it with term insurance if you need more coverage. Remember, you won't get your premiums back, and at some point you'll want to stick around to start profiting from them.

The Best Policy at the Best Price

The obvious way to compare costs of different life insurance policies is to compare the premiums charged by different companies for the same coverage. That works fine for term insurance, but not for whole life. Dividends, cash values, interest you could have earned elsewhere, and the number of years a policy is kept in force also play important roles in determining the actual cost. And it is nearly impossible to tell in advance how your premium is divided among insurance coverage, commissions, and company profits, how much goes into the cash-value fund, and how much interest you'll earn on the cash value. A handful of companies use something called the Barnes Standard as a way of disclosing policy costs to insurance pros and financial planners, but consumers are pretty much in the dark.

SHOP FROM HOME FOR LIFE INSURANCE

One of the most convenient ways to get comparative quotes on term insurance is to use one of the national quote services. They are, in effect, insurance agents, meaning they are paid commissions by the companies they represent. To improve your chances of finding the lowest premiums for the coverage you want, check with at least two national quote services and an independent agent before making your choice. The listings show toll-free numbers and, when they exist, addresses for Web sites.

TERM POLICIES

InstantQuote	www.instantquote.com	888-223-2220
MasterQuote	www.masterquote.com	800-337-5433
LifeRates of America	www.liferatesofamerica.com	800-457-2837
TermQuote	www.termquote.com	800-444-8376
Quotesmith	www.quotesmith.com	800-556-9393
QuickQuote	www.quickquote.com	800-867-2404
SelectQuote	www.selectquote.com	800-343-1985
ConsumerQuote USA	www.consumerquote.com	800-552-7283
InsuranceQuote Services	www.iquote.com	800-972-1104
Quicken InsureMarket	www.quicken.com/insurance	800-811-8766

CASH-VALUE POLICIES

In shopping for whole-life insurance, it's a good idea to check with financial planners and insurance agents. A few companies sell directly to the public or through fee-only planners.

Veritas	www.veritas.ameritas.com	800-745-6665
USAA	www.usaa.com	800-531-4440

The cost of whole-life insurance is all over the lot. Careful shopping can pay off big.

There is some help available, though. Any agent will gladly produce a "net cost" calculation for you. That adds up all your premiums over a period of 10 or 20 years, subtracts anticipated dividends and cash value, then subtracts that number from total premiums to produce a startlingly low net cost of coverage. But the net-cost method ignores the fact that you could have done something else with the money and perhaps earned even more than the policy paid you in dividends.

Insurance industry analysts have tried to incorporate this factor into newer formulas that produce a couple of esoteric numbers called interest-adjusted net-cost indexes. By adding a certain level of assumed earnings—say, 5 percent—to the cost of your premiums, these indexes account for the possibility that you might have chosen to invest the money at that rate.

The "interest-adjusted surrender cost" is a measure of the true anticipated cost of keeping a policy in force for 10 or 20 years and then surrendering it for its cash value. The "net payment cost index" assumes you hold on to the policy until you die. Most states require agents to provide these numbers for cash-value policies if you ask for them. Interest-adjusted costs vary according to the type of policy and your age at purchase. Armed with these numbers, you can compare the costs of different policies within the same company and among different companies. What you'll discover is that the cost of whole-life insurance is all over the lot. Careful shopping can pay off big.

Ask the agent for the 10- and 20-year interest-adjusted surrender costs per $1,000 of face amount for the specific policy being recommended. Ask also for comparable data for the same kinds of policies issued by two other companies. The agent doesn't have to furnish information on competitors' policies but should be able to obtain approximate figures for some companies from manuals widely used in the insurance business. If the agent won't or can't help, call other companies yourself.

Useful though they are, the interest-adjusted net-cost indexes are not an invariably accurate guide to what a policy will actually cost. They are based on the assumption that the cash values will earn a certain amount per year. When interest rates are higher or lower than that, the relationships between premiums and cash values are thrown out of whack, especially in the later years. But the distortions affect all policies, so you can still use the indexes as a relative measure of comparative policy costs over the years, provided the issue dates and death benefits are the same.

Second-to-Die Insurance

The idea behind second-to-die insurance is to make sure of having enough cash on hand to pay estate taxes. The estate of high-bracket couples can easily be eaten up by taxes when the second spouse dies (see Chapter 30). Second-to-die insurance provides the cash to pay estate taxes and thus protect the couple's ultimate heirs, probably their children.

Because the premiums are based on two life expectancies rather than one, second-to-die insurance should be a lot cheaper than a policy covering a single life, or two separate policies covering each life. But don't take that for granted. Price each of those combinations before buying this coverage.

How Safe Is the Insurance Company?

Imagine paying premiums on a policy for years and years, and then watching helplessly as the company goes broke before you can collect. Ever since two of the nation's largest insurers—Mutual Benefit Life and Executive Life—collapsed in the early 1990s (along with several smaller companies), it's been clear that no one should take an insurance company's health for granted. The professional rating agencies, whose job it is to judge the financial soundness of insurance companies and make the results public, missed the warning signs back then. They have attempted to toughen their standards and they remain, for better or worse, the

The idea behind second-to-die insurance is to make sure of having enough cash on hand to pay estate taxes.

Pension-fund investors look to rating companies for clues to insurer solvency.

best defense consumers have against being stung. Before you buy any policy, check the health of the issuing company by learning how it is graded by major rating agencies.

Making Sense of the Ratings

You can get insurance-company ratings in libraries, from agents, or directly from the rating agencies. They're easy to get, but not so easy to decipher. To illustrate: An A+ is the second highest grade from A.M. Best, but fifth from the top on Standard & Poor's and Fitch's scales. Moody's Investors Service's fifth-best rating is A1. Weiss Research, the newest entrant in the rating business, gives its top mark (A+) to very few companies, reflecting a definition of financial stability that differs from the other agencies. Even a B+ from Weiss is high praise, while a B+ from others should be a cause for concern. The raters also differ on what information they use to arrive at their ratings. With so many different ways of looking at things, be sure to check a rating with more than one company. This guide will help you make sense of the different systems.

A.M. BEST. Best has been rating insurers about half a century longer than anyone else. As with most raters, Best starts its analysis with the thick financial statements insurers file with state regulators, then conducts meetings with senior management. In these meetings, analysts are privy to confidential, nonpublic information about company operations.

The rating scale ranges from A++ (superior) through D (below minimum standards), with E and F ratings for companies that are under state supervision or in bankruptcy. Best publishes ratings only with the insurer's permission and will withhold a low rating on request. Take that into account if you come across a company that isn't rated by Best.

Best's annual compilation of ratings and commentary, *Best's Insurance Reports,* is available in many libraries. Or you can check Best's Web site at http://www.ambest.com.

STANDARD & POOR'S, MOODY'S, AND FITCH. These are the companies that pension-fund investors look to for clues to insurer solvency. All three built their reputations on rating bonds and in the 1980s began rating insurers' ability to pay claims, too. The rating scales start with AAA at the top (Aaa in Moody's case), then step down to double As, single As, triple Bs (or Baa), and so on. S&P and Fitch use pluses and minuses within each category after AAA; Moody's uses 1s, 2s, and 3s (an Aa1 rating from Moody's, for instance, is equivalent to an AA+ from the other two). On all three scales, ratings below BBB– (Baa3 for Moody's) are considered below investment grade, or "vulnerable" to adverse economic or underwriting conditions.

You can get individual ratings of claims-paying ability (AAA through D) at no cost from S&P's ratings desk at 212-438-2400 or search online (http://www.standardandpoors.com). Moody's (212-553-0377; http://www.moodys.com) and Fitch (800-853-4824, ext. 199; http://www.fitchibca.com) also give out single ratings over the phone and are searchable online at no cost.

WEISS RESEARCH. Martin Weiss includes in his statistical analysis a measure of how well insurers would fare, given their financial position today, in "average" and "severe" recessions. So a company with a lot of liquidity and low-risk securities would be rated higher than a company that would have to drop a weak product line or upgrade the quality of assets to address a financial crisis. Weiss doesn't meet with company officers and doesn't factor in a subjective judgment on the quality of management.

The Weiss ratings look like a typical academic bell curve. Only a relative handful earn As or Bs, reflecting good financial health. Many more fall into the C (average/fair) range. (Unlike the same grade from other raters, a C from Weiss is not all that terrible.) The bottom-rated companies get a D (weak), E (very weak), or F (failed). The companies that get a B+ or better earn a spot on Weiss's list of companies that are recommended for safety.

To find companies in good health today, limit yourself to insurers that rate an A++ or A+ from Best, a B or above from Weiss, or at least an AA from S&P, Moody's, or Duff & Phelps.

Weiss's Web site (http://www.weissratings.com) offers a free list of the strongest and weakest insurers in various categories. You can purchase an individual rating online for $14.99 or by phone (800-289-9222) for $19, charged to your credit card. A one-page report on a company costs $27. You may get more information at the company's Web site.

When Should You Worry?

No high rating will ensure safety for years down the road. But to find companies in good health today, limit yourself to insurers that rate an A++ or A+ from Best, a B or above from Weiss, or at least an AA from S&P, Moody's, or Duff & Phelps. That leaves you plenty of competitive policies to choose from. If you already hold a policy or annuity, it's a good idea to check at least two of the ratings annually.

Making Sure the Right People Collect

Most people don't run into beneficiary difficulties with their life insurance, perhaps because their lives generally follow the anticipated course. A husband designates his wife as beneficiary; he dies; she receives the money as he intended. However, you can't be sure that even well-conceived beneficiary arrangements won't be upset by later events. To avoid problems, get familiar with these essential points.

Naming Beneficiaries

A policy owner can name anyone he or she chooses as beneficiary—relative, friend, business associate, charity. You can also change beneficiaries unless you have previously named someone as the irrevocable beneficiary. In that case you must obtain the beneficiary's permission. Irrevocable designations result most often from divorce and separation settlements. Beneficiaries can be changed merely by filling out a company form and sending it to the company.

If you die without having recorded a living beneficiary with the company, the proceeds will be paid into your estate or sometimes to surviving children, depending on the terms of the policy.

DESIGNATING YOUR BENEFICIARIES. The normal procedure is to name a primary beneficiary and a secondary, or contingent, beneficiary in case the primary should die before you do. You can even select a third beneficiary to receive the money in the event neither the primary nor secondary beneficiary survives you.

If you name two or more beneficiaries of equal rank, the funds will be divided equally unless you provide otherwise. Two primary beneficiaries, for example, would receive 50 percent each.

LEAVING IT TO YOUR SPOUSE. To avoid confusion, a wife or husband should be identified by his or her given name. Mrs. John Nelson, for example, should be described as "Mrs. Jane Nelson" or "Jane Nelson, wife of the insured." For further specification, her premarital surname could be added—for example, "Mrs. Jane Smith Nelson." If a woman has kept her premarital surname, then of course the policy should use it.

LEAVING IT TO THE KIDS. "My children" or "children of the insured" or some similar collective designation usually suffices because it usually covers all present and future children, including adopted children. However, a broad description might have to be modified to cope with a specific situation, such as stepchildren.

LEAVING IT TO A MINOR. When you name a child as beneficiary, legal problems may arise if the proceeds of your insurance have to be paid while he or she is still a minor. To protect itself against future claims, the insurance company will want a valid receipt for payments, and a minor may not be considered legally qualified for that purpose. State laws vary considerably, but in some cases the court may decide to appoint a guardian to receive and take care of the funds.

The normal procedure is to name a primary beneficiary and a secondary, or contingent, beneficiary in case the primary should die before you do.

You can move life insurance out of your estate by making the beneficiary the owner of the policy. That means you give up the right to the cash value and the right to change the beneficiary.

To avoid those difficulties, you can appoint a trustee to accept the insurance money and administer it for the child's benefit while he or she is a minor. The trustee could be directed in the trust agreement to pay the child any funds remaining at the time the child reaches his or her majority. You can also appoint a successor trustee to take over if the first becomes unable to serve.

Working the Tax Angles

The beneficiary of a life insurance policy gets three big tax breaks:

- **No income tax** has to be paid on the money.
- **The funds don't have to go through** the often time-consuming and possibly expensive probate procedures required for assets that are transferred by a will.
- **The state may exempt** part or all of the money from its estate tax or inheritance tax.

Life insurance proceeds may not be completely tax-free because the money is included in the estate of the policy owner when federal estate taxes are figured. But it's possible to move life insurance out of your estate by making the beneficiary of the policy the owner of the policy. That means you give up the right to the cash value and the right to change the beneficiary. You could also transfer ownership of the policy to an irrevocable living trust, whose terms normally can't be changed (see Chapter 30).

By taking either of these steps, you in effect make a gift of the insurance to someone else and may have to pay a gift tax. If you think you need estate-tax planning, don't try doing it on your own with ready-made forms. See Chapter 30, and consult an experienced estate-planning lawyer.

Picking the Payoff Method

Life insurance proceeds are usually paid out in a lump sum. But insurance companies also offer several alternative arrangements. As a policy owner, you can select one of these settlement options for your beneficiary. If you make no choice, the beneficiary can elect one within a certain period after your death. These are the options commonly available:

INTEREST ONLY. The funds are left on deposit with the insurance company, which guarantees a minimum rate of interest but normally pays more. Interest is paid to the beneficiary, who can be given the right to withdraw principal as desired.

INSTALLMENTS FOR A FIXED PERIOD. The proceeds are paid out in equal amounts for as long as the money lasts. Again, the company usually adds extra interest to its guaranteed rate.

LIFE INCOME. The beneficiary is guaranteed a lifetime income based on his or her age and on the amount of the proceeds. The company may allow the beneficiary to use the proceeds to buy one of its regular annuities at a discount.

Which should you choose? Consider installment and annuity plans if you're protecting a beneficiary who doesn't have the experience to manage a large sum. But be aware that a beneficiary can often invest the money safely at a better rate than the insurance company offers. In most cases, you should leave the choice of a settlement option to the beneficiary.

> In most cases, you should leave the choice of a settlement option to the beneficiary.

Mass-Market Life Insurance

You can hardly turn on the television or open the mail without discovering that, by virtue of some sort of affiliation or another, you're eligible for a special deal on life insurance. You may have a credit card or a mortgage or an alma mater or a profession that puts you in the select group eligible for the special rates.

In theory, buying insurance this way should save you money by cutting out the middleman—the life insurance agent who must be paid a commission for the work done on your policy. Sometimes insurance sold through the mail is indeed cheaper. But mail-order or TV-sold policies don't necessarily deliver on the promise, and in fact very often they don't.

Some mail-order policies are sold to professional, fraternal, and trade associations, which may use sales commissions from their insurance programs to raise funds for the organization instead of passing on lower premiums to their members.

A large number of mass-marketed plans are offered by brokerage firms that specialize in mail-order sales of life, health, and other types of insurance. If you buy directly from such a company, you get an individual policy, just as you would if you bought one from an agent.

If the insurance comes through an association or other sponsoring group, your coverage is governed by the seller's master contract with the insurer or the broker. That distinction has two very important ramifications for the buyer.

First, individual policy rates are guaranteed; association and group-plan rates are not. All term policies are renewed periodically, and rates are stepped up in line with the policyholder's age. Renewal premiums for individual policies can't be increased any faster than that. With association plans the insurer reserves the right to raise the rates beyond those normal increases. Your premium might never be increased, but you can't be sure of it.

Second, if the individual policy is automatically renewable each year, as most are, you can keep the insurance in force up to the ultimate termination age simply by paying the premiums. With association and group plans the insurance normally stops if you leave the group, and the coverage can be maintained only by converting the term policy into a higher-premium cash-value policy.

Mail versus Regular Rates

The bigger question is this: Do the claimed economies of selling by mail or TV or the Internet actually produce savings for the buyer?

CASH-VALUE QUESTIONS

Q: *My wife and I have four cash-value policies that we bought in the early 1990s. We're thinking about dropping them because monthly premiums total more than $100 and we don't want the expense. What are the tax consequences of cashing out the policies?*

A: You owe income tax on the amount you receive that exceeds the total you paid in premiums over the years. In your case, you may be off the hook entirely, because after ten years there's a good chance you've paid more in premiums than you've earned in cash value.

Q: *I've been using my life insurance dividends to buy additional paid-up insurance. Is this a smart move?*

A: Yes, if you need the insurance and can't get it cheaper elsewhere. There's no medical exam and you don't pay any commissions. But consider your other options: You could use part of your dividends to pay current premiums, take the rest in cash, and buy term insurance to meet your additional needs; or you could use part of the dividends to pay premiums on your current coverage and let the rest accumulate as cash value. Later, if you need the cash, you can borrow it from your policy or cash in the policy.

Sometimes. By calling the quote services listed in the box on page 279, you can get a wide array of policies to compare with each other and with agent-sold policies. But it would be virtually impossible to compare them all. You can get some clues about the competitiveness of the rates by the company's attitude toward the medical qualifications of its applicants.

Medical Qualifications

The application form for a policy often asks questions that the company uses to evaluate your acceptability. Your replies will probably be cross-checked against data that may be on file with the Medical Information Bureau, through which companies swap information. You may be asked to have a medical examination at the company's expense.

However, some plans are sold without any medical conditions: You are guaranteed acceptance if you pay the premium. To avoid being swamped by applicants who are dying or otherwise present high risks, the insurers may employ one or all of several safeguards:

■ **The full face value isn't paid for** deaths that occur during the first two years the policy is in force, maybe longer.

■ **The premium is set considerably above** rates for medically screened plans sold through agents.

■ **The policy is offered only** during limited enrollment periods.

■ **Only a modest amount** of insurance is available.

Mail-order insurance companies set premium rates on the basis of sales costs as well as actuarial considerations. Only 1 to 2 percent of the people solicited by mail actually buy the insurance, and that is often regarded as a good return. Therefore, the rates have to take into account the costs of mailing to the other 99 or 98 percent who fail to respond to the first solicitation. Association plans may produce a higher response because of the sponsor's endorsement, but the insurer has to figure in fees to brokers and others involved in the deal. The same sort of situation applies to policies marketed by television: TV time is expensive, and the company may be sharing part of the revenue from each order with the television stations on which it advertises.

Plans that require no medical qualifications will be priced to cover the inevitable poor risks the companies assume, so there's no point in buying that kind of policy unless you have a condition that would make a medically screened policy prohibitively expensive. Try first to obtain regular insurance, either by mail or through agents, at standard premiums.

Buying Health Insurance

Deciding whether to buy health insurance is a no-brainer. Think of what would happen if you didn't have insurance and someone in your family suffered a serious illness requiring extended medication or a long hospital stay. How quickly would snowballing medical bills wipe you out?

Conclusion: You should have as much health insurance as you can reasonably afford. That's a clear and simple enough rule. Unfortunately, nothing else about health insurance is either clear or simple. Your choices are more complex than ever. Rising costs and the efforts to control them are affecting your options almost daily. On top of that, employees are being asked to pay for a bigger portion of their companies' health insurance premiums, and insurers are trying to steer you to doctors and hospitals who have agreed to hold down costs, thus restricting your choice of health care providers. What to do? The smart thing to do is to learn about each kind of coverage you'll encounter because you'll probably have to choose among them, and the choice you make can have a major impact on your finances. (Most of the following discussion refers to group coverage. For help if you're on your own, see the box on page 295.)

Fee-for-Service: Health Coverage the Old-Fashioned Way

Under fee-for-service, which is the kind of coverage your parents remember, you choose the doctor or the hospital or the clinic, and the in-

Comprehensive major medical is a policy that combines basic and major-medical insurance in one plan so that there are few gaps in coverage.

surance pays for part or all of the cost according to a schedule laid out in the policy. The "Blues"—Blue Cross and Blue Shield—are the best-known providers of this kind of health insurance, although not the only ones. It may be offered at group rates through an employer or an affinity group such as a trade association, or it may be offered at individual rates. Either way, it is the most expensive kind of health insurance around.

Fee-for-service policies are usually divided into two parts: The cost of visits to the doctor, hospitalization, surgery, and other medical expenses are often referred to in policies as basic benefits. When that runs out, the major-medical part of the policy takes over.

Just the Basics

MEDICAL. This covers you for doctors' visits in and out of the hospital. In addition, some plans cover such services as diagnostic tests and various laboratory procedures. Some exclude physician coverage for routine physicals and well-baby care, and pay only if the doctor diagnoses an illness.

HOSPITALIZATION. This will cover you for daily room and board and regular nursing services while in the hospital. You'll also be covered for certain hospital services and supplies, such as X rays, lab tests, and drugs.

SURGICAL. This coverage pays for specified surgical procedures in or out of the hospital.

When Major Medical Kicks In

At some point, your basic coverage hits the policy ceiling and stops. Major medical provides backup coverage that picks up where basic leaves off. It pays the bulk of the bills in case of a lingering illness or serious injury, often protecting you against huge medical bills that climb to $250,000 or more. Million-dollar limits on major-medical policies aren't uncommon these days.

Comprehensive major medical is a policy that combines basic and major-medical insurance in one plan so that there are few gaps in coverage. Increasingly, both employer-sponsored and individual plans combine coverage into comprehensive policies.

Different Ways Policies Pay

Having the right kinds of protection doesn't necessarily mean that you are well covered. Most every policy, no matter how good it is, limits the benefits it will pay. The trick is to make sure the benefit limits you choose keep pace with the ever-rising cost of medical care. There are two basic types of benefit payout methods:

USUAL, CUSTOMARY, AND REASONABLE. The plan will probably limit coverage to "medically necessary" treatments and to "usual, customary, and reasonable" (UCR) fees for that treatment in your area, as determined by the insurance company. Some services may be fully covered within these guidelines, others only partially covered. For example, 100 percent of your hospital bills may be paid but only 75 percent of your medical and surgical costs. And should your doctor's fee be above the usual range for your area, you'll have to make up the difference. Benefits may be paid directly to the doctor or hospital, but in the case of routine visits, you may have to pay up front and file paperwork for reimbursement. Often, the doctor's office will do the filing for you.

PREDETERMINED COSTS, WITH LIMITS. An indemnity, or scheduled, type of policy pays specific dollar amounts for each covered service according to a predetermined schedule or table of benefits. These schedules tend to become out-of-date even before the ink is dry on the policy. That means you could wind up digging deeper into your pocket to make up the difference between what the insurance company pays and what the doctor or hospital charges. Perhaps for this reason, this kind of policy is less common than it used to be.

What's Covered?

With either type of policy you can't be sure that you're adequately insured unless you know exactly what's

> Most every policy, no matter how good it is, limits the benefits it will pay. The trick is to make sure the benefit limits you choose keep pace with the ever-rising cost of medical care.

covered, and that may not be completely clear to you. Some health insurance companies are trying to use plain language in their policies, but as you read through yours, you may wish the company would spell out exactly what a term means. For instance:

What does coverage for a preexisting condition really mean? Are you covered for a preexisting condition you didn't know about when you took out the policy, or just for known conditions that the insurance company agrees to accept? How long after a policy is in force will the insurance finally kick in for a preexisting condition? Under the Health Insurance Portability and Accountability Act of 1996 (HIPAA), you can't be denied coverage for preexisting conditions if you are moving from one group plan to another or from a group plan to individual coverage. The law protects you if you have been in a group plan for at least 12 months continuously (defined as a break of no more than 63 days) and have exhausted any coverage you have had through COBRA, the federal law that lets you extend employer-provided coverage for up to 18 months after you leave the job. Some state laws extend HIPAA coverage to people moving from one individual policy to another.

How broadly does a company interpret such terms as "not medically necessary" and "not reasonable and customary"? You can get an idea of the restrictions by reviewing the policies or the brochures provided by your employer or the insurance agent.

Deductibles, Copayments, and Limitations

Conceivably, you could buy health insurance to cover the expense of bandaging a cut thumb. But who needs that kind of insurance? You can pay those bills yourself. Insuring such minor medical care, even routine visits to your doctor, is what makes your health insurance more expensive.

Catastrophic accidents or illnesses are something else. You want insurance because you couldn't afford to pay for them yourself. And naturally you want the pro-

FINDING A POLICY WHEN YOU'RE ON YOUR OWN

Most health insurance is provided by employers, who pay the premiums themselves or pass along the benefit of group rates to their employees. But if you're on your own, finding affordable care gets tougher.

Find out whether you're eligible for a group plan through membership in a club, professional or fraternal society, or other organization. If you are not, consider joining some group that offers a group plan.

Look into interim insurance plans for people who don't qualify for group coverage but expect to in the near future. New college graduates often find themselves in this situation. Such stopgap policies are offered for 60, 90, or 180 days. Contact insurance agents to see what's available. A couple of companies that offer such coverage are Assurant Health (800-553-7654; http://www.assuranthealth.com) and Golden Rule (800-444-8990; http://www.goldenrule.com). The premium will vary according to the coverage, where you live, and the size of your family. It could be several hundred dollars per month for family coverage.

Look into health savings accounts. HSAs, which are described on pages 306-307, permit individuals and families to pay for medical insurance with tax-deductible dollars and accumulate in a tax-sheltered account money that can be used to pay the deductible on the policy.

To control costs, investigate the trade-offs between the deductible and the copayment. If you're in good health, you're generally better off with a policy that has a high deductible and put premium savings into an HSA. Depending on the details of the insurance policy, those in poor health or without excess cash flow will probably be no worse off if they choose an HSA option, although they may end up spending all the money in their account each year.

Don't overlook COBRA coverage if you are leaving a job that provided employer-sponsored insurance. COBRA is described in the box on page 301.

tection to be as cheap as possible because the cheaper the protection is, the more of it you can afford. That's why health insurance is sold with a system of deductibles and copayments.

DEALING WITH DEDUCTIBLES AND COPAYMENTS. A deductible is the amount you pay—say, $1,000 a year—before the insurance company makes any payments at all. The copayment, also called coinsurance, is the share of the bill you pay above the deductible, with the insurance company paying the rest, up to the policy limits.

Deductibles can vary within a policy, with certain services having higher deductibles than others.

Say you incur a $6,500 hospital bill. Your policy has a $500 deductible and a 20 percent copayment on bills up to $2,500. Your out-of-pocket cost would be $1,000—the $500 deductible (assuming you hadn't already met it), plus 20 percent of $2,500, or another $500. The insurance company would pay $5,500.

The higher your deductibles and coinsurance, the lower your premium. Deductibles can vary within a policy, with certain services having higher deductibles than others. Deductibles that apply to the family as a whole are usually preferable to individual deductibles for each family member. With the former, once one or two members have met the deductible, any illness or injury striking other family members is covered immediately. In an employer-sponsored group policy, you may not have a choice.

Court cases in recent years have put the spotlight on cases in which policyholders have been forced to pay their share of medical bills based on the full price of the treatment, while the insurance company paid its share based on a privately negotiated reduced rate. Say you have an insurance policy that requires you to pay 20 percent of your medical bills. You have a medical procedure that costs $1,000 and you pay $200 (your 20 percent share). You assume that the insurer has paid the remaining $800. But your insurer has privately negotiated a deal with the hospital that reduces the cost of the procedure to $800, so the company pays only $600. Your 20 percent copayment just turned into a 25 percent copayment.

If you suspect that this is going on, ask both the insurer and the doctor or hospital to tell you the negotiated rate, then figure your share from that figure. Send that amount to the provider with a letter explaining that you are paying your portion of the "actual" fee, and send a copy of the letter to your insurer. If the insurer balks, file a complaint with your state's insurance department.

DEALING WITH POLICY LIMITATIONS. Various limits and exclusions are written into every policy. For instance, there may be a limit to how many days you can stay in the hospital for a particular treatment and still be covered. There is a limit to how long you can take to meet the deductible and reach the point at which the insurance begins to pay. If you don't reach that point within a stated time, often a year, you have to start counting all over again.

Most policies put a ceiling on the total amount they will pay for a single claim, or during a single year, or during your lifetime. For family coverage, an annual limit of $500,000 or $1 million is worth a few more dollars a month in premiums than a policy with a $100,000 limit.

Many plans also dictate the hospitals or doctors you can go to or require you to pay more for visiting a provider not under contract with the policy. That's what's called managed care, and it is described a little later in this chapter.

You are not covered for care in military or other government hospitals or for illnesses and accidents covered by workers' compensation.

Keeping the Policy in Force

A group plan will renew automatically as long as your employer pays the premium and the insurance company chooses to keep the policy in force, but you have to be careful about the renewability terms of an individual policy. Some companies retain the right to terminate your coverage when your policy period is over—as they might, for instance, if you have a lot of expensive claims. Your best bet is a noncancelable type of health policy that will cover you at the same premium and benefit level up to a certain age—say, 65—as long as you pay the premiums.

Your next-best bet is a guaranteed-renewable policy. It's like a noncancelable policy in that the company can't refuse to cover you as long as you pay your premiums and no acts of fraud are involved. But it differs in that premiums can be raised if the entire class to which you belong—meaning your occupation, age group, or gender—gets a premium increase.

Your policy might limit how long you can stay in the hospital for some treatments.

If you have PPO coverage, you agree to use providers your insurer and employer have contracted with at discount rates.

Protection against Catastrophic Costs

The copayment terms of major-medical plans are typically 80/20 or 75/25. That means that the company pays 80 or 75 percent of the cost of a claim and the policyholder pays 20 or 25 percent of costs above the deductible. Deductibles typically range from $200 to $4,500, or even more.

As health care costs spiral upward, so do those out-of-pocket expenses. Once, if insurance covered 80 percent of your costs, that seemed adequate, but today it's very easy to run up a $100,000 hospital bill. With 80 percent coverage you'd have to pay $20,000.

To protect against such bills, your policy should have stop-loss protection. No matter how high the bills run up, or for how long, you pay no more than the stipulated amount in any year.

Here's how one such plan might work: After the policyholder pays a $400 deductible, the insurance company pays 80 percent of the first $5,000 of covered expenses during a five-year benefit period. The company pays 100 percent of any additional expenses, up to $1 million. Thus the policyholder's obligation would be capped at $1,400—the $400 deductible plus 20 percent of $5,000—unless the total exceeds $1 million.

Insurers offer various choices of stop-loss limits. As with deductibles, the higher the limit, the lower the premiums.

Managed Care #1: Preferred Provider Organizations

As long ago as the 1970s, preferred-provider organizations began changing the rules of fee-for-service care. PPOs steer employees to cooperating doctors and hospitals that have agreed to a predetermined plan for keeping costs down.

For your part, if you have PPO coverage, you agree to use providers that your insurer and employer have contracted with at discount rates. You can usually use any doctor you want, even one who isn't a member of the PPO, but you'll pay the difference between the nonmember's bill and the PPO's discounted rate. Even if your nonmember doctor accepts the PPO rate, your plan may make you pay extra simply because he or she is not a member of the plan.

Because a PPO usually eliminates or reduces deductibles and coinsurance, joining could save you money if you stay with its list of approved providers. But a PPO could complicate a decision to use a specialist or facilities outside your home area. Check any such deals to make sure you're covered without a penalty if you get sick or injured in another town.

Managed Care #2: Health Maintenance Organizations

Health maintenance organizations are booming, partly because the government has encouraged their growth. By law, if you work for a company with 25 or more employees that has a health plan and the company is approached by a qualified HMO, the company must not only offer the prepaid HMO but also kick in at least as much of the premium as it would for an alternative insurance plan.

How They Work

With traditional fee-for-service medicine, as we have seen earlier, you go to your doctor when you believe you have a problem. He or she may decide that you should see one or more specialists or go to a lab or the hospital for special tests. You set up appointments in various locations and fill out insurance forms so that you can be reimbursed for your payments.

In contrast, at an HMO you pay in advance for your care. The HMO handles just about all your medical and hospital needs, but without the blizzard of paperwork and with hardly any deductibles or copayments. The idea is to make services easily available,

An HMO handles just about all your medical and hospital needs, but without the blizzard of paperwork and with hardly any deductibles or copayments.

often in a clinic-like setting, and to encourage you to come in soon enough to prevent a minor condition from becoming serious.

Not All HMOs Are Alike

Beyond that general description, HMOs differ in the way they are organized and how they deliver services and pay doctors. In one type, doctors are paid a salary regardless of how many patients they see or treatments they prescribe. Because there is no incentive to give unnecessary service, the reasoning goes, the organization incurs fewer costs and patients' premiums can be held down.

When comprehensive services are provided in this fashion and given under one roof, the HMO is called a staff model or group practice plan. Care is provided by a primary-care physician or a nurse practitioner who hears your medical complaints first and then decides whether you should see a specialist or be hospitalized.

In another type of HMO, called an individual practice association (IPA), doctors earn a fee based on services rendered, usually in their own offices, or a monthly fee per HMO patient, regardless of whether the patient is seen or not (called "capitation"). The prepaid premium does away with bills and insurance forms, just as in a regular HMO, but because care is usually not centralized, you and your doctor still have the obligation of locating medical facilities as they are needed. Still, as with a traditional HMO, the amount you pay should not depend on the level of services you use.

IPA physicians are paid from premium income, and usually receive less than their standard fee. The difference goes to cover the plan's expenses. If sufficient economies are realized, the cash pool or parts of it may be distributed to participating doctors. If the plan runs short of cash, payments to physicians may be reduced so that members don't have to make up the deficit with higher premiums.

A third type, called an open-ended HMO, is a hybrid. This type extends conventional fee-for-service coverage to members. Enrollees get all the benefits of

WHEN COBRA KICKS IN TO PROTECT YOU

If you leave a job that provided health insurance and aren't soon to be covered under new employment, you may have the right to continue your coverage for 18 months or more (29 months if you're disabled) under a federal law called COBRA (the letters stand for Consolidated Omnibus Budget Reconciliation Act, the 1986 law that created the protection). You don't qualify for COBRA if your company has fewer than 20 employees, or if you work for a church or the government of a U.S. territory or the District of Columbia. Federal employees are covered by different rules, and some states provide protection for people to whom COBRA doesn't apply. If you do qualify, you must pay the employer's premium, plus a 2% administrative fee. COBRA can help if you get bumped from a group health insurance plan under the following circumstances:

You lose or leave your job for reasons other than gross misconduct, or your hours are cut so that you no longer qualify for coverage under the employer's plan.

You and your dependents are covered under your spouse's group plan and your spouse dies or becomes eligible for Medicare, or you get divorced. This coverage lasts 36 months.

You are too old to continue coverage under a parent's group plan. Under COBRA, you can get 36 months of coverage.

Your spouse and dependents have group coverage as part of your retirement package and your employer files for Chapter 11 bankruptcy protection. As long as your employer stays in business, you can continue coverage until you die or find another policy. If you die, your spouse and dependents can continue COBRA coverage for up to 36 months.

Your new policy has a waiting period for coverage. You can continue coverage under your old policy until the waiting period is past.

---

prepaid care but also have the option of going outside the plan to see another physician, typically under another insurer, and paying for the privilege in copayments.

Reasons to Join an HMO

If you have the option of joining an HMO, don't worry that you might have to deal with just any doctor who happens to be on duty when you have a medical problem. The choice of doctors is limited to those on staff or under contract, but you or members of your family will usually have a choice of which doctor you see first when you have a medical complaint. However, in many

In a well-run HMO you are encouraged to come in for periodic checkups and to make appointments when needed.

instances, patients see a nurse practitioner first. The nurse prescribes treatment or refers you to one of the staff specialists; your doctor will hospitalize you when necessary, using one of the hospitals associated with the group. You may have to accept a stand-in in an emergency or if your own doctor is off duty, but that happens in fee-for-service plans, too.

In a well-run HMO you are encouraged to come in for periodic checkups and to make appointments whenever justified. Most plans cover routine visits, checkups, major illnesses requiring hospitalization, anesthesia, lab work, X rays, children's immunizations, and physician and surgeon services. But details vary among plans.

Because of the economies achieved in HMOs through preventive medicine and cost control, there is additional cash, at least in some of them, to expand preventive and support services. These include courses in prenatal care, physical fitness, weight control, and smoking cessation. Some groups provide guidance in reducing the risk of chronic ailments or controlling such disorders as high blood pressure and diabetes.

Studies indicate that HMO members' health care bills are lower than average and that members tend to go to the hospital less and lose less time from work than patients under traditional care. But it's not clear whether the difference is because of wiser planning or because HMOs tend to attract people who are healthier to begin with.

Reasons to Hesitate

HMOs are not to everyone's liking. If your employer offers the option, listen to the explanation, read the information, and think about whether joining would be a good idea. Pinning down the benefits you can count on is important, but you should also find out when you can get back into your company's conventional insurance program without loss of coverage if you become disenchanted. Most plans offer an open enrollment period once a year.

Even though some HMOs are responding with more flexible plans, choosing among the ones available still requires your careful consideration. Here are some tips:

Know what you're giving up. To some people, the main drawback of an HMO is having to give up their present doctor, along with easy access to specialists and hospitals outside the plan, then having to pick a new one from the HMO's list. That may sound like a fair trade-off for lower costs, if you understand the rules from the start. But a lot of people don't. Although HMOs reimburse for emergency care out of town, outpatient nonemergency care outside the plan's geographical area may not be covered. If the plan has no reciprocal arrangement and you travel a lot, consider other health care plans.

Some HMOs assign nurse practitioners and medical aides to deal with routine complaints. That could make you uncomfortable if you prefer to have a physician handle your medical concerns. To keep costs under control, most HMOs require you to see doctors within the plan unless some special care is unavailable or your HMO doctor can make a referral. If you want a second opinion, you'll probably have to pay for the privilege yourself.

Consider your medical needs. The makeup of your family and the extent to which an HMO covers services that are important to you are key considerations. A family with two children needing vaccinations and care for common childhood illnesses and a mother requiring obstetrical and gynecological checkups might find an HMO worthwhile. But a couple in their 20s with no kids could find that a simple indemnity plan is better for them. Someone else who expects extended psychiatric treatment might think twice about an HMO; they generally limit mental-health therapy to 10 to 20 visits per year and only if the HMO approves it.

Consider convenience. Most HMOs tend to be concentrated in metropolitan areas. Be sure the HMO you're

The makeup of your family and the extent to which an HMO covers services that are important to you are key considerations in selecting an HMO.

HOW TO CHECK UP ON YOUR HEALTH PLAN

It's never been easy to shop for an HMO. Many of them release information selectively and standardized "report cards" are still in the development stages. But the number of quality-of-care resources is increasing. Check out the following:

Best's Insurance Reports. A.M. Best Co., which has been evaluating the financial soundness of insurance companies for more than 100 years, began rating HMOs in the 1990s. In evaluating financial strength and the ability of HMOs to meet ongoing obligations to their members, Best also looks at key consumer issues, such as how an HMO approaches preventive care and what credentials it requires of participating physicians. Best assesses how an HMO balances services against costs—reviewing, for instance, how often doctors see patients and how many

days members stay in the hospital. It also considers how many new members are signing on and how many old ones are leaving—an indication of how satisfied you might be with the plan. (You can access ratings for HMOs at Best's Web site, www.ambest.com. Ratings are free and detailed reports cost $75.

Consumer's Guide to Health Plans for Federal Employees. The Center for the Study of Services, a nonprofit consumer group in Washington, D.C., rates every health insurance plan available to federal employees in the U.S., both fee-for-service plans and HMOs, for quality and access to care (202-347-7283; www.checkbook.org; $10.40).

Joint Commission on Accreditation of Healthcare Organizations. This

thinking of joining is within a reasonable distance of your home or office.

Size up the quality of care. Look for HMOs with open houses and tour them, noting the condition of facilities. If it's an IPA-type (page 300), set up a get-acquainted meeting with one or more of the primary-care physicians. Find out whether physicians tend to stay in the plan, and ask the HMO for biographies listing doctors' specialties and credentials. Most doctors with active practices are certified in their specialties by national boards. There is no reason to expect less in an HMO.

Check out the plan's reputation. Ask the HMO for the names of members who can tell you how it rates with them. Be wary of any that refuse. Also ask for financial

nonprofit group prepares accreditation and performance reports on 18,000 health plans, hospitals, and other health care organizations nationwide (630-792-5800; www.jcaho.org; free).

National Committee for Quality Assurance (NCQA). This nonprofit group evaluates health plan quality through accreditation reviews and standardized measures of health plan performance. Its HEDIS (Health Plan Employer Data Information Set) is the basis for many plans' "report cards." NCQA has reviewed about half of the country's HMOs. You can view its ratings online at www.ncqa.org or www.healthchoices.org.

SEARCHING FOR A NEW DOCTOR?

Ask your employer or insurance company for educational and professional information about doctors you're considering. You can also search for a doctor online, at several sites:

■ **AIM DocFinder**
(www.docboard.org). The National Association of State Medical and Osteopathic Board Executive Directors has a database that includes doctors in 20 states.

■ **AMA Physician Select**
(www.ama-assn.org). The American Medical Association's database on more than 690,000 doctors lets you search by specialty and location in all 50 states.

■ **Health Pages magazine**
(www.thehealthpages.com). This Web site lets you search for information about physicians, dentists, and managed-care health plans in your city or county.

statements, which are an indicator of the organization's fiscal health.

Assess the plan's costs. HMO members must pay some out-of-pocket costs, which average hundreds of dollars a year.

The A.M. Best Company, which is well known for its ratings of insurance companies, also rates the financial stability of HMOs. Check your library for a copy of *Best's Managed Care Reports—HMO* for evaluations of some of the nation's HMO providers, or search the Web site at http://www.ambest.com.

Managed care is everywhere. PPOs, HMOs, and regular fee-for-service plans are often mixed together by employers as part of a "managed care" system designed to help control rising health insurance costs.

With a flexible spending account, you pay medical expenses from pretax income, reducing those expenses by the same percentage as your top tax bracket.

Details differ, but the layers of complexity that managed care adds to your health insurance choices makes it especially important to read the literature you're given, ask questions about anything you don't understand, and apply the guidance in this chapter before making your decisions. Unfortunately, there are no shortcuts.

Flexible Spending Accounts

Flexible spending accounts (FSAs) are set up by an employer and allow you to divert part of your salary each year into the accounts, and use it to pay for qualified medical or dependent-care expenses. The main advantage of such plans is that you wind up paying expenses such as policy premiums, deductibles, copayments, and qualified out-of-pocket expenses from pretax income. This has the effect of reducing those expenses by the same percentage as your top federal tax bracket, plus your state tax levy.

There is a catch: This is a use-it-or-lose-it proposition. You forfeit any money in the reimbursement account that remains unspent at the end of the year. (A modification gives a company the option of offering its employees a grace period of two and a half months in which they can use up the money in the account.) This means that you should estimate carefully at the beginning of the year and err on the conservative side.

Health Savings Accounts

Because insurance costs are so high, it makes sense for healthy individuals and families to go with a high deductible health insurance policy and stash the premium savings in a health savings account (HSA). These plans became available in 2004 and are available both for the self-employed and company employees.

To qualify for an HSA, you must be under age 65 and purchase a health policy with an annual deductible of at least $1,000 for an individual or $2,000 for a family. This policy must be your only health insurance.

Once the policy is in place, you may set up an HSA and contribute up to the amount of your policy's deductible. If you are age 55 or older by the end of the year, you may contribute $500 beyond the deductible.

Money you put into the account can be deducted on your tax return—whether you itemize deductions or not. Earnings in the account grow untaxed, just as in a 401(k) or IRA. But unlike retirement plans, you can dip into an HSA at any age—tax-free—to pay for medical expenses, including your policy deductible and co-payments and many charges that are not typically covered by health insurance, such as over-the-counter drugs, vision and dental care, long-term-care insurance premiums, and future Medigap premiums.

Unlike flexible spending accounts, HSAs allow unspent money to be rolled over from year to year. You will owe income tax on earnings if funds are used for non-health-care purposes, and a 10 percent penalty will be imposed on any nonqualified withdrawal before age 65.

You can't have an HSA if you use a flexible-spending account to pay health care costs with pretax dollars or if you have other medical coverage (say, through a spouse's policy). However, if your FSA restricts reimbursements to wellness care (such as annual physicals) and vision and dental care, you can have an HSA, too.

After age 65 any that's left in the HSA may be withdrawn penalty-free for any purpose, but earnings not used to pay medical bills will be taxed.

Unlike flexible spending accounts, health savings accounts allow unspent money to be rolled over from year to year.

What If You Can't Work? Why You Need Disability Insurance

Disability insurance, which pays you when you can't work because of illness or injury, can be crucial to you and your family. Millions of people have some form of disability coverage from private or employer-sponsored programs. But only a fraction of those people have long-term coverage, which pays benefits usually up to age 65. The Social Security dis-

The protection you get from any disability plan depends to a large extent on how strictly it defines disability.

ability income program also offers disability insurance, but only for severe, long-term disability. Most claims filed under that program are rejected.

The protection you get from any disability plan depends to a large extent on how strictly it defines disability. The plan may dictate, for instance, that you're not entitled to benefits unless you are totally disabled. That can be interpreted to mean either you are unable to perform every duty pertaining to your occupation or that you are unable to engage in any type of paid work.

Some policies offer residual coverage, which pays you part of the difference in income if you can manage to work part-time. Residual coverage is considered better than partial disability coverage, which pays a fixed amount for only six weeks to a year.

You will have to shop around if you want to buy an individual, private disability policy to supplement whatever coverage you may have from other sources. The premiums for these plans are high, ranging from a few hundred dollars a year to more than $2,000.

Insurers won't cover your entire salary because they want you to have some incentive to return to work. Generally, they won't pay benefits totaling more than 70 to 80 percent of your income, no matter how much insurance you buy. Most professionals working for a medium-size to large company have long-term disability coverage of about 60 percent. Benefits paid under an employer's plan are taxable, while those paid under a private plan are tax-free.

If you're at least partially vested under your company's pension plan, find out whether it would provide some income to reduce your need for individual coverage. If you have a group policy at work and wish to increase your coverage, check with your group insurer. They can most easily supplement—and avoid duplicating—the protection you already have, and you might be entitled to a group discount, possibly saving you anywhere between 10 and 30 percent of your premium. Then check with several insurance companies because premiums and policy provisions differ considerably.

Limitations on Coverage

Disability coverage is usually subject to a couple of important limitations. If your company provides coverage under a group plan, you may not be able to buy a personal policy. Many employers pay all or most of the cost of group policies. But you can't take the coverage with you when you leave the company—unlike group term life insurance, which can usually be converted into an individual cash-value policy.

Social Security provides long-term-disability protection, but it lays down what are probably the toughest qualifying standards in the field:

- **Unless you become disabled before age 24,** you must have worked 1.5 years during the 3-year period ending with the quarter your disability began.
- **There must be a physical or mental condition** that prevents you from doing any gainful work.
- **The disability must last at least 12 months** or entail a condition expected to result in death.
- **You must wait a minimum of five months** before receiving any benefits.

The law requires state officials to determine an individual's eligibility under those and other federal guidelines. A national review is conducted occasionally to check the uniformity of state decisions.

Medicare

You qualify for Medicare coverage if you're at least 65 and eligible for Social Security (see Chapter 29) or railroad retirement benefits. It's also possible to qualify if you are under 65, if you have been receiving Social Security disability income for at least 24 months or have chronic kidney disease.

Medicare has traditionally been a two-part program, called A and B, but in 1998 it sprouted a third wing, Part C. And starting in 2006, the Medicare prescription drug plan, also known as Part D, will begin.

- **Hospital insurance,** called Part A coverage, is free. It helps pay for stays in the hospital, nursing-home care

If you have a group disability policy at work and want to increase coverage, check with your insurer to avoid any duplication.

(if needed following a hospital stay), and home health care under certain conditions.

- **Medical insurance,** or Part B of Medicare coverage, pays a set percentage of approved charges for doctors, home health aides (under certain circumstances), hospital outpatient treatment, laboratory tests, X rays, physical therapy, and certain kinds of medical equipment. The premium for this coverage—$78.20 a month in 2005—is deducted from your monthly Social Security check. You also pay a $110 deductible each year before Medicare begins paying.
- **Medicare Advantage,** formerly Medicare+Choice, which is also called Part C, offers Medicare Managed Care Plans, Medicare Preferred Provider (PPO)

FEATURES TO LOOK FOR IN A DISABILITY POLICY

Before you start contacting companies about disability insurance, take the time to familiarize yourself with these essential terms:

Guaranteed renewable. This means the insurance company can't cancel your insurance as long as you pay the premium. Most companies will cancel your policy in any event when you reach age 65. And guaranteed renewable doesn't guarantee that your rates will remain the same. Your premium can be increased, depending on a company's experience with those in your class— determined by such factors as age, occupation, and income level.

Guaranteed future insurability. This feature permits you to hike coverage to match future salary increases without having to pass a medical exam.

Noncancelable. This feature protects you from cancellation of the policy and from in-

creases in premium rates beyond the schedule stated in the policy.

Waiting, or elimination, period. This is the time you have to wait for payments to begin after the onset or diagnosis of an injury or disease. The longer the delay, the lower your premium will be. Waiting periods may range from 30 to 180 days, or even a year. One way to save money is to figure out how long savings and other income sources can carry you before you would need benefits to begin. The first check won't arrive until a month after the elimination period ends.

Benefit period. This is the length of time the policy will pay disability benefits; the longer the period, the higher the premiums. For instance, a plan that pays to age 65 could

Plans, Medicare Private Fee-for-Service Plans, and Medicare Specialty Plans. You must have Medicare Parts A and B to join these plans. You may pay lower copayments and get extra benefits such as coverage for days in the hospital. If you chose a Medicare Advantage program, you do not need a Medigap policy, since Medicare Advantage plans generally cover many of the same benefits as a Medigap policy (described beginning on page 313).

■ **Medicare's prescription-drug program (Part D),** beginning in 2006, requires a monthly premium of about $37 and a yearly deductible of up to $250. You will also pay part of the cost of your prescriptions in the form of a copayment. If you already have a policy,

cost 40% more than a policy from the same company that promises payments for only five years.

Cost-of-living rider. Under this policy addition, both the amount of benefits and the amount of money you're allowed to earn without forfeiting benefits can be indexed to keep abreast of inflation. It takes effect after you start receiving benefits and may raise your premium 20% to 25%.

Incontestable clause. An optional provision, this clause states that the insurance company may not contest the validity of the contract after it has been in force for two or three years. This can be important if you have a preexisting medical condition. If you disclose the condition on your application and the company does not disclaim it at that time or within the two-or three-year period, the company

must honor subsequent claims. If you are unaware of a medical problem or don't consider it serious, you may fail to disclose it on your insurance application. Yet your condition could later cause serious illness. Some insurance companies may consider it to be an illness that began before you had coverage; if you don't have the incontestable clause in your contract, you won't get paid.

Coordination of benefits. This provision integrates disability income with various other insurance sources so that you can't collect more than 100% of the allowable benefits.

Waiver of premium. If the policy includes this feature, you won't have to pay any premiums while you're disabled. Such a provision lasts for the duration of the contract. It is well worth having.

You can enroll in Medicare starting three months before your 65th birthday. Early enrollment will ensure that coverage starts the first day of the month you turn 65.

you'll have to decide by May 15, 2006, if you want to keep that coverage. After that, you will have to pay more for your Medicare prescription drug plan or Medicare Advantage prescription drug premium and you will lose your right to switch to another policy.

If your employer covers retiree prescriptions and coverage is at least as good as Part D, you are better off not switching. If your employer later drops this coverage, you will still be able to enroll in Part D without penalty as long as you can show Medicare a "certificate of credible coverage" from your company. You can obtain more information about Part D by visiting Medicare's Web site (http://www.medicare.gov) or by calling 800-633-4227.

If you're 65 but not eligible for the free coverage under Medicare Part A because you haven't contributed to Social Security long enough, you can buy it for a premium (about $205 to $375 a month in 2005), depending on how long you contributed to Social Security. Medicare also charges deductibles and copayments. To help pay them, many people buy so-called Medigap insurance (unless they have chosen one of the Medicare Advantage programs).

When to Enroll in Medicare

You can enroll in Medicare starting three months before your 65th birthday. Early enrollment will ensure that coverage starts the first day of the month you turn 65. If you enroll within three months after the month you turn 65, coverage will kick in on the first day of the month after the month you enroll.

Counting the three months before the month you turn 65, the month of your birthday and the three months after that, you have a window of seven months to enroll and start your coverage almost immediately. If you miss this window, you'll have to wait for the next general enrollment period, which is January 1 through March 31 of each year. In that case, your Medicare coverage won't begin until the following July. On top of that, your Part B premium will be increased by 10 percent for each year you delay enrolling.

If you continue to work after age 65 and are covered under your employer's health care plan (or if your spouse is working and you are covered under his or her plan), the 10 percent penalty doesn't apply. In the meantime, you should go ahead and apply for Part A coverage, since it is free.

For more information about Medicare, you can call 800-633-4227, or visit the Medicare Web site sponsored by the Health Care Financing Administration (http://www.medicare.gov).

As good as it is, Medicare pays for only about half of the medical costs of people 65 and older. How do people pay the rest? That's the subject of the next section.

Medicare pays for about half of the medical costs of people 65 and older. Medigap insurance helps cover the rest.

How Medigap Insurance Plugs the Holes

Medicare-supplement, or Medigap, insurance is designed to plug the holes in Medicare. It is sold by insurance companies, and federal rules that standardize the coverage make comparing policies a snap.

Under the rules, each policy must conform to one of ten defined packages of benefits, which are labeled A through J. Furthermore, all Medigap insurers must offer the basic package, policy A, that contains the core group of benefits. Companies must use uniform language to describe the policies, and sales literature must identify policies by the appropriate letter.

For six months after you sign up for Medicare Part B, you can choose any of the Medigap policies you want. Regardless of your health, the company must cover you. After the six-month window has closed, companies aren't obligated to accept you (although most will). If you already have Medigap coverage and want to switch to a better package, you won't have to wait for preexisting conditions to be covered.

TIPS FOR BUYERS OF MEDIGAP INSURANCE

COMPARE PRICES

Benefits in each policy must be identical to those in other policies in the same category, but prices vary a lot from company to company. In North Carolina, for instance, premiums for a 65-year-old woman ranged recently from $1,200 to $2,800 for policy F.

Premiums can vary based on your age, sex, and where you live. For example, in a recent year Mutual of Omaha charged a 65-year-old male nonsmoker living in San Diego $1,356.23 for policy A but asked only $933.01 from a man the same age in western Nebraska. Cost of living policies can vary in the same state. For example, if that same man lived in Lincoln, Nebraska, the policy would have cost $1,027.66. Female nonsmokers in the same areas would pay $1,179.93, $811.72, and $894.06, respectively.

A few policies, including the AARP's group plan, have one premium for a given area regardless of age.

Insurers can't adjust their rates on the basis of your health status. But they can accept only applicants who meet strict health standards and thus pose less risk. Such a company will probably charge a lower premium than a less discriminating company. If you're healthy, that practice works in your favor.

SHOP FOR STABILITY AND SERVICE

Choose a company that has a solid reputation for financial stability and customer service, and avoid companies that you've never heard of. A company with a system for transferring claims electronically from Medicare to the Medigap carrier may save you paperwork hassles. Some state insurance departments track the number of complaints that companies receive from consumers and provide that information upon request.

LOOK FOR MEDICARE SELECT

Various insurers offer discounted Medigap premiums in exchange for enrollment in a combination managed-care/fee-for-service program. To get the discounts, you have to agree to use health care providers that have been selected by the plan.

KNOW YOUR RIGHTS

Consumers in every state are guaranteed a 30-day free look. If you're dissatisfied with the policy and you return it within 30 days of receiving it, you're entitled to a full refund.

You can get more information about Medicare and Medigap insurance from any Social Security office.

In addition, The Medicare Rights Center publishes *Filling the Medicare Gaps*, which explains the pros and cons of each plan. Send $8.00 to Medicare Rights Center, 1460 Broadway, 17th Floor, New York, NY 10036, or visit www.medicarerights.org.

All ten policies may not be available in Massachusetts, Minnesota, and Wisconsin—states that are exempt from the federal rules because they established standardized Medicare-supplement policies before the federal government stepped in.

Policy A is the least expensive and should be the most competitively priced of the ten packages because all companies have to offer it. It pays for hospital charges that are not covered by Medicare, which limits coverage to 60 days. For 2005, the policy covered a copayment of about $228 for hospital days 61 to 90, and $456 for days 91 to 150. It also covered the full cost of up to 365 additional hospital days during your lifetime, the 20 percent copayment of Medicare's allowed amount for physician charges (after you paid the first $110 yearly deductible), and the first three pints of blood (Medicare coverage kicked in after the three-pint deductible). Policy A is a good choice if your aim is to cover catastrophic costs.

Policy J, at the other end of the scale, pays all that plus:
- **the hospital deductible** under Medicare Part A, recently about $912;
- **the $110-a-year Part B deductible** for doctors' services;
- **the copayment for days 21 through 100** for skilled care in a nursing home—about $114 per day;
- **50 percent of outpatient prescription drug costs,** up to $1,250 a year (after a deductible of $250);
- **up to $1,600 a year** for short-term custodial care at home following surgery, injury, or illness;
- **up to $120 a year** for preventive health screenings;
- **80 percent of the cost of emergency care** needed while traveling in a foreign country, after a $250 deductible.

Other policies offer something in between A and J. Odds are you can quickly narrow your search to only four of the packages: A, D, G, and H.

Policies D and G cover custodial care at home following an illness or injury, and includes the copayment for nursing-home care.

Policy G is attractive if you use nonparticipating physicians—those who charge more than the amount approved by Medicare.

Long-term-care premiums can range from $1,000 to $6,000, depending on age and care level.

Policy H is the least expensive package that includes prescription-drug coverage.

If your income is limited, also consider Policy B, which costs $200 to $300 more a year than Policy A but covers the deductible for each hospital stay, a valuable benefit that can easily pay for itself.

Annual premiums for the packages range from about $800 for Policy A to almost $4,000 for Policy J. See the box on page 314 for shopping tips, and make sure you don't pay for features you don't need.

Two new Medigap policies begin in 2006. Plans K and L each provide coverage for "catastrophic" expenses. Once out-of-pocket costs for medical expenses covered by Medicare Parts A and B exceed $4,000, Plan K will pay the balance. Plan L will work the same way, but the out-of-pocket limit is $2,000. The new plans roll out for sale in each state as the states insurance departments approve them.

Long-Term-Care Insurance

Most older Americans have no insurance to cover the incredibly expensive long-term care often necessary when chronic illness or disability strikes late in life. Nursing-home costs alone can run $60,000 to $80,000 a year. At the most expensive centers the bill can approach twice that much.

Most people pay these costs from their own pockets. Medicare and Medigap insurance pick up very little of the tab. What's more, they cover only nursing-home skilled care, not the lesser levels of intermediate and custodial care that most people actually require.

The rest of the cost of long-term care is borne by Medicaid, the welfare program financed jointly by the federal and state governments. But before a person can become eligible, his or her assets, including life savings, must be pared down to a minimum. That has left many beneficiaries virtually impoverished.

For those who think far enough ahead, private insurance is available to ease the burden. More than 150 insurance companies offer policies designed to cover a large chunk of the costs of long-term care. For an annual premium that can range from $1,000 to $6,000, depending on the level of care you insure and your age when you buy the policy, you can cover a specified stay in a long-term-care facility and, in an increasing number of instances, be reimbursed for certain home health services.

These are essentially indemnity policies. That means insurers pay a fixed amount—say, $150 a day—rather than a percentage of the fees, as with comprehensive insurance. An indemnity policy tends to become outdated almost as soon as you sign the agreement. If it has no index for inflation, it's up to you to peer down the road and try to gauge the amount of protection you would need to make a dent in future bills.

Premiums start out at relatively modest levels for those in their 50s and then rise steeply, making the insurance costly or even prohibitive. For instance, a policy sold in 2005 cost a couple who were both age 55 about $1,200 to $1,400 a year for a $150 daily benefit per person, with a 5 percent annual inflation adjustment. A 65-year-old couple would pay $2,000 to $2,300 a year each for the same policy. Buying at a younger age locks in the lower rate if the policy provides for a level premium and guarantees your insurability before a disqualifying condition or disease has had a chance to develop.

How the Policies Pay—or Don't Pay

Generally, benefits become available once you meet three of the following conditions:

- **You are unable to perform two of six basic activities** of daily living (such as bathing or dressing) or you show signs of severe cognitive impairment, such as those associated with dementia.
- **Your doctor or other health professional certifies** that your condition is expected to last at least 90 days.
- **You pay for long-term-care services** for the number of days in your waiting period.

> Long-term-care policies are essentially indemnity policies. That means insurers pay a fixed amount—say, $150 a day—rather than a percentage of the fees.

The more closely a policy can be tailored to the beneficiary's needs, the more sense it will make in the long run.

Then, depending on the beneficiary's condition and terms of the policy, care proceeds through several stages.

SKILLED CARE. This is medically necessary care provided by licensed, skilled medical professionals—nurses and therapists, for example—working under the supervision of a doctor. Restoring the patient to a condition approximating the state of health before the illness or accident is the goal.

INTERMEDIATE CARE. This also requires supervision by a physician and skilled nursing care, but it is needed only intermittently rather than continuously over a prescribed period.

CUSTODIAL CARE. Even if they escape disabling illness and injury, many elderly people reach a stage when performing such simple tasks as bathing, dressing, and eating is difficult. Supervised custodial care, which is the nursing-home service in greatest demand, can help. Benefits cover mainly room and board plus payments for assistance with the activities of daily living.

HOME HEALTH CARE. Depending on the policy, benefits for home health care may range from homemaking and chore services to occupational therapy and laboratory services.

How to Compare Policies

Like any competing products, long-term-care policies have contingencies and options that may fit the needs of one person but not another. Whether you consider such coverage for yourself or help an aging family member decide, it's essential to have the facts. The more closely a policy can be tailored to the beneficiary's needs, the more sense it will make in the long run. A plan that does not cover all levels of care—including custodial—is of very limited value. Options to look for: a waiver of premiums once benefits start or three to six months later; and language guaranteeing renewal of the policy (renewal at the company's option is more

HEALTH INSURANCE FOR PETS

Pet health insurance has become more popular in recent years as people find themselves spending more on veterinary bills. The bond between pet and owner is such that many owners will spare no expense to treat even serious illnesses. If a pet needs surgery or simply has a persistent skin disorder or infection, costs can mount quickly.

Pet health insurance may make sense for you, especially if you insure your pet when he or she is young and before problems develop. Pet policies offer basic fee-for-service coverage: You visit the vet or animal hospital of your choice, pay the bill up front, then submit a claim. Depending on the plan, reimbursement may be 70% to 100% of the bill, after the deductible (usually $50 to $100 per incident). Most insurers limit the amount they'll pay per incident and per year. Premiums on the policies average about $200 annually. With pet insurance, premiums are based on specific risks such as age, health, and genetic makeup, and various levels of coverage are available.

Not surprisingly, the lowest-priced insurance is available for pets that are fit, frisky, and free of incipient problems, and live in areas where veterinary costs are low. If the animal barks or meows, so much the better. Only a few companies, including Veterinary Pet Insurance (VPI), cover birds, ferrets, and other more exotic pets.

To save money, consider a discount plan, which slices a straight percentage off the cost of services from participating providers. Pet Assure, with 2,000 participating vets nationwide, enrolls everything from quarter horses to cockatiels, for an annual fee of $100 for a single pet and $150 for "family coverage." That gets you 25% off every bill, no matter how extensive the treatment. Before signing up for a pet policy be sure to read the fine print. You may not be covered for big illnesses such as feline leukemia unless pets test negative and have been vaccinated annually; hereditary or genetic conditions also aren't covered; and premiums may increase as your pet ages.

Here's a list of some of the insurance and discount plans available. Make sure the insurer gets good grades from a reputable ratings company, such as A.M. Best.

REGULAR PLANS (DISCOUNTS SOMETIMES AVAILABLE)
PetCare Pet Insurance (866-275-7387; www.petcareinsurance.com).
Petshealth Care Plan. (800-807-6724; www.petshealthplan.com).
Veterinary Pet Insurance (VPI) (800-540-2016; www.petinsurance.com).

DISCOUNT PLAN
Pet Assure (888-789-7387; www.petassure.com). $100 annually for one pet, $150 for the family plan (up to 4 pets).

likely to protect the seller than you). Here are other points to compare.

WHERE WILL CARE BE DELIVERED? A so-called facilities policy pays only for those services provided in a skilled-

Pass up any policy that excludes "mental disorders" unless the seller satisfies you that organically based mental disease such as Alzheimer's is covered.

nursing facility, even if the care given is intermediate or custodial. A so-called care policy will cover levels of care given in less intensive surroundings if it otherwise complies with standard definitions. Language in the policy may require that care be provided in a skilled-nursing facility or licensed nursing home. The proportion of such institutions varies from state to state. Ask local officials from agencies on health or aging for the makeup of various long-term-care facilities to help you evaluate competing policies.

IS THERE A HEALTH SCREEN? The insurer will want to know the state of the beneficiary's health; stretching the truth could later invalidate the policy. It is safe to assume that applicants with a recent record of illness or institutionalization will not be acceptable candidates for insurance, although this is not usually stated directly in the policies.

WHEN DO BENEFITS BEGIN AND END? Even the best policies have restrictions that define when care can begin and under what circumstances. Most older policies required a stay in a hospital or skilled-nursing facility before you could claim other benefits. Newer policies are less likely to require a stay to trigger benefits. Between discharge from the hospital or the occurrence of the triggering medical event and entry into a nursing home there is usually a delay, called a waiting or elimination period, of 20 or even 100 days before benefits begin. This period serves as a sort of deductible, with the beneficiary picking up the tab. The policy should clarify this, and you should be told what levels of care are covered and for how long.

DOES THE POLICY EXCLUDE ANY MEDICAL PROBLEMS? Like conventional health insurance, long-term-care policies carry exclusions for preexisting conditions, which usually won't be covered for six months or a year after a policy is in force. Nearly half of all nursing-home patients are confined because of Alzheimer's disease or other organically related mental disorders. Pass up any policy that excludes "mental disorders" unless the seller satisfies you that organically based mental disease is covered.

The National Council on Aging, 300 D St., SW, Suite 801, Washington, DC 20024 (202-479-1200) offers *Planning for Long-Term Care,* Item No. SC100 ($14.95), which covers planning, insurance coverage for long-term care, and various levels of available care, such as assisted living and nursing-home care. To order, call 800-373-4906 or check the Web site at http://www.ncoa.org. The National Association of Insurance Commissioners, 2301 McGee, Suite 800, Kansas City, MO 64108-2604 (816-783-8300; http://www.naic.org) will send you a free copy of its guide, *A Shopper's Guide to Long-Term-Care Insurance.*

Dental insurance is more a way of keeping small problems from becoming large ones than it is of guarding against the unexpected.

Insurance for Healthy Teeth

Dental insurance is a different breed of cat. When you buy coverage for medical bills, you're paying for protection against an unknowable future event, a medical problem that could even mean bankruptcy. Basic dental policies cover the recurrent and predictable, such as exams, cleanings, and cavities that nearly all of us have at one time or another. So dental insurance is more a way of keeping small problems from becoming large ones than it is of guarding against the unexpected.

Most dental policies are sold to groups, such as company employees, members of unions and associations, and school groups. In every group some participants are bound to need little dental care, some a lot. Sharing the risk in this way helps control the costs. If the choice of whether to sign up were left to individuals, those with known problems would more likely be customers than those with sound teeth.

Can you buy individual coverage? It used to be difficult, but now several companies such as Aetna, GE, and Uni-Care offer programs nationwide, while others operate regionally. You can check the National Association of Dental Plans' Web site at http://www.dentalplans .com to compare individual policies.

Dental coverage is available in some HMOs, but don't assume all dental work is free after the premium is paid. Like regular dental insurance, HMO coverage stresses improvement in oral health. That means that preventive measures, such as examinations, cleaning, and fluoride treatments, are usually covered in full to encourage their use. More extensive work—fillings, caps, and the like—often is covered only after you shell out a deductible. Orthodontic benefits have lifetime limits, and plans impose annual limits for all types of dental care.

There are also dental HMOs that offer preventative and restorative dental care delivered by a network of dentists and specialists. You can find dental HMOs in most metropolitan areas, but they are not available everywhere. Dental HMO plans usually provide standard preventative care at no cost to the patient but require copayments (deductibles you pay out-of-pocket) for other procedures. You must choose a dentist who participates in the plan, and you receive no reimbursement if you go outside the plan.

Think Twice About This Insurance

Chapter 21

You'll find more kinds of insurance on the market these days than ever. That's good news because there are probably more perils lurking to insure ourselves against. Most new kinds of coverage are legitimate, creative spin-offs of traditional policies. But some provide coverage of questionable value. And some are merely new ways of marketing old ideas. Deciding what you need and don't need isn't always easy. This chapter takes a look at some insurance you probably don't need—because it duplicates coverage you may already have, because it's too expensive for what you get back in benefits, or because it covers minor expenses you can, in most cases, easily cover yourself.

Life Insurance on Kids

No matter how you look at it, buying life insurance for young children isn't an efficient way to spend your money. You'd be better off putting the money in stocks for the child, or in premiums for increased insurance coverage for the family breadwinners, whose death would reduce the family income. Yet, year in and year out, parents insure their children for billions of dollars, often in mistaken solicitude for the child's welfare. The sales pitch for insuring kids—and the arguments against it—go something like this:

SALES PITCH: *It costs very little to insure a child, so why not take advantage of this bargain?*

YOUR REPLY: Of course it costs very little, because the chance of death in the near future is very low. Why should I pay all those premiums for all those years?

SALES PITCH: *By buying a whole-life policy for a child at an early age, you lock in a low premium. That makes it easier for the child to pick up the premiums later, and you'll both pay less over the long haul.*

YOUR REPLY: Prove it. I'll concede the first point, but show me on your premium schedule the difference in total premiums for the child starting at age 16 and starting at age 25 and paying until age 65 in both cases.

SALES PITCH: *I thought you'd never ask. Assuming you keep both policies until age 65, I calculate that you'd save the equivalent of several years' premiums by buying at age 16, when premiums are very low, compared with buying at age 25, when premiums will be higher.*

YOUR REPLY: Okay, now show me what the result would be if I took all the premium money for all those years and invested it at a modest rate of return—say, 5 percent.

SALES PITCH: *Um . . . okay, I concede that you'd accumulate more than the face value of the policy because you wouldn't be paying anything to insure your child's life. It stands to reason that the company must charge something for insuring your child's life for those years. But suppose when your child gets older he takes a job or develops a health problem that makes him ineligible for insurance or for insurance at regular rates. You can guard against that dangerous possibility by insuring now.*

YOUR REPLY: Not likely. A minority of applicants have to pay higher premiums and few get turned down. My child will probably be buying insurance in his late 20s or early 30s. Odds strongly favor his being able to get all the protection wanted at standard premiums.

SALES PITCH: *Well, you have to admit that a child's policy will help defray burial expenses.*

YOUR REPLY: True, but my bigger worry is an expensive, lengthy serious illness that might cause my child

---

WHY YOU MIGHT WANT TO INSURE A CHILD

The decision to insure a child must overcome several impressive objections before it becomes justifiable from a hard-nosed financial point of view. But in considering ways to help your children, you might not want to limit yourself to cold economic calculations. What seems an extravagance from one point of view might make sense when viewed as a gift. And you can accomplish some important long-term objectives by insuring your child early in life.

- **You can start** off his or her adult career with a low out-of-pocket expense for life protection he or she is bound to need. The lifetime premium cost may be more, but that extra cost represents your gift to your child.
- **You can protect** your child against the risk, however small, of not being able to buy insurance at standard rates as an adult.

- **By carefully selecting** the kind of insurance you buy, you can give children a base on which to build their own insurance programs later. With inflation constantly eroding the value of each dollar of insurance bought now, they will need a good start.

---

to die young. Maybe I should use the money to beef up my catastrophic health insurance coverage.

NET: No knockouts, but you win on points. Still, there are reasons you—or someone else, such as a grandparent—might want to buy a life insurance policy to cover a child, strictly as a gesture of generosity. Those reasons are described in the box above.

Credit Life Insurance

Credit life insurance is sold through lenders—banks, auto dealers, finance companies, retailers—in connection with their loans and charge accounts. It covers the lender if you die before you've paid off your debt. There are several reasons to think twice about buying this kind of insurance.

- **It's expensive.** The next time you get one of those invitations from your mortgage lender to buy life insurance to cover your mortgage at special rates for special customers like you, toss it. If you do need insurance to cover the debt, a term life policy will invariably be cheaper, especially if you're in your 20s or 30s.

At a cost of only a few hundred dollars a year, hospital indemnity insurance seems cheap, but it isn't.

■ **A credit life policy pays off the loan** even if that might not be the best financial decision for your survivors—who might want to keep the mortgage and use the insurance money to pay hospital bills, for instance.

■ **If you're single with no heirs to worry about,** credit life is probably superfluous. Life insurance is supposed to protect your surviving family from claims against your estate. If you have no family, you end up protecting only the creditor—who, in the absence of such insurance or other assets in your estate, would probably just repossess the car, the TV, or the boat.

Often a creditor can require you to have insurance as security for a debt, but state laws generally make it illegal to require you to buy it from a particular company. You have the option of pledging an existing policy or buying coverage elsewhere. If the lender requires the insurance and you buy it from the lender, its cost has to be included in the loan's finance charge and annual percentage rate. You end up paying to insure not only the loan principal and all finance charges, but also the insurance premium. You are actually insuring the insurance.

That said, there are circumstances when credit life might make sense. If you want to insure a small, short-term loan—say, $2,000 for two years—credit life may be your only choice. It also might be a reasonable buy if you can't meet the health requirements for other insurance coverage or if at your age other policies cost even more than credit life. Some creditors deal with more than one insurer, so rates available to you may vary.

The price of credit life, usually decreasing-term coverage, is generally expressed as cents per $100 of initial coverage per year of the loan. This gives you a means for comparing costs of credit life policies with each other and with conventional term life insurance as well.

Hospital Indemnity Insurance

This pays you a predetermined amount for every day you're in the hospital. At a cost of only a few hundred dollars a year, it seems cheap, but it isn't. One study found that some insurance companies were paying out less than 20 cents in benefits for every $1 they received in premiums. A 50-cent payout ratio is considered more acceptable by insurance-industry standards, suggesting that hospital indemnity premiums could be a lot cheaper.

And what do you get? Policies often pay only about $200 a day if you wind up in the hospital. Measured against average hospital bills of $1,000 or more, that's better than nothing, but it's not much.

Even though it could be cheaper and its benefits are limited, hospital indemnity insurance isn't a high-priced item. The most important thing is not to substitute it for comprehensive health insurance.

Dread-Disease Insurance

These policies cover only specified ailments, such as cancer or multiple sclerosis. The biggest rap against them is that they often duplicate coverage already being paid for in comprehensive health insurance policies. In no case should such policies be purchased as anything other than a supplement to a broad health insurance package, and then only after careful review and cost comparisons with your coverage.

The price for dread-disease insurance sounds cheap, perhaps two or three hundred dollars a year. (Some firms will even pay back your premiums every ten years if you don't develop cancer.) If you are diagnosed with cancer, you may get a check for a lump sum, plus other payments toward the cost of hospitalization, chemotherapy, and further treatments. The hospitalization coverage suffers the same shortcomings as indemnity policies, and most cancer treatment is done on an outpatient basis. If the policy pays for expensive procedures such as surgery or chemotherapy, the benefit still falls way short of what you would actually need.

Individual cancer policies have been banned from sale in several states on the grounds that they provide minimal economic benefits. If they're legal where you live and you're tempted to buy, study the coverage

The biggest rap against dread-disease policies is that they often duplicate coverage already being paid for in comprehensive health insurance policies.

Credit card insurance is among the most expensive insurance you can buy.

carefully and compare it with what you already have under a comprehensive health care policy.

Student Accident Policies

Accident insurance offered through your child's elementary or secondary school typically costs less than $40 a year for schooltime coverage and $90 to $150 for 24-hour coverage. Not onerous, but you get what you pay for. The policies usually pay limited amounts for specific injuries, and many have a $25,000 payment ceiling—too low to cover the cost of major injuries. Some student policies kick in only after your family plan has paid for a claim, although you could recoup some of your family-coverage deductible or copayments. Even if the policy pays on top of additional coverage, the benefits you collect from other policies will almost certainly be reduced by the same amount, so your combined benefits won't exceed your expenses.

Credit Card Insurance

This coverage is typically offered in a flyer that comes with your credit card bill. It pays off your credit card balance not only if you die but also if you become disabled, or even if you lose your job. The premiums are only a few dollars a month, but compared with the benefits, this is among the most expensive insurance you can buy. Instead, put those few dollars a month toward paying down your balance.

Investments for Today and Tomorrow

How to Have Investing Smarts All the Time

You want a home of your own, an education for your kids, a comfortable retirement someday, and a little fun along the way. These are the routine, standard-issue dreams we all seem to be born with. To achieve them, we must become investors. Saving up for things is a good habit to cultivate for a lifetime, but saving up isn't enough because you can't possibly earn enough interest to get you where you want to go.

A brilliantly executed program of saving—putting your money into certificates of deposit, money-market funds, or savings bonds—is capable of earning 5 percent to 6 percent in a good year. Consider that 3 percent or so is a reasonable expectation for inflation (some would say that's optimistic) and that taxes will nick 25 percent or so of what remains, and you can see what you're up against: 5 percent quickly becomes about 1.5 percent after inflation and taxes. You're going to have to do a lot better than that.

To drive the lesson home: Suppose you start with $1,000 in a CD earning 5 percent compounded daily and set aside $250 a month for a new certificate earning the same. Keep it up for 10 years and you'll have a little more than $41,000, before taxes. In 20 years you'll have about $107,000 (because of compounding, the 20-year return is more than twice the 10-year return).

That's not too shabby, but it won't buy you that condo on the golf course, especially at prices 20 years down the road, plus pay for the kids' college between now and then. You've got to increase your return, and you do it by becoming an investor, not just a saver. That means you're going to have to take some risks.

Successful investors operate from a plan based on their goals, how long they have to achieve them, their tolerance for risk, and what they can afford to set aside for an investment program.

Investing seemed like a pretty sure thing in the 1990s, when the stock market was regularly piling up returns of 20 percent and more. Elated investors exchanged high fives, congratulating each other on their genius. But let's face it: You didn't have to be a genius to make money in such markets. You didn't even have to pay very close attention to what you were doing. And if the stock market were capable of pounding out returns like that indefinitely, you could put all your money in an index fund (see Chapter 25) and throw away this book.

Alas, as the drop at the turn of the century and plunge following the events of September 11 showed, the stock market doesn't work that way. There is no endless summer; you need an investment approach for all seasons. Stocks should be a major part of it, but you have many other choices. Interest rates, inflation, corporate profits, and consumer and investor psychology affect the prospects for different kinds of investments in different ways at different times. And brokerage firms, banks, insurance companies, and others who would like some of your money are ingenious at devising new products that let you take advantage of the changes.

How much more will you need to earn than you could get through saving alone? You should aim for an average return of 10 to 12 percent per year on your investments. You won't make it every year, but that's an achievable range if you plan your approach thoughtfully and stick to your plan.

You're Going to Need a Plan

Successful investors don't jump around from one place to another according to what's hot and what's not. They operate from a plan that's based on their goals, how long they have to achieve them, their tolerance for risk (both financial and psychological), and what they can afford to set aside for an investment program. You want to make money, of course, but you also want to be able to sleep at night. Here's how to do it.

Set Exciting Goals

Chapter 1 described the importance of short-term goal setting when drawing up a budget for the year ahead. Investment goals tend to be long-term: enough to pay college tuition starting in 10 years, for instance, or enough to retire on in 15 or 20 years. In fact, it's this long-range outlook that causes many people to set such vague, halfhearted goals that they fail to maintain the discipline necessary to reach them.

If you set merely "retirement" as a goal, what will motivate you to get there (besides, of course, the relentless passage of time)? To build motivation into your goal setting, try going a few steps further: Where would you like to live when you retire? How much will it cost? What would you like to do? Travel? Sail the Caribbean? Play golf? How much income will you need in addition to your pension? This kind of thinking lets you add some flesh to your bare-bones goal to "retire someday." You can set a goal something like this: "Our goal is to retire at the age of 58 to a three-bedroom house near the Grand Canyon in Arizona, with room for the grandchildren who will come to visit. We want to spend at least two months of the year traveling in the U.S. and Europe, and we'll need $3,000 a month to supplement our pensions and Social Security." Now you've got some goals you can pin a price tag on, and a nice mental picture to remind you of why you're pouring all that money into delayed gratification.

Adopt a Clear-Cut Strategy

Brokerage firms, mutual funds, and the financial press produce lots of useful information. But you don't have to read much of it before you realize how contradictory it can be. The developments used to explain yesterday's drop in stocks may be the same ones cited for today's rise. One expert recommends buying utility stocks and selling computer stocks; another advises us to sell utilities and buy computers. No wonder we're confused.

View this day-to-day crystal-ball gazing with clear-eyed vision and create your own strategy based on your own goals, risk tolerance, and psychological make-

> **Investment goals tend to be long-term: enough to pay college tuition starting in 10 years, for instance, or enough to retire on in 15 or 20 years.**

To make sure your investment plan remains on track, sit down once a year or so and update the values of what you own, including the equity in your home.

up. For example, three different investors might devise strategies like the following.

- **Sticking with stocks.** "Stocks offer the best returns over the long run. I have more than a decade to ride out any market dips, so I'm going to play the averages and put 90 percent of my money in the stock market. The rest I'll keep in savings, insured certificates of deposit, and money-market funds."

- **Rooted in real estate.** "I think that rental real estate, despite its occasional setbacks, offers the best chance of long-term gain and steady income. I know the local market well, and I'll try to keep 40 percent of my assets in real estate and diversify the rest, putting some in the money market for liquidity and some in big-company stocks to balance the risks in real estate."

- **Spreading the risks.** "I don't have a clue what's going on in the investment markets and I don't have the time to keep up, so I'll spread my money across a wide range of investments in the hope that gains in some categories will offset losses in others. I will invest 60 percent in stock-oriented mutual funds, 20 percent in corporate bonds, 10 percent in money-market funds and CDs, and 10 percent in shares of a real estate investment trust."

These are made-up scenarios, of course. Your own plan may look nothing like them, but you should go through the thought process so that investment decisions you make will be guided by your own strategy, not that of a broker or advisor trying to sell you something. A successful strategy can probably be summarized in three or four sentences, just like the ones above.

Pay Attention

As time passes, investment plans have a way of taking on a life of their own. Interest rates rise and fall. Big-company stocks pass in and out of favor. Real estate markets plunge and soar. To make sure your investment plan is still on track, sit down once a year or so and update the values of what you own, including the equity in your home. Compute each type of investment—stocks, bonds, mutual funds, and so forth—as a percentage of the total. If you haven't achieved an asset mix to your liking, this exercise will show you which parts have to be increased and which cut back. As the years go by, the percentage mix of your investments will change without you lifting a finger, as some parts of your portfolio rise in value and others fall. This makes a periodic review imperative. Money-management software, such as *Microsoft Money* or *Quicken,* makes it a snap.

Control Your Risks

The risks you are prepared to take will influence the kinds of investments you make and the return you should expect. These rules will keep you in a comfortable risk zone. (And, once again, let you sleep at night.)

1. Don't invest until you're ready. Your investment portfolio should be built on a solid foundation of sure things: sufficient insurance coverage and several months' income tucked securely away in interest-bearing CDs or a money-market fund. Only when you have that cushion are you ready to start investing.

2. Invest aggressively for the long term and conservatively for the short term. Stocks should be thought of as investments for achieving your long-term goals. For short-term goals—that is, money you'll need within two or three years—stick with CDs and other sure bets.

3. Don't invest very much money in anything that still leaves you uneasy after you have investigated its strengths and weaknesses. The bigger the promised reward, the bigger your risk. This doesn't mean you should never take big risks; just don't take big risks with big chunks of your money.

4. Don't buy anything you don't know how to sell. Some so-called investments, such as collectibles and gemstones, are easy to buy but may take specialized assistance to sell because there are no organized national resale markets, as there are for stocks and bonds.

> The risks you are prepared to take will influence the kinds of investments you make and the return you should expect.

Dollar-cost averaging won't automatically produce a profit, but it smooths out the market's ups and downs.

Make Investing a Habit

Dollar-cost averaging is a reliable way to smooth out the ups and downs of the stock market. You invest a fixed amount on a regular schedule, paying no heed to the level of prices at the time. The amount can be $25 a month, $50 a month, $500 a month—whatever fits your budget. Your fixed number of dollars will automatically buy more shares when prices are low than they will when prices are high. As a result, the average purchase price of your stock will be lower than the average of the market prices over the same length of time.

Dollar-cost averaging won't automatically produce a profit. But by investing on a regular schedule and sticking with your plan, you're virtually guaranteed to do better in a generally rising market, with the usual number of ups and downs, than investors who try to sell at the top and buy at the bottom. History shows that the odds are strongly against that kind of timing.

How can you buy small amounts of stock on a regular basis without going broke paying the commissions? There are a couple of ways.

First, a growing number of companies are willing to sell shares directly to investors, thus allowing you to bypass brokers' commissions. These programs also make you eligible to participate in the company's dividend reinvestment plan, or DRIP. For a list of companies offering such plans, check The Moneypaper Inc.'s Directinvesting.com (800-388-9993; http://www.directinvesting.com) or Sharebuilder.com (877-595-0014; http://www.sharebuilder.com).

Second, no-load mutual funds (see Chapter 25) are ideally suited for dollar-cost averaging. There are no sales commissions when you buy, and you can invest a small (or large) amount of money on a regular schedule, even if your dollars buy fractional shares. Funds will let you have money transferred regularly from a bank account, thus creating for you an enforced investment plan that will grow as the years go by.

Don't Get Stuck in a Rut

The time may come when you want to revise your strategy. Retirement, for instance, may be a time to lighten up a bit (but not entirely) on stocks and emphasize income-oriented investments such as bonds.

Avoid abrupt changes in direction, and don't try to time the market. You can change your asset mix gradually by allocating new investment money from savings, dividends, and interest to the category you want to increase.

Don't Fool Yourself

Investment expectations are easy to exaggerate by fixating on an investment's most favorable period—the stock market in the 1990s, for instance, or the real estate markets in the 1970s. On average, a total return of 10 to 12 percent per year on your investments—that is, the sum of dividends and interest plus price increases of your holdings—is a reasonable, achievable expectation. Some years you will do better, some years worse.

You'll have ups and downs, so keep in mind the trade-off between risk and reward. A conservative investor sacrifices potential gain in order to limit potential losses. An aggressive investor sacrifices safety in hopes of a bigger gain.

How Not to Get Ripped Off

There's hardly a legitimate investment that isn't considered fair game by crooks. They sell low-priced stocks, precious metals, rare coins, commodity contracts, diamonds, real estate—you name it and someone will find a way to make a scam out of it.

Investment rackets often originate in telephone "boiler rooms," where squads of high-pressure salespeople canvass the nation with get-rich-quick schemes. Sometimes the approach is low-key; sometimes it's so pressure-packed that usually sensible people get rattled into parting with their money. Whatever the approach, the message is the same: You can make a lot of money or save a lot in taxes by taking advantage of the rare opportunity you're being offered, and you'd better move fast.

A few of these scams are so comical that it's hard to believe anyone would fall for them. But people have been sold shares in companies claiming to be in the

There's hardly a legitimate investment that isn't considered fair game by crooks. You name it and someone will find a way to make a scam out of it.

Deal only with well-established local or national firms whose reputations you trust. If there truly are fantastic deals to be had, these companies will be aware of them.

business of developing underwater home sites, pelts from giant rabbits, and electronic asparagus cutters. We all like to think we'd never fall for anything as laughable as that, and we probably wouldn't. But the crooks are often so clever, talking jargon and spinning out scenarios so fast, that their victims aren't sure what's happening to them. To guard against becoming one of those victims, approach any unfamiliar investment with the following rules firmly in mind.

Deal Only with Established Businesses

Hard as it may be to believe, a poultry-stand operator in Baltimore once allegedly bilked customers out of $4 million by selling them diamonds, second mortgages, and other "investments" he never owned. A parking-lot attendant in Pennsylvania was charged with swindling police officers by luring them into phony deals with promises of 40 to 50 percent returns.

Moral: Confine your dealings to well-established local or national firms whose reputations you trust. If there truly are fantastic deals to be had, you can bet these companies will be aware of them.

Don't Fall for Inflated Promises

The surest tip-off to a rip-off is the promise of big profits, real fast, with little or no risk. If the pitch sounds too good to be true, watch out.

Don't Buy What You Don't Understand

Penny or microcap stocks, oil and gas deals, commodity contracts, art prints, rare coins—these are all specialized areas in which the experts make money sometimes and the amateurs almost always lose. If you don't understand what you're dealing with, seek the advice of someone who does—an accountant, lawyer, or tax advisor. Meanwhile, don't be pressured into a purchase.

Check Out the Seller

Contact the appropriate organization to see if complaints have been filed against the firm you're dealing with.

■ **Stockbrokers and mutual funds:** National Association of Securities Dealers (800-289-9999; http://www.nasdr

.com); ask for the Central Registration Depository report (CRD) on the broker. Or check its searchable data base online. For a more detailed report, call the securities regulation office of the state in which the broker operates (see pages 518 to 523).

- **Business opportunities:** Federal Trade Commission, CRC-240, Washington, DC 20580 (877-382-4357; http://www.ftc.gov). But be aware that the FTC will not tell you about complaints unless it has acted on them.
- **Land sales:** Interstate Land Sales Registration, U.S. Department of Housing and Urban Development, 451 7th Street, SW, Washington, DC 20410 (http://www.hud.gov).
- **Commodities contracts**: Commodity Futures Trading Commission, Office of Public Affairs, Three Lafayette Center, 1155 21st St., NW, Washington, DC 20581 (http://www.cftc.gov); or National Futures Association, 800-621-3570 (in Illinois, call 312-781-1410) or online at (http://www.nfa.futures.org).
- **Anything that comes in the mail:** Criminal Investigations Service Center, Attn: Mail Fraud, 222 S. Riverside Plaza, Suite 1250, Chicago, IL 60606-6100 (800-275-8777; http://www.usps.gov) or contact your local postal inspector. You can also report suspected fraud online.

If you get suspicious, get out fast. Stop payment on your check. Demand your money back. Threaten to go to the authorities.

If you get suspicious, get out fast. Stop payment on your check. Demand your money back. Threaten to go to the authorities. This sort of fuss works more often than you might think. A crook doesn't want some disgruntled victim making a lot of noise and attracting the attention of the authorities. So if you think you're being ripped off, holler.

Hiring Help:
How to Pick a Financial Planner

Investment markets change fast and it's hard to keep up. In addition, it's not always easy to take a dispassionate view of your own financial situation and decide on the proper mix of insurance, investments, and

If you'd like someone to make broad-based investment suggestions based on extensive knowledge of your financial situation, you may be in the market for a financial planner.

the like. A good stockbroker can help, and the next chapter describes how to choose one you'll like. But if you'd like someone to make broader-based investment recommendations based on extensive knowledge of your financial situation, you may be in the market for a financial planner.

Candidates aren't hard to find; just look in your local Yellow Pages. You can also get names of planners in your area from the profession's major membership organizations listed on the opposite page.

After you have the names, select at least three candidates. Visit the office of each and ask for a detailed statement of fees and services, a résumé, and references. Your purpose is to compare them on the following points.

Experience

Financial planning is a wide and varied field, and some of the people in it do not match the popular image of the sage, seasoned counselor. Nevertheless, your planner should have, at the very minimum, a few years of experience in planning or allied fields, such as accounting, securities analysis or trading, or law.

Credentials

Many practitioners have managed to pull themselves above the crowd by taking courses and passing examinations that lead to a professional designation.

Certified Financial Planner (CFP) is probably the best-known credential. Graduates must take a series of courses, pass a two-day, ten-part exam, and complete three years of work experience to earn the CFP designation. In addition, the planner must complete 30 hours of continuing education every two years to keep the credential. The coursework usually takes a couple of years or more to complete and covers virtually all aspects of financial planning for individuals.

Chartered Financial Consultants (ChFC) have earned the designation from the American College in Bryn

Mawr, Pennsylvania, which also grants an insurance-business certification, Chartered Life Underwriter. The ChFC has successfully completed an eight-course sequence over a period of two to four years and passed two-hour exams on each.

Master of Sciences in Financial Services (MSFS) is also conferred by the American College, after 36 credits of coursework. Twelve of the credits are earned by attending two weeks of study at the college.

Registered Financial Consultants (RFC) have met the requirements of the International Association of Registered Financial Consultants, which confers the designation on planners who meet certain academic and work-experience guidelines.

These titles do provide some assurance that the planner took the trouble to take the courses to raise his or her level of skill and knowledge in the field.

Access to Experts

No one person, however well trained, has the encyclopedic knowledge required to deal in depth with all the problems that can affect an individual's financial affairs. That would require knowing as much about, say, estate

---

HOW TO FIND A QUALIFIED FINANCIAL PLANNER

■ **For a directory** of fee-only practitioners, contact the **National Association of Personal Financial Advisors,** 3250 North Arlington Heights Road, Suite 109, Arlington Heights, IL 60004; 800-366-2732; www.napfa.org.

■ **For names of CPAs** who have earned the credential of Accredited Personal Financial Specialist (PFS), contact the **American Institute of CPAs**, Personal Financial Planning Division, 201

Plaza 3, Harborside Financial Center, Jersey City, NJ 07311-3881; 201-938-3828, option 1, or 888-777-7077.

■ **The Financial Planning Association** has a registry service you can use to get names of members in your area. Contact it at 800-322-4237 or visit its Web site at www.fpanet.org, where you can do an online search. The site also features consumer information related to financial planning.

Unless you're dealing with a fee-only firm, expect to get suggestions that you purchase a product the planner sells. There's nothing wrong with that, provided the product is suitable for you.

planning and insurance as commodity futures. Instead, a planner should be able to demonstrate that he or she consults regularly with experts in a variety of fields.

Fees and Commissions

There is no standard fee system or scale in the planning business. At one end of the spectrum are the planners who work only for fees, much like lawyers. At the other end are the firms that operate entirely or almost entirely on commissions. In between are the larger number, who depend on a combination of fees and commissions. In some cases the planner might partly credit commissions against the fee to encourage the client to buy insurance or other financial products through the planner's company.

A planner who feels confident of being able to sell a high-commission product might gamble on a low fee. Assume, for instance, you're charged $1,000 for a complete plan plus a certain number of hours of interviews and consultation time. If you put $20,000 in a mutual fund with a 5 percent sales charge, or load, your planner would make $1,000, and only $19,000 would buy shares in the fund.

Unless you're dealing with a fee-only firm, you can expect to get suggestions that you purchase an investment or insurance product that the planner sells. There's nothing wrong with that, provided the product is suitable for someone in your financial situation and compares favorably with the scores of others you might buy elsewhere.

If the product is insurance, for example, and the policy is right for you and competitively priced, you might as well buy it from the planner. But your attitude should be different about mutual funds and securities. You'd want to think twice about buying a load fund when there are so many no-load funds available, for instance. And why buy the stocks recommended by the planner at a standard commission rate when you can use a discount broker? It's up to you to decide whether the quality of the planner's service is worth the cost.

How to Make Money in Stocks

There's really only one reason to take on the risks that go with investing in stocks: the hope of a higher return on your money than you could get elsewhere. And it's not an unreasonable hope. Over your adult lifetime, stocks will almost certainly outperform virtually any other investment you could make. That doesn't mean that stocks will beat, say, bonds or real estate in any particular year, or even any particular decade. The stock market was a lousy place to be for most of the 1970s, for instance. Along with most other so-called financial assets, stocks went virtually nowhere while "hard" assets—real estate, gold, and even diamonds—seemed to be making a lot of people rich. Then, stocks soared starting in the early 1980s, swooned when the 1990s arrived, then soared again, more than making up for their disappointing decade before first dropping at the turn of the century, plunging in the aftermath of September 11 and then starting back up.

Stocks are capable of generating spectacular returns and equally spectacular losses from time to time. Over the long haul, the returns have far outweighed the losses; since 1961, stocks have returned an average of more than 10 percent per year. They offer a chance to share in the economic growth of the country by owning a piece of the companies that are making it happen. And they can play an important role in diversifying your investment assets and thus spreading your risks.

Although it's possible to profit from a rising market without ever having to select a single stock (see the description of index funds in Chapter 25), as an investor

Earnings per share is the bottom line you hear so much about. It is the company's net income divided by the number of common-stock shares outstanding.

your main concern isn't merely the general direction of the stock market. You should also know how to pick good stocks. This chapter will show you how.

What Makes a Good Stock?

From magazines and newspapers, radio and television, we're all bombarded regularly with stock recommendations from experts of all kinds. Even if every single one of them were worthy of our confidence, we can actually afford to buy only a handful of stocks. But which ones? By knowing how to use the basic tools that stock analysts use to separate the good from the bad, you should be able to find the stocks most likely to meet your goals and strategy. Take a look at the yardsticks professional money managers use to measure security values. You can use them, too.

First, some basic definitions. Stocks come in two principal varieties: common stock and preferred stock. Both represent an ownership share in the company that issues them. Common stock may or may not pay dividends; preferred stock, because it gives investors first crack at a company's dividends, is generally bought for the income it produces, rather than the chance that the price will go up. Common stocks are where the action is, and when people talk about "stocks" they are almost always referring to common stocks.

So how do the pros sort out the good stocks from the bad? By comparing the following characteristics.

How Much Does the Company Earn?

This is the bottom line you hear so much about. It boils down the company's year (or quarter) into a nice, neat number from which the company can't hide. Earnings per share is the company's net income (after taxes and after funds are set aside for preferred-stock dividends) divided by the number of common-stock shares outstanding. Earnings reports sometimes differentiate between income produced by regular operations and income resulting from unusual transactions, such as the sale of a subsidiary.

When a company is described as growing at a certain rate, it's usually the earnings that are being used as the measure, and successful pros look for companies with a strong record of rising earnings.

How Does the Price Relate to Earnings?

Divide the current price of a stock by its earnings for the past 12-month period and you have the price-earnings ratio—or the price-earnings multiple, as it is often called. The "P/E" is probably the most widely used analytical tool among stockpickers, and for good reason: It tells you what investors think of a particular stock compared with other stocks and compared with the stock market as a whole. Actually, there are two ways to express a P/E ratio. The most common way is to use the previous year's earnings; the number is called a "trailing" P/E. Sometimes analysts use their earnings forecasts to calculate a potential P/E for a company, in which case it is called an "anticipated" P/E or something similar.

The fact that investors are willing to pay 20 times earnings for one stock and only 12 times earnings for another seems to indicate that the first stock is more highly regarded than the second, and you wouldn't go too far wrong thinking of it that way. Perhaps investors feel more confident that the first company will be able to increase its earnings, increase them faster or pay higher dividends than the second company.

Still, a company's P/E ratio doesn't provide an investment clue until it's compared with P/E values of the same company over past years, the P/Es of other companies in the same business, and the P/E of stock indexes representing the market as a whole. A stock selling for $10 a share with earnings of 10 cents a share may seem cheap. But its P/E of 100 actually makes it vastly more expensive than a $50 stock with earnings of $2.50 a share (a P/E of 20).

A stock with an especially high P/E in relation to similar stocks or the market as a whole may be the victim of unrealistic expectations on the part of investors. Even a slight stumble could send the price tumbling. The idea is to buy your stock at the lowest possible P/E. As other

> The "P/E" is probably the most widely used analytical tool among stockpickers, and for good reason.

Investors buy a stock not for what it can do for them today, but for what they hope it will do for them tomorrow.

investors begin to recognize the stock's potential, they may bid up the price (and thus the P/E). That is your hope, of course, but reality doesn't always oblige. Sometimes a rise in earnings per share may actually be accompanied by a drop in the price. Why? Because expectations were that earnings would climb even higher than they actually did. Remember: Investors buy a stock not for what it can do for them today, but for what they hope it will do for them tomorrow. If it doesn't live up to expectations, investors will tend to bail out.

How Does the Price Relate to Book Value?

Simply put, a company's book value is the difference between its assets and its liabilities—what it owns and what it is owed, minus what it owes. This is sometimes referred to as shareholder's equity. Dividing book value by the number of outstanding shares gives you the book value per share, another useful reference point for a stock.

Theoretically, book value represents the amount stockholders would receive for each share they own if the company were to shut down, sell all its assets, pay all its debts, and go out of business. (Few companies whose shares are widely traded ever shut down, but the list of bankruptcies and near-bankruptcies that dot the history of American business makes the point: Stuff happens.)

Stocks may be recommended as cheap because they are selling below book value or very little above. Such stocks sometimes become takeover candidates, attracting the attention of other companies, which see a chance to buy them up on the cheap—and that can drive up the price of the shares and thus reward investors who spotted the bargain sooner.

However, it's possible a company's stock is selling below book value not because it is an undiscovered bargain but because that company or its industry has fallen on hard times. You need more information to go on before you start buying. (See the box on the next page.)

What's the Return on Book Value?

A company's total annual net (after-tax) income, expressed as a percentage of total book value, measures how much the company earns on the stockholders' stake in the enterprise. Return on book value, also called return on equity, varies from company to company and from industry to industry, and it fluctuates with economic conditions. One year's return on equity means little, but by comparing several years' results for the company and its industry, you can spot trends and get an idea of how well the company is managing its assets.

WHERE TO FIND OUT ABOUT STOCKS

Company annual reports
Basic information about the company, including audited financial data for the most recent year and summaries of prior years. Available from brokers and from investor-relations offices of individual companies.

Analysts' reports
Commentaries by brokerage firms' research departments, with forecasts and data to accompany recommendations to buy, sell, or hold stocks that the firm follows. Available from brokers.

Value Line Investment Survey
Data on more than 1,700 stocks, including historical prices, earnings, and dividends, along with analysis and recommendations, with weekly updates. Available from libraries or from Value Line. A print version is $75 for a trial subscription and $598 a year; an online version is $65 for the trial and $598 a year. Order at 800-634-3583 or www.valueline.com.

Standard & Poor's Corp.
S&P Stock Reports offer a wealth of current and historical data in the monthly *S&P*

Stock Guide, a compendium of similar data on more than 7,500 stocks, but with no analysts' commentary. Available from libraries, brokers, or by subscription from S&P, 55 Water St., New York, NY 10041; 800-221-5277 or www.standardpoors.com.

Mergent Manuals and handbooks
These come in eight volumes containing current and historical data on thousands of companies. *The Handbook of Common Stocks* covers about 900 stocks, and the *Dividend Record* keeps track of current dividend payments of most publicly traded companies. Available from brokers, libraries, or from Mergent Inc., Customer Care Center-Consumer Accounts, 10475 Crosspoint Blvd., Indianapolis, IN 46256; phone: 877-762-2964; fax: 800-597-3299; online at www.mergent.com.

Financial newspapers
The stock listings of *The Wall Street Journal, Barron's,* and *Investor's Business Daily* contain current information on prices, dividends, yields, and price-earnings ratios, as do the stock listings of most daily newspapers.

Knowing a stock's volatility gives you some idea of the kind of behavior you can expect from it in relation to the market.

What's the Total Return?

Investors tend to think of their gains and losses in terms of price changes and forget about dividends. But both price changes and current income should be taken into account to evaluate investment performance. Together they show your total return, which is the only fair way to compare stocks that pay dividends with stocks that don't and to compare results from stocks with results from bonds, Treasury bills, and other alternatives.

How Much Debt Does the Company Carry?

A company's debt-equity ratio, which is its book value divided by its debts, is a pretty good measure of its fiscal health because the more it pays out to debt service—as interest on bonds, for instance, or on lines of credit with banks—the less it has available to pay dividends, invest in the future, or set aside as a cushion for business downturns. Most companies do carry some debt, and what's acceptable in one industry may not be acceptable in another. Always be sure to compare debt-equity ratios of similar companies. Other things being equal, the lower the debt the better.

How Volatile Is the Stock?

A stock's past volatility, which can be measured with some precision, is as good a gauge of its future risk as you're going to get. At the least, knowing a stock's volatility gives you some idea of the kind of behavior you can expect from it in relation to the market. Some stocks' prices move slowly and within a relatively narrow range; others bounce up and down a lot. Analysts have developed several measures of price volatility. Perhaps the most easily understood is the *beta*, which tells you how much a stock characteristically moves in relation to a change in a stock-market index, usually the Standard & Poor's 500. A stock with a beta of 1.0 moves in step with the index. A stock with a beta of 1.1 historically rises or falls 10 percent more than the index. A stock with a beta of 0.9 is less volatile; it would be expected to go up 9 percent if the market rose 10 percent or down by

HOW STOCKS ARE TRADED

Most stocks are bought and sold on one of the major exchanges. The New York Stock Exchange (www.nyse.com) is probably the best known because the biggest companies tend to be traded there. Also, it's usually on the floor of the NYSE where the television cameras get their pictures of frenzied trading on days when stocks soar or plunge. Almost 3,000 stocks are "listed" on the NYSE, which means they are bought and sold there, no matter where the investor happens to place the order.

The stocks of even more companies are traded on Nasdaq ("nazz-dak"; www.nasdaq.com), a national computerized system that once was considered a place for small companies to trade. It still is, but today Nasdaq also counts corporate giants such as Intel and Microsoft among its clients. A smaller number of stocks are listed on the American Stock Exchange and on the regional stock exchanges, which are located in Boston, Chicago, Philadelphia, San Francisco, and other cities. Some stocks listed on the NYSE are also traded on the regional exchanges. The "over-the-counter" market is a telephone-and-computer-linked network on which the shares of thousands of smaller, unlisted companies are bought and sold each day.

9 percent if the index fell 10 percent. Once thought to be an arcane measure best left to the green-eye-shade crowd, betas are now commonly reported by such stock-ranking services as *Value Line Investment Survey* (see the box on page 347).

Getting a Little Technical

The concepts described so far—P/E ratios, book value, and so forth—are derived from the fundamental financial strengths and weaknesses of a company, and using them as tools for spotting stock values is called fundamental analysis. From time to time you may come across buy or sell recommendations that reflect what is known as technical analysis. Technicians examine the whole market or individual stocks and try to forecast price movements by examining previous price changes, the ratio of advancing to declining stocks, and a wide and sometimes bewildering range of other statistical data. To technicians these factors, often plotted on charts, reveal the basic forces that they believe influence prices of individual stocks and the market as a whole.

If you're essentially a conservative, buy-and-hold type, look for "blue chips"— big companies with consistently high earnings and a record of increasing dividends.

Technicians speak their own language, particularly when referring to chart patterns they feel have special significance: heads and shoulders, channels, saucers, wedges, pennants, double bottoms. Many investors have no faith in such patterns, and most don't understand them, but technical analysis does command respect in the investment business, and committed adherents of fundamental analysis often check a stock's technical position before acting. You should know a little about technical analysis, but unless you plan to make a lengthy study of its methods, don't go nuts trying to decipher it.

What's Your Plan?

By yourself you can't possibly sort through the thousands of stock issues traded on the various exchanges and over the counter, searching for a few to buy. Once in a while you may come across an interesting company through business or personal contacts. For the most part, though, you have to look for investment prospects among the recommendations of the brokerage firms and financial publications. Sifting through their leads will be much easier if you first take the time to decide on an overall investment approach. Then you can see how suggested stocks might fit into it. The following approaches aren't mutually exclusive. Many successful investing plans contain elements of each; balance is the key.

Buying and Holding

Investors in this category hold their stocks for a long time—five or ten years or more. They sit tight during market declines (or use them as opportunities to buy more stocks at lower prices), confident that the inherent strength of their companies will ultimately reward them with higher earnings, dividends, and prices.

If you're essentially a conservative, buy-and-hold type (for most people this is the most sensible attitude), look for "blue chips"—big companies with consistently high earnings and a record of increasing dividends.

Counting on Diversity

J. Russell Holmes, who delved into stock returns produced over a 107-year period, concluded that one of the three keys to succeeding in the market was to think in terms of portfolios, not individual issues. (The other two, according to Holmes, are taking time to select issues with growth potential and holding stock for the long term—10- to 15-year periods.)

How many stocks does it take to diversify enough? That depends on several factors. One study indicates that you need a minimum of ten separate issues if you're dealing with high-quality companies. Another way to spread the risk would be to buy just a few individual stocks and buffer them with shares in mutual funds, or to stick with mutual funds exclusively because their portfolios usually hold no fewer than several dozen issues.

Betting on One Industry

Certain industries grab the headlines from time to time because of economic or social trends, technological developments, or marketing innovations. This can create whole new industries seemingly overnight—managed health care and computer software, for example.

The opportunity to profit from such industries lies in discovering the winning companies before the boom starts or while it is in its early stages. You get maximum *oomph* from so-called pure-play companies, those that specialize in the field and so stand to gain most. Many big corporations are so highly diversified that gains in any one product may not substantially increase total profits. In the best of circumstances, you might find a company that turns into a growth leader that you can hold for the long haul.

Workers in a particular industry are better placed than outsiders to spot opportunities there, so look first in your own field. Trade journals sometimes provide clues, and many professional analysts read them religiously.

Swinging for the Fences

When you're hoping for the big score, the long-term qualities of a stock aren't as important as the near-term

Your broker can be your most valuable source of help in making good investment decisions. An inept or unresponsive broker can make your life miserable, and cost you money.

potential. You're looking for home runs: sexy companies selling stock to the public for the first time, corporations likely to be bought out or to buy out another company, "concept" companies promoting some new product or service, or turnaround stocks that have been severely depressed and are expected to snap back.

You can speculate even with a conservative stock by the way you buy and sell it. Buying on margin (financing part of the purchase with a loan from the broker) and selling short (selling shares borrowed through the broker in the hope of replacing them later with shares bought at a lower price) increase the risk and the potential return.

This sort of activity should be confined to a small part of your investment portfolio, because the actions that you hope will boost your reward—buying start-ups, borrowing money to buy more, betting on a decline in a stock's price—are the very actions that will boost your loss if you're wrong.

How to Find the Right Broker

If you make the right choice, your broker can be your single most valuable source of help in making good investment decisions. By the same token, an inept or unresponsive broker can make your life miserable, as well as cost you money. The first decision you need to make is whether you want a traditional broker at all, or whether you'd rather do your thinking for yourself, or get your advice elsewhere and use a brokerage firm only to execute your trades.

Brokers differ in several ways. There are full-service and discount firms; national, regional, and local firms; and firms that operate only online or over the phone. All sell more than stocks: They sell municipal bonds, unit trusts, tax shelters, and annuities. But the chief distinction is between full-service and the discount firms.

Full-Service Brokers
Whether regional outfits known mostly in their own area of the country or national giants, these companies

are the places to go if you want access to a small army of research analysts who study firms and industries in search of good investments and pass along their recommendations to you through your broker, who gets paid a commission when you buy or sell. Individual brokers assigned to your account will be called financial consultants or something similar. Rarely are they officially referred to as brokers.

Full-service firms offer a wide range of customer services, including research reports, individual advice, asset-management accounts (see Chapter 4), consolidated account statements, and seminars on retirement planning, tax shelters, and other investment-related topics. Among their most popular programs are so-called wrap accounts, in which the firm manages a portfolio of mutual funds or stocks you select. You may get advice as part of the package and you pay no commissions to buy and sell in the account, instead paying an annual "wrap" fee of .75 to 1.5 percent of your assets if you own funds. For wrap accounts containing stocks, the fee may be 3 percent or so. This fee structure makes wrap accounts attractive for investors in mutual funds that charge

---

FULL-SERVICE BROKERS

A. G. Edwards & Sons
877-835-7877
www.agedwards.com

Prudential
800-778-4357
www.prudential.com

Edward Jones
314-515-2000
www.edwardjones.com

Smith Barney
800-232-4454
www.smithbarney. com

Merrill Lynch
800-637-7455
www.ml.com

UBS Financial Services
800-354-9103
www.ubs.com

Morgan Stanley
866-742-6669
www.ms.com

If you have a good working relationship with a broker, and he or she helps you make your investment decisions, commissions shouldn't be a major concern.

sales commissions, but a bit on the expensive side for investors in stocks, especially buy-and-hold investors who don't generate enough commissions to cover the wrap fee.

If you have a good working relationship with a broker, and he or she provides valuable help in making your investment decisions, then commissions shouldn't be a major concern. Most people select a brokerage firm for reasons that have nothing to do with commissions, anyway—perhaps its office is conveniently located, its research reports have been useful, or the account executive is helpful. Factors such as these can easily compensate for the commissions, especially for relatively modest investors.

Because they offer so many services, full-service brokers may excel at some and fall back a bit on others. In recent studies, *Kiplinger's Personal Finance* magazine found little difference in commissions for similar trades. (In fact, prized customers—those with big accounts who make lots of trades or who use a number of the firms' products or services—can often get discounts on commissions, anyway.) Where the full-service brokers separate themselves from the competition is in areas such as stock picking, asset allocation, and breadth of research.

Discount Brokers

Today the offices of the major discount firms, such as Charles Schwab and Fidelity Brokerage Services, are virtually indistinguishable from the offices of their full-service brethren, complete with stock tickers, libraries of investment information, all-in-one accounts, plush chairs, and computer terminals for checking on the value of your holdings. But here you get execution of your order—no research, no handholding, no advice. (Most firms do make helpful literature available, often including research reports from other sources, such as Standard & Poor's, Value Line, and Morningstar.) Salespeople are paid a salary, not commissions. Most discounters also offer a long list of account services identical to those of the full-service brokers.

DISCOUNT BROKERS

These brokers maintain walk-in offices, although most also offer online trading.

Ameritrade
800-669-3900
www.ameritrade.com

JB Oxford
800-782-1876
www.jboxford.com

StockCross
800-225-6196
www.stockcross.com

BrownCo
800-822-2021
www.brownco.com

JH Darbie
800-606-8844
www.jhdarbie.com

T. Rowe Price
800-225-5132
www.troweprice.com

Cutter
800-536-8770
www.cutterco.com

Saturna Brokerage Svs.
800-728-8762
www.saturna.com

TD Waterhouse
800-934-4448
www.tdwaterhouse.com

Dreyfus
800-421-8395
www.dreyfus.com

Charles Schwab
800-225-8570
www.schwab.com

USAA
800-531-8343
www.usaa.com

Fidelity
800-343-3548
www.fidelity.com

Scottrade
800-619-7283
www.scottrade.com

Vanguard
800-992-8327
www.vanguard.com

H&R Block
Financial Advisors
800-472-5625
http://investment-center
.hrblock.com

Muriel Siebert & Co.
800-872-0711
www.siebertnet.com

Wachovia
800-326-4434
www.wachovia.com

They can all save you money over the full-service shops. Competition is fierce, and which is "best" depends on what you need. If the best price is what you're after, you'll have to call around to find it, but be aware that the firm charging the lowest fees may not be the best for other services you might want, such as issuing and delivering stock certificates (which you'd need if you wanted to enroll in a dividend reinvestment plan, for instance), or making mutual funds available with no transaction fees.

Before you sign on with a discount broker, find out whether there is a minimum charge for transactions; the fee could wipe out savings from a small trade.

Many discounters are members of the New York Stock Exchange, with offices in several cities around the country. They have toll-free telephone numbers for distant clients, and most offer online trading. Discounts, depending on the size of the transaction, can amount to as much as 80 percent of what you'd pay a full-service broker, although 20 to 30 percent is a more representative saving. You can commonly save about 50 percent on transactions in the $5,000 range.

Some discounters operate through banks and savings and loan associations. The larger firms have walk-in offices in major cities. But before you sign on, find out whether there is a minimum charge. Some firms set a $20 to $45 minimum fee regardless of the size of the trade. On small trades, that could wipe out the savings you might be anticipating.

Online Brokers

A growing number of active investors are bypassing conventional brokerage offices entirely and doing all their trading online. More than 11 million investors traded online in 2005. The implications of this trend aren't lost on the discount brokers who have jumped into the field with both feet. Schwab is the online market leader. But competitive pressures are strongest from firms created expressly for the online environment, such as Ameritrade and E*Trade Financial. All told, a couple of dozen firms offer trading via the Internet.

The attractions of online trading are price and convenience. Commissions for electronic trading tend to be the lowest around. You can easily shop for the best rate and can make your trades any time of day or night just by sitting down at your computer. Most firms will also let you trade by phone through a customer-service representative, though they may charge extra for that. Some full-service brokers have Web sites and offer information online but are reluctant to undercut their staff brokers by offering online trading.

You can also buy and sell mutual funds via online brokers. A recent Kiplinger survey found that one size doesn't fit all. The study evaluated which brokers

MAJOR ONLINE BROKERS

Accutrade
800-882-4887
www.accutrade.com

American Express
800-297-5300
www.americanexpress
.com/trade

Ameritrade
800-454-9272
www.ameritrade.com

Brown & Co.
800-822-2021
www.brownco.com

E*trade Financial
800-387-2331
www.etrade.com

Fidelity
800-343-3548
www.fidelity.com

Harris Direct
800-825-5723
www.harrisdirect.com

Merrill Lynch
800-637-7455
www.ml.com

Morgan Stanley
866-742-6669
www.dbdirect.com

Muriel Siebert & Co.
800-872-0711
www.siebertnet.com

Scottrade
800-619-7283
www.scottrade.com

TD Waterhouse
800-934-4448
www.tdwaterhouse.com

would be best if you had $50,000 to invest versus $500,000. Two brokers shared the number one spot.

The best Internet broker for customers with $50,000 to invest was relatively little-known Muriel Siebert & Co. Among the criteria that helped Siebert finish in first place were the firm's first-class service and its high scores for ethical standards.

But for those with over $500,000 to invest, Fidelity was best because it excelled in the research it provided clients, and its Web site was deemed best of the bunch.

The number two spot went to Scottrade, a fast-growing company that offers good service while keeping fees low for modest investors, and Murial Siebert for investors with bigger accounts.

If low fees are your main concern, Scottrade was the winner. It charged just $7 for a market order and $12 for a limit order. What's more, it tacked on virtually no nuisance fees for such things as transferring an IRA or obtaining a copy of a canceled check. Brown & Co. had lower commissions—$5 for a market order

Before you sign up with a broker on the basis of commissions alone, ask about annual service charges. Some firms levy an annual fee to keep small investors away.

and $10 for a limit order—but imposed more incidental fees than almost any other broker.

Do you want to choose from as many funds as possible? Ameritrade had the most no-load funds, just shy of 3,000. Next, in order, were USAA, Fidelity, Waterhouse, Siebert, Schwab, Harris, Brown, and Scottrade. All offered close to 2,000 or more no-loads. But E*Trade offered only 1,100 funds, and Merrill had just 400.

To help you choose a broker that meets your needs, go to http://www.kiplinger.com, click on "Tools" then "Stock Tools" then "Which Online Broker is Best for You." You can also access online broker sites directly, using a Web browser such as Netscape or Microsoft Internet Explorer, or through commercial services such as America Online and CompuServe.

Opening Your Account

It is simple enough to open an account with any broker by walking into the office, calling for an application, or submitting one online.

Before you sign up on the basis of commissions alone, ask about annual service charges. Some firms, wishing to limit their business to well-heeled investors, levy an annual fee to keep the small ones away. It's important to shop around. A trade of one size may be cheaper at, say, Fidelity than at Siebert, while another transaction will cost less at Siebert than at Fidelity.

One rule of thumb you can use in comparing fee schedules at either full-service or discount brokerages is that a firm whose commission is calculated on the basis of the number of shares traded rather than the price of the shares should be cheaper for trading big blocks of higher-priced stocks.

If You Need to Tangle with Your Broker

When things go seriously wrong with a broker, your first instinct is rarely to sue the firm. Good thing, because the vast majority of broker-investor agreements, which you sign when you open your account, contain a clause that says you can't sue. Instead, you must submit your complaint to binding arbitration. (Older broker-investor agreements may not contain the clause.)

Luckily, most complaints against brokers can be settled with a letter or a phone call. Serious complaints—for instance, churning of your account (which means a pattern of buying and selling by the broker for the purpose of generating commissions) or high-pressure tactics that result in your choosing inappropriate investments—might require arbitration, so you should know something about it. Any member of a securities exchange or of the National Association of Securities Dealers (NASD) is subject to a uniform binding arbitration procedure, whether the squabble is over a few hundred dollars or several thousand—even if the dispute isn't over money at all but over a matter of procedures or ethics.

The NASD, the Municipal Securities Rulemaking Board, and all of the stock exchanges are known as self-regulatory organizations (SROs) and are overseen by the Securities and Exchange Commission, in Washington, D.C. The SEC doesn't arbitrate disputes but refers them to the arbitration program run by the SRO involved in the dispute.

Before it comes to that, the SEC, NASD, and most of the SROs will try to mediate. They'll send your complaint to the brokerage firm, ask for a written explanation, and try to get both sides to agree to a settlement. If that doesn't work, you must decide whether to seek arbitration. If you do, the process will be conducted by the appropriate SRO, or it may be heard by representatives of the independent American Arbitration Association.

The various forums follow similar rules. Your initial filing fees for AAA arbitration start at $500, while those of the industry-subsidized SROs start at $15. Fees are usually nonrefundable. Cases take several months to complete.

You can hire a lawyer to plead your case, but with or without a lawyer, you have no right to sue later if the arbitrator or panel of arbitrators rules against you.

The vast majority of broker-investor agreements contain a clause that says you can't sue; you must submit to binding arbitration.

A firm cannot refuse to cooperate with the arbitration process, but it can file a counterclaim if it believes your contentions are frivolous.

To file a claim, you must first get the forms from the director of arbitration of the appropriate exchange. Just about any exchange could have jurisdiction because most securities firms are members of all major exchanges, some or all of the regional boards, and the NASD.

A firm cannot refuse to cooperate with the process, but it can file a counterclaim if it believes your contentions are frivolous. You won't get anywhere, for example, just because you lost money on a broker-recommended stock, unless you can show that the broker promised you its price wouldn't fall or held back negative information.

If your case involves less than $5,000, the exchange will put it through a simplified arbitration procedure. The one arbitrator assigned will rule from the evidence submitted but is unlikely to call a hearing.

If your claim is for more than $5,000, the procedure becomes more like a trial. The exchange will schedule a hearing in a nearby large city at a convenient date and appoint a panel of arbitrators. You and your lawyer, as well as the respondent, can call witnesses. The arbitrators and the counsel for either side can subpoena people and documents. The proceeding takes place under oath and all documents are kept confidential.

The arbitrators will not rule on the spot but will mail their decision to you and the responding firm, usually within 30 days. You may or may not get an explanation with the ruling, which can include a monetary award. The decision is final.

For more information, contact the director of arbitration at the NASD, 33 Whitehall St., New York, NY 10004 (http://www.nasd.com), or the NYSE, 11 Wall St., Fifth Floor, New York, NY 10005 (http://www.nyse.com).

Investing with a Club

Serious investing is hard work. It takes careful research, attention to detail, and nearly constant alertness to shifting economic tides. Most of the time, not much happens: An excellent investment choice may take from several months to several years to fulfill its potential. Meanwhile, the job can be tedious, discouraging—and lonely. That's why hundreds of thousands of people around the country band together to form investment clubs.

A typical club has about 15 members—friends, neighbors, or coworkers, usually—and meets once a month to consider its portfolio decisions. Members are assigned different tasks. One team may be responsible for tracking economic conditions; another may report on the investment climate; a third may present charts, graphs, and other material to back up specific investment recommendations, which are usually decided by majority vote.

To fund the portfolio, club members typically pitch in about $85 a month, although in some clubs the amount may be a little smaller or much larger. With the money, a typical club accumulates a portfolio of about 15 stocks, ownership of which the members share in proportion to their contributions to the investment kitty.

For most members, the club is not the only place they invest. In fact, they tend to have individual portfolios that are much larger than what they have tied up in the club. That makes investment clubs popular with brokers, who like the thought of serving all those individual members' portfolios.

How well do clubs do? BetterInvesting, formerly known as the National Association of Investors Corp. (NAIC) reports that over the years many of its member clubs regularly beat the S&P 500 stock index— and that's about as well as professional portfolio managers do. Teamwork is very important to the success of an investment club. All members must work to move the club forward to avoid member burnout. Each member has a role and responsibility to the club. BetterInvesting has found that if club members aren't willing to share responsibilities within the club and work together to achieve success, the club will fail in the first two years.

You can get guidance in starting and running an investment club from BetterInvesting, P.O. Box 220,

A typical investment club has about 15 members— friends, neighbors, or coworkers, usually—and meets once a month to consider its portfolio decisions.

One major requirement for successful investing is to keep mistakes to a minimum.

Royal Oak, MI 48068; 877-275-6242; http://www .betterinvesting.org.

Stupid Stock Tricks

It has been said that the winners of tennis matches, football games, even battles, are those who make the fewest mistakes. Or, to put it another way, the winners are those who manage not to lose. The same could be said for the stock market. One major requirement for successful investing is to keep mistakes to a minimum.

What are the most common ways investors go wrong? *Kiplinger's Personal Finance* magazine has examined this question over the years and counts eight mistakes that recur with unnecessary frequency. Forewarned is forearmed.

1. Not having an investment plan or philosophy. This error takes various forms. Without the guidance of a long-range objective, you fail to decide in advance what type of company you want to own stocks in—long-term-growth companies, cyclical firms, or speculative ones. You don't decide whether you want current income or capital gains. You shoot from the hip. If by chance you do have a plan, you abandon it when the market is bursting with optimism or sulking with pessimism.

2. Not taking the trouble and time to be informed. Failing to get information about a company before investing in it is the most common form of this mistake. Some investors actually buy stock in a company without knowing what the company makes and what the future might be for that kind of product.

3. Not checking on the quality of your advice. Many investors don't check on brokers or advisors before doing business. They don't investigate, for example, their educational background, how long they have been in business or have been handling other people's money, how well they have done. They don't ask to see sample accounts.

In the words of the manager of a large mutual fund complex, "Following the advice of a mediocre broker is known as a 'cut flower' program. The broker keeps picking flowers and selling them to you. When one bunch withers, he sells you another."

4. Investing money that should be set aside for another use. Too often people tie up money that should be available for emergencies or for purchase of a new car or some other predictable expense. If you invest what should be emergency funds in stocks, you may be forced into selling stocks at a time not of your own choosing. Fate often decrees that this will be a period of low prices when you must take a loss.

5. Being optimistic at the top and pessimistic at the bottom. Optimism and bullishness are infectious, as are pessimism and bearishness. Thus, even when the market is high by such standards as the ratio of prices to earnings, people go right on buying. They do it because everyone seems to be buying, or because they extrapolate recent trends and assume that what has been happening will continue to happen, or because they mistakenly think there is an exact correlation between the stock market and business conditions. Conversely, people grow increasingly pessimistic as the market drops and tend to reach the bottom of the pit when stocks are cheapest. This may be when you should be buying, or at least holding on to what you have.

6. Buying on the basis of tips and rumors. There's hardly any chance that the average investor will get advance or inside information about any company whose stock is publicly held. And even if you do, it probably won't do you much good. Professional speculators are watching the market news all day long, ready to buy or sell on a minute's notice. There are also specialists in each stock listed on the various exchanges. At any rumor about a company or any unusual change in the volume of trading, the specialist calls up the company's management and gets the facts. So remember, no matter

> **If you invest what should be emergency funds in stocks, you may be forced into selling stocks at a time not of your own choosing.**

Some investors grow as attached to their stocks as they do to their pets. That can be a big mistake.

how hot a tip you hear, plenty of people knew it before you did.

7. Becoming sentimental about a stock or an industry. Some investors grow as attached to their stocks as they do to their pets. As a result, they hold on to companies long after the potential for growth and profit has passed. A similar mistake is to fail to sell a stock because you hate to admit that you were wrong to buy it in the first place.

8. Buying low-priced stocks on the theory that they will show the largest percentage gains. A low-priced stock may be a bargain, but not necessarily because it is low-priced. The price of a stock is what the marketplace believes a company to be worth divided by the number of shares outstanding. A stock that sells for peanuts does so because that's what the market thinks it's worth. Period.

What You Should Know About Bonds

Bonds sound boring, but they're not. Nor are they a nice safe haven for rich and retired folks who never want to lose money. They have a role to play in your investment plan for several important reasons.

First, bonds aren't stocks. Well-selected stocks, as we have seen in the previous chapter, tend to go up over the long run. But in the short run they can—and from time to time certainly will—go down, sometimes through no fault of their own. And the very same kinds of things that depress stock prices, such as a recession or sluggish business conditions, tend to boost bond prices. This makes them ideal for diversifying and thus controlling your investment risks.

Second, bonds usually produce a steady stream of income you can reinvest or use for living expenses. The price may go up or down, but barring default on the part of the issuer, the income from a bond remains the same. Municipal bonds can generate tax-free income.

Day-to-day changes in interest rates are what put spice in the life of bond investors. Consider what happens to a bond's market price as interest rates do a normal amount of bouncing around.

Say you buy a $1,000 bond issued to yield 7 percent, or $70 a year. Then interest rates rise to 8 percent. If you want to sell your 7 percent bond, other investors aren't going to pay full face value for it because they could get 8 percent interest on a new bond. Thus, your bond loses market value. If you sell it, you'd have to sell it for something less than the $1,000 you paid for it.

Now suppose rates fall. If new bonds are offering 6 percent, then your 7 percent bond looks pretty good.

In their basic form, bonds are IOUs— receipts for money borrowed from the investor.

If you sell it, you can get more than face value and make a profit. More on this later.

The marketplace for bonds and bond-like investments is wide and diverse, and it contains opportunities to hedge against inflation, trim taxes, even lock in profits that are virtually guaranteed.

A Primer for Bond Buyers

In their basic form, bonds and other credit instruments, such as notes, bills, and commercial paper, are IOUs—basically, receipts for money borrowed from the investor. They bind the issuing organization to pay a fixed amount of interest periodically (usually semiannually) and repay the full face amount on the maturity date, which is set when the instrument is issued.

Governments and corporations regularly finance their operations by issuing such credit instruments. Agency securities are issues of various government-sponsored organizations, such as Fannie Mae. Municipals, also known as tax-exempts, are issued by state and local governments.

General obligation municipal bonds are secured by the full taxing power of the issuing organization. Revenue bonds depend on revenues from a specific source, such as bridge or road tolls. Some municipals are secured by revenues from a specific tax.

Secured corporate bonds are backed by a lien on part of a corporation's plant, equipment, or other assets. Unsecured bonds, known as debentures, are backed only by the general credit of the corporation. Zero-coupon bonds are issued at a big discount from face value and pay no interest until maturity.

Corporations also pay a fixed annual amount on preferred stock when profits permit, but preferred shares represent an ownership stake in the corporation, not a debt. However, because of the fixed return, the price of preferred stocks tends to fluctuate in response to interest-rate changes, more like bonds than like common stocks.

Some bonds, debentures, and preferred stocks are convertible into the corporation's common stock at a fixed ratio—a certain number of shares of common stock in exchange for a certain amount of bonds or preferred shares. Convertibles may sell at lower yields than nonconvertibles because of the possibility that the owner can make a profit on the conversion.

How Much They Cost

The standard face value for bonds is $1,000 or $5,000. Some are issued in larger denominations but very few come in smaller denominations. You buy them through a broker, or, in the case of U.S. Treasury bonds, you can buy them directly through the government.

How You Own Them

Bonds and notes usually must be registered with the issuing organization in the name of the owner, just like common stock. Usually ownership is in book-entry form, meaning the issuer keeps a record of buyers' names but no securities actually change hands. Treasury bills are issued this way. Bearer bonds, which are no longer issued, are unregistered and presumed to belong to anyone who holds them, like money. You clip and mail in coupons to get the interest.

When They Pay Interest

Most bonds pay interest semiannually. Many mutual funds and unit trusts that invest in bonds pay dividends monthly as a convenience to shareholders. Discount securities, such as Treasury bills and savings bonds, pay interest by deducting it from the sales price, or face value at the time of issue, then paying full face value at maturity.

Why Maturity Counts

When bonds reach their maturity, they pay back the face amount. Bonds that mature in two years or less are usually dubbed short-term bonds; maturities of up to ten years are called intermediate; and bonds maturing in ten or more years get the long-term label. Many

When bonds reach their maturity, they pay back the face amount.

Whatever their maturity, bonds usually can be "called," meaning redeemed, by the issuer at a specified date before the scheduled maturity.

bonds are issued with 20- to 30-year maturities. Notes usually run about seven years. The lines separating the categories aren't hard and fast, however, so it's important to check the number of years to maturity for any security you're considering.

Whatever their maturity, bonds these days usually can be "called," meaning redeemed, by the issuer at a specified date before the scheduled maturity. An issuer may call in its bonds if, for instance, interest rates fall to a point where it can issue new bonds at a lower rate. It has been customary to pay owners of called bonds a small premium over the face value.

How They're Taxed

Interest and capital gains on corporate credit instruments are normally subject to federal, state, and local income taxes. Income from Treasury and agency securities is subject to federal income taxes, but all Treasury and some agency securities are exempt from state and local income taxes. Interest on most municipal bonds is exempt from federal income taxes. Most state and local governments exempt interest on their own bonds but tax income on securities issued by other states. Because of their tax advantage, municipals pay a lower interest rate than taxable bonds.

Different Kinds of Yields

The coupon rate is the fixed annual interest payment expressed as a percentage of the face value of the bond. A 9 percent-coupon bond, for instance, pays $90 interest a year on each $1,000 of face value. The payment is set when the bond is issued and does not change as the bond's price fluctuates. A bond investor should be familiar with other kinds of yields as well.

Current yield is the annual interest payment expressed as a percentage of the bond's current market price. Thus, a 10 percent-coupon bond selling for $1,100 has a current yield of 9.1 percent ($100 interest divided by the $1,100 price times 100). The same bond selling for $900 has a current yield of 11.1 percent.

Yield to maturity takes into account the current yield and the eventual gain or loss it is assumed the owner will receive by holding to maturity a bond selling at a discount or a premium. If you pay $900 for a 10 percent-coupon bond with a face value of $1,000 maturing five years from the date of purchase, you will earn not only $100 interest a year but also an additional $100 five years later when the bond is redeemed for $1,000 by its issuer. By the same token, if you buy that bond for $1,100, representing a $100 premium, you will lose $100 at maturity. The loss, however, could be more than offset by the extra interest earned on a premium-priced bond if its coupon rate exceeds the current yield available on comparable securities. Tax considerations could also make the capital loss worth taking. For bonds selling at a discount, the yield to maturity probably provides the best estimate of total return.

Yield to call is computed the same way as yield to maturity, except that it is assumed the bond will be redeemed at the first call date for the face value plus the call premium.

How Bond Prices Are Listed

If you look up bond prices in the financial pages of a newspaper, you'll find them identified by the abbreviated name of the issuer, the coupon rate, and the maturity date. The more common price lists give only the current yield, but your broker can get the yields to maturity and call for you. Prices are reported as a percentage of face value. To get the actual price, multiply the decimal equivalent of the percentage by 1,000. Thus, an AT&T 7 percent bond maturing in 2008 might be reported as ATT 7s08 101, meaning the issue is selling at the time of the listing for $1,010 (101 percent) per $1,000 face value, a small premium that produces a current yield of 6.9 percent.

How Interest-Rate Changes
Affect Bond Prices

Because the amount of interest paid on a bond or note commonly remains fixed for the life of the issue,

Generally, the shorter its maturity, the less a bond's market value is affected by changes in interest rates.

the bond adjusts to interest-rate movements by changes in price.

To see how that works, consider a newly issued $1,000 bond with a coupon interest rate of 8 percent—$80 a year. If interest rates rise to 9 percent after the bond is issued, you can sell your 8 percent bond only by offering it at a price that will deliver a 9 percent current yield to the buyer, who would otherwise have no incentive to buy your 8 percent bond in a 9 percent market. So the price becomes whatever $80 represents 9 percent of, which is $889. Thus, you lose $111 if you sell.

By the same token, if interest rates decline to 7 percent while you're holding your 8 percent bond, you can sell it for whatever $80 represents 7 percent of, which is $1,143. That's a $143 capital gain. Congratulations.

These examples oversimplify the relationship, because in the actual marketplace prices are also strongly influenced by the time remaining to the bond's maturity or possible call. But the underlying principle is the same: *As interest rates rise, bond prices fall; as interest rates fall, bond prices rise.* Generally, the shorter its maturity, the less a bond's market value is affected by changes in interest rates. This table shows how the time remaining to maturity affects the market value of a bond yielding 8 percent when interest rates rise one and two percentage points.

Years to maturity	Loss of market value if rates rise:	
	one point	two points
2.50	−2 %	−4 %
10.00	−7	−13
30.00	−10	−19

Why Quality Counts

When you set out to buy bonds, it's tempting to look for the highest available yields. But yield figures can be misleading unless you also take into account the quality of the bond itself. If there's any doubt about the ability of the bond issuer to pay off on time, high yield could be poor compensation for the risk. In general, small investors should stick with high-quality bonds. But what is high quality? And how high is high enough?

What the Safety Scale Means

At the top of the safety scale stand all those issues for which the U.S. government has a direct obligation to meet interest and principal payments. The government, after all, is the only borrower on the market that can print money to pay its debts, if necessary.

Below that lofty level lies a vast array of securities issued by U.S. agencies, corporations, and local governmental units—states, counties, cities. There you will find bonds ranging in quality from those that are nearly as solid as U.S. government issues to those close to or already in default.

Bonds, like people, have credit ratings. The difference is that bond ratings are made public and can quickly be checked by anyone. Most widely traded bonds are rated by at least one of the major agencies in the field—Moody's Investors Service (http://www.moodys.com) and Standard & Poor's Corp. (http://www.standardandpoors.com). Fitch also rates bond issues for default risk. Their judgments can be valuable provided you know what they mean and how they affect market prices. The rating categories they use are shown in the table at right.

Standard and Poor's AA, A, BBB, BB, and B ratings are sometimes supplemented with a plus (+) or a minus (–) sign to raise or lower a bond's position within the group. Moody's applies numerical modifiers in each generic rating classification from Aa through Caa. The modifier 1 indicates that the obligation ranks in the higher end of its rating; a 2 indicates a midrange rank; and a 3 indicates a ranking in the lower end of the generic rating category.

The investment grades include bonds ordinarily bought by individuals and institutional investors seeking stable income and safety. BBB/Baa is the lowest rating that qualifies for commercial bank investments. It's a borderline group for which, in Standard &

BOND RATINGS	
S&P	**MOODY'S**
Investment	**Grades**
AAA	Aaa
AA	Aa
A	A
BBB	Baa
Speculative	**Grades**
BB	Ba
B	B
CCC	Caa
CC	Ca
D	C

Rating agencies try to track the financial condition of issuers and update their ratings if necessary.

Poor's words, adverse economic conditions or changing circumstances are more likely to lead to a weakened capacity to pay interest and repay principal than for bonds in higher-rated categories.

Dipping below BBB/Baa takes you into speculative territory. Because of their higher risk of default, such bonds must pay higher yields. They are often gathered into the portfolios of so-called high-yield bond mutual funds. "High yield" is the marketing name for what most people call junk bonds.

Moody's and Standard & Poor's don't always agree on a bond's rank. It's not unusual for them to rate an issue one grade apart. If you see this happening, take it as a sign of uncertainty about the company that issued the bond.

How Ratings Affect Price

Credit ratings play a big role in determining the relative levels of bond prices. Normally you pay a higher price (and thus receive a lower yield) with each notch you move up the quality scale. A triple-A usually costs more than a double-A with comparable characteristics, a double-A costs more than an A, and so on. The higher the quality, generally, the lower the yield. Few investment-grade issues (those above junk ratings) have ever defaulted. But there have been enough cases to reinforce the attractiveness of the highest ratings.

The rating agencies try to track the financial condition of issuers and update their ratings if necessary. In fact, many issues are either upgraded or downgraded each year, so you must check current ratings when buying bonds that have been on the market for some time.

Buying and Selling Bonds at a Discount

A "discount bond" sells for less than its face value, or par, which is the price the issuing company or governmental agency will ultimately pay when it redeems the bond from the owner at maturity.

A deep-discount bond is one selling at a large discount.

Sometimes bonds are issued at a discount in an effort to attract buyers. But most discounts develop mainly as a result of changes in interest rates. To understand how that happens, start with a hypothetical 30-year corporate bond with a $1,000 face value issued 20 years ago with a 5 percent coupon interest rate. That means it has been paying $50 a year (5 percent of $1,000) for the past 20 years and is now 10 years away from maturity.

You wouldn't give the owner $1,000 for that bond today because rates have risen since then, and you expect to earn more than $50 for each $1,000 you invest in bonds now. At what price would that 5 percent bond become a good buy? Finding out takes some math, but not much.

First, Compare the Current Yield

The current yield is the annual interest payment divided by the current price. To put it another way, the current price is the annual payment divided by the current yield. Let's assume that other bonds you could buy are yielding 6.9 percent. The bond you're considering buying must match that or you should pass it up. What price for the $1,000 bond would make it yield 6.9 percent to the buyer? Here's the math: Price = 50/0.069 = $725 (rounded off). So $725 would be a fair price for this bond.

Next, Find the Yield to Maturity

Here's the situation so far: The 5 percent bond pays $50 a year, no matter what you pay for it. In addition, the company that issued the bond will redeem it in ten years at its par value of $1,000, which is $275 more than the current price suggested by current interest rates. You won't realize the $275 for ten years, but for mathematical convenience let's say you receive the discount as equal installments of $28 for each of the ten years. The percentage figure that tells you how much you are earning from interest payments plus the annual payout of a tenth of the discount is the yield to maturity. Unfortunately, you don't simply add and then divide.

Sometimes bonds are issued at a discount to attract buyers. But most discounts develop as a result of changes in interest rates.

Bond dealers use bond tables and programmed calculators to compute yields to maturity, and some handheld financial calculators can do it. But you can approximate the yield to maturity with the following shortcut formula:

$$\frac{\text{annual interest payment} + \text{annually accumulated discount}}{\text{average of par value and current price}} \times 100$$

For the bond in the example:

$$\frac{50 + 28}{860} = \frac{78}{860} = .09069 \times 100 = 9.06\% = 9.1\%$$

The same formula can be used for bonds for which you pay a premium. In those cases you would subtract the annually accumulated premium from the annual interest payment.

Don't worry about following this exercise too closely. It's presented not as a mathematical model for you to use, but as an example of the kinds of considerations that affect the value of a bond you might buy or sell at a discount.

Before You Buy Any Bond

While there are many factors you need to keep in mind when you're evaluating bonds, if you follow these few general buying tips, you'll be more likely to select good ones.

Update the Credit Rating
A bond's quality rating may be revised after it is issued because of a change in the issuer's financial health. Many bonds have been on the market a long time, so it's important to check current ratings.

Be Sure There's an Easy Exit
Although you may buy a bond firmly intending to hold it to maturity, it usually doesn't make sense to freeze yourself into an investment. Ordinary investors should

restrict themselves to investment-grade bonds that can be priced and sold easily to other investors.

Watch Your Maturities

Often you can select bonds that will mature exactly when you need large sums—say, for college expenses or, at retirement, for reinvestment in bonds with high current yields to supplement your pension income. Also, remember that the further away a bond's maturity date, the riskier it is as an investment.

How "Zeros" Can Add Up

With a conventional bond you can typically expect to receive an interest payment every six months. Zero-coupon bonds, on the other hand, credit you with regular interest but don't actually pay any until maturity. You buy the bond at a substantial discount from its face value, then collect the full value years later. Zeros usually come in denominations as low as $1,000 and are sold at discounts from face value of 50 to 75 percent, depending on the maturity. You can buy a zero-coupon bond to pay for college bills ten years down the road, sock it away, and forget about it until you withdraw the money. You're paying tomorrow's bills today, at a big discount.

There's one big gotcha, though. Even though you receive no annual interest, the IRS requires that you report the phantom payments just as if you were getting the checks. You owe tax each year on the prorated difference between what you paid for the bond and what you'll receive when it matures. This makes zeros attractive chiefly to people with IRAs, on which they needn't pay tax until they take the money out. Zeros are available as municipal bonds, which also spare you the annual reporting chore. Most are Treasury issues, which escape state income taxes. Zeros are also an attractive way to give financial gifts to kids, who will probably be taxed at a lower rate than you would be.

Zero-coupon bonds credit you with regular interest but don't pay any until maturity. The IRS requires that you report the phantom income payments as if you were getting checks.

Because they can't be matched for safety, securities issued by the U.S. government and its agencies are the choice of many conservative investors.

Zeros carry the usual market risks for investors, with this added kicker: The company that issues a zero could conceivably default without ever having paid you a penny of interest.

Uncle Sam's Bonds

Because they can't be matched for safety, securities issued by the U.S. government and its agencies are the choice of many conservative investors concerned with preservation of their capital. There are dozens of government issues to choose from. Some, such as Treasury bills, are readily salable in the open marketplace; others, such as U.S. savings bonds, are less liquid. Yields on government issues usually run a little lower than on high-grade corporate issues because they are safer. Here's a rundown of the most popular government debt instruments.

Best for Short-Timers: Treasury Bills

T-bills usually mature in one year or less, and new ones are sold weekly. Minimum purchase is $1,000. Some bills run for a year and are sold every four weeks. When first issued, T-bills are auctioned off to the public on a discount basis, then redeemed at maturity for the full face amount. If the auction determines that the rate is 5 percent, for instance, a buyer would pay $9,500 for a $10,000 bill, then collect $10,000 when it matures.

This "auction," or "discount," rate actually understates the yield when compared with other securities. You normally pay full face value when bonds are first issued, but the investor here is laying out only $9,500 to collect $500 in interest. To account for this difference, the rate on T-bills is often stated in terms of "bond-equivalent yield." To find the bond-equivalent yield for a T-bill, calculate the relationship between the amount of interest paid and the cash you actually had to lay out to get it. In the example above, assuming this is a one-year bill, the bond-equivalent yield would be 5.26 percent (500 ÷ 9,500).

In addition to their safety, T-bills, along with other Treasury securities, are exempt from state and local income taxes. They are issued in book-entry form, meaning you don't actually receive any certificates, just a notification that you own them.

The Treasury Department has made buying bills (and other Treasury securities) much easier than it used to be. If you have a touch-tone phone, you can call 800-722-2678 and buy government debt by authorizing a debit from your bank account. If you have access to the Internet, you can go to http://www.publicdebt.treas .gov and buy online. It's also possible to buy the old-fashioned way (and the way you must buy four-week bills), by stopping by or writing to a Federal Reserve bank or branch (see the listing on pages 524-525) and asking for the forms and instructions. Commercial banks and brokers will make the purchase for you, but their fee—usually $50 or so—cuts into the yield.

T-bills, along with other Treasury securities, are safe, and are exempt from state and local income taxes.

Beat Inflation, If Any: Treasury Notes

Notes run for two to ten years. They are coupon issues in much the same way as corporate bonds are. As with T-bills, you can purchase them directly through a Federal Reserve bank or branch, or you can have a broker or a commercial bank do it for you. Interest is paid semiannually, the notes are not callable prior to maturity, and the minimum purchase is $1,000.

Notes were pretty much forgotten by individual investors until 1997, when the government started selling Treasury inflation-protected securities, or TIPS for short. These are five- or ten-year notes whose interest is determined by the inflation rate, with the principal adjusted every six months to reflect the change. This can result in less current interest than a standard T-note, but a bigger payoff at maturity. You are guaranteed to stay on top of inflation.

Treasury Bonds

T-bonds generally carry maturity dates more than ten years after issue. Maturities used to be as long as 30 years, but the Treasury department stopped offering 30-year bonds in 2001. Most cannot be called early by the Treasury. Minimum purchase is $1,000.

Among the most popular of agency securities are those backed by Ginnie Mae, which helps create a secondary market for home mortgages.

U.S. Agency Securities: Close Enough to the Real Thing

A number of U.S. government agencies and federally sponsored enterprises issue debt securities. They usually do not carry the full faith and credit of the government, but this difference is really quibbling because it's doubtful that the government would allow one of its agencies to default on an obligation. Nevertheless, the difference is usually reflected in the relative yields of agency versus Treasury debt instruments. Agency issues, being the "inferior" risk, pay a bit more, despite the additional fact that some agency securities—but not all—are exempt from state and local income taxes, just like Treasury issues.

A description of the various securities available would amount to a description of the issuing agencies' functions. Each has its own financing needs, each goes to the markets to fulfill them, and each pays the going rates. Some issue short- as well as long-term debt instruments. Most float mainly intermediate-term issues. Minimum-purchase requirements vary greatly, ranging from $1,000 to $25,000. Purchases must usually be made through brokers, who can supply a listing of the securities available.

Ginnie, Fannie, and Freddie: Mortgage-Backed Securities

Among the most popular of agency securities are those backed by the Government National Mortgage Association, or Ginnie Mae (http://www.ginniemae .gov), which helps create a secondary market for home mortgages. Ginnie Mae doesn't actually issue securities. It insures pools of FHA and VA mortgages assembled by mortgage bankers and other lenders. Ginnie Mae insurance has no loopholes: If a borrower on a mortgage in the pool fails to make a monthly payment of principal and interest, the agency will make good if the issuer of the security doesn't. Because the FHA and VA mortgages in the pool are also backed by the federal government, your investment should be doubly secure against default.

Ginnie Mae securities are called pass-through certificates and come in minimum denominations of $25,000. But for as little as $1,000 you can buy into a Ginnie Mae mutual fund or unit trust sponsored by a number of fund managers and brokerage firms. Some pass along only the interest payments and use the principal to invest in more mortgages. Others pass along both interest and principal to investors.

Freddie Mac (http://www.freddiemac.com) participation certificates (issued by the Federal Home Loan Mortgage Corp.) and Fannie Mae securities (issued by the Federal National Mortgage Association) round out the market for mortgage-backed securities from quasigovernment agencies. Denominations start at $1,000. Fannie Maes and Freddie Macs are not obligations of the federal government but carry the guarantee of the agency.

Mortgage-backed securities can be a solid addition to an investment portfolio, but many investors don't seem to understand the risks. As with bonds, their market value declines as interest rates rise. But Ginnies, Fannies, and Freddies carry another risk: As mortgage rates go down (an event you would expect to enhance the value of securities bought at higher rates), homeowners tend to refinance to take advantage of the situation. And when they refinance, their mortgages get paid off and drop out of the pool. Investors get the principal back, but the lucrative return goes up in smoke. This has the perverse effect of driving the price of Ginnie Maes and similar issues down at the very time that the price of bonds is going up.

Meanwhile, because you're at the mercy of thousands of homeowners making independent decisions about when to refinance, the principal comes back to you in unpredictable chunks. Your cash flow is erratic and so is your yield. To compensate for this uncertainty, mortgage pools have generally had to pay a percentage point or two more than Treasury bonds, which are much more predictable.

Mortgage-backed securities can be solid additions to investment portfolios, but many investors don't seem to understand the risks.

Unless you feel at home with interest-rate floaters, inverse floaters, and other derivatives, resist your broker's invitation to jump aboard the CMO bandwagon.

Collateralized Mortgage Obligations: Take a Pass

CMOs attempt to take some of the uncertainty out of the situation by building in some protection against early prepayments. Backed by Ginnie Maes, they pay interest monthly or quarterly. A typical CMO is divided into several different maturities, called tranches—short, intermediate, and long term, with finer divisions in between. As prepayments are received, they're used first to pay off the short-term investors, then the intermediate-term investors, and then long-term investors, until the entire issue is retired. The minimum investment in a CMO is usually $1,000. A variation on the CMO idea, the real estate mortgage investment conduit, or REMIC, may contain mortgages that are not backed by government agencies. Today, most CMOs are issued in REMIC form. Note that although CMOs and REMICs may protect your income stream, they are not immune to the ups and downs in value caused by fluctuations in interest rates.

The problem with CMOs is their complexity and the tendency of their packagers to load them up with derivative schemes that make their risks very difficult to anticipate. Unless you feel at home with interest-rate floaters, inverse floaters, and other derivatives, resist your broker's invitation to jump aboard the CMO bandwagon.

U.S. Savings Bonds

Savings bonds come in three varieties: EE bonds and I bonds, which are vehicles for savings, and HH bonds, which were created to produce income for their buyers.

EE Bonds

Uncle Sam has changed the rules on EE bonds frequently. EEs purchased today pay a fixed rate of interest, which will apply for the 30-year life of each bond, including a 10-year extended maturity period (unless a different rate or rate structure is announced and applied at the start of the extension period). Interest is compounded semiannually, with a three-month interest penalty if you cash in the bonds before five years. Bonds issued earlier may earn different rates, depending on when you bought them. Rates for new bonds are set May 1 and November 1, with each new rate effective for all bonds issued through the next six months. You can get current rate information by calling 800-722-2678 or on the Web at http://www.savingsbonds .gov. EE bonds are sold at a 50 percent discount from face value in denominations of $50, $75, $100, $200, $500, $1,000, $2,500, $5,000, and $10,000.

Savings bonds are sold at banks and other financial institutions or through payroll-deduction plans. There is no sales charge or commission.

I Bonds

You can take the "I" in the name to stand for inflation-adjusted. The interest paid by I bonds actually comes in two parts: You get an underlying fixed rate, which is announced when the bonds are issued, plus a second rate that is equal to the level of inflation. Thus, if the flat rate is 1.5 percent and inflation is 3 percent, then I bonds would pay 4.5 percent that year. The interest is compounded semiannually. You must keep bonds for at least one year before you can redeem them and at least five years if you don't want to forfeit three months of accrued interest. For example, if you cash in an I bond after 18 months, you'll receive 15 months of interest. They will earn interest for 30 years.

Unlike EE bonds, which sell at a 50 percent discount and gradually grow to their face value, I bonds sell for face value right from the start. Denominations start at $50 and climb in several steps to $10,000. The maximum you can purchase in one year is $30,000.

Potential savings-bond buyers shouldn't be put off by the relatively low fixed rate paid by I bonds. Consider them an inflation hedge and think of them this way: With a fixed rate of 1.5 percent and low inflation, your return will be low but you'll still be beating inflation by 1.5 percent, year after year. If inflation soars to,

> **You can take the "I" in the name to stand for inflation-adjusted. The interest paid by I bonds comes in two parts: an underlying fixed rate plus a second rate equal to the level of inflation.**

Savings bonds are not transferable, meaning you can cash them in but you can't sell them to someone else.

say, 10 percent, the return on your I bonds will be 11.5 percent. Feel better?

HH Bonds

The Bureau of the Public Debt stopped issuing HH bonds in 2004, citing the high cost and relatively few takers. Bondholders who exchanged E or EE bonds for HH bonds before the deadline will earn interest on HH bonds until they reach final maturity in 2024.

Why People Buy Savings Bonds

If it's yield you're after, you'll never be happy with savings bonds. Other factors usually motivate buyers.

AS SAFE AS CAN BE. Savings bonds are backed by the full faith and credit of the U.S. government, so there is no safer place to put your money. Payment of the interest and principal is guaranteed. Lost, stolen, damaged, or destroyed bonds can be replaced free. For more information, write to the Bureau of the Public Debt, Savings Bond Operations Office, Parkersburg, WV 26106-1328 (http://www.publicdebt.treas.gov). Ask for an application to replace lost or stolen bonds, or obtain the application online and mail to this address.

Savings bonds are not transferable, meaning you can cash them in but you can't sell them to someone else. Their market price doesn't rise when interest rates fall or fall when rates rise. Savings bonds will never have to be cashed in for less than you paid for them.

CONVENIENT, SORT OF. Payroll savings plans sponsored by employers make it easy to accumulate savings bonds. This convenience is attractive to savers who need an incentive to put something aside on a regular basis. Savings bonds can also be easily purchased at banks and other financial institutions. It's not quite so easy to redeem savings bonds. When that time comes, try a full-service bank or financial institution. Most are paying agents for the bonds. You'll have to sign the request for payment on the back of the bonds in the presence of a certifying officer at the bank, provide your Social Security number and mail the bonds to the Federal Reserve Bank that services your area.

With so many different interest-rate schedules, it is often difficult to figure out what your bonds are worth, particularly if you've been buying them for several years. For help with this, you can try a bank, or you can use the Savings Bond Wizard on the Bureau of the Public Debt's Web site, http://www.publicdebt.treas.gov.

TAX ADVANTAGED, DEFINITELY. To begin with, the interest on savings bonds is exempt from all state and local income taxes. And although the exemption doesn't extend to federal taxes, your options for paying the federal tab create opportunities to increase your effective return considerably.

For EE bonds you can (1) pay the tax each year as the interest accrues or (2) postpone the day of reckoning until you cash in the bond or dispose of it (by giving it away, for instance) or until it reaches final maturity. Here's how investors in certain circumstances can profit from these options.

ADVANTAGES FOR PARENTS WITH YOUNG CHILDREN. If you'd like to start, say, a college fund for a child, you might take advantage of the option to report the interest on EE bonds as it accrues. You simply purchase bonds in the child's name (list yourself as beneficiary in case something happens to the child, but don't make yourself co-owner). This will make the child liable for the tax. And because the child probably won't have enough income to incur any tax liability for several years, the income from the bonds will accumulate, for practical purposes, tax-free.

You set up this arrangement by filing a federal income-tax return in the child's name when you first start the program and stating on the return that your child will be reporting the interest yearly. Report all the interest earned up to then. This establishes your intent. No further returns are necessary until the child's bond interest plus other income reaches the level at which a return would be required by law. At

The interest on savings bonds is exempt from all state and local income taxes.

Parents who buy EEs to pay for their children's college education get a special break.

that time the child need pay tax on only that year's interest. Previously accrued interest escapes tax.

Parents who buy EEs to pay for their children's college education get a special break: If the proceeds are used to pay for qualifying tuition and fees for your child attending a college, university, or technical or vocational school, the interest may be completely tax-free, provided certain conditions are met.

The conditions are these: Bonds must be purchased in the parent's name. The government says you must buy them after your 24th birthday and redeem them in the year that the qualifying expenses are paid. There is also an income test: For 2005, the break was phased out starting at adjusted gross income of $91,850 on a joint return, and was gradually scaled back until it was gone completely at $121,850. (For single parents, the phase-out zone ran between $61,200 and $76,200.) But those ceilings are indexed to inflation, so they aren't very meaningful for long-term savings plans.

ADVANTAGES FOR RETIREES. Taxpayers with high incomes can take advantage of the option that allows postponing the federal income tax on EE bond interest until the bonds are cashed in. Say you belong to a defined-benefit pension plan financed in part by your own contributions. When you retire, the taxable portion of your pension benefits may be reduced until you've recovered your contributions. Cashing in your bonds during that period may permit you to escape some of the tax on their interest because your taxable income will be comparatively low. (Defined-contribution plans, such as 401(k)s, don't qualify for this feature.)

The Enduring Allure of Municipal Bonds

Municipal bond is a catchall name that describes the debt issues of cities and towns, states and territories, counties, local public-housing authorities, water districts, school districts, and similar governmental or quasigovernmental units. Because the interest paid is exempt from federal income taxes and, usually, income taxes of the state in which the bond is issued, municipals can pay less interest than corporate bonds of comparable quality and still deliver the same (or better) after-tax yield. The higher your tax bracket, the more valuable this tax-exempt feature becomes.

A simple formula can show you exactly how valuable tax-free income can be. Say you have a choice between a taxable corporate bond yielding 7 percent and a tax-free municipal bond yielding 5 percent. Which is the better deal? The answer depends on your tax bracket. What you're looking for is the taxable equivalent to your tax-free yield. Here's how to figure it:

The higher your tax bracket, the more valuable the tax-exempt feature of municipal bonds becomes.

$$\frac{\text{tax--free rate}}{1-\text{ federal tax bracket}} = \text{taxable-equivalent yield}$$

Say your taxable income is $60,000. Whether you're single or married, that puts you in the 25 percent bracket. Thus, your taxable-equivalent yield would equal the tax-free rate (5 percent in this example) divided by 1 minus 0.25, or 0.75. The answer: 6.67 percent. In this case, you're better off with the taxable bond.

But what if you're in the 33 percent bracket, a neighborhood you enter at about $151,000 of taxable income if you're single, around $183,000 or so if you're married and file jointly. Run the numbers again: The equation now says to divide 5 by 0.67, which produces a taxable-equivalent yield of 7.46 percent. In the 33 percent bracket, a 5 percent tax-free yield is better than a 7 percent taxable yield. That's what makes munis most attractive to people in the upper brackets. For those in the highest bracket, 35 percent, the taxable-equivalent yield is 7.59 percent.

Another aspect to investing in munis can make them even more attractive, depending on where you live. Most states don't tax the interest on bonds issued by municipal authorities within their own borders. A few states don't tax municipal-bond interest regardless of where it comes from. These breaks on your state

Whatever type of muni you're considering, ask your broker for an official statement from the issuer. This should describe in detail the bond, the project, and the municipality.

income taxes can boost your taxable-equivalent yield significantly, especially if you live in a high-tax state.

Just like corporate issues, munis vary in quality according to the economic and financial soundness of the project or the creditworthiness of the issuer. To serve as quality guides for investors, Standard & Poor's Corp. and Moody's Investors Service study available financial data and determine credit ratings for municipal-bond issues. Bonds considered least risky are rated AAA by S&P and Aaa by Moody's. These triple-As are considered prime investments. Next in quality comes S&P's AA, the equivalent of Moody's Aa, followed by the A rating used by both services, then BBB (Baa by Moody's), BB (Ba), and so on down the line. Bonds rated below BBB or Baa are considered speculative issues and might be risky investments over the long run.

It stands to reason that the higher a bond's rating—in other words, the safer an investment it appears to be—the lower the interest it needs to pay to attract investors, and vice versa. Thus, the riskiest bonds tend to yield the most.

Every revenue-bond project is different and needs to be analyzed on its economic merits. There are also special legal and financial agreements that can be significant to investors. Whatever type of municipal bond you are considering, ask your broker for an official statement from the issuer. This should describe in detail the bond, the project, and the municipality. (If the bond is a new issue, your broker is required to give you a statement.) This document, unlike a corporate prospectus, has no standardized format. And unlike corporations, municipal-bond issuers are not required to provide regular financial information to bondholders.

Different Ways to Buy Munis

The investment packagers of Wall Street have responded imaginatively to the public's demands for tax-free income from municipal bonds. Years ago they figured there was a market for a product that would help guide investors through the sprawling marketplace of municipal debt, where thousands of governmental units compete for billions of dollars of investors' money. The result was the appearance in 1961 of the first municipal-bond unit trusts. They made available, for a small sales fee, portions of a fixed portfolio selected by the fund's professional underwriters. The minimum investment in most cases was $5,000.

Then, in 1976, the mutual fund idea came to municipals. The minimum investment dropped to only $1,000, or less. For that you got a slice of a portfolio of bonds that the fund's managers would buy and sell to take advantage of market conditions.

There's a third way to acquire a portfolio of municipal bonds—the old-fashioned way, by buying your own instead of letting someone else choose them for you. If you are in the market for munis, you'd do well to compare the different ways of acquiring them. You could discover that some prominent features of particular methods fade in importance while others you might have overlooked begin to loom large.

However you choose to own your muni bonds, you should shop for the highest yield consistent with the risks you're willing to take. Let's assume for a moment that each of the three options mentioned earlier—individual bonds, unit trusts, and mutual funds—offers precisely the same yield. Will your earnings be the

---

TWO TYPES OF MUNICIPAL BONDS

Revenue bonds. Repayment is generally tied to particular sources of revenue, such as bridge or highway tolls, or to specific taxes, such as those on alcohol or cigarettes. Uses of revenue bonds include financing of construction projects such as waterworks, airports, rapid transit systems, and sports complexes. Industrial revenue bonds, although issued by governmental units, are designed to raise construction capital for private corporations. They are backed by the credit standing of the corporation, not the issuing government, and their tax-free status may be limited.

General obligation bonds. These pledge the faith and credit of the government that issues them, meaning that the taxing authority of the issuer stands behind the bond to insure payment of interest and principal.

same, whichever you buy? The answer is no, and the reasons lie in the costs associated with the different forms of ownership.

INDIVIDUAL BONDS. If you buy the bonds directly from a broker, the commission is likely to be included in the cost and thus reflected in the yield. Brokerage houses normally sell bonds from their own accounts, and when they raise the price to add in their sales charge, they usually recalculate the yield to reflect that additional cost. This means that when they sell, for example, a bond issued to yield 5.25 percent, the brokerage might promise investors a return of only 5 percent. Part of that missing 0.25 percent would be lost to the dealer's commission. From your point of view, you are purchasing a bond yielding 5 percent.

UNIT TRUSTS AND MUTUAL FUNDS. Unit trusts and mutual funds don't always work that way. Trusts, and funds that levy sales charges, or loads, carry fees that reduce your actual return because the commission is deducted from your gross investment. If you buy $10,000 worth of a unit trust charging a typical 4.5 percent sales commission, what you get is $9,550 worth of bonds earning interest for you. The same thing happens with a mutual fund charging a load.

There are other costs involved as well. Mutual funds, including the no-loads, require the services of investment advisors to manage portfolios (see Chapter 25). For this the managers generally take 0.5 to 1 percent—or more—of the fund's average net asset value as a fee. This reduces your return by the same amount. A mutual fund earning 6 percent on its portfolio and keeping 0.5 percent for management can pay out only 5.5 percent to its investors.

Because unit trusts normally don't trade in the market once the portfolio is set, they don't need managers. But they do require trustees and administrators, who must be paid. Their fees generally amount to about 0.1 percent of net asset value. Thus, a trust earning 6 percent on its portfolio will return 5.9 percent to its investors, whose initial investment has already been reduced by the sales commission they paid to get in.

Advantages of Funds and Unit Trusts

To give them their due, muni-bond mutual funds and unit trusts do have some very attractive features. Funds, for example, offer the opportunity to ride along with rising interest rates if their managers are alert enough to spot the signals. The risk with mutual funds lies in the possibility that a fund's managers will make the wrong decisions or wait too long to make the right ones, thus depressing the fund's net asset value and leaving you with a loss if you have to sell your shares. But funds and trusts have other advantages over individual bonds.

INSTANT DIVERSITY. In a unit trust or a mutual fund you get another measure of protection that is difficult to obtain on your own: diversity. Consider a unit trust consisting of 16 different issues. Because the great majority of individual bonds sell in $5,000 minimums, you'd need a portfolio worth at least $80,000 to buy that much diversity on your own. You can buy a piece of some trusts for as little as $1,000.

EASY LIQUIDITY. Mutual funds redeem their shares on demand, and unit trusts generally maintain a secondary market for units. There's also an active market for individually held bonds, but you usually have to pay a premium if you want to sell only one or two.

CONVENIENCE. To calculate what this is worth to you, consider what would be involved in maintaining your own portfolio of municipals. You'd need a place to safeguard them, probably a safe-deposit box. You'd have to watch the papers and other sources if you owned any callable bonds. Interest is nearly always paid semiannually, whereas most unit trusts and mutual funds let you choose monthly or quarterly distributions instead. In addition to professional selection

Since interest on municipal bonds is tax-free, muni zeros are a nearly perfect long-term investment with a predictable return.

and management, that's the sort of service funds and unit trusts are selling you.

Zero-Coupon Municipals

Zero-coupon municipal bonds are sold at a big discount from face value and pay no current interest, just like the corporate zeros described earlier. A potential disadvantage of corporate zeros held outside an IRA or other tax-deferred account is that you must pay tax on the interest that accrues each year even though no interest is actually paid until the bond matures. Municipal zeros eliminate that worry and constitute a nearly perfect long-term investment vehicle with a predictable return.

As with other bonds, risks lie in the possibility that interest rates will rise substantially while you own zeros, thus reducing their current market value. There is some risk of default, which you can minimize by paying attention to safety ratings. And there is risk with some bonds that they will be called prior to maturity. If that happens, you lose one of the investment's biggest attractions: the certain knowledge of what it will be worth on a particular date in the future.

Insurance for Your Munis

All municipal-bond investments entail some degree of risk. The bonds are rated on the same scales used for judging the quality of corporate bonds, but issuers aren't required to reveal as much about their financial affairs as corporations are. Municipal bonds have had an excellent safety record over the years, but there have been near-defaults by some large cities and a number of actual defaults, the best known being by the Washington Public Power Supply System (WPPSS, or Whoops).

Since then, Orange County, California, and the city of Bridgeport, Connecticut, have declared bankruptcy, throwing a scare into holders of their bonds, and bond-backed projects have fizzled into default in parts of California, Colorado, and Texas. These episodes have made insured municipal bonds attractive to many safety-conscious investors.

To insure bonds, an issuer or underwriter pays an insurance premium of anywhere from 0.1 to 2 percent of total principal and interest. In return, the insurance company agrees to pay principal and interest to bond-holders if the issuer defaults. Policies cannot be canceled; they remain in effect over the life of the bond.

In the case of a unit trust, insurance is usually purchased for the entire portfolio rather than for each individual bond. As long as a defaulted issue remains in the fund, shareholders have the same guarantee of principal and interest payments as owners of individually insured bonds. Bonds in the trust that have already been insured by the issuer don't carry portfolio insurance as well.

The first municipal bond was insured by the American Municipal Bond Assurance Corporation (AMBAC) in 1971. The Municipal Bond Insurance Association (MBIA), another major insurer, began operations in 1974. Others have come along since then.

Once a bond is insured, it is assigned an AAA rating by S&P, even if the bond has, say, a BBB rating based on its own creditworthiness. So it's important to remember that a broker selling an AAA-insured bond may actually be selling a BBB security with insurance.

Will having insurance affect your yield? Yes. Issuers of riskier bonds need to offer higher yields to attract investors. Because insured issues carry a relatively low risk, their yields will be about 0.2 to 0.4 percentage point lower than a comparably rated uninsured issue. Lower interest costs, as well as increased marketability of insured bonds, are the reasons that issuers are willing to pay the one-time insurance premiums.

The main advantage of an insured municipal-bond trust is that a defaulted issue in the portfolio will continue to pay interest and return principal at maturity. If you hold on to your shares until the defaulted issue matures, you'll feel no adverse effect. But if you decide to sell before then, having a defaulted bond, even in an insured portfolio, could affect the value of your shares on the secondary market.

Municipal-bond insurance guarantees only that your principal and interest will be repaid in the event of a default; it does not guarantee the market value of a bond. An unexpected downgrading in the issuer's credit

A broker selling an AAA-insured bond may really be selling a BBB security with insurance.

rating or a default by the issuer, as well as interest-rate changes, could affect the market value of insured bonds.

Swapping Munis to Save Taxes

For the great majority of investors, a bigger risk than default is getting locked into a return that looks fine at the beginning but turns out to be inadequate in the face of rising interest rates. If you have to sell the bond under those circumstances, you'll suffer a capital loss.

You can ease the pain somewhat by performing what is known as a tax swap. Tax swapping is especially suited to munis and can be a valuable year-end tax-saving move. You merely sell your devalued bonds and reinvest the proceeds in bonds from a different issuer paying the higher, current rate. This gives you a capital loss for your tax return and, ignoring commissions, keeps your bond income at the same level.

Example: Say you are holding $5,000 in munis purchased in January and yielding 4 percent. That gives you an annual income of $200. By December, rates have climbed to 6 percent. You are still earning $200 from your bonds, but their market value is now down to $3,333. You sell the bonds, take a $1,667 loss, and reinvest the proceeds in 6 percent bonds issued by another municipality. Since 6 percent of $3,333 is $200, you've maintained your level of income while achieving a capital loss that can be used to shelter investment income from other sources.

But note: The IRS considers a transaction a "wash sale" if you sell a bond or other security and within 30 days acquire a "substantially identical" one. Losses from wash sales are not deductible. Relying on small differences between issues, such as maturity dates or interest rates, could put you on shaky ground, so be sure to check with your broker or tax advisor before undertaking a tax swap. Mutual funds and unit trusts, because each has a different portfolio, are ideally suited for tax swaps.

TAX-FREE MONEY-MARKET FUNDS. You could also choose among a vast collection of tax-free money-market funds. They own short-term notes issued by state and local governments and their agencies: bond anticipation notes (BANs), tax anticipation notes (TANs), revenue anticipation notes (RANs), grant anticipation notes (GANs), tax and revenue anticipation notes (TRANs), and temporary loan notes (TLNs). Because they stick with short maturities, tax-free money funds usually pay less interest than their longer-term cousins, but they offer many of the advantages of taxable money-market funds, including instant liquidity through check writing.

Tax-free money-market funds are offered by all the major brokerage houses and mutual fund families. Among the largest offered by fund families are: Dreyfus BASIC Municipal Money Market (800-645-6561; http://www.dreyfus.com), Fidelity Tax-Free Money-Market (800-343-3548; http://www.fidelity.com), T. Rowe Price Tax-Exempt Money Fund (800-225-5132; http://www.troweprice.com), and the Vanguard Tax-Exempt Money Market Fund (888-662-7447; http://www.vanguard.com). Funds and brokerages commonly also offer single-state municipal-bond money-market funds, which pay income that's tax-free at the state as well as the federal level.

Making It Big with Mutual Funds

For individual investors with neither a lot of money nor a lot of time to devote to investing, mutual funds offer advantages that simply aren't available anywhere else. Instead of picking stocks or bonds one at a time, you can invest in a collection of them designed to match your investment goals. You can afford a high-priced, celebrity money manager with a fabulous track record. And, as with stocks, you can monitor performance on a daily basis. It's a combination that's hard to beat.

MANAGEABLE MINIMUMS. You can buy into a lot of funds for an initial investment of $500 to $1,000. Minimums lower than $500 are rare. And regardless of their initial purchase requirements, most funds will take smaller amounts once you become a shareholder, and many will permit you to start smaller if you open an individual retirement account (IRA), or set up a program of automatic periodic investments.

INSTANT DIVERSIFICATION. A share in a mutual fund gives you partial ownership of a professionally managed portfolio of dozens of stocks, bonds, or other securities. Diversification doesn't insulate you against market movements, but it does help to soften the impact of wide price swings that may affect individual securities.

EASY LIQUIDITY. Mutual funds are by definition "open-ended." That means they are constantly issuing new shares and redeeming old ones. When you want to

Mutual funds use the money from their shareholders to buy stocks or bonds or a combination of stocks, bonds, and other financial instruments.

sell your shares, the fund is required to buy them back. Transactions can be accomplished through the mail or, in the case of many funds, by telephone or online.

AUTOMATIC REINVESTMENT PLANS. Virtually all funds automatically reinvest dividends and capital gains earned by your account. Reinvesting like this boosts the pace at which your money grows.

AUTOMATIC INCOME PLANS. Most funds will arrange automatic periodic payouts of earnings or principal or both for shareholders who want regular income from their account.

How Funds Work

Mutual funds use the money from their shareholders to buy stocks or bonds or a combination of stocks, bonds, and other financial instruments. Most funds offer shares to the public continuously, either directly, through advertisements, or through stockbrokers and other dealers. Funds that sell directly to the public may or may not charge a sales commission, or load. Funds sold through brokers almost always charge a load, although that has been changing since the introduction of so-called wrap accounts, as described in Chapter 23. Here's how funds operate.

Professional Managers Pick the Portfolio

Although individual managers tend to get all the publicity, mutual funds are actually run by management companies that administer their day-to-day operations, choose their staffs, and select the fund's investments. Many funds are managed by brokerage firms or investment counselors who also serve other clients. Some management companies administer a family of funds offering a variety of investment styles. Within a family, you can usually exchange shares in one fund for shares in another at no charge.

Investment Objectives Are Clear

The majority of funds invest in common stocks or bonds or both, but some buy gold or other kinds of assets. Some concentrate on only one industry, such as health care or technology. Portfolios are assembled to meet specific objectives: safety of capital, high income, moderate capital appreciation, or fast growth, for example. The riskiest funds use such techniques as short selling, buying on margin, or investing in risky derivatives in an attempt to boost performance or hedge other investments.

A fund's investment policies, plus other details of how it operates, are spelled out in its prospectus, which is available on request and must be given to each prospective buyer.

Shares Are Priced Daily

The value of a fund share is expressed in terms of its net asset value (NAV), which is the fund's total net assets (the value of its portfolio minus any money the fund owes) divided by the number of shares outstanding. Because net asset value rises and falls with the market prices of a fund's holdings, the funds calculate a new price at the end of each day. A few specialized funds value their shares hourly. The price at which you buy shares or sell them back to the fund is based on the next calculated net asset value following receipt of your order. When you invest by dollar amounts, your purchase will probably include a fractional share. For instance, $1,000 will buy 61.728 shares of a no-load fund with a $16.20 asset value, assuming no sales commission is charged.

Shareholders Get the Profits

A fund makes money from dividends and interest on the securities it owns and from capital gains made on the sales of those securities or other investments. If its portfolio selections are bad or the market turns sour, the fund will probably lose money. Virtually all income left after payment of management fees and other expenses is distributed to shareholders.

A fund's investment policies, plus other details of how it operates, are spelled out in its prospectus.

Some mutual funds impose a sales charge when you purchase shares. These "loads," as they're called, reduce the amount of your investment that goes to work for you.

Sales Loads and Other Charges

Some mutual funds impose a sales charge when you purchase shares. Although these "loads," as they're called, vary a great deal, 5.75 percent isn't unusual. (Try to forget for a moment that a broker who tried to charge that much on a stock purchase would soon be out of business.) This load reduces the amount of your investment that goes to work for you. If you invest $1,000 in a fund charging a 5.75 percent load, $57.50 will be deducted as a sales charge and $942.50 will be invested in the fund's shares. A 5.75 percent sales charge thus works out to about 6.1 percent of your net investment in such a case.

Thousands of funds, including virtually all money-market funds, charge no up-front sales fee and are known as no-load funds. They have no salespeople, so you have to reach them by mail or by telephone. In other respects, they operate like the load funds.

Some funds have a sales load of only 2 or 3 percent. That sounds low, but the irony is that low loads are often charged by companies that sell shares directly by mail or telephone—companies that don't need loads to pay outside commissions.

Sometimes the mutual fund tables in newspapers show two prices: the net asset value or "bid" price (the price at which the fund will buy a share back from a shareholder), and the "offering" or "asked" price at which you can buy a share. The offering price includes the maximum sales charge. With no-load funds the bid price is identical to the asked or offering price.

There are a number of other possible charges you'll have to check before you'll know how much it will cost you to own a particular fund.

Deferred Loads

These fees are deducted from your account if you redeem shares before a specified period elapses from the date you bought them. The amount of the charge and any conditions under which you may be exempt should be explained in the prospectus, but the descriptive language may be confusing. A key point to check is whether your entire interest in the fund or just the amount you originally invested for shares is liable to this charge. If increases in net asset value, capital-gains distributions, or dividends are exempt, you know going in the maximum charge you face and that your profits are shielded.

Redemption Fees

Slightly different from deferred loads, redemption fees are more worrisome if you are investing for capital gains rather than dividend or interest income. A redemption fee is levied against the net asset value when you sell, so it nips profits as well as the amount you invested.

Marketing Fees

Many funds take a special deduction from assets for advertising, marketing, and other expenses, including commissions to brokers. These are called 12b-1 fees. Most 12b-1 fees amount to less than one-half of 1 percent of assets, but some are higher. If a fund charges no sales fee but levies a 12b-1 greater than 0.25 percent of assets, by law it can't call itself a no-load fund.

Management Fees

The fund's professional managers are paid an annual fee, commonly 1 percent or so of the fund's average assets but sometimes much more. (Fees tend to be higher for stock-oriented funds than for bond-oriented funds.) The rate may be stepped down as the fund's assets increase—the larger the fund gets, the smaller the percentage the managers take as their fee. Some funds use an incentive system, periodically adjusting the fee according to the fund's performance compared with the stock market as a whole: The better the performance, the higher the fee. The sum of all management fees, and the 12b-1 fee, if any, is the fund's expense ratio, an important term to remember.

How to Pick a Winning Fund

Although a mutual fund saves you the trouble of having to select the individual investments in a portfolio, it doesn't eliminate the risks that go

Thousands of funds, including virtually all money-market funds, charge no up-front sales fee and are known as no-load funds.

You'll want to diversify with selections from several fund groups; your choices will depend on your risk tolerance and length of time you have until you'll need the money.

with investing. If you choose a lousy fund, you take the loss just as surely as if you had chosen its portfolio yourself. So know what you're getting into. Mutual funds are not all alike. Some are conservative, some are terribly risky, most fall somewhere between the extremes. When setting out to select a fund, your first task is to formulate your own investment objectives. (If you haven't done that yet, read Chapter 22.) Then look for funds that seem to fit with your objectives.

The box on page 403 lists several sources of solid information about mutual funds. Use these sources to compile a roster of funds that seem to meet your investment objectives, then proceed as follows:

- **Call each fund to get its prospectus** and annual report (or order it through the fund's Web site.)
- **Compare your candidates on past performance** over several years, in good markets and bad, not just for the past year or two.
- **Check to see that the managers** who compiled that wonderful record are still running the fund.
- **Check each fund's volatility score** (different publications rate them in different ways) to see how much risk you're taking on. Other things being equal, a fund that beats the market while taking few risks is a better bet than a fund that beats the market by taking big risks.
- **Finally, compare the funds' fee structures,** looking especially for outsize loads that will cut the amount of money you have working for you at the start, and for overly ambitious 12b-1 fees, which can nibble your account to death, year by year.

Different Strokes for Different Folks

The following major groupings of funds offer more options than you'll probably ever use. You'll want to diversify with selections from several groups, and your choices will depend on your risk tolerance and length of time you have until you'll need the money. These definitions match the groupings you'll usually see in quarterly or annual rankings of fund performance in many newspapers and magazines.

Aggressive-Growth Funds

These strive for big profits, generally by investing in small companies and developing industries or by concentrating on volatile issues. Some use speculative techniques, such as trading with borrowed money and short selling. The greater the drive for high profits, the greater the risk.

Growth Funds

These look for long-range capital gains by buying the stocks of companies that supposedly have unique characteristics enabling them to grow faster than inflation.

Growth-and-Income Funds

These funds have much the same objective as growth funds, but they put greater emphasis on capital preservation and try to produce more current dividend income for shareholders. These funds invest in bonds, preferred stocks, and high-yielding common stocks.

Specialized, or Sector, Funds

Some funds concentrate their investments in one or two fields or industries. They may invest largely in stocks of utility companies, U.S. government securities, bank shares, or stocks of gold mines.

Index Funds

The opposite of the narrowly focused sector funds, index funds assemble portfolios designed to track as precisely as possible one or more broad stock or bond index. Funds that track the Standard & Poor's 500 are perhaps the best known, but there are many others. When the market is moving relentlessly upward, as it did for most of the 1990s, index funds are tough to beat.

International and Global Funds

International funds are U.S.-based but invest in securities of companies traded on foreign exchanges. Global

> **The greater a fund's drive for high profits, the greater the risk.**

Most money-market funds allow you to draw checks on the balance in your fund.

funds reserve the right to mix in some U.S. issues as well. They are good places to be when the value of the dollar is falling because their holdings may be denominated in foreign currencies and investors profit from the favorable exchange rates on those currencies.

Bond Funds

These can be either taxable and nontaxable (muni) funds. Within the taxable category are high-quality (investment-grade) and high-yield corporate-bond funds, global-bond funds, mortgage funds, and U.S. government-bond funds. Muni funds are either high-quality or high-yield. High-yield funds specialize in lower-rated bonds that must pay more interest to attract investors. High-quality funds stick to top-rated corporate or municipal issues. Single-state municipal-bond funds invest exclusively in the bonds issued within a particular state to deliver yields free of federal and state taxes, and sometimes local taxes as well.

Money-Market Funds

Money-market funds invest in U.S. Treasury bills, commercial paper (essentially the IOUs of corporations), certificates of deposit, and other more esoteric short-term debt instruments. They usually credit interest to your account daily; most allow you to draw checks on the balance in your fund. Money-market funds are discussed in detail beginning on page 407.

How to Tell How You're Doing

The mutual fund tables in the newspapers list daily net asset values, or price. The price of your shares is a key concern, of course, but you need more information than that to be able to judge how your fund has been performing. Suppose that the price shows virtually no change for some extended period—say, a year. That does not necessarily mean that the fund's value to you didn't change. You might have collected dividends and capital gains during that period. In fact, a capital-gains payment acts to depress the

SOURCES OF MUTUAL FUND INFORMATION

Several personal-finance and investment magazines rank the top-performing mutual funds on a monthly basis and rank most funds on an annual basis. Among the popular periodicals covering funds on a regular basis are *Business Week, Forbes, Kiplinger's Personal Finance* magazine, *Money, Mutual Funds,* and *SmartMoney. Barron's* publishes fund rankings quarterly. All provide information on their Web sites: businessweek.com offers a mutual fund interactive scoreboard and selected stories free, and you must subscribe for access to the rest of the site; forbes.com, kiplinger.com, money.com, and smartmoney.com all offer free financial information, portfolio tracking, and calculators; barrons.com offers financial information and portfolio tracking for a fee.

The following publications and services provide comprehensive directories to funds, usually arranged according to investment objectives. Where indicated, these guides can also be valuable sources of information on fund performance. They are available in libraries, directly from the publisher, and, in some cases, on the Internet or in bookstores.

Mutual Fund Fact Book

A guide to statistics and trends in the mutual fund industry, published by the Investment Company Institute (ICI), an industry association. You can read it on the institute's Web site or buy a hard copy. No performance information. Updated annually ($30; 401 H St., NW, Suite 1200, Washington, DC 20005; 202-326-5800; www.ici.org). ICI's Web site also provides a list of mutual fund families that are members of the Institute, with phone numbers and Web addresses when available.

Individual Investor's Guide to Low-Load Mutual Funds

Comprehensive information on about 900 no-load funds, compiled by the American Association of Individual Investors, whose members get the book free. Includes performance records, risk ratings, and information on portfolio holdings. Updated annually

($30; 625 N. Michigan Ave., Chicago, IL 60611; 800-428-2244; www.aaii.org).

Kiplinger's Mutual Funds

An annual newsstand guide to choosing the best funds, with advice for novices and experienced investors alike ($5.95; 1729 H St., NW, Washington, DC 20006, 888-547-5464, www.kiplinger.com).

Morningstar Mutual Funds

A compendium of mutual fund analysis updated every other week. Covers 1,700 funds ($549; Morningstar Inc., 225 W. Wacker Dr., Chicago, IL 60606; 800-735-0700; www.morningstar.com).

Value Line Mutual Fund Survey

A biweekly publication analyzing the performance of more than 2,000 mutual funds ($345/yr., Value Line Publishing, 220 E. 42nd St., New York, NY 10017; 800-634-3583; www.valueline.com).

To get the true measure of a fund's performance, you need to take dividends and capital-gains payments into account along with changes in the price. The result is total return.

fund's price because the fund is actually paying out money that was previously included in its portfolio.

You can't get the true measure of a fund's performance, therefore, unless you take dividends and capital-gains payments into account along with changes in the price. What you really need to know is the fund's total return. That's what the funds promote, and that's the basis used in comparing the performance of one fund with another.

On your own, you can compute your fund's performance in several ways and get different answers. For an idea of how a return varies depending on the approach you use, consider this simplified illustration:

The fictional HotShot Fund, a no-load, growth-oriented fund, starts the year with a net asset value of $10 a share. After six months, a market rally pushes HotShot's value to $15 a share. The fund sells assets and distributes $5 a share in capital gains. This returns its NAV to $10. The shareholders have a choice of taking the $5 in cash or reinvesting it in the fund.

In the second half of the year, HotShot's investments continue to do well. It ends the year at $20 a share. Because it is a growth-oriented fund, assume it pays no cash dividends. If you ignore the capital-gains distribution, the fund jumped 100 percent—from $10 to $20 a share.

A better approach is to include the $5 in the return even if you took the money in cash. The $5 plus the $10 increase in the ultimate price of a share means the $10 at the start of the year is worth $25 at the end. That's a 150 percent increase.

Another way to figure total return, and probably the most accurate, is to assume that the $5 distribution is reinvested in HotShot shares. The $5 goes back into the fund when shares have a $10 NAV, so you now have one and one-half shares instead of one. Each share is worth $20 at the end of the year, for a total of $30—a 200 percent return on the original $10.

The key to understanding the total-return concept is to think about the total wealth generated from your initial purchase, not just the market price of one share at the end of the measurement period.

Should You Be Open to Closed-End Funds?

Closed-end funds also pool shareholders' capital for investment, but they don't issue new shares and they don't redeem old ones when investors want to sell. You buy the shares on a stock exchange or in the over-the-counter market and sell them the same way, paying a commission to a broker.

Because the market, not the value of the underlying assets, determines the price of closed-end funds, it is possible for their shares to sell at discounts from their net asset values—the equivalent of a stock's selling for less than book value. Some sell at premiums from time to time. No one seems to have a completely satisfactory explanation for either phenomenon. The discounts don't automatically make the shares a bargain, because you usually have to accept a discounted price when you sell them. You could profit if for some reason the discount narrows, but you could lose if the discount widens. Closed-end funds, like mutual funds (which are open-ended), invest in diversified or specialized groups of securities.

Over the years, several closed-end funds have converted to open-end funds, either voluntarily or under pressure from dissident investors. Because mutual fund shares are priced at NAV, and closed-ends often sell at a discount, open-ending can hike the worth of a closed-end fund investment 10 percent, 15 percent, or more overnight.

In recent years there has been an explosion in closed-end offerings. The boom has been fueled by investors' desire to enlist the expertise of certain high-profile money managers who were starting such funds and to cash in on foreign stock markets. Closed-end funds operating in Mexico, Korea, Taiwan, Japan, Australia, France, Italy, Ireland, Spain, and other countries provide access to those countries' markets.

In considering a closed-end fund, the safe route is to stick with funds that have been around long enough to establish a track record of consistent performance. It's not a good idea to buy a fund immediately after it

The market, not the value of the underlying assets, is what determines the price of a closed-end mutual fund.

An exchange-traded fund's portfolio represents a slice of the market—an index, a sub-sector of an index, or a particular industry.

has been issued because hard selling by brokers may generate a lot of early interest in a fund, which tends to inflate its price. It's also not a good idea to buy closed-ends as a means of playing short-term market swings because the discounts and premiums serve to exacerbate the effect of price changes.

Well-managed closed-end funds can be a sensible place to look for dividends. Consider this: If a fund with a net asset value of $10 sells at a 10 percent discount, you can get $10 worth of assets earning dividends for only $9. That kind of leverage isn't available in many places.

Exchange-Traded Funds

Exchange-traded funds (ETFs), the fastest-growing segment of the fund industry, have grown from none a dozen years ago to more than 175 ETFs holding about $228 billion in assets. Like closed-end funds, ETFs own a fixed portfolio of securities and can be bought and sold any time of the day that the stock market is open. Unlike closed-ends, ETFs don't tend to develop significant discounts or premiums.

An exchange-traded fund's portfolio represents a slice of the market—an index, a subsector of an index, or a particular industry. You buy and sell them through a broker, even sell them short or buy them on margin, just like ordinary stocks. ETFs also come in more varieties than conventional index funds and tend to cost even less than the least costly traditional index fund.

The biggest drawback of ETFs is the brokerage commission you pay each time you buy or sell one. So investors engaged in dollar-cost averaging are usually better off using regular index funds rather than ETFs. But if you plan to buy and sell in large chunks and you trade through a discount broker, a commission of $10 or so may be inconsequential.

The major reasons to consider them are:

LOWER MANAGEMENT FEES—due in part to the economics of indexing, which minimizes the need for managers and analysts.

LOWER TAXES—Because ETFs and index funds don't buy and sell very much, there is rarely any reason to distribute anything except dividend income, which is minimal.

SOPHISTICATED TRADING OPPORTUNITIES—If you want to bet against the market in which an ETF concentrates, you can sell it short. If you want to leverage your investment, you can borrow from your broker and buy an ETF on margin. What's more, you can impose stop-loss and limit orders that trigger, say, an automatic sale if an ETF you own falls to a certain price that you specify in advance.

Money-Market Funds: Keeping It Short

Money-market mutual funds originally grew popular as a place to park money temporarily between more lucrative investments. But occasional sharp rises in short-term interest rates and the volatility of the investment markets in general has made them a permanent fixture in many portfolios. There's no price volatility, and you can become an investor for as little as $1,000, although a more typical minimum initial investment is $2,500.

What They Are, What They Own

Money-market funds got their name because they invest in securities known as money-market instruments. The money market is the collective name given to deals by which the government, banks, big corporations, securities dealers, and others borrow and lend money for short periods. The deals may be for overnight or for a few days, but are never more than a year; otherwise, they're not part of the money market. The average maturity of a money-market fund can't exceed 90 days.

Each fund's prospectus describes the types of instruments and investment techniques it may use, and its quarterly financial statements report current hold-

Occasional sharp rises in short-term interest rates and the volatility of the investment markets in general has made money-market funds a permanent fixture in many portfolios.

ings. The makeup of the portfolio determines the yield and safety of your investment. These are the principal instruments you're likely to find in a fund portfolio.

TREASURY BILLS AND NOTES. Bills are issued with maturities of four weeks, three months, six months, nine months, and one year. Notes run longer, but they, like bills, are widely traded and can be bought when they are close to maturity. Treasury issues constitute direct obligations of the federal government, so they rate tops in safety.

OTHER GOVERNMENT SECURITIES. The funds may also buy short-term securities issued by individual government agencies or government-sponsored organizations. Some are backed by the full faith and credit of the federal government; others are guaranteed only by the agencies, but they rank just below Treasuries in safety because it's assumed that the government would not permit an agency to default.

COMMERCIAL PAPER. Essentially, these are IOUs issued by corporations to raise funds for limited periods, usually 60 days or less. Paper is rated for quality by credit-analysis firms according to the issuing company's financial strength. Standard & Poor's top rating is A-1; Moody's is Prime-1.

BANKER'S ACCEPTANCES. These loans originate largely in import and export transactions in which the buyer gives the seller a note payable by the buyer within a fixed period. If the bank financing the transaction accepts the note, thus guaranteeing payment at maturity and making the draft salable in the open market, it becomes a banker's acceptance. A money-market fund can buy the acceptance at a discount and get paid the full amount at maturity.

CERTIFICATES OF DEPOSIT. The money market deals in large-denomination, negotiable certificates, not the relatively small amounts familiar to savers. Domestic CDs are issued by U.S. bank offices. Yankee CDs are issued by branches of foreign banks in the U.S.; Eurodollar CDs are sold by U.S. bank branches in Europe and are payable in U.S. dollars.

REPURCHASE AGREEMENTS. Repos work in a couple of different ways. In their most common form, they are created when a bank wishes to borrow money for a short while, maybe only one day. The bank sells Treasury bills it is holding to a money-market fund with a promise to buy them back the next day at a higher price or a specified interest rate. In effect, the repurchase agreement amounts to a loan with Treasury securities as collateral.

There is also a reverse repurchase agreement in which the transaction goes the opposite way: The fund sells its bills to a bank and agrees to buy them back. Here it's the fund that is borrowing money from the bank. A fund may leave itself the option of executing reverse repos as a means of handling heavy shareholder redemptions. The borrowed money can be used to pay shareholders' withdrawals so the fund doesn't have to sell portfolio securities.

How Safe Are They?

Money-market funds are very safe, but they aren't guaranteed. Because most funds hold several kinds of securities, the risk often depends on what those securities happen to be and how large they loom in the portfolio.

For maximum safety, look for a fund with a high proportion of U.S. government securities, CDs from well-known domestic banks, and top-rated commercial paper. Some investors prefer the funds that invest exclusively or chiefly in U.S. and U.S.-guaranteed securities—Capital Preservation fund, Fidelity U.S. Government Reserves fund, Merrill Lynch U.S. Government Securities fund, and several others.

Why the Yields Change and the Price Doesn't

Occasionally one or more funds report surprisingly high yields compared with most other funds. Sometimes this

> For maximum safety, look for a money-market fund with a high proportion of U.S. government securities, CDs from well-known domestic banks, and top-rated commercial paper.

MONEY-MARKET FUNDS: A SAMPLER

	MINIMUM INITIAL DEPOSIT	MINIMUM CHECK SIZE	
AXP Cash Management Fund www.americanexpress.com	$2,000	No checks	800-297-5300
Dreyfus Liquid Assets www.dreyfus.com	2,500	500	800-645-6561
Dreyfus Worldwide Dollar Money Market www.dreyfus.com	2,500	500	800-645-6561
Fidelity Cash Reserves www.fidelity.com	2,500	500	800-343-3548
Merrill Lynch Ready Assets www.ml.com	2,000	No min.	800-637-7455
Oppenheimer Money Market www.oppenheimerfunds.com	1,000*	500	888-470-0862
Prudential Money Market Assets www.prudential.com	1,000	500	800-225-1852
Scudder Cash Reserves Fund www.scudder.com	1,000	No checks	800-621-1048
T. Rowe Price Prime Reserve www.troweprice.com	2,500	500	800-225-5132
UBS CashFund www.ubs.com	1,000**	500	800-221-3260
Vanguard Prime Money Market www.vanguard.com	3,000	250	888-662-2739

GOVERNMENT-ONLY FUNDS

Capital Preservation (American Century) www.americancentury.com	2,500	100	800-345-2021
Dreyfus 100% U.S. Treasury www.dreyfus.com	2,500	500	800-645-6561
Fidelity U.S. Government Reserves www.fidelity.com	2,500	500	800-343-3548
Merrill Lynch USA Government Reserves www.ml.com	2,000	No min.	800-637-7455
Reserve U.S. Government www.reservefunds.com	1,000	No min.	800-637-1700
Vanguard Federal Money Market Reserves www.vanguard.com	3,000	250	800-662-2739

TAX-FREE FUNDS

Calvert Tax-Free Reserves www.calvertgroup.com	2,000	250	800-368-2748
Dreyfus Municipal Money Market www.dreyfus.com	2,500	500	800-645-6561

* $500 with auto deposit signup for $50/month ** No initial deposit required with signup for $50 a month auto deposit

happens because the fund temporarily suspends its management fee in order to propel itself to the top of performance charts and thus attract attention. In the long run, though, much of the difference results from the fund managers' investment acumen. For instance, if a fund manager thinks interest rates are headed down, he can delay the effect on his portfolio by lengthening the average maturity of his holdings, delaying for a time the need to invest in those new, lower-rate securities. If he thinks rates are going up, he shortens maturities so he'll be in the market when it happens.

But timing is not the whole story. Differences in yields can also stem from differences in the way funds compute the value of their portfolios. Funds maintain a fixed net asset value, usually $1. Interest income and profits from the sale and redemption of securities are paid out in the form of dividends. And the dividends buy additional shares to add to your account.

However, a portfolio's value really fluctuates every day as short-term interest-rate changes raise or lower the market price of the securities in the portfolio. The funds insulate their net asset values from those price changes by using different valuation methods, and the choice can have an effect on their yields, especially over a short measurement period such as a week. Over longer periods, the differences tend to wash out, underlining the futility of chasing yields based on technical factors such as valuation methods. Over the long haul, superior management will make the important difference.

Costs—and Perks—of Ownership

Variations in fees and services may appear trivial, but they sometimes produce unnecessary costs and annoying delays. Normally you deal with funds directly, although in a few cases you may have to go through the brokerage firm that sponsors the fund and perhaps open an account with the firm. If you buy shares through a bank or a broker other than the sponsoring broker, you might be charged an additional fee. In the normal course of events, though, your management fee buys you a bundle of convenient services.

MANAGEMENT FEES. Money-market funds do not charge sales fees. Some funds, though, charge account-maintenance fees of a couple of dollars a month. All charge management fees, which average about 1 percent. Some charge considerably more, and higher fees come directly out of the pockets of investors. You can check on fees in the prospectus.

CHECKING PRIVILEGES. This is one of the most attractive features of money-market funds. Most allow you to write checks on your account balance, usually in minimum denominations of $250 or $500, and most give you the checking plan at no extra cost. By all means, sign up for it when you open an account.

Unit Investment Trusts

When you buy into a unit investment trust, you get part ownership, measured in units, of a fixed portfolio of securities. Unit trusts are a popular way to buy tax-exempt bonds and are also used by brokerage firms to package offerings of corporate bonds, utility stocks, and pools of government-backed mortgages known as Ginnie Maes. They were described briefly in Chapter 24.

For investors who want to put money into a particular type of security, unit trusts provide professionally selected, diversified portfolios that can usually be bought in multiples of about $1,000. Because the trusts hold on to their original securities instead of trading them, the bond investor gets a fixed dollar return that won't change much for a long period. Trusts don't dissolve and return the remaining capital to investors until most of the bonds in the portfolio have been redeemed.

The ability to lock in a certain rate is attractive if you want a steady, assured income or think interest rates will decline, thereby increasing bond prices. Of course, if interest rates increase, you'll be stuck with a low-level return that lowers the value of your units. Those are the risks faced by anyone who buys fixed-income securities.

Unit trusts are sold so casually that many investors mistakenly assume they are interchangeable pieces of the same product, differing only in yield and type of security. Actually, trusts are far more complex than they seem, as anyone who reads a prospectus quickly learns, and they can differ significantly.

The Right Way to Buy a Unit Trust

Brokerage firms try to sell out unit trusts within a matter of days after they are registered with the Securities and Exchange Commission. As a result, investors often have to place their orders before they receive a prospectus, relying on advance information from their brokers.

Often you can't get more than a few sketchy details in advance—the approximate yield, the sales charge, the distribution of the bonds according to quality rankings (AAA, AA, etc.), and a summary description of the issues in the portfolio. But there are a lot of other facts you should know. For instance, if you're trying to lock in a high yield for the long term, you'll want to know the call provisions of the bonds in the portfolio. Bonds with short-term call dates give the issuers greater freedom to call the bonds for redemption if interest rates decline; the high-rate bonds can then be paid off with funds raised by selling new bonds at lower rates.

You have an opportunity to check those and other details when you receive the prospectus with your bill. If the information given to you earlier by the broker turns out to be incorrect, you can ask to have your order canceled. Brokers may comply as a matter of good customer relations even when no mistake has been made. To avoid misunderstandings, make clear when you place the advance order that it's conditional on your satisfaction with the prospectus.

Getting Out

Although they are not obligated to do so, as prospectuses carefully point out, unit-trust sponsors maintain a secondary market for their own units and are pre-

Check out details of the trust when you get the prospectus with your bill. If they're incorrect, you can ask to have your order canceled.

pared to buy or sell them as they would other securities. Thus, the easiest way to get rid of your units is to sell them back to the broker.

Investing in Real Estate

One major difference between real estate and practically any other investment you could make is that it is bought and sold on local markets, not national ones. You don't have to live in Atlanta or Denver or San Bernardino to buy or sell rental property there, but it surely helps. Settlement on the property will take place there, and the deal will close according to various local and state laws. That means real estate can be a more cumbersome investment than, say, stocks or bonds, which are traded on national marketplaces with no more trouble than a phone call or the click of a computer mouse.

Nevertheless, great fortunes have been built on real estate, and although several rounds of tax reform have left it less seductive these days than it used to be, it's still got a lot going for it.

The Lure of Leverage

It is not unheard of to use OPM—other people's money—to buy stocks and other investments by borrowing part of their purchase price. In real estate, OPM is practically a way of life. You use OPM (or leverage, in the lingo of the trade) when you take out a mortgage to buy a house, an apartment, or a commercial building. The bigger the mortgage as a proportion of the property's value (and the smaller your down payment), the greater your leverage. And it's leverage that produces the spectacular profits you hear about in real estate.

Despite some tightening up over the years, real estate has been showered with tax breaks that few investments can match.

Say you pay cash for an $160,000 condo and sell it a few years later for $200,000. The $40,000 gain represents a 25 percent return on your $160,000 outlay. Not bad. But what if you had invested only $40,000 of your own money and borrowed the other $120,000? In that case your result is considerably better: You made $40,000 on a $40,000 investment, for a gain of 100 percent. Now we're talking. (This example obviously ignores the mortgage payments you made along the way, but you get the point.)

Unfortunately, leverage can also magnify your losses. For example, if you are forced to sell the $160,000 condo for $140,000, the $20,000 loss wipes out half of your $40,000 investment—a 50 percent loss even though the value of the property declined by only about 13 percent. That's why leverage should be considered a two-edged sword. Investors who live by it sometimes die by it. The keys to avoiding a slow and agonizing death: well-selected properties and enough other financial resources to be able to wait out bad real estate markets.

Tax Breaks in Real Estate

Despite some tightening up over the years, real estate has been showered with tax breaks that few investments can match. Chiefly, the breaks fall into two categories.

Deductible Expenses

If you own stocks and bonds, you can deduct the cost of professional advice, portfolio-management fees, and other expenses of generating profits only to the extent that they exceed 2 percent of your adjusted gross income. For an income of $50,000, that means the first $1,000 comes entirely out of your own pocket.

According to the tax laws, your stocks and bonds are strictly personal, but your rental property puts you in the real estate business. That means your operating costs, mortgage-interest (but not principal) payments, real estate taxes, and other expenses can be deducted from rental income, just as you would offset income with expenses in any business. In other words, if you own rental real estate, you can deduct every qualified cent you spend to find and keep tenants and maintain the place. You even get a mileage allowance for driving over to unclog the sink—and don't forget to deduct the cost of the drain cleaner.

Depreciation

Real estate's crowning tax break is depreciation: the right to deduct each year a certain portion of the value of the building, simply because you own it. You don't have to spend a cent for repairs or maintenance to claim your depreciation allowance. The property needn't be deteriorating physically. The fact that the building's market value is rising doesn't stop you from claiming your deduction for depreciation. If you buy the property from someone who has already depreciated it, you can start the depreciation cycle all over again, as can the buyer after you.

Your depreciation deduction is a classic tax shelter because it shields part of your current rental income from current taxes. What's more, if you have income from other sources (within certain limits described below) and you meet a few not-so-tough tests, you can use depreciation on rental property to shield up to $25,000 of that income, to boot.

The IRS says that residential real estate, such as a house or an apartment, must be depreciated over a period of 27.5 years, meaning that each year you get to deduct 1/27.5 (about 3.64 percent) of the price you paid for the building. Commercial properties, such as office buildings and stores, put into service on or after May 13, 1993, are depreciated over 39 years. Every time the property changes hands, the depreciation schedule starts all over again. (Investors who put their properties into service in earlier years when more generous rules were in effect get to stick with those depreciation schedules.) The current schedule isn't generous, but it can turn a losing property into a winner, as the following simplified example shows.

Real estate's crowning tax break is depreciation: the right to deduct each year a certain portion of the value of the building, simply because you own it.

A negative cash flow would be the kiss of death for most investments, but not necessarily for real estate. Depreciation is the ace up our sleeve.

Let's go back and buy that $200,000 condo we described a couple of pages ago. We take out a $160,000 mortgage at 7 percent (rates are usually higher for mortgages on investment properties than on owner-occupied homes), which means monthly payments of $1,064. The condo fee adds another $150 to the monthly outlay, and property taxes, insurance, maintenance, and repairs add up to another $150. Total out-of-pocket expense: $1,364 a month. We advertise to rent the place out and discover to our chagrin that we can get only $1,350 a month. Our simplified annual balance sheet before taxes looks like this:

Expenses: $1,364/month x 12 months = $ 16,368
Income: $1,300/month x 12 months =   15,600
Cash flow: – $ 768

A negative cash flow would be the kiss of death for most investments, but not necessarily for real estate. Depreciation is the ace up our sleeve. It kicks in to generate tax savings that can convert a pretax loss into an after-tax profit.

Let's apply the 27.5-year depreciation schedule to this example. The property cost $200,000, but the land on which our building sits is not depreciable and must be subtracted from the total before the depreciation allowance is applied. The IRS has no cut-and-dried formula for this, but allowing 20 percent of the total for land is safe enough. That leaves $160,000 against which to apply depreciation.

As mentioned earlier, a 27.5-year depreciation schedule translates to about 3.64 percent per year (you actually get a little less in the first year, but let's ignore that technicality to keep the example simple). So your depreciation deduction each year is $5,824. In the 25 percent tax bracket, that saves you $1,456 in taxes you don't have to pay. Apply that against your negative cash flow of $768 and you actually squeak through the year with an after-tax positive cash flow of $688—not a princely sum considering you put up $40,000 as a down payment, but a positive return nonetheless. And in a higher bracket, your tax savings would be larger. The sharp-eyed reader will note that our return would be even higher because we haven't taken into account the deduction for mortgage interest—about $930 a month in the first year. But you must lay out the interest payments in order to deduct them. The deduction for depreciation involves no outlay of cash.

Despite the ability of depreciation to turn a loser into a winner, a better property would be one that returned a positive cash flow—that is, an annual profit—or at least broke even, before taxes. A positive cash flow could be offset by the depreciation, thereby giving you cash in your pocket with no tax liability. That's the nirvana real estate investors dream of. If you have more depreciation than you need to offset income from the property, then maybe you can use it to shelter income from other sources. But note that word "maybe."

Limits on Deductions

In order to claim all the real estate deductions you have coming in the year you incur them, the law says that your income must qualify as "active." It is automatically considered to be active if you are a real estate professional, which, according to the IRS definition, means that more than half the services you perform during the year are in real estate–related businesses and you spend more than 750 hours a year working at it.

If you do not meet these requirements, your rental activity will be considered "passive" by the IRS, and current deductibility will be limited. But all is not lost. You can still deduct real estate losses, including depreciation, against current rental expenses, such as maintenance, interest, and property taxes. Beyond that, you can deduct up to $25,000 in rental losses against other income, including salaries, provided you meet certain requirements. To meet the requirements, you must be actively involved in the management of the property, which has been interpreted to mean that you set the rent, approve tenants, and decide on capital improvements. If your adjusted gross income is more than $100,000, you will be denied 50 cents of the loss

> While depreciation can to turn a loser into a winner, you're better off with a property that returns a positive cash flow.

An exchange allows you to trade your investment property for a similar one without having to pay taxes on profits until you sell the second property or stop exchanging properties.

allowance for every dollar over $100,000, until it disappears entirely at $150,000 of income. Actually, these losses are never gone completely because you get to save any disallowed amounts and apply them against rental or other "passive" income in future years. If you don't get a chance to use them that way, you can add disallowed amounts to the cost basis of the property when you sell it, thus reducing any profit and any tax you'd owe on the profit.

Meanwhile, adding to your profits will be all that depreciation you claimed along the way, because Uncle Sam wants it back when you sell. You're required to add up the depreciation you've claimed and subtract it from the original cost basis of the property. This has the effect of increasing your profit, and thus the amount of tax you owe on the sale. And profit attributable to depreciation after May 6, 1997, is taxed at 25 percent rather than the 20 percent rate for other long-term gains. This can be a rude surprise to investors who, after years of merrily depreciating a property, discover that their tax bill upon sale is a whopper even when the price appreciation of the property has been modest—or, in some cases, even if the price has gone down! As a result, many decide to parlay one property into another via a tax-deferred exchange.

Exchanging Rental Properties

An exchange allows you to trade your investment property for a similar one of equal or greater value without having to pay taxes on any profits until you sell the second property or, if you continue exchanging properties, until you sell the last one and don't purchase another.

The economics of these deals, called 1031 exchanges (or, sometimes, Starker exchanges) are tricky. You'll need to hire a real estate or tax lawyer who specializes in tax-deferred exchanges. Though the tax code requires the properties to be of "like kind," the term is very liberally defined. Exchanging one rental house for another qualifies, but so does trading raw land for an apartment building. It's the nature of the property that matters, not its condition, degree of development, or even its location, except that you can't exchange property in the U.S. for property in another country.

Proceeds from the sale must be held by a qualified intermediary, a person who is not a relative or agent, otherwise the proceeds will become taxable and you'll have only 45 days after selling your property to identify a suitable replacement property.

You must close on the replacement property within the "exchange period," which ends within the earlier of 180 days after the date on which you sold your property or the date for the taxpayer tax return for the taxable year in which the sale took place. (This 180-day rule is strict and is not extended if the 180th day should happen to fall on a weekend or legal holiday.) You can see how tricky this is and why professional help is a must.

You can also do a 1031 exchange when you sell your personal residence if you have been depreciating for a home office and your profit from the sale would be more than the tax-free amount allowed ($500,000 for couples and $250,000 for singles). But the only way to take advantage of both breaks is to swap your home and its office for a similar home and office of equal or greater value.

Pick a property that's typical, not one so special that it will appeal only to tenants with tastes that match your own.

Selecting Profitable Rental Properties

- **Pick a property that's typical,** not one so special that it will appeal only to tenants with tastes that match your own.
- **If you are buying from another investor,** ask to inspect the record of income, expenses, and occupancy for the past few years to make sure they back up what the seller is telling you.
- **Compare prices of similar properties** to make certain the property you're considering isn't overpriced.
- **Compare rents for similar units nearby.** Be skeptical of a seller's assurance that you can raise the rent once you take over. If it's so easy, why didn't that owner do it?

A real estate investment trust is to real estate what a mutual fund is to stocks and bonds.

- **Make sure the agreement you sign** requires the seller to turn over tenants' security deposits when you settle on the property.
- **Examine existing leases** before closing so you know how long they have to run, who the tenants are, and how long they've been there.
- **Be wary of investing in property** on which maintenance has been put off. The seller's income and expense statements could show a handsome return because the owner hasn't spent enough for repairs.
- **Check for violations of local code.** You don't want to get stuck with the expense of correcting them.
- **Keep loan payments affordable** so you won't get hurt by occasional vacancies.

Real Estate Investment Trusts

There is a way to extend your reach in real estate beyond the local marketplace and diversify across many different properties at the same time. A real estate investment trust (REIT) is to real estate what a mutual fund is to stocks and bonds. A shareowner in a REIT participates with other shareholders in the pooled ownership and professional management of income-producing properties, such as apartment houses, shopping centers, office buildings, warehouses, or a combination of these; in the pooled ownership of mortgages on such properties; or in a mixture of buildings and mortgages. Shares are sold by brokers and traded on the major stock exchanges or over the counter every day, which makes REITs the most liquid form of real estate investment you can find.

Types of REITs

You should be familiar with the distinction between equity REITs and mortgage REITs. Equity REITs own income-producing properties. Mortgage REITs provide long-term mortgages and short-term construction loans. REITs in the lending business often demand some piece of the projects they finance and withdraw from the market when conditions are weak.

Hybrid REITs have a portion of their investments in mortgages and a portion in equity positions.

Tax advantages

Federal tax laws allow REITs to pay no taxes on income or gains if they distribute at least 90 percent of earnings to shareholders and meet a number of other specific conditions. Because they pass along nearly all of their earnings, REITs are attractive to investors seeking relatively high dividends as well as rising share prices. Mortgage REITs tend to pay out a little more than equity REITs, but both generally pay high dividends.

Sometimes dividends are paid not from earnings but from shareholders' equity. They are designated as returns of capital and treated as a refund of part of your investment. Instead of paying income taxes, you deduct the payment from the cost basis of the shares when you sell the stock. Be careful of REITs paying their shareholders this way, as the technique can be used to artificially inflate the yield in order to attract investors.

Risks in REITs

The risk in equity trusts is that markets in which they hold properties will turn sour, leaving them with empty buildings, no tenants, and thus no rental income to pass along to shareholders. Mortgage trusts can be damaged by upswings in interest rates, which tend to hurt mortgage demand, and by recessions, which may impair mortgage borrowers' ability to repay their loans.

How to Find a Good REIT

Study the annual reports of REITs that interest you. Once you've narrowed your choices, ask the companies for copies of the 10-K reports they are required to file with the Securities and Exchange Commission. Check the following:

DIVIDEND HISTORY. Check especially on the consistency of payouts, and compare different REITs on this point.

> **Mortgage trusts can be damaged by upswings in interest rates, which tend to hurt mortgage demand, and by recessions, which may impair borrowers' ability to repay their loans.**

Limited partnerships are a lot easier to buy than to sell. They are difficult to understand. They charge high fees to investors and can create tax-filing headaches. Avoid them.

LOCATION OF PROPERTIES AND TENANT MIX. Watch out for inflated predictions of rent increases; overly optimistic outlooks for condominium sales or conversions; heavy investment in old open-air shopping centers in well-to-do areas; aging apartment complexes, which are expensive to maintain; and dependence on a few tenants or on one-industry towns.

On the plus side, look for strong investments in recession-resistant industries; a good geographic mix or a solid position in local markets you can keep an eye on yourself; and relationships with grade-A tenants such as major retailers and the U.S. government.

APPRAISALS. An annual report may show the properties' current appraisals. Take those figures with a grain of salt. A trust that liquidates properties won't necessarily get top dollar on the open market. On the other hand, impressive differences between the book value of a REIT's holdings and their current market values may make the trust attractive for takeover by big investors looking to buy real estate assets at bargain prices. If that bids up share prices, investors should benefit.

NONPERFORMING LOANS. Trusts state the proportion of loans not earning interest or in default. If a trust forgoes too much income or has to keep repossessing property, its loan selection should be questioned.

Real Estate Limited Partnerships

In a real estate limited partnership, money put up by investors is used to buy land, mortgages, apartments, office buildings, shopping centers, or other property. The organizer and manager of the program—an individual or a company—assumes the role of general partner and receives fees and commissions for the service, plus a share of any profits. Investors are called limited partners, because their liability for losses is limited to the amount they invest.

Limited partnerships are a lot easier to buy than to sell. They are difficult to understand. They charge high fees to investors and can create tax-filing headaches. Avoid them.

The Risks in Raw Land

If you buy undeveloped property, whether as an investment or a place to live, vacation, or retire, you may be taking risks you didn't expect. Tens of thousands of buyers in virtually every state have invested thousands of dollars in land that is worth much less than they paid for it, and in a number of cases it is worth nothing at all on the resale market. They are stuck with property that has no sewer, water, or electric lines. It may not support a septic tank and a well, or the expense of those improvements could double the cost of the plot. The land might be subject to periodic flooding. Local ordinances might effectively prohibit building there at all.

In the meantime, the tax news is bad, too: Land isn't depreciable, and the deduction for the interest you pay on the loan to buy the land is limited to the amount of taxable income you get from the land and other investments.

There really isn't much to protect you except your own awareness. Some laws at the federal level and in some states and localities are designed to protect buyers. Overall, however, crackdowns generally come only after buyers have been gulled.

One federal statute—the Interstate Land Sales Full Disclosure Act—is designed to protect consumers in the market for land. It covers companies offering more than 100 subdivision lots across state lines, with certain exemptions. Consumers are also protected by the Real Estate Settlement Procedures Act (RESPA), which is aimed at helping consumers become better shoppers for settlement services and at eliminating kickbacks and referral fees that unnecessarily increase the costs of certain settlement services.

The companies affected are required to file with the federal Interstate Land Sales/RESPA Division a statement of record, which is a detailed description of the lots for sale or lease, plus financial and legal infor-

SMART STEPS BEFORE YOU BUY RAW LAND

If you are seriously considering buying a piece of undeveloped property, take your time and follow this procedure.

Write for and read the useful pamphlets available from the Interstate Land Sales/ RESPA Division, Room 9154, 451 Seventh St., SW, Washington, DC 20410, or search its online topics by going to www.hud.gov, selecting search/index, and clicking on "Interstate Land Sales."

Ask one or more independent brokers in the area whether they would be willing to list the property and what its selling price would be.

Visit the property. Don't buy anything sight unseen.

Make sure that any representations about property improvements and the services that will be provided are added to the sales contract and signed by the sales manager. If he or she won't sign it, you shouldn't either.

Find out whether the land can actually be used as a home site. Write, phone, or visit the appropriate offices of the local government. Ask what kinds of permits must be obtained before you can build on the property and whether sewer and water hookups are available.

Call HUD, the office of your state's Attorney General, and the Better Business Bureau to determine if any complaints have been filed against the developer or if any investigations are in progress.

Check to see whether environmental considerations might limit the use of the land. Is radon present? Is the property on wetlands? Are hazardous chemicals on the land or near it?

Determine whether the developer's bonds for improvements—swimming pool, utility lines, and the like—are the surety kind, so that if he or she goes bankrupt the money will still be available. Escrow accounts can also be used for this purpose. A corporate bond for further improvements is only as good as the corporation itself.

Finally, take the time to read the property report, the sales contract, and all other papers thoroughly. Then take them to a lawyer who deals in land transactions for an evaluation before you sign anything.

mation. The company must also file a shorter version, called a property report, which includes information on sewers, water lines, possible flooding conditions, legal problems, and so forth. The property report should be required reading for any prospective buyer, and the law insists that you be given a copy before you sign a sales contract.

Walk On By: Investments You Can Live Without

This chapter looks at a number of investments that strike us as unsuitable for most individuals. They may be too risky, too costly, too difficult to monitor, or simply too unrewarding. Most share significant drawbacks in comparison with stocks, bonds, and other so-called financial assets. Some pay no income while you hold them, you may have to buy at retail prices and sell at wholesale, and you must pay to store and insure the assets while you're waiting for the price to rise.

Gold's Lost Luster

Gold, despite its reputation, has not always been a reliable long-term hedge against inflation. Its price today is only a little more than 70 percent what it was in 1980, even without adjusting for general price inflation of more than 50 percent since then. Inflation has been no friend of gold.

And what of the claim that gold is a store of value in times of global uproar? When economic chaos, war, or other troubles threaten to erupt, people are said to turn to gold, thus driving up its price. But over the past couple of decades we have lived through the worst U.S. single-day stock-market crash in history. At times, our banking system seemed on the verge of collapse. The Japanese stock market did collapse. The world confronted the fall of the Berlin Wall, the dissolution of the Soviet Union and the subsequent outbreak of civil wars, unimaginable terrorist atrocities, and multinational wars in the Middle East. Through all that, gold moved up a little, down a little, but mostly

Efforts to demonstrate that gold is a good hedge against inflation or an effective counterbalance to the risks in stocks don't work if you extend the numbers past about 1984.

sideways. Why? One reason is the growing tendency of central banks to sell their stores of gold when the price rises, thus adding to supply and serving to keep the price down. Efforts to demonstrate that gold is a good hedge against inflation or an effective counterbalance to the risks in stocks don't work if you extend the numbers past about 1984.

Even those who favor gold as a hedge against the possibility of disasters ahead suggest limiting your exposure to 5 to 10 percent of your investable assets. At that level, even a doubling in price wouldn't have much impact on your wealth. Why tie up your money, thus forfeiting other opportunities, for so modest a promise?

Silver: Not as Good as Gold

The arguments for owning silver are even less persuasive than the arguments in favor of gold. For one thing, the silver market is considerably smaller. It is so small, in fact, that the buying and selling of relatively few very wealthy individuals can influence the price. It happened in 1980 when an attempt was made to corner the market, and it happened on a more modest scale when superinvestor Warren Buffett bought more than $130 million worth of the metal in 1997 and 1998, not because he thought it offered a good long-term investment, but because he saw a temporary imbalance in supply and demand, and figured he could profit from it.

Industrial usage plays a more important part in the market demand for silver than it does for gold, most of which is used in jewelry. When silver prices rise, industrial users, such as manufacturers of film, electronic parts, batteries, and other products, have a strong incentive to find substitutes or recycle what they use. Either action is eventually reflected in market demand for the metal, which declines. Meanwhile, rising prices also spur faster production from the world's silver mines, thus adding to supplies. The combination of less demand and more supply is quickly reflected in the price: It goes down.

Many silver investors base their hopes for profit on the belief that the world is running out of the metal. Although the demand for silver has sometimes exceeded supplies, that has not been true for some years. In fact, the world's supply of silver is more ample than its supply of gold.

In short, the world is not running out of silver—not for some time, at least—and industrial demand and investor interest are likely to remain the chief forces influencing its price. The first fluctuates, and there's been precious little of the second in recent years.

Many silver investors base their hopes for profit on the belief that the world is running out of the metal. It's not.

Collectibles: Buy What You Like

Collecting can combine the thrill of a treasure hunt with the joy of acquiring things you like. And the folklore of collecting is filled with tales of fabulous finds. Somebody discovers that the shade of an old lamp that had hung for years in a church rectory is a genuine Tiffany worth thousands of dollars. A baseball card picturing Honus Wagner, Hall-of-Fame shortstop for the Pittsburgh Pirates, turns out to be one of the most valuable of its kind. (Wagner, a nonsmoker, forced a cigarette company to stop using his picture in its advertising, and fewer than 20 of the cards are known to exist.)

Unfortunately, not everyone comes out a winner. Prices of collectibles can skid as well as climb. The market has always been heavily salted with fakes and flawed merchandise. When something becomes popular, forgers may grind out reproductions in massive quantities. Schlock, such as certain commemorative medals and limited-edition offerings, is also in abundance.

Collectibles pay no interest or dividends. They often entail costs for insurance and storage. They may be hard to sell. You often have to buy at retail prices and sell at wholesale prices, meaning the value of your piece must climb by 50 percent or more before you break even on your "investment." And what looks like solid profits may evaporate under the hard light of analysis. Say you pay $1,000 for a Victorian clock and

Collect what you like and what interests you. Someday it may be worth more than you paid for it. But don't think you're investing; you're just enjoying yourself.

sell it at an auction five years later for $1,500, less $300 for the auctioneer (commissions typically run between 10 and 25 percent). Your net gain is $200, about 4 percent a year.

Collect what you like and what interests you. Someday it may be worth more than you paid for it. But don't think you're investing; you're just enjoying yourself.

Stock Options: Opt Out

Stock options investors buy on the open market shouldn't be confused with the lucrative stock options some companies grant their employees. There are essentially two kinds of stock options offered to investors. A call gives its holder the right to buy a particular stock at a specified price anytime before the option expires. Whoever sells (or "writes") the call agrees to sell the stock at the specified price. A put gives its holder the right to sell a stock at a specified price within a specified time and obligates its seller to do the buying. As a rule, calls are bought and puts are sold by traders who think the price of the underlying security will rise. Sellers of calls and buyers of puts think the price will fall, or at least remain the same.

Puts and calls are standardized contracts covering 100 shares of the particular underlying stock. Each stock exchange specifies a list of stocks against which puts and calls can be sold and bought. For the most part, the stocks represent big, nationally known corporations, such as AT&T, IBM, Sears, and others.

The price specified in the contract is known as the exercise or striking price, which is set near the current market price of the stock in $5, $10, or $20 multiples. If the stock is selling for $48 per share, the exchange might place the striking price at $50 per share. An option with a later expiration date might have a $55 striking price.

There's no doubt that sharp, attentive investors make money in options. They do it by watching closely and turning over their positions frequently. The rewards depend on daring, skill, and luck. What's more, the time and energy involved aren't worth the trouble unless you buy and sell options on a regular basis. Because the activity creates a lot of bookkeeping and day-to-day market watching, trading in options is inconsistent with a long-term investment plan.

Furthermore, commissions on options are higher than on regular stock trades. Depending on the size of the transaction, they can run as high as 10 percent—an expense your profits will have to make up.

In short, buying and selling puts and calls, like driving an 18-wheeler, isn't necessarily dangerous if you know what you're doing. But most people have neither the time nor the knowledge.

The time and energy involved in options aren't worth the trouble unless you buy and sell them on a regular basis.

No Future in Commodities

What you trade in the commodities futures markets is not a product but a standard agreement to buy or sell a product at some later date at a particular price. Commodities range from soybeans to orange juice, from cattle to pork bellies, from cotton to copper. The big attractions of futures markets are leverage and the promise of a fast turnaround. Investors can buy into a contract for 2 to 10 percent of its dollar value, and in some cases may be in and out of the deal within a week.

Probably the strongest arguments against amateur investors getting involved in commodities futures are the studies showing repeatedly that most commodities traders lose money. If some are amateurs and some are professionals, who do you think the losers are likely to be? This speculating technique requires paying close attention to the markets and having an expert's knowledge of esoteric subjects. Leverage can generate spectacular losses virtually overnight. Futures contracts were developed to protect commodities producers from the vagaries of crop failures and surpluses. Leave this game to them. For amateurs, commodities are really speculations, not investments.

Taxes You'll Pay (or Not) on Your Investments

No matter how cleverly you invest your money, the true measure of your investment success is your after-tax return—what you get to keep after the government claims its share. And what you get to keep depends on where you put your money. The earnings from savings accounts and certificates, for instance, are taxed differently than the profits from stocks, bonds, or mutual funds. This chapter will survey some more of the tax traps and opportunities in the various kinds of investments described in other chapters.

Tax Angles on Savings Accounts

Interest you earn in a savings account is fully taxable in the year you earn it, whether you withdraw the money or let it compound inside the account.

On certificates of deposit, the IRS also usually demands its share as the interest is earned. An exception lets you postpone the tax bill if you put your savings in a CD that matures in a year or less. In that case, the interest is taxed in the year the certificate matures. If you invest in a six-month CD in September, for example, the interest earned on it during the current year won't be taxed until the following year, when the certificate matures. For deposits with longer maturities, the interest is taxed in the year it is credited to your account.

Your bank, credit union, or savings and loan will send you a notice each year showing how much interest to report to the IRS. (The IRS gets a copy, too.) If you withdraw funds from a CD before it matures and have to pay an early-withdrawal penalty, you can

The kiddie tax was clearly designed to prevent families from shifting income to children as a tax-saving strategy. Still, it doesn't entirely eliminate the opportunities.

deduct such a penalty whether or not you itemize other deductions on your tax return.

Working Around the Kiddie Tax

The same rules generally apply to interest earned inside a custodial account set up for your children, but there's a complication: the so-called kiddie tax. If a child under age 14 has unearned income over a certain amount, the excess is taxed at the parents' top rate. ("Unearned" income is basically earnings from investments, while earned income is from a job.)

The kiddie tax slaps the parents' tax rate onto a child's unearned income in excess of $1,600. For a child under 14, the first $800 of investment income is tax-free and the next $800 is taxed at the child's rate, probably 10 percent. Then the parents' rate, which is probably 25 or 28 percent, kicks in. (The trigger point for the kiddie tax is indexed to rise with inflation.)

The kiddie tax was clearly designed to prevent families from shifting income to children as a tax-saving strategy. Still, it doesn't entirely eliminate the opportunities. In an account earning 8 percent, for example, the balance in your child's name could reach above $20,000 before the earnings would be threatened by the kiddie tax. Assuming $1,600 in interest is the child's only income, the first $800 would be tax-free and the 10 percent tax on the remaining $800 would be about $80. If that same money were invested in the parents' name, and the earnings taxed in the 28% bracket, the tax bill would be $448. In five years, that $368 annual savings amounts to $1,840. In ten years, you'd save $3,680 by saving that $20,000 in the child's name instead of yours. The kiddie tax is repealed in the year your child turns 14; it doesn't apply to any income received that year.

Learning to Love Your Basis

When you start buying stocks, bonds, mutual funds, and other more adventuresome instruments, you need to know something about "basis." Your basis is essentially the amount of your investment in a piece of property such as a share of stock, a bond, or a mutual fund share. When you sell the investment, your basis is what determines whether you have a profit or a loss.

Sounds simple, but it's not. Not only is the basis affected by how you acquire an investment, but the basis of different investments can change while you own them. You must keep track of the basis of every investment you own, and that means keeping good records.

Your basis depends in part on how you obtained the property in the first place.

If you bought it, your basis begins as what you pay, including any commissions. If you buy 100 shares of SureThing Inc. for $40 a share and pay a $100 commission, your tax basis in each share is $41—the full $4,100 acquisition cost divided by the number of shares you purchased. Thus, you should hang on to the purchase confirmation form.

If you got it as a gift, the basis depends in part on whether you eventually sell for a gain or a loss. If you sell for a profit, your basis is the same as the basis of the previous owner—he or she passes on the basis along with the property. But if the sale results in a loss, the basis is either the previous owner's basis or the value at the time of the gift, whichever is lower. In other words, you don't get to deduct any decline in value that occurred before you got the gift, but you do have to pay tax on any gain that occurred before you got it.

If at the time of the gift the property is worth more than the benefactor's basis, all you need in your records is his or her basis. It becomes your basis. But if the property has declined in value, your records will need to show both the previous owner's basis and the value at the time of the gift.

Say, for example, that a rich and generous uncle gives you 200 shares of stock for which he paid $10,000 but which are worth just $8,000 at the time of the gift.

> **You must keep track of the basis of every investment you own, and that means keeping good records.**

If you inherited it, your basis is "stepped up" to the value of the asset on the date of death. However, in 2010 the rules will change.

If the stock rises in price so that you eventually sell it for $12,000, your basis for determining gain is $10,000—your uncle's basis. If the share value continues to fall and you sell for less than $8,000, however, the basis for figuring your loss is the $8,000 value of the stock at the time of the gift. If you sell for an amount between $8,000 and $10,000, you have neither a gain nor a loss.

If you inherited it, your basis is "stepped up" to the value of the asset on the date of death. (When large estates are involved, the value on a date within six months after death is sometimes used.) This means that the tax on any profit that built up during the previous owner's lifetime is forgiven. You'll be taxed only on income and capital gains that accrue after you inherit the asset. If its value falls and you then sell, you can deduct the loss. This rule also applies if you become the sole owner of property after the death of a joint owner. When a husband and wife jointly own stock and one spouse dies, for example, the survivor's basis becomes his or her half of the original basis plus half of the stock's value at the time the joint owner died. In community-property states, the full value may be stepped-up. If you inherit property, be sure to pinpoint the stepped-up basis to hold down your tax bill.

Note that starting in 2010, a carry-over basis will apply. That is, your basis for inherited property will be the lesser of the previous owner's basis or the property's fair market value on the date of death, which means that any appreciation while he or she was alive will be taxed to you when you sell the asset. Of course, there will be exceptions. The executor will have the power to step up the basis of assets in the estate by a total of $1.3 million—wiping out the tax on that amount of gain. For assets left to a spouse, an additional $3 million of basis could be stepped up. The executor will be responsible for deciding which assets get this treatment and for reporting the basis adjustments to the IRS.

Capital Gains and Losses

In addition to tracking the basis of your investments, you also have to keep an eye on the calendar. The critical distinction is between long-term gains—from investments held for more than 12 months—and short-term gains from investments held for 12 months or less.

How Gains Get Taxed

The maximum tax rate for most long-term capital gains is 15 percent if you are in the 25 percent bracket or higher. (If you're in the 15 percent tax bracket, tax on long-term gains is just 5 percent and will fall to 0 percent in 2008. If the capital gain itself pushed you from the 15 percent bracket to the 25 percent or higher bracket, then the amount of the profit that would fall in the 15 percent bracket gets the 5 percent rate; the rest is taxed at 15 percent.) Short-term gains are still taxed in your top tax bracket, which can be as high as 35 percent.

Investment real estate doesn't get full advantage of the new long-term rates. Instead, a 25 percent tax rate applies to profits that result from depreciation deductions. The new rules also do not apply to profit from collectibles, such as stamps, antiques, and coins. A top rate of 28 percent still applies to profits from the sale of collectibles owned more than one year.

How Losses Are Deducted

If your investments produce a loss, the government will help absorb it—up to a limit. Losses can be used to offset any amount of capital gains, but no more than $3,000 of losses beyond that can be deducted against other income, such as your salary. Leftover losses, though, can be carried forward and deducted in future years.

Say that during the year your investments produce $10,000 of capital gains and $14,000 of capital losses. The losses would more than offset all the gains, so you'd owe no tax on the profits. But only $3,000 of the excess $4,000 in losses could be deducted against other income. In the 25 percent bracket, that would save

If your investments produce a loss, the government will help absorb it— up to a limit.

Profits from the rising price of stocks are safe from the IRS until you sell. Postponing a sale from December to January allows you to delay reporting the profit for a full year.

you $750 in taxes. The leftover $1,000 loss gets carried over to the next year.

The deductibility of capital losses makes your portfolio fertile ground for tax maneuvering, especially at year-end. Although you should not let tax factors dictate your buy or hold decisions, neither should you ignore the possibility of converting a paper loss to a real one to offset gains or other income.

DON'T WASH AWAY YOUR LOSSES. Say you own stock showing a big paper loss. You expect the shares to recover, but you could use a tax deduction this year. So you sell the stock to take the loss, then buy it right back. Result: You get the tax deduction you sought and you still own the stock.

Pretty clever—provided you waited more than 30 days after the sale before you bought back the shares. Buy them back any sooner and the IRS will deny the tax loss. It considers the deal a wash since you wind up with the same stock in your portfolio.

You trigger the wash-sale rule if you buy "substantially identical" securities within 30 days before or after the sale of securities showing a loss. There's no precise definition of substantially identical, but it definitely covers shares in the same company whose shares you just sold.

You can skirt the wash-sale rules fairly easily by using mutual funds with similar objectives but different portfolios. For instance, you could sell a Scudder growth fund at a loss and immediately buy a T. Rowe Price growth fund to position yourself for an anticipated market upturn.

Saving Taxes on Stocks

Unlike interest on savings, which generally gets taxed in the year it's earned, profits from the rising price of stocks are safe from the IRS until you sell. This gives you important flexibility. Postponing a sale from December to January, for example, allows you to delay reporting the profit for a full year. Accelerating a sale, on the other hand, might allow you to use a loss in a year when it would be most beneficial.

Making the most of this advantage requires keeping careful records so you can calculate your basis correctly and pinpoint the profit or loss from a potential sale.

As noted earlier, the basis can change while you own an investment. If a company in which you have invested declares a stock split, for example, your basis in each share will drop because your original basis will be spread over both the old and new shares. Assume you own 100 shares, each with a $40 basis, and the company declares a two-for-one split. That suddenly makes you the owner of 200 shares. Your original $4,000 investment does not change, however, so your basis in each share drops to $20 ($4,000 ÷ 200). The holding period for the shares you received in the split is the same as for the original shares. If you have owned the shares for more than 12 months at the time of the split, the new shares immediately qualify for long-term treatment.

Controlling Taxes on Capital Gains

Keeping track of the basis is essential for successful tax planning. It's particularly important when you buy shares of the same stock or mutual fund at different times and prices. When you decide to sell some of the shares, being able to identify which ones to part with permits you to control the tax consequences of the deal.

Let's say you bought 100 shares of SureThing stock in January 2004 for $2,400, giving you a basis of $24 per share (for convenience, we're ignoring commissions in this example). In January 2005, you purchased 100 more shares, this time for $2,800. Your basis in each new share is $28. In January 2006, you purchased another 100 shares for $3,000, giving each of those shares a basis of $30.

When the stock hits $40 a share in May 2006, you decide to sell 100 shares. If you simply tell your broker to sell 100 shares, the IRS's FIFO rule (first in, first out) comes into play. It's assumed that the first shares you purchased—the 2004 group with the $24 basis—are the first ones sold. That would create a

Keeping track of the basis is particularly important when you buy shares of the same stock or mutual fund at different times and prices.

If the company gives you the choice of taking a dividend in stock or in cash, the dividend is taxable in the year you receive it even if you take the shares.

long-term taxable profit of $16 a share, or $1,600. At the 15 percent tax rate, that would cost you $240.

A better idea is to sell the shares purchased in 2005 for $28 dollars a share. That would produce a profit of $1,200 and the tax bill would be only $180. (You wouldn't sell the $30 shares because that would produce a short-term gain, which is taxed as ordinary income and doesn't get the capital-gains rate.)

In either case you'd get $4,000 from the sale, but your tax bill would be quite different. In most cases, you'll want to structure the sale to produce the smallest taxable profit. It's possible, though, that circumstances will warrant selling the asset with the lowest basis first—if, for example, you have sufficient losses to offset the larger gain. As this example shows, you also have to watch the calendar to guarantee preferential long-term-gain treatment.

Controlling Taxes on Dividends

Dividends you receive from stock you own are usually fully taxable. Sometimes you even owe tax on dividends you never see. For instance, dividends invested through a dividend reinvestment plan count as taxable income even though you never lay hands on the money. What's more, if the plan allows you to buy shares at a discount from market value, the discount counts as taxable income, too, in the year of purchase. The basis of your shares is what you paid plus the discount on which you were taxed.

When companies pay dividends in shares of stock instead of cash, the value of the stock dividends is generally not taxable that year. Instead, the new shares dilute your basis in the old shares. Say you have 100 shares of stock with a basis of $2,500, or $25 a share, and you get a stock dividend of 10 shares. The $2,500 basis is then spread over the 110 shares, giving each one a basis of $22.73. The effect is that you'll pay tax on the value of the stock dividend when you sell the shares because you report a higher profit due to the reduced basis.

If the company gives you the choice of taking a dividend in stock or in cash, the dividend is taxable in the year you receive it even if you take the shares. The market value of the shares counts as income, but the basis of your original shares stays the same, and your basis in the new shares is the amount you have to include in income.

Saving Taxes on Bonds

Corporate bonds generally pay interest every six months, and it is taxable in the year you receive it. If you buy a bond at face value and hold it to maturity, tax on the interest is all you owe. But, as discussed in Chapter 24, you can buy bonds at a premium (more than face value) or at a discount (below face value). Either situation complicates your taxes, particularly when it comes to keeping track of your basis.

When You Buy Bonds at a Discount

When you buy bonds at a discount from face value, the tax rules that apply depend on the type of discount involved and when the bond was issued.

Original-issue-discount (OID) bonds are, as the name suggests, issued for less than face value. This basically means part of the interest will be paid when the bond is redeemed for more than its original price rather than in regular payments over the life of the bond. You have to wait for your money, but the IRS doesn't want to wait for its share of it. Each year that you own the bond, you have to report as interest income a portion of the original discount amount. (The method you must use to calculate how much to report depends on when the bond was issued, but each year the issuer should send you a 1099-OID form showing the taxable amount.) Good records are critically important here. The portion of the original-issue discount you report as income each year increases your basis in the bond. If you fail to keep track, you could wind up paying tax on the same income twice—once as original-issue discount interest and later as part of the profit on the bond.

Market-discount bonds usually sell at a discount because interest rates have risen since they were issued, or because the safety-rating agencies have downgraded the

> **If you buy bonds at a premium (more than face value) or at a discount (below face value) your taxes are complicated, particularly when it comes to keeping track of your basis.**

Even though you don't see the money, interest on zero-coupon bonds is taxed as it accrues, so you must report and pay tax on the interest your investment is assumed to have earned each year.

issuing company's rating. For bonds issued after July 18, 1984, the difference between what you pay for a market-discount bond and its redemption value is considered to be interest that will accrue between the time you buy the bond and the time it matures. You can wait until you dispose of the bond via sale or redemption to report that interest income, or you can figure how much interest accrues each year and report it annually. If you opt to report a portion of the market discount annually, your basis in the bond increases by the amount reported as interest income. You're probably better off waiting.

Zero-coupon bonds pay no interest until maturity. Issuers compensate investors for their patience by issuing zeros at steep discounts from their redemption value. A new 20-year zero with a face value of $10,000 and a yield to maturity of 4.44 percent, for example, would sell for $413 today.

Because a zero-coupon bond is really nothing more than the OID idea carried to its extreme, the OID rules apply. Even though you don't see the money, interest is taxed as it accrues, so each year you must report and pay tax on the interest your investment is assumed to have earned that year. The bond issuer or your broker should send you a notice showing how much to report.

This "imputed" interest hikes your basis in the bonds and, again, it's up to you to keep track. Consider this example: You buy zeros for $10,000 that are called (redeemed early by the issuer) three years later for $11,000. During the intervening years, you report $1,408 of imputed interest. That raises your basis to $11,408, so even though the bonds are called for $1,408 more than you originally paid, you actually have a $408 loss. (On zero-coupon municipal bonds, accruing interest raises your basis even though the imputed interest is not taxable.)

When You Buy Bonds at a Premium

When you buy a bond for more than its face value, as you might to capture above-market rates, the IRS gives you a choice of how to deal with the premium. You can spread it over the life of the bond, claiming a tax-saving deduction each year. Or you can wait until you sell or redeem the bond to crank the premium into your tax calculations.

The latter is by far the simpler way. Wait until you sell or redeem the bond and report the premium all at once. If you redeem the bond at face value, you can claim a capital loss equal to the size of the premium.

When You Buy between Interest Payments
The price of bonds sold between semiannual interest dates includes the interest accrued since the last payment date. For the seller, that part of the price is interest income and should be reported as such rather than being counted as part of the price of the bond when determining gain or loss on the sale. For the buyer, the "purchased interest" is not part of the basis. Rather, when you receive your first interest payment on the bond, part of it is considered a nontaxable return of part of your investment rather than taxable interest.

Say you purchase a $10,000, 8 percent bond midway between semiannual $400 interest payments and you pay $10,200 for the bond and the $200 of accrued interest. When you get the first $400 interest payment, half of it is considered a return of your investment. (You report the full amount on your tax return, though, then subtract $200 as "accrued interest." If you don't, you'll overpay your tax.) Your basis in the bond is $10,000.

Uncle Sam's Bonds
When you invest in U.S. government obligations, you get a break compared with corporate bonds: The interest on Treasury bills, notes, and bonds is exempt from state and local income taxes. You have to take this benefit into account when comparing yields.

Assume you live in a state with an 8 percent state-tax rate and can choose between investing $10,000 in a corporate bond yielding 7 percent or a $10,000 Treasury bond yielding the same. Either investment will generate $700 of interest annually and will cost you $175 in fed-

The interest on Treasury bills, notes, and bonds is exempt from state and local income taxes. You have to take this benefit into account when comparing yields.

Municipal bonds enjoy the best of all federal tax rates: 0 percent.

eral taxes if you are in the 25 percent bracket. On the T-bond, that's all you'd have to pay. With the corporate bond, however, your state would want its 8 percent, or $56. Because the state tax is deductible on your federal return, you get back 25 percent of that $56, so the actual extra cost would be $42.

Treasury bills, which are issued with 4-week, 13-week, 26-week, and 52-week maturities, offer the chance to defer income from one year to the next. The bills are issued at a discount, with the interest paid when they are redeemed at face value. The tax isn't due until the year the bill matures. If you sell a T-bill before maturity, part of the sales price is accrued interest and must be reported as interest income rather than being counted in the capital gain or loss.

The interest on Treasury notes and bonds, which is paid every six months, is taxable in the year you receive it. When T-bonds and notes are purchased at a market discount or premium price, the same basic rules apply as for corporate bonds.

Mortgage-Backed Bonds

If you invest in bonds guaranteed by the Government National Mortgage Association (GNMA), part of each payment you receive will be totally tax-free. As discussed in Chapter 24, Ginnie Maes represent an investment in a pool of home mortgages. As homeowners make their monthly payments, you get your share of the interest and principal. The principal portion is a return of your investment and is therefore tax-free. You should get a statement showing a breakdown between taxable interest and nontaxable return of principal.

Municipal Bonds

These enjoy the best of all federal tax rates: 0 percent. Although you must report municipal-bond interest to the IRS each year, it is almost never taxed. (One exception allows the IRS to tax interest from "private-activity" bonds owned by a taxpayer who is subject to the alternative minimum tax.)

Although the interest on these bonds is tax-free, the IRS wants its cut if you sell municipal bonds for a profit: Capital gains are fully taxable. By the same token, if you sell a municipal bond for less than your basis, the loss is deductible.

Cost basis is usually figured the same way as with taxable bonds. However, if you buy a tax-exempt bond at a premium, you must amortize the premium over the period you own the bond. This gradually shrinks your basis in the bond but you can't deduct the amortized amount, as you can with taxable bonds. If you buy a bond originally issued at a discount—including a zero-coupon municipal—you increase your basis each year by the amount of the interest accruing on the bond, but you don't have to report that amount as income. When you buy a municipal bond at a market discount, however, different rules apply. Your basis doesn't change. When you redeem the bond at face value, the difference between your purchase price and the face value is a taxable capital gain.

"Swapping" Bonds to Save Taxes

Bond swapping is a maneuver that may allow bond investors to generate a tax loss without affecting the income stream from their fixed-income investments. What you do is sell bonds that have fallen in value—due to rising market interest rates—and reinvest the proceeds in other bonds. Consider this example:

Assume you own $100,000 worth of AA-rated bonds with a 7 percent coupon yield, a maturity date in 2020, and a current market value of $84,750. You bought the bonds at par (face value), so selling at the current price would produce a $15,250 capital loss. Suppose, too, that you can buy $100,000 face value of AAA-rated bonds with a 7 percent coupon and a 2019 maturity, for $83,612.

Consider the result if you decide to sell one set of bonds and buy the other: Since they have the same par value and coupon rate, your annual income remains the same. Your bond rating increases from AA to AAA. You pull $1,138 out of the investment—the difference between what you got for the old bonds and what you paid for the new ones. And you can claim a $15,250 tax

Bond swapping is a maneuver that may allow bond investors to generate a tax loss without affecting the income stream from their fixed-income investments.

To protect yourself from overpaying your taxes on mutual fund income, set up a separate file for each fund you own and faithfully keep it up-to-date.

loss. If it offsets gains that otherwise would have been taxed at 25 percent, you save $3,812.50.

If you have bonds that show a paper loss, your broker should be able to help you find attractive candidates for swapping that won't run afoul of the wash-sale rule discussed earlier in this chapter.

Saving Taxes on Mutual Funds

The professional management you get when you invest in mutual funds handles some of the tax work for you. The fund worries about the fluctuating basis of the stocks or bonds it owns. That spares you the hassle of amortizing bond premiums, for example, or adjusting your basis to account for stock splits. But funds don't spare you all the tax-related work.

Except for money-market funds, the price of mutual fund shares fluctuates just like the price of individual stocks and bonds. When you redeem shares, you need to know your tax basis in order to calculate your taxable gain or loss. You also need to know how long you've owned the shares to know whether you have long- or short-term gains or losses. To protect yourself from overpaying your taxes on fund income, set up a separate file for each fund you own and faithfully keep it up-to-date.

Your basis in shares begins as what you pay for them. When you invest in a no-load fund, your basis is the share's net asset value on the day you buy. If you buy into a load fund, the commission counts as part of your basis.

Tax Complications with Funds

Capital gains you don't see. From time to time, funds declare capital gains but retain the profits and pay tax on them rather than distributing the gain to shareholders. Such undistributed capital gains increase your basis in the shares. Even though you didn't get a dime, you have to report the gain as income. You also get to claim a credit for the amount of tax paid by the fund on your behalf. Finally, you raise your basis in the shares by the difference between the undistributed gain and the credit you claim. If all this sounds like a lot of trouble for nothing, take comfort in the fact that claiming the tax credit cuts your tax bill now, and raising the basis reduces your tax bill when you sell.

Nontaxable fund income. Funds occasionally make a payment that doesn't come out of earnings or profits. Such "return of capital" distributions are sometimes called tax-free dividends or nontaxable distributions, but they do reduce your basis in the shares, thus increasing the gain or diminishing the loss when you sell.

Reinvested dividends and capital gains. If you have your dividends and capital gains reinvested in additional shares of your fund, as most investors do, then you'll be buying new shares every time the fund distributes income. Your basis in the new shares is their cost at the time of purchase. If $72.75 in dividends and gains buys you 5.89 shares, for example, the basis of each share is $12.35 ($72.75 ÷ 5.89).

It's important to keep careful track of all this. If you don't, here's the potential threat: Say you invest $5,000 in a fund and each year have $500 of dividends and capital gains reinvested in additional shares. After five years, you redeem all your shares for $10,000. What's your gain? An investor who simply compared the redemption amount to the original investment would pay twice as much tax as necessary. Because the $2,500 that's been reinvested raised your basis by that amount, the gain is just $2,500, not $5,000. (And besides, you will have paid tax on those distributions already!)

Selling only some of your shares. Good recordkeeping habits really pay off when you sell only part of your fund holdings. In deciding which shares to sell, you can pick the ones that will produce the best tax result.

Redeeming shares with the highest basis will produce the lowest taxable gain. But because your shares are pooled in a single account by the mutual fund,

> **Good record-keeping habits really pay off when you sell only part of your fund holdings. In deciding which shares to sell, you can pick the ones that will produce the best tax result.**

Unless you tell a fund which shares to sell, the first-in, first-out rule applies— and that could cost you money.

who knows which ones got sold? You do, if you've kept good records. If you direct the fund to sell specific shares, the basis of those shares determines the tax consequences of the sale. (Keep records of your sale order, including a copy of a letter to the fund identifying the shares to be sold by the date of purchase and price paid, and a copy of the fund's confirmation of the sale. If you order the sale by phone, keep a copy of a letter to the fund confirming your instructions.)

If you just tell the fund to sell a certain number of shares without specifying which ones, the first-in, first-out (FIFO) rule will govern which ones those are. FIFO assumes that the first shares you bought are the first ones sold. If the shares have been appreciating gradually, that ensures that those with the lowest basis are assumed to be sold—and that leaves you with the highest taxable profit.

If you prefer, you can use the average-basis method for figuring gain or loss on the sale of your shares. There are actually two average-basis methods. With the single-category method, you find the total basis of all the shares you own of a fund, then divide it by the number of shares and arrive at the average basis. The double-category method is similar, but you divide the shares according to whether you have owned them long term (more than one year) or short term (one year or less). To use the short-term average basis, you must have written confirmation that you advised the fund at the time of the trade that you were redeeming shares from the short-term group. Otherwise you use the long-term average basis.

The specific-identification method gives you the most flexibility but if you normally use the FIFO method, you should check whether the average-basis method can work to your benefit. However, once you start using average basis, you must use it for all future redemptions from the fund.

Switching funds. Switching from one fund to another, even within the same family, creates what the tax people like to call a "taxable event." To switch, you must sell the shares in the fund you're leaving. Unless you're moving out of a money-market fund, the switch is likely to produce a taxable capital gain or a deductible loss.

How Fund Income Is Taxed

Knowing how the IRS treats fund income can save you trouble and money.

Income from money-market and taxable bond funds is considered dividend income for tax purposes, even though the source of the income is interest. If you accidentally report such income as interest, you'll probably hear from the IRS, which will have been told by the fund that it paid you dividends.

Interest from a municipal-bond fund escapes federal income tax. It may be taxed by your state, however, although interest from bonds issued within your state are probably exempt from state taxes, too. The fund statement will probably show what percentage of the income you received was attributed to home-grown issues.

You may get some state-tax savings on income from a fund that invests solely or partially in U.S. government securities. That interest would be free of state tax if you owned the obligations directly, and most states allow it to retain its tax-free status when it comes from a fund. Check with your state tax department.

Ordinary dividends are taxable in the year paid, whether you take them in cash or have them reinvested in new shares. Knowing when a stock fund declares dividends—its ex-dividend date—is important. When the dividend is declared, the share value drops by about the same amount. If you invest in the fund just before the ex-dividend date, the dividend you get will be taxable for that year, even though it amounts to a refund of part of your purchase price. Better to buy after the ex-dividend date. The price of the shares will be lower by the amount of the dividend, and you won't owe taxes on the dividend.

> **Ordinary dividends are taxable in the year paid, whether you take them in cash or have them reinvested in new shares.**

Earnings within a cash-value life insurance policy grow tax-free. Taxes aren't due until you cash in the policy, and then you owe taxes only on the amount by which the cash value exceeds your premiums.

Capital-gains distributions—your share of long-term profits from portfolio trades during the year—are considered long-term gains regardless of how long you have owned the fund. This is easy enough to understand for stock and corporate-bond funds, but investors in tax-free bond funds are sometimes confused by taxable capital-gains distributions. Such payouts are taxable because they represent your share of the profits realized when bonds within the portfolio were sold.

If you own shares in a fund holding foreign securities, you may be in line for a foreign-tax credit. Your year-end statement from the fund will show the amount of foreign tax paid on your behalf. You must include that amount in your taxable income for the year, but you can either write it off as an itemized deduction or claim a foreign-tax credit. The credit—now easier to claim than ever before—is almost always worth more.

Taxes on Life Insurance Proceeds and Annuities

Sometimes a very substantial part of the premiums paid for cash-value life insurance are used by the company to pay not for insurance but for investments that build cash value. As described in Chapter 19, policyholders may have a choice of stock and bond mutual funds and other investments. The key tax break is that earnings within the policy are allowed to grow tax-free. Taxes aren't due until you cash in the policy, and then you owe taxes only on the amount by which the cash value exceeds your premiums.

Annuities are another insurance product with tax advantages. The contract serves as an impenetrable wrapper that keeps the tax collector's hands off your earnings. No tax is due until you withdraw your funds, presumably in retirement. In exchange, you agree to leave your money invested until you reach age 59½. Pull the money out early and the earnings are not only taxed but also subject to a 10 percent penalty. The penalty doesn't apply to policyholders who are disabled, nor to any payment that is part of a series of periodic payments based on your life expectancy.

The penalty is designed to dissuade investors from trying to use annuities as short-term tax shelters. Once you reach age 59½, though, the tax penalty disappears, although insurance companies generally apply penalties of their own if annuity buyers withdraw funds during the early years of a contract. See Chapter 29 for more on annuities.

Deduct Your Investment Expenses? Maybe

If you borrow money to make an investment, the interest on the loan is usually deductible if the purpose of the investment is to generate taxable income. But if you borrow in order to invest in tax-free bonds, the interest is not deductible. Nor do you get the deduction if you borrow to buy a single-premium life insurance policy or an annuity. The government doesn't want to subsidize loans used to purchase tax shelters. Interest on money borrowed to invest in a passive investment activity, such as a real estate limited partnership, is an expense of the passive activity and therefore deductible only to the extent of passive income (see Chapter 26).

The deduction for investment interest you pay is limited to the amount of investment income you report. If your investment income for the year is $5,000, for example, your investment-interest deduction can't exceed $5,000. For this purpose, investment income includes interest and dividends, but not capital gains. Any interest you are unable to deduct because of the cap can be carried forward to future years and deducted when you have sufficient investment income.

A number of investment expenses are deductible, but don't count on getting much benefit from any of them. The IRS considers them "miscellaneous" expenses, which means you can deduct them only to the

If you borrow money to make an investment, the interest on the loan is usually deductible if the purpose of the investment is to generate taxable income.

extent that all of your miscellaneous expenses exceed 2 percent of your adjusted gross income (that is, your gross income after "adjustments," such as IRA contributions, but before itemized deductions). If your AGI is $80,000, for example, the first $1,600 of your miscellaneous expenses don't count.

If you cross the threshold, the following expenses of investing may be tax deductible in whole or in part:

- **Rental fees for a safe-deposit box** used to store taxable securities;
- **Investment counseling or management fees;**
- **Subscriptions** to investment-advisory newsletters;
- **The cost of books** (including this one) and magazines purchased for investment advice;
- **State and local transfer taxes** on the sale of securities;
- **Fees paid to a broker** or other agent to collect bond interest or stock dividends. (Commissions paid to brokers when you purchase stock aren't deductible. They are added to the basis of the shares.)
- **Cost of travel** to see your broker to discuss investments. If you drive your own car, deduct the actual cost or the IRS standard rate, which was 40.5 cents for 2005. In either case, you can add in what you pay for parking or tolls.

Your Retirement and Estate Planning

Part 7

Money Enough to Retire On

Chapter 29

et's call it the Great American Retirement Income Challenge and divide it into two parts: 1) How much money will you need to live financially worry-free when you retire? 2) Where will you get it?

How Much Will You Need?

When you retire, you'll tend to spend less on clothing, commuting, Starbucksing, and other daily expenses associated with earning a living. If you have kids, they'll probably be on their own, freeing up a big chunk of your income.

Unfortunately, other expenses have a way of taking up the slack. For instance, studies show that retirees spend significantly more on health care—no surprise there. They also spend more on gifts, household maintenance, and other things. All this makes the Great Retirement Income Challenge especially—well, challenging.

Some estimates hold that you can keep your standard of living with as little as 40 to 60 percent of your preretirement income. Yeah, right. Maybe Michael Jordan could get by on that, but chances are your income is a little less than his, so you'd better plan on replacing a higher proportion of it. In fact, 75 or 80 percent might be a more realistic neighborhood. On top of that, even though inflation has been tame for several years now, it's still true that a dollar of income tomorrow won't be worth as much as a dollar of income today. The bottom table on page 483 lets you estimate inflation's impact on your future income.

Before you try to devise a way to generate the do-it-yourself portion of the nest egg, estimate how much income you can reasonably expect from other sources.

Where Will You Get It?

So where will you get that kind of money? It will probably come from a combination of places: Social Security, a pension plan perhaps, and your own saving and investing. Before you try to devise a way to generate the do-it-yourself portion of the nest egg, you need to estimate how much retirement income you can reasonably expect from pensions and Social Security. The worksheet on page 459 will help you do that.

Your company's human resources or benefits office can give you the information you need about future pension payments, and you can get an estimate of what to expect from Social Security from the Social Security Administration's "Social Security Statement." The SSA sends this form annually to everyone over age 25.

If you're under age 25 or want to check your records before you receive the statement, contact the Social Security Administration and request an estimate form. Call 800-772-1213 and ask for Form SSA-7004, "Social Security Statement." Or go online at http://www.ssa.gov to request the form or fill out another one, submit it online, and the SSA will send the statement. You'll receive your estimate two to four weeks after you return the completed form. You can also use the online calculator to estimate benefits yourself. If you want more than one estimate—to see how retiring at different ages affects your benefits or those of other members of your household—use the online calculator to enter different scenarios, photocopy the form, or send in more than one request and vary the factors.

If you plan to retire before age 62, you can't count on all your long-term savings and investments to contribute income right away. The worksheet reflects the fact that pension benefits are rarely available before age 55, Social Security benefits can't start before age 62, and IRA funds are generally tied up until age 59½.

How to Use the Worksheet

The worksheet assumes that you want to live on 80 percent of your preretirement income and that you'll be able to earn 8 percent per year on the investment assets you build between now and then without depleting your capital. (The 8 percent assumption about earnings is lower than the assumption you should make while building capital, because it reflects the fact that once you are retired, you'll want to keep your money in lower-risk investments that produce a higher level of income.) Odds are that you'll have to dip into capital on some sort of regular basis.

Now begin to plug in your numbers.

SAVINGS AND INVESTMENTS. Begin with what you have in your retirement fund today and use a future-value multiplier from the table below to see what it will be worth in the future. If you have $50,000 now, you plan to retire in 15 years, and you expect your savings and investments to yield 6 percent a year after taxes, multiply $50,000 by 2.4—the figure where the 15-year row and 6 percent column intersect. That's $120,000.

WHAT YOUR MONEY WILL BE WORTH IN THE FUTURE

This table shows how much your current savings and investments will be worth in the future, assuming they grow at various annual rates of return. It also can be used to calculate how inflation will affect your living expenses. Say you plan to retire in 20 years and expect your investments to grow 10% a year between now and then. Find 20 years in the left-hand column and 10% on the horizontal scale across the top. The place where the two columns intersect shows a multiplier of 6.73. That tells you that

$1,000 in your retirement account today will grow to $6,730 in 20 years, assuming a 10% annual return (6.73 × $1,000 = $6,730).

But in 20 years, you'll need more than $1,000 to have the purchasing power of $1,000 today. How much more? First make an assumption about inflation—4% a year is a reasonable estimate for the next 20 years. Where the 4% column intersects with 20 years, the multiplier is 2.19. That means that you'll need $2,190 in 20 years to match the purchasing power of $1,000 today.

				RATE OF RETURN					
YEARS	**4%**	**5%**	**6%**	**7%**	**8%**	**9%**	**10%**	**11%**	**12%**
10	1.48	1.63	1.79	1.97	2.16	2.37	2.59	2.84	3.11
15	1.80	2.08	2.40	2.76	3.17	3.64	4.18	4.78	5.47
20	2.19	2.65	3.21	3.87	4.66	5.60	6.73	8.06	9.65
25	2.67	3.39	4.29	5.43	6.85	8.62	10.82	13.59	17.00

It's highly unlikely that taxes will cut into your profit if you sell your home, unless you have been in it a long time, or live in an area where home values have skyrocketed.

If the nest egg generates 8 percent a year, you can count on it for $9,600 toward your retirement needs.

EQUITY IN YOUR HOME. This line assumes that you will use your home equity as a source of income—either by selling your home and renting or by "buying down" to a smaller place and investing the freed-up equity to generate income. (A "reverse mortgage" is another way to do it, as described on page 499.) Begin with the current value of your house and apply a future-value multiplier from the table on the previous page to estimate its value when you'll sell it. If you don't have a feel for where values are headed where you live, use 4 percent. Subtract any mortgage you'll still have outstanding at that time and enter the result on line 2. Since Congress has declared that the first $250,000 of profit from the sale of a home is tax-free—$500,000 if you file a joint return—it's highly unlikely that taxes will cut into your profit, unless you have been in your home a long time, or live in an area where home values have skyrocketed.

INDIVIDUAL RETIREMENT ACCOUNTS. Consider this money tied up until you reach 59½, although there are exceptions, as discussed later in this chapter. Apply a future-value multiplier from the table to the current value of your IRAs (and other resources, too).

KEOGH ACCOUNTS. You can tap a Keogh without penalty starting at age 59½ (age 55 if you close the business funding the plan), with the same exceptions as you get in an IRA. Complete this line the same as you did line 3.

401(K) AND PROFIT-SHARING PLANS. Money in employer-sponsored 401(k) and profit-sharing plans can be withdrawn without penalty as early as age 55 if you leave the job. If you roll over a distribution into an IRA—to avoid paying all the tax at once—the money will be controlled by the IRA rules described later in this chapter. In 2006, employers can offer Roth 401(k)s, described on page 468, that have many rules similar to Roth IRAs.

EMPLOYER-PAID PENSION BENEFITS. Outside of the government and military service, defined-benefit plans rarely pay anything before age 55. Your human resources office should be able to estimate what you can expect and when you can start collecting it. You can probably count on your benefits increasing for each year past age 55 that you delay retirement, provided you stay with the same employer. If you leave that company, your pension will almost certainly be frozen at the level you had earned before leaving. If you have a defined-contribution pension plan, the value of your account would probably keep growing after you left because you would keep it invested.

SOCIAL SECURITY BENEFITS. You can't collect Social Security retirement benefits before age 62, and if you choose to begin at that age checks will be reduced to as much as 70 percent of what you'd get if you waited until your full retirement age. The age for receiving full benefits and the reduction for early retirement is

---

WHERE WILL THE MONEY COME FROM?

A: Your Goal: Current income x multiplier from table on page 457 x 0.80 = $_____

B: Anticipated resources at crucial ages:

Resource	Current Value x Multiplier from Table, Page 457	Age 50-54	55-59	60-62	62+
1. Investments	$_____ x 0.08 =	$_____	$_____	$_____	$_____
2. Equity in home	_____ x 0.08 =	_____	_____	_____	_____
3. IRAs*	_____ x 0.08 =	XXXX	XXXX	_____	_____
4. KEOGHs	_____ x 0.08 =	XXXX	_____	_____	_____
5. 401(k)s	_____ x 0.08 =	XXXX	_____	_____	_____
6. Pensions	_____ x 0.08 =	XXXX	_____	_____	_____
7. Social Security	_____ x 0.08 =	XXXX	XXXX	XXXX	_____
Totals		$_____	$_____	$_____	$_____
Shortfall (A minus B)	$_____	$_____	$_____	$_____	

*You can withdraw your own contributions to the new Roth IRA penalty-free before age 59½.

increasing gradually until it reaches 67 for those born in 1960 or later. Use the estimate you requested from the Social Security Administration to complete this line.

What If You Come up Short?

Completing the worksheet almost certainly generates bad news: a substantial shortfall that makes retirement look like a swan dive into poverty. In a sense, the worksheet is stacked against you because it is based only on the growth of what you've accumulated so far and does not take into account any future savings.

Say you're hoping to retire in 20 years, and you face an annual shortfall of $24,000, or $2,000 a month. Use the first table on page 483 to calculate the size of the nest egg it will take to generate that much income for a given length of time. If you'll need the extra $2,000 a month for 30 years, for example, your additional nest egg must total $272,560, if you assume it will earn 8 percent a year after you retire. That means you'll have to invest enough over the next 20 years to total $272,560 when you retire.

(A mathematical footnote: A nest egg of $272,560 may not seem to be enough to generate an income of $2,000 a month if it earns 8 percent, because 8 percent of $272,560 is only $21,804, which amounts to $1,817 per month. The apparent discrepancy is explained by two factors: First, the unexpended portion of the nest egg continues to earn interest, so drawing out $2,000 per month depletes the fund by something less than $2,000. Second, the schedule assumes you will exhaust the fund in 30 years, so it's okay to nick the principal a little each month.)

How Much Time Do You Have?

You can use the table on the opposite page to figure out how much extra you need to start saving each month to accumulate your retirement fund. Assuming a 10 percent annual yield, you can see that $100 a month invested over 20 years will build a nest egg of $76,570 ($10 a month invested for 20 years at

10 percent = $7,657 × 10 = $76,570). Dividing the amount you need—$272,560—by that figure gives you 3.6. Multiply that by 100 and you can see that you need to sock away $360 a month over the next 20 years to meet your goal.

Fortunately, that's not necessarily an extra $360 a month. Part of it may be covered by money you are already putting away in IRAs and other plans, plus future contributions by your employer to a job-related account. Also, the amount you need to come up with yourself probably drops as the years go by and other retirement income kicks in. If you needed the extra $2,000 a month for five years instead of 30—to tide you over for the years between an early retirement at age 50 and age 55, perhaps—the monthly savings required over 20 years would drop from $360 to $129.

What kinds of investments offer the best hope of achieving your retirement goals? A core portfolio of individual stocks (or stock-oriented mutual funds) is ideal for a long-term goal such as retirement. Other chapters in this book describe how to go about selecting them. In general, the more time you have, the more risk you can afford to take.

If Retirement Is 20 or More Years Away

With 20 years or so to go, an aggressive-growth mutual fund such as those listed in Chapter 25 would be appropriate for a portion of a portfolio dominated by growth

HOW $10 A MONTH WILL GROW

This table shows how much you'll have at the end of the period indicated if you save or invest $10 a month, assuming various annual rates of return. Results for other amounts can be calculated as multiples of $10.

Years	8%	9%	10%	11%	12%
10	$ 1,842	$ 1,950	$ 2,066	$ 2,190	$ 2,323
15	3,483	3,812	4,179	4,589	5,046
20	5,929	6,729	7,657	8,736	9,991
25	9,574	11,295	13,379	15,906	18,976

stocks (or funds that specialize in them); zero-coupon bonds (especially zeros sheltered in IRAs and other retirement plans described in this chapter); well-selected real estate (provided it meets the criteria spelled out in Chapter 26); and other long-term investments.

If Retirement Is Ten Years Away

There's still plenty of time to recover from market reversals, but it's also time to think a little more conservatively. Market peaks present opportunities to move money out of risky aggressive stocks and into dividend-paying growth stocks with reinvestment plans. You can give your mutual fund portfolio a less risky profile by moving into growth-and-income, equity-income, and balanced funds. At this point in your life, consider moving about 20 percent of your portfolio into cash, meaning money-market funds, certificates of deposit with various maturities, and Treasury bills. You give up the chance that a soaring market will reward you, but you also give up the risk that a plunging market will punish you.

If Retirement Is Only Five Years Away

When you get to within five years of retirement, it's important to be conservative, but it's also important to remain diversified. Hang on to some growth stocks or growth-stock funds, especially those that pay good dividends. If interest rates look high, buy bonds; if rates decline, you'll have the choice of selling them at a profit or keeping them for the high income they provide. If you own rental real estate that has appreciated in value, look for opportunities to take the gain so you can move the money into a more liquid investment that will produce more income in retirement.

Checking Up on Your Pension

Working for a company with a pension plan does not necessarily mean that you are a member of the plan, or that you will actually get a pension, or that the pension will be as much as you think. It's important to know what you've got.

The best time to check out a company's pension plan is before you're hired; if you have more than one offer, the details of pension coverage could influence your decision. Even after you're hired, pay attention to the plan. The company will amend it as laws and regulations change, and your benefits will be affected.

You should be able to find most of the information you need in the plan's annual report to members and in what's called the summary plan description, both of which the company must provide to employees. Although the law doesn't require employers to offer any pension benefits at all, companies that do have plans must meet the disclosure, funding, and administrative standards of the Employee Retirement Income Security Act (ERISA), which was enacted in 1974.

If the plan summaries leave questions unanswered, you might be able to get some clarification from the company's pension officer or from your union. The ultimate authority is the plan's formal agreement, but you'll need a lot of patience (and possibly a law degree) to wade through it successfully. Before you try that route, track down a pension officer and get the answers to the following ten crucial questions.

1. What Kind of Plan Is It?

Essentially, there are two types of employer-sponsored pension plans.

DEFINED-CONTRIBUTION PLANS. In this increasingly common arrangement the company (and usually you, too) contributes a specified amount each year to a fund that's invested in securities, mutual funds, or some sort of insurance contract. When you retire, you get the money in your account as a lump sum or the company uses it to purchase an annuity, or income stream, for you. You get only as much annuity income as your money will buy, and the amount is not guaranteed. Defined-contribution pension plans include 401(k) and 403(b) plans, deferred profit sharing, and stock-bonus programs.

Even after you're hired, pay attention to your pension plan. The company will amend it as laws and regulations change, and your benefits will be affected.

With a defined-contribution plan you take the risks. It's possible the investments in the fund won't do well, thus reducing the amount available to you when you retire.

Notice that with a defined-contribution plan you take the investment risks. It's possible that the investments in the fund won't do well, thus reducing the amount available to you when it comes time to retire.

DEFINED-BENEFIT PLANS. This kind of plan uses a mathematical formula to determine your pension, and it's up to the employer to contribute enough to the fund to provide the income prescribed by the formula when you retire. The benefit is usually tied to years of service and salary. The more generous plans base the pension on your salary in the final few years of service, when you're likely to be earning most. Less favorable plans tie the pension to your average earnings for all years of service. In the overwhelming majority of defined-benefit plans, employees needn't make any contributions.

2. When Do You Become a Member?

Ordinarily, you can't join the plan until you've met certain age and service requirements. In general, federal law decrees that you must become a member—and thus begin the all-important process of vesting (see question 4)—no later than age 21 with one year of employment. That's the minimum. A company can write a plan that makes you a member sooner, but don't count on it.

3. How Fast Do You Earn Benefits?

Once you become a member of a plan, you start building up your rights to pension benefits year by year. In a defined-contribution plan, your accrued benefit at any point is easy to understand: It's the amount credited to your account. The accrual process is more complicated for defined-benefit plans because your pension isn't a special sum set aside for you but a monthly income that will be paid years down the road.

Some plans credit their members with a set percentage of income for each year of employment. Another common formula is based on a ratio of actual service to the maximum time you could spend in the plan. For example, say you join the plan at age 35 and, therefore, could work another 30 years until reaching the plan's normal retirement age of 65. (Defined-benefit plans need a "normal" retirement age as a basis for calculating benefits. It's often 65, but that doesn't mean you can be required to retire at that age.) If you leave the company after 20 years of covered service, you will have participated for two-thirds of the potential accrual period and will be entitled to two-thirds of the estimated pension you would have qualified for at your full retirement age.

4. How Fast Will You Be Vested?

Even after you've accrued part of a pension, you are not automatically entitled to benefits. You do own any money you contributed to the plan yourself, plus whatever your contributions have earned, but you don't completely own the accrued benefit created by the employer's contributions until you're 100 percent vested. The plan's vesting schedule is critical. If you are only 20 percent vested, then you own 20 percent of the accrued benefit. If you leave the company without being vested at all, you have no rights to that pension. Upon retirement you will receive zip, nothing. If you change jobs frequently, it's possible to work a lifetime for companies with pension plans and not earn much of a pension.

The vesting requirements for employer matching contributions to defined contribution plans were tightened in 2002 to require either full 100 percent vesting in three years or an additional 20 percent vesting each year under a graduated schedule that fully vests with the completion of six years of service.

5. What Do You Lose If You Leave?

Each plan lays down rules defining your pension status when you have a "break in service"—from a layoff, say, or extended leave—or if you fail to work a full year. ERISA, the law governing these things, says that a full year is 1,000 hours of service and that a break in service occurs if you work fewer than 500 hours in a year. ERISA protects employees who might miss extended periods because of pregnancy, birth, or adoption of a

You don't own the accrued benefit created by your employer's contributions until you're fully vested.

THE COST OF EARLY RETIREMENT: A TYPICAL SCENARIO

Current Age	Average Pay Last Five Years	Years of Service	Pension Benefit Starting at Age 65	Pension Benefit Starting at Age in Left-Hand Column
55	$60,000	20	$14,400	$10,080
56	61,800	21	15,574	11,369
57	63,654	22	16,805	12,772
58	65,564	23	18,096	14,295
59	67,531	24	19,449	15,948
60	69,556	25	20,867	17,737
61	71,643	26	22,353	19,670
62	73,792	27	23,909	21,757
63	76,006	28	25,538	24,006
64	78,286	29	27,244	26,426
65	80,635	30	29,029	29,029

Assumptions:

1. Pay increases at 3% each year you continue working.

2. Pension formula is 1.2% of final five-year average pay times years of service.

3. Pension is reduced 3% per year for retirees below "normal retirement age" 65.

Source: Hewitt Associates

child. In such cases, up to 501 hours of the leave must be counted as service if failing to count them would create a break in service.

6. What Will You Get If You Retire Early?

You will get a smaller monthly income than you would at the usual retirement age of 65, but how much smaller? A number of things will affect it. The accrual period will be shorter. Your final salary may be lower than if you worked another few years. And normally the pension is reduced by an actuarial formula that takes into account the likelihood that you will receive the pension for more years. The effect of these adjustments will vary with the provisions of the plan, but they can be substantial. The table above demonstrates how early retirement might reduce the pension of a worker under a more-or-less typical pension plan.

7. What If You Work after Age 65?

You can't be forced to retire because of age. Most plans, though, have designed benefits for a so-called normal retirement age of 65. Your plan must recognize service after that age by including the additional years of service in the pension computation.

8. What Will You Get If You're Disabled?

Most companies have a long-term-disability program that pays a monthly income until you become eligible for retirement. An alternative is to put employees on a retirement pension if they become disabled after they work for the company a prescribed number of years. The plan will specify any disability benefit to which you're entitled.

9. What Are the Death Benefits?

When you retire from a company with a defined-benefit plan, you will probably be offered a choice of annuities that will pay an income or a lump sum to your spouse or other survivor after your death. For married retirees, the law requires that a joint-and-survivor annuity (defined later in this chapter) automatically be used if you make no other choice. You can elect not to receive the joint-and-survivor annuity, provided you do so in writing and your spouse agrees to the waiver in writing. A joint-and-survivor annuity will reduce your pension payments to compensate the plan for the added cost of paying survivor benefits for an undetermined number of years after your death. Still, it provides an important safeguard for the surviving spouse, who will be assured of additional income to supplement his or her Social Security benefits.

10. Do You Have Any Inflation Protection?

Probably not. Very few private pension plans adjust benefits after retirement to compensate for cost-of-living increases. The handful that do usually limit the annual rise to a relatively small amount—say, 3 percent. Some companies, though, have made voluntary increases for retirees from time to time.

> Very few private pension plans adjust benefits after retirement to compensate for cost-of-living increases.

The Growing Role of the 401(k)

As defined-benefit plans have become increasingly expensive for companies to sponsor, more and more have turned to 401(k) plans instead. (Public-school teachers and employees of nonprofit organizations may encounter the 403(b), a close cousin.) These plans get their rather awkward-sounding names from the sections of the Internal Revenue Code that authorize them. They give employees the option to divert a portion of their salary to a tax-sheltered investment account set up by the employer. Most firms allow you to contribute between 2 and 15 percent of pay each year, and the IRS agrees to postpone taxing the portion of the pay you agree to postpone receiving. Earnings accumu-

THE NEW ROTH 401(K)

Starting in January 2006, companies may amend their 401(k)s to include the new Roth 401(k). Rules for Roth 401(k)s are similar to those for Roth IRAs: Pay-ins do not reduce taxable income because they are made with after-tax dollars. Withdrawals from them are tax-free, including earnings on the account, if you take them after more than five years and after you reach age 59½. (For more on Roth IRAs, go to page 480.)

But there are important differences, most of them favorable. The Roth 401(k) pay-in cap will be higher than for a Roth IRA. The standard 401(k) limits will apply—a $15,000 maximum for 2006 plus up to an additional $5,000 for participants over age 50. The 2006 ceiling on pay-ins to Roth IRAs seems paltry by comparison—$4,000 plus up to $1,000 extra for individuals who are age 50 or older. Note that any Roth 401(k) pay-ins will count toward the regular 401(k) cap. You won't be able to contribute the maximum to both types of accounts.

No income limitations apply to contributions to Roth 401(k)s, unlike the $160,000 adjusted gross income ceiling for regular Roths. Distributions will generally have to be made after you reach age 70½, unlike for Roth IRAs, which do not require any lifetime withdrawals. It appears the age 70½ rule could be circumvented by rolling the balance of the Roth 401(k) over to a Roth IRA, but the IRS hadn't ruled on this when this book went to press.

Contributions to Roth 401(k) plans will have to be segregated from deferrals to regular 401(k)s, along with earnings on each account. Matches of employee Roth 401(k) contributions aren't tax favored. The matches go in a special account and are taxed as income when paid out.

Roth 401(k)s are set to lapse after 2010. But Congress is likely to make them permanent, given the number of firms expected to hop on the Roth 401(k) bandwagon.

late tax-free until you take the cash. Meanwhile, the company may match your contribution in whole or part.

A 401(k), because it is a defined-contribution plan, takes the investment risk off the company's shoulders and puts it on yours. Still, the attractions are considerable. Say you make $50,000 a year and work for a company that allows you to put up to 10 percent of your salary in a 401(k), and say you contribute the maximum. You benefit twice, and possibly three times: First, you're taxed on only $45,000, which saves you $1,250 in tax if you're in the 25 percent bracket; second, your $5,000 goes to work in a tax-sheltered account, meaning that whatever it earns as the years go by is shielded from tax until you withdraw it, presumably in retirement; and third, any amount that your company puts in as a match is pure gravy. If your employer adds 50 cents for every dollar you put in, that's an immediate 50 percent return on your investment.

In 2005, you could put up to $14,000 in your plan, and the maximum rises to $15,000 in 2006. A "catch-up" provision for workers age 50 or older permits them to contribute even more each year, an additional $4,000 in 2005, and $5,000 in 2006. Your company can contribute more, up to a combined contribution of $42,000 or 25 percent of your pay, whichever is less. (The $42,000 is not indexed and includes some after-tax contributions.) Most companies set lower limits, however. You are immediately vested in the money you contribute, but the company's contributions will probably be vested over a period of years, on one of the schedules described earlier.

Although the company plan determines the maximum contribution, you decide how much, if any, to trim your pay. If financial demands increased, you could suspend contributions and have 100 percent of your pay show up in your paycheck—not counting withheld tax, of course.

Choosing Where the Money Goes

Your choices of where to invest your 401(k) set-asides are determined by the company. They may include the company's own stock; a list of mutual funds including

You are immediately vested in the money you contribute to a 401(k), but the company's contributions will probably be vested over a period of years.

You may be able to tap your 401(k) account early by taking a loan against your balance, which you must repay within five years.

stock, bond, or money-market funds; or a guaranteed-investment contract, or GIC (sometimes called a "stable value" fund). Just a few years ago, about 47 percent of employee funds went into superconservative GICs when that choice was available. This is changing. In 2004, the Employee Benefits Research Institute reported that as of year-end 2003 almost 70 percent of 401(k)-plan balances were invested directly or indirectly in equity securities, 10 percent was in bonds, and 18 percent in money-market or other stable-value investments.

If you are tempted to put a large percent of your 401(k) money into a GIC, be aware that the promised interest rate is usually low compared with the return you could get by stepping up the risk a little and choosing a stock-oriented mutual fund, if it's offered. You can diversify your funds among the plan's investment alternatives, and you should periodically assess how your account is performing. The further away you are from retirement, the more of your 401(k) money should be in stock-oriented funds because of their superior long-term results. (Buying their own company's stock through the 401(k) plan can be a good deal for employees of companies with a bright future, but for some of the potential drawbacks, see the section on ESOPs on pages 472-473.)

Getting the Money Out

Because the aim of 401(k) plans is to encourage saving for retirement, the IRS puts restrictions on your ability to get at the money. You can't have it back until you leave the company, when you can roll the money into an IRA or into your new employer's 401(k) plan, if the rules of the new plan permit it.

A major exception to the no-early-withdrawal rule lets employees tap the money they've contributed to their accounts in the event of financial hardship. Just what qualifies as a hardship is not always clear, but the rules have gotten tougher in recent years. You must be able to prove that you're facing an immediate and substantial financial need and that you don't have another source of money. Even if you meet the hardship definition, withdrawals before age 59½ are subject to a 10 percent penalty. And, of course, you'll owe regular income tax on the withdrawn amount.

You may be able to tap your account early by taking a loan against your account. If your plan permits it, you can borrow as much as half of your account balance, up to a maximum loan of $50,000. Most plans require you to repay the loan within five years unless you use the money to buy a home, in which case there is no time limit.

When you borrow from your 401(k) account, the plan will deduct the amount of the loan from your account balance and set up a repayment schedule at a specified rate of interest. As you repay, the money is added back to your balance. Because you are, in effect, borrowing from yourself and paying yourself interest, some plan participants think of 401(k) loans as "free money." But these loans aren't free. The real cost consists of loan set-up fees you pay, plus the lost earnings on the funds while they are out of your account. For instance, if you were to pay interest at 10 percent over a period during which the rest of the account earned 15 percent, your true cost of the loan would be 15 percent—the 10 percent you're paying out of pocket plus the 5 percent your money's not earning, plus the loan set-up costs. That's not free. (If, on the other hand, the market were to plunge, generating losses for plan participants while you were paying yourself 10 percent interest, you might want to congratulate yourself for your good timing.)

If you leave the job in the year you reach age 55, or later, you can take your money with no penalty, although you'd probably want to roll it directly into an IRA to avoid the big tax bill. (If you take possession of the money, your employer will have to withhold 20 percent for the IRS. You won't get the money back until you file your tax return, showing that you have rolled the money into a qualified plan.) If you leave before that, you can avoid the penalty and the tax by rolling the money into an IRA. In addition, you are permitted to use all or part of the money without penalty if you need it to pay medical bills that exceed 7.5 percent of your adjusted gross income, if you are

If you leave the job in the year you reach age 55, or later, you can take your 401(k) money with no penalty, although you'd probably want to roll it directly into an IRA to avoid the big tax bill.

The advantage of an employee stock ownership plan to employees is that they acquire stock of the company they work for at either no cost or reduced cost.

disabled, or if you elect to receive the money in a series of equal installments based on your life expectancy.

SIMPLE 401(k)s

Firms with fewer than 100 employees can establish what's called a SIMPLE plan, short for "savings incentive match plan for employees." The company sets a percentage of each employee's pay that can be contributed to the plan, up to a maximum of $10,000 a year per employee (in 2005). The employee chooses where the money goes, just as in a conventional 401(k).

In exchange for the simplicity of the plan, the employer must agree to contribute to workers' accounts, matching up to 3 percent of pay contributed to the plan, or, at a minimum, 2 percent of everyone's pay, even those who don't participate in the plan themselves. Workers are vested immediately in the employer's contributions. All contributions—the workers' and the company's—escape taxation that year and grow tax-deferred as long as they remain in the account.

The SIMPLE 401(k) is a nice cross between an IRA and a 401(k). It allows a smaller maximum annual contribution than a conventional 401(k)—$10,000 versus $14,000 in 2005, for example—but more than twice the limit of an IRA. Rules governing the plan are essentially the same as for a 401(k), with the exception that bailing out within the first two years of joining the plan raises the 10 percent early-withdrawal penalty to a whopping 25 percent.

Employee Stock Ownership Plans

In an employee stock ownership plan (ESOP), employees buy stock in their company through payroll withholding or some other method, or the corporation contributes shares of its stock to funds that allocate the shares to employees based on their annual compensation.

The advantage to employees is that they acquire stock of the company they work for at either no cost or reduced cost. Employees owe taxes on the value of the stock only when it is distributed to them. In the meantime, the stock can appreciate tax-free, and when employees take possession of the stock, they can continue the tax-favored treatment by rolling it over into an IRA.

As retirement programs go, ESOPs have a couple of potential drawbacks. Because all or most of your stake is invested in one company, you lose the protection of a diversified investment portfolio. And because you are already counting on the company to provide you with your preretirement income, you should think twice about whether you want to depend on its stock price to provide your income in retirement as well.

Profit-Sharing Plans

Some profit-sharing plans pay the money directly to employees each year in the form of cash, meaning employees owe taxes on it and it's up to them to decide how to invest it (or spend it). Most plans, though, defer the payout until you leave the company, directing the money into an account that grows year by year. You owe no tax until you withdraw the money, which is usually invested in the meantime by professional investment counselors under the supervision of the trustees of the plan or an investment committee. A small percentage of profit-sharing plans give employees a voice in the selection of investments.

Some plans invest part of their funds in the company's own stock. That can prove an advantage or disadvantage to the employee, depending on the company's dividend-payment policy (if the stock held by the plan earns dividends), and on whether the stock appreciates or declines in value as the years go by.

Although they lack the guarantees of regular pension plans, profit-sharing programs make it possible to accumulate sizable retirement funds when you work a long time for a successful company. Many plans are offered in combination with other retirement plans. The ideal arrangement would be a program that combined a defined-benefit pension plan with deferred profit sharing.

Most profit-sharing plans defer the payout until you leave the company, directing the money into an account that grows year by year. You owe no tax until you withdraw the money.

If one spouse has no earned income, you can open a separate spousal IRA.

Individual Retirement Accounts

Anyone with earned income to report on a tax return is eligible to set up a tax-sheltered IRA. You can put aside up to $4,000 a year of your earnings, and the maximum rises to $5,000 a year in 2008. Workers age 50 or older may make a "catch-up" contribution—an extra $500 in 2005 and $1,000 in 2006. (For calculations here, we use $4,000.) And, you can deduct all of it from your taxable income if you or your spouse are not covered by a pension plan or you meet certain income tests. Even if you don't qualify for the deduction, you owe no taxes on the earnings in the IRA until you withdraw the money.

This is the real beauty of the IRA: Your earnings accumulate tax-free, supercharging the already powerful effect of compound interest. A series of $4,000 nondeductible IRA contributions earning at a rate of 10 percent per year compounded annually over a 20-year period will grow to about $252,000. If the earnings were taxed annually in the 25 percent bracket, the account would grow to only about $186,200.

Married couples filing jointly for 2005 with adjusted gross incomes up to $70,000, and singles and heads of households with adjusted gross incomes up to $50,000 got the full deduction whether they were covered by a company retirement plan or not. Above those levels, the deduction was phased out at a rate of $10 for every $50 above the thresholds. Thus it was gone completely for covered couples with $80,000 of AGI, and singles and household heads with $60,000 of AGI.

The income limits—and the phase-out zones—are scheduled to increase year by year, topping out at $80,000 to $100,000 for joint returns, and $50,000 to $60,000 for singles in the year 2007. (See the table on the opposite page.) If you are not covered by a retirement plan at work, you can deduct your contributions to a regular IRA regardless of your income.

If one spouse has no earned income, you can open a separate spousal IRA for that spouse and contribute a total of $8,000 a year to the two accounts, as long as neither account gets more than $4,000 in a single year. And

CAN YOU DEDUCT YOUR IRA CONTRIBUTION?

These are the scheduled phase-out zones under which taxpayers covered by a retirement plan at work will qualify for a full or partial deduction of contributions to a regular IRA (as opposed to a Roth IRA, for which no one can deduct contributions). If your income is below the lower figure, you can deduct your entire contribution. If your income falls within the phase-out zones, you get a partial deduction, which will be determined by the IRS. A higher phase-out zone applies in determining whether contributions to a spousal IRA are deductible. In that case, the phase-out zone is $150,000 to $160,000.

Year	Single Return	Joint Return
2005	$50,000–60,000	$70,000–80,000
2006	50,000–60,000	75,000–85,000
2007	50,000–60,000	80,000–100,000

because there's no minimum age requirement to open an IRA, parents can open one for their children and fund it by matching earnings from babysitting, paper routes, and other after-school jobs. The IRS doesn't care if it's parents' money being funneled into the account, provided the child has earned at least that much money.

(What constitutes "earned" income? Generally, it means compensation for working: wages, salaries, bonuses, sales commissions. Alimony also counts. Rental income, capital gains, and dividends don't count, nor does income from an annuity or a pension.)

If you withdraw money from an IRA before you reach age 59½, you're subject to a 10 percent penalty tax, plus regular income tax on the amount withdrawn, except under certain circumstances.

■ **If you pay certain college** or other higher-education bills for yourself, your spouse, your child, or grandchild, you escape the penalty (but owe the tax) on early withdrawals. Qualified expenses include tuition, fees, books, supplies, and required equipment. For students attending at least half time, room and board also qualify.

■ **If you withdraw up to a total of $10,000** to buy or build a first home for yourself, your spouse, a child, a

Because dividends and other earnings that accumulate in IRAs won't be taxed right away, it may make the most sense to make your contributions as early in the year as possible.

grandchild, or your parents, you also escape the penalty. You do owe income tax on the withdrawal, however, at your usual rate.

■ **If you withdraw money to pay medical expenses** that exceed 7.5 percent of your adjusted gross income and to pay for your health insurance during a long period of unemployment, you owe tax but no penalty.

■ **If you withdraw funds to convert your regular IRA** to a Roth IRA (described later in this chapter), you owe tax but no penalty. To be eligible to convert, your adjusted gross income must be less than $100,000.

You may not make contributions to a regular IRA in the year you reach age 70½ and you must begin withdrawing money from a regular IRA (as distinguished from a Roth IRA) no later than April 1 in the year following the year you reach age 70½. Thus, if you reach age 70½ in 2008, you must begin withdrawing your IRA money by April 1, 2009. When you do withdraw the money, it will be taxed as ordinary income if you took the deduction when you put it in; only the earnings will be taxed when you make mandatory withdrawals from a nondeductible IRA.

Contribute on Your Own Schedule

You can make each year's contribution in one lump sum or in regular or irregular installments. (Want to make monthly contributions, thus taking advantage of dollar-cost averaging, as described in Chapter 22? Just send a check for $333 to your IRA each month.) Still, because dividends and other earnings that accumulate in IRAs won't be taxed right away, it may make the most sense to make your contributions as early in the year as possible.

IRAs can be opened and contributions made any time before the April 15 deadline for filing your federal tax return for the previous calendar year. There's a 6 percent penalty tax for overages, and the excess counts as taxable income when you withdraw it. Alternatively, you can absorb excess contributions by contributing less in a subsequent year. You still owe the 6 percent penalty, though.

IRA investments must be made through a custodian or trustee—in practice, a company that supervises the account and reports to you and the government each year. Banks, credit unions, mutual funds, and others that provide IRA plans have standard IRS-approved custodial or trustee arrangements. All you have to do is complete a simple form. You can maintain more than one IRA account with the same or different companies (but contributions to all of them can't exceed the yearly maximum).

Move Your Money Around

Despite the penalty for premature withdrawals, you are not required to keep your money in the same IRA from the time you open the account until you reach age 59½. The rules offer great flexibility for shifting the money around. There are two ways to do it: direct transfers and rollovers.

DIRECT TRANSFERS. Funds can be transferred directly from one custodian or trustee to another—from a bank IRA, for example, to one sponsored by a mutual fund, or from one mutual fund to another. In a direct transfer, you never take possession of the money. You can move your IRA money around and open and close accounts at will using this method. However, charges imposed by plan sponsors, such as fees to set up an IRA or early-withdrawal penalties if you cash a bank CD before it matures, may make frequent shifts costly.

ROLLOVERS. If you take possession of the funds during a transfer (you close an account with a stock mutual fund, for example, and then put the money in an insurance company's IRA), the law calls the transaction a rollover. You can use this method only once each year for each account. After you withdraw the funds, you have 60 days to complete the rollover. Any money that isn't contributed to a new account within that time is considered a premature distribution, and it will be fully taxed as ordinary income and trigger the 10 percent penalty, assuming you're under age 59½. If you

> You can maintain more than one IRA account with the same or different companies (but contributions to all of them can't exceed the yearly maximum).

The opportunities for IRA money are almost unlimited. You can find sponsors offering almost every imaginable investment.

plan to do a rollover, do it directly from one institution to another without taking possession of the funds. Most institutions will send you the necessary forms.

Choosing Your Investments

The opportunities for IRA money are almost unlimited. You can find sponsors—banks, S&Ls, credit unions, mutual funds, insurance companies—offering almost every imaginable investment, the relative merits of which you will find described in the investment chapters of this book.

If you want to put together your own portfolio rather than rely on mutual fund managers, you can do it with a self-directed IRA. These accounts, usually set up through brokers, let you choose what you want to invest in, such as stocks and bonds of individual companies. You decide what and when to buy and sell, but if you wheel and deal too much, commissions can eat up a lot of your nest egg. The fees attached to this type of account demand close attention, especially in the early years, when it holds a relatively modest amount.

If you want, you can even fill your self-directed IRA with gold, silver, palladium, and platinum bullion, or gold, silver, and platinum coins. It would be foolish to waste the tax advantages of an IRA on such investments, however. The only way to make money on precious metals and coins is to sell them for more than you bought them for—in other words, to take capital gains. But when you withdraw these gains from your IRA, they will be taxed as regular income. You may discover that you have swapped a 25 percent tax rate for a 28 percent or higher rate. Better to reserve your IRA for investments that generate taxes over the years, so you can take full advantage of the opportunity to defer the tax and thus enhance the compounding effect.

Municipal bonds also have no place in an IRA. First, their earnings are already tax-free; second, higher yields are available from other issues; and third, when you begin to withdraw money from your IRA, it will be taxed and you will have converted the tax-free income of a municipal bond into the taxable income of an IRA distribution.

LIFE EXPECTANCY DIVISORS FOR IRA DRAWDOWNS

Your Age	Uniform Lifetime	Joint Life and Last Survivor Expectancy										
		59	60	61	62	63	64	65	66	67	68	69
70	27.4	28.1											
71	26.5	27.9	27.2										
72	25.6	27.7	27.0	26.3									
73	24.7	27.5	26.8	26.1	25.4								
74	23.8	27.4	26.6	25.9	25.2	24.5							
75	22.9	27.2	26.5	25.7	25.0	24.3	23.6						
76	22.0	27.1	26.3	25.6	24.8	24.1	23.4	22.7					
77	21.2	27.0	26.2	25.4	24.7	23.9	23.2	22.5	21.8				
78	20.3	26.9	26.1	25.3	24.6	23.8	23.1	22.4	21.7	21.0			
79	19.5	26.8	26.0	25.2	24.4	23.7	22.9	22.2	21.5	20.8	20.1		
80	18.7	26.7	25.9	25.1	24.3	23.6	22.8	22.1	21.3	20.6	20.0	19.3	

Source: Internal Revenue Service

When It's Time to Take the Money Out

Not only will the government penalize you if you dip into your retirement fund early, but also it will impose a stiff penalty if you don't withdraw the money fast enough later on (except in a Roth IRA, for which there is no requirement to withdraw, as described later). Between the time you reach age 59½ and the year you turn 70½, you can withdraw without penalty as much or as little as you want from your IRA. Once you reach approximately age 70½, there are minimum withdrawal schedules based on your life expectancy—or on that of you and your beneficiary if she or he is more than ten years younger. The schedules, part of which are shown in the table above, are designed to make sure you make a serious effort to deplete the account (so the government can finally tax the money) before you die.

To figure out how much you need to withdraw from a regular IRA, you need to divide your account balance by your life expectancy. Things get a little complicated because statistically the longer you live the longer you are expected to live. So you need to recalculate your minimum withdrawal every year. And

Although Roth contributions aren't tax deductible under any circumstances, withdrawals after age 59½ are completely tax-free.

life expectancy depends on your marital status and beneficiary.

For example, if you are unmarried, married with a spouse not more than ten years younger, or married but whose spouse is not the sole beneficiary of your IRA, refer to the "Uniform Lifetime" column in the table on page 479 to determine life expectancy. If you are 72, you're expected to live another 25.6 years, so you'd divide your account balance by that figure. Next year, you'll be 73, and your life expectancy becomes 24.7 years. And so forth.

If you have named a sole beneficiary who is more than ten years younger than you, you'll need to use the rest of the table. Find his or her age at the top and read down the appropriate column to where it intersects with your own age. That's your age divisor you'll use to divide into your account balance to see how much you are required to withdraw.

If you don't withdraw as much as you should each year, the IRS will slap you with a 50 percent penalty tax. Assume, for example, that two men own IRAs, each of which have grown to $300,000. The first man is supposed to withdraw about $13,000 in a particular year. If he took out only $10,000, the 50 percent penalty would apply to the $3,000 not withdrawn and cost him $1,500. The second man withdrew $15,000, so there would be no penalty because he had withdrawn more than the minimum amount.

For a more complete table of divisors, plus a description of the various permutations that can result from complications such as multiple beneficiaries, see IRS Publication 590, *Individual Retirement Arrangements*. You can order it by phone at 800-829-3676 or view it and download it from the IRS Web site, http://www.irs.gov.

Roth IRAs

Like a regular IRA, a Roth must be funded from earned income—in general, money you get paid for performing work. As with a regular IRA, contributions are limited to $4,000 a year and will rise to

$5,000 a year in 2008, with the same contribution deadlines. As with a regular IRA, money in a Roth grows tax-free until you take it out.

For most people, though, it's the differences between a regular IRA and a Roth IRA that makes the Roth so attractive.

■ **Although Roth contributions** aren't tax deductible under any circumstances, withdrawals after age 59½ are completely tax-free.

■ **You can withdraw** the total of your annual contributions at any time without incurring a penalty or tax. Note that this rule applies only to your contributions to a Roth, not the account's earnings. If your withdrawals reach the point at which you're dipping into earnings, you may owe the penalty and tax if you're under age 59½. The tax and penalty are both waived on up to $10,000 of earnings withdrawn—after the account has been opened for five years—for the purchase of a first home.

■ **You can continue to contribute** to the account after age 70½.

■ **There is no requirement** that you begin withdrawing money from a Roth IRA at age 70½ or any other age. If you wish, you can leave the money there until you die.

■ **If you die** with a balance in your account, it goes to your heirs tax-free. In a regular IRA, the beneficiary owes income tax on the balance.

Not everyone is eligible for a Roth IRA, although the great majority of taxpayers do qualify. If your income tops $150,000 on a joint return or $95,000 on a single return—whether as an individual, head of household, or surviving spouse—you begin to lose your Roth eligibility. (Married persons filing separately aren't eligible no matter what their income.) The phase-out zone stretches to $160,000 for joint returns and $110,000 for singles. If your income falls somewhere in that zone, your maximum contribution is reduced according to a prorated schedule: If you're halfway through the zone, your limit is cut in half; if

> You can withdraw the total of your annual Roth contributions at any time without incurring a penalty or tax.

Convert from a traditional IRA to a Roth? The decision depends on whether you'd be better off paying the tax now or later.

you're two-thirds into the zone, it is cut by two-thirds, and so forth.

Open a Roth?

There are some circumstances under which the Roth IRA has clear advantages over the old-style IRA. More commonly, it's a tough call. If your situation is such that you can't deduct your contributions to a regular IRA, then by all means open a Roth and pour in the money. If you can deduct regular IRA contributions, the picture gets murky. You have to choose between a tax deduction now and tax-free income years from now, when you may or may not be in a lower tax bracket. Perhaps the other attributes of the Roth—the lack of a mandatory withdrawal schedule, the tax-free inheritance for a loved one—will tip the balance in its favor.

Convert Your Old IRA to a Roth?

The arguments in favor of a Roth are compelling, which raises a natural question if you have been merrily contributing to a regular IRA all these years: Should you convert to a Roth? The law lets you do it if your adjusted gross income is $100,000 or less, regardless of your filing status (except that married couples filing separately can't convert).

If you do convert, you'll be spared the 10 percent penalty on early withdrawals, but you will have to pay income tax on the amount involved (except for the amount of nondeductible contributions you've made to the regular IRA account). If you've been pouring cash into an IRA for many years, the prospect of paying income tax on all that money can be daunting.

The decision to convert depends on whether you'd be better off paying the tax now or later. If you expect to be in a higher tax bracket when you retire, then it makes sense to convert and pay the tax now at the lower rate. If you expect that your bracket will be the same—and you'd have to deplete IRA funds to pay the tax now—converting would ultimately make no difference in your spendable income later on. If you expect to be in a lower bracket when you start withdrawing

NUMBERS YOU'LL NEED TO PLAN YOUR RETIREMENT

The first table shows how large a fund you'd need to yield $100 a month over a number of years when invested at various rates. Let's say you needed the money over 20 years, during which you can earn 9%: You'd start with $11,114 (where the 20-year and 9% columns meet). To generate $500 a month, you'd need 5 times that amount, or $55,570.

You can also use this table to find out what you'd get monthly from a hunk of cash you'll draw down over your retirement. Say you have $250,000, on which you figured you could earn 9% over 20 years. Tracing the 20-year and 9% columns gives you $11,114—the amount that will yield $100 per month. Your fund is 22.5 times greater, so your payout would be 22.5 times greater than $100, or $2,250 monthly.

The second table shows how much you'd have to save monthly at various interest rates over a number of years to accumulate $1,000. For example, to build your kitty over 20 years by investing in a 9% account, you'd need to save $1.49 a month. To accumulate $55,000, you'd need to save 55 times $1.49, or $81.95.

The last table shows what inflation can do to your retirement expenses. Start with your estimated expenses for your first year of retirement. To see how they'd grow after 5 years of 5% inflation, find where those columns intersect and multiply your original expense figure by the number shown there.

How Much Capital You'll Need to Yield $100 a Month for the Period Indicated at Interest Rate Indicated

Years	5½%	7%	8%	9%	10%	11%	12%
5	$ 5,235	$ 5,050	$ 4,932	$ 4,817	$ 4,706	$ 4,599	$4,496
10	9,214	8,613	8,242	7,894	7,567	7,260	6,970
15	12,238	11,125	10,464	9,860	9,306	8,798	8,332
20	14,537	12,898	11,955	11,114	10,362	9,688	9,082
25	16,284	14,149	12,956	11,916	11,005	10,203	9,495
30	17,612	15,030	13,628	12,428	11,395	10,501	9,722

Monthly Investment Needed to Accumulate $1,000 Over the Period Indicated at Interest Rate Indicated

Years	5½%	7%	8%	9%	10%	11%	12%
5	$14.45	$13.89	$13.52	$13.16	$12.81	$12.46	$12.12
10	6.24	5.76	5.43	5.13	4.84	4.57	4.30
15	3.57	3.14	2.87	2.62	2.40	2.18	1.98
20	2.29	1.91	1.69	1.49	1.31	1.14	1.00
25	1.55	1.23	1.04	0.89	0.75	0.63	0.53
30	1.09	0.81	0.67	0.54	0.44	0.35	0.28

Inflation's Effect on Your Figures

Years	3%	4%	5%	6%	7%	8%	9%	10%
5	1.16	1.22	1.28	1.34	1.40	1.47	1.54	1.61
10	1.34	1.48	1.63	1.79	1.97	2.16	2.37	2.59
15	1.56	1.80	2.08	2.40	2.76	3.17	3.64	4.18
20	1.81	2.19	2.65	3.21	3.87	4.66	5.60	6.73
25	2.09	2.67	3.39	4.29	5.43	6.85	8.62	10.82
30	2.43	3.24	4.32	5.74	7.61	10.06	13.27	17.45

your IRA money, then you might as well leave well enough alone and not convert.

Variable Annuities

That billions and billions of dollars reside in variable annuities is a tribute to the sales ability of the insurance industry and, too often, the gullibility of its customers.

Built around a life insurance policy, a variable annuity offers a range of investment products into which the buyer can direct part of his or her premiums. There is no limit on how much you can invest each year. Contributions aren't deductible, but taxes on any earnings are deferred until the money is withdrawn.

This deferral is both a plus and a minus. Over time, most of the gain from a stock mutual fund should be in the form of capital gains, but all the earnings that come out of an annuity are taxed as ordinary income. So the highest-income annuity holders wind up paying as much as 35 percent when they start taking income from the account, instead of the 15 percent top rate that applies to capital gains outside the account. (In fairness, it should be pointed out that the same kind of tax transformation takes place within a regular IRA or other tax-sheltered account.)

Typically, the life insurance coverage guarantees that if you die before you start withdrawing money from the annuity, your heirs will get at least as much as you invested, even if your investment portfolio has lost money. This guarantee sounds nice, but investors rarely lose money over the period of years during which they are paying into the annuity, so many wind up paying for life insurance their heirs never collect.

Meanwhile, in addition to premiums, you're paying typical annual fees of 2 percent—nearly double those of the average mutual fund. There's also a yearly contract charge of $25 or so. There are surrender charges, too, if you decide to take your money out. These penalties average 5.5 percent and generally phase out after you've been in the annuity for a few years. There's also a 10 percent penalty for withdrawing earnings before age 59½, although it doesn't apply if you switch to another annuity, are disabled, or base a series of withdrawals on your life expectancy.

If you die with money in the account, your heirs owe tax on the earnings built up during your lifetime. Outside an annuity, the part of the inheritance attributable to unrealized capital gains would be tax-free.

When Variable Annuities Make Sense

Despite all this, a variable annuity could deserve a place in your retirement savings plan under the following circumstances.

- **You are contributing the maximum** to your 401(k) or 403(b) plan at work, or, if you are self-employed, to a Keogh or SEP-IRA (see the next section). These are superior tax shelters because you can deduct your contributions and you don't have the insurance costs of an annuity.
- **You are contributing the maximum** to deductible and even nondeductible IRAs. A nondeductible IRA gives you the same tax break as a variable annuity without the extra costs, although you can't invest more than $4,000 a year in an IRA (rising to $5,000 in 2008).
- **You won't need the money** you invest in a variable annuity before age 59½. This is to make sure you won't get hit with the 10 percent early-withdrawal penalty.
- **You plan to contribute** for at least ten years before you begin tapping the annuity. It will take that long for the tax advantages to overcome the extra costs.
- **You plan to take the payout** from your annuity as a steady stream of monthly payments throughout retirement. Although you'll be offered the option of withdrawing the annuity in a lump sum, the tax hit means doing so is almost always a bad idea. You'd have to pay regular income tax immediately on all the earnings that have built up over the years. Better to pay those taxes gradually, meanwhile leaving the rest of the money in the account to grow tax-deferred.

Although you'll be offered the option of withdrawing the annuity in a lump sum, the tax hit means doing so is almost always a bad idea.

Favored by many professionals, as well as moonlighting consultants and freelance writers, Keogh plans can be used even if you participate in a company pension program and have an IRA.

Retirement Plans If You're Self-Employed

IRAs and Roth IRAs are excellent retirement-saving vehicles, but the annual limit on contributions won't allow you to build a nest egg big enough to fund a comfortable retirement. You need to set aside more than that, especially as retirement gets near. And if you work for yourself, or for a company with only a few employees, the business probably can't afford a generously funded pension plan. Congress has created IRA-like instruments especially for situations like this.

Keogh Plans

Self-employed workers with an eye on retirement have the late U.S. Representative Eugene Keogh of New York to thank for a wealth of tax-favored possibilities. When John Kennedy was in the White House, Congressman Keogh pushed through legislation that extended to the self-employed many of the advantages previously reserved for employee retirement plans. Favored by doctors, dentists, architects, lawyers, and other professionals, as well as moonlighting consultants and freelance writers, Keogh plans can be used even if you're already participating in a company pension program and have an IRA. Annual contributions are deductible from taxable income in the year in which they're made. Brokerage firms, banks, mutual funds, and other types of financial companies offer standardized Keogh accounts, most of which are no more difficult to open than an IRA.

DIFFERENT KINDS OF KEOGHS. With a money-purchase Keogh plan, the annual contribution limit boils down to 25 percent of self-employment income, to a maximum contribution of $42,000. The catch is that you are required to choose a fixed percentage of income and make that contribution each and every year. If, for example, your plan calls for a 25 percent contribution, you have to deposit that amount even if business has been lousy that year.

A profit-sharing Keogh is more flexible and therefore favored by part-timers whose self-employment income isn't very reliable. The maximum deductible contribution is 25 percent of net self-employment income per year, up to a maximum annual contribution of $42,000. Actually, because the 25 percent is applied to net income minus the Keogh contribution and minus the deduction self-employeds get for 50 percent of their self-employment tax, the maximum contribution is reduced to an effective rate of only about 20 percent of net income. You can try to figure it out yourself, or you can use tables prepared by the IRS and published in Publication 590, *Individual Retirement Arrangements.*

You can often contribute more with a defined-benefit Keogh, a plan designed to produce a preset amount of retirement income. With a defined-benefit plan you decide how much you would like to receive in annual retirement income, up to a maximum amount ($170,000 in 2005), and then work backwards from that figure to design a contribution schedule to achieve it. You can contribute up to 100 percent of self-employment income. (The actual limit in 2005 was the average of self-employment income during your three highest-earning years, or $170,000, whichever was less.) These plans are especially attractive to self-employed people who have the money to fund big annual contributions to a Keogh but relatively few years to go until retirement. The rules and calculations are complex, and you should get the help of an accountant or lawyer to set up such a program.

TAX ADVANTAGES OF A KEOGH. Dividends, interest, and other earnings accumulate tax-free. Neither the contributions nor earnings are subject to tax until the money is withdrawn at your retirement.

You can't start dipping into your Keogh funds without incurring a 10 percent penalty until you're 59½, unless you become disabled, use the funds to pay catastrophic medical bills, or withdraw the money as part of a series of roughly equal payments tied to your

You can tap Keogh funds penalty-free at age 55 if you close the business that generated the self-employment income.

The advantage of a SEP over a Keogh is that it is simpler to administer; the paperwork burden isn't quite so onerous. And it's flexible.

life expectancy (same as the IRA rules). You may also get the funds penalty-free as early as age 55 if you close the business that generated the self-employment income. But you don't have to start drawing from the fund until after you reach age 70½. Keogh funds may be paid out in a lump sum, or installments or annuity payments, and you're taxed accordingly. The payouts, though, cannot be scheduled to exceed your life expectancy or the life expectancies of you and the beneficiary you name in the plan. As with IRAs, the government wants its tax money eventually.

You can buy an annuity to fulfill the payout requirement, or you can keep the account intact and arrange for your own annuity-type payments to come out of it. The proper installments can be calculated from IRS tables prepared for that purpose.

If you have any full-time employees, they must be included in your Keogh plan. You may include part-timers, provided you include all the eligible ones.

Simplified Employee Pensions

A simplified employee pension, or SEP, is a kind of combination IRA and Keogh. The annual contribution limit is about 25 percent of net self-employment income, the same as for profit-sharing Keoghs, up to a maximum of $42,000 per year. Again, net means the amount that's left after you subtract your contribution and the offset for any Social Security taxes paid on self-employment income. For simplicity's sake, figure 20 percent of net income—not counting those two factors—is the limit. The rules governing deductibility of contributions, tax-deferral of earnings, penalties for early withdrawals, and distribution minimums after age 70½ are the same as for IRAs. Because of the IRA connection, they are sometimes called SEP IRAs or Super IRAs.

The advantage of a SEP over a Keogh is that it is simpler to administer; the paperwork burden isn't quite so onerous. And it's flexible: Like a profit-sharing Keogh, a SEP lets you vary the contribution from year to year or skip it entirely if the profits aren't there.

Finally, like Keoghs, SEPs can be especially valuable for moonlighters with sideline businesses who are in search of a way to cut their current tax bill and save for retirement at the same time.

SIMPLE IRAs

The acronym stands for "savings incentive match plan for employees." SIMPLE plans were created for companies with fewer than 100 employees, which, of course, includes companies run by the self-employed.

A self-employed individual can make tax-deductible contributions of up to $10,000 a year (for 2005) to a SIMPLE IRA, even if it's every penny of self-employment income. For moonlighters, this limit gives the SIMPLE plan a distinct advantage over either a money-purchase Keogh (you'd need $50,000 of income in order to contribute $10,000).

The rules governing SIMPLE IRAs are much the same as those governing other IRAs, with a significant kicker: The 10 percent penalty for withdrawing contributions before age 59½ jumps to 25 percent for SIMPLE plan contributions withdrawn within two years of starting the plan. (See the discussion of SIMPLE 401(k)s earlier in this chapter.)

Social Security: Don't Sell It Short

Social Security, which gets much of the credit for driving down the poverty rate among America's senior citizens, has become a political hot potato in recent years. Depending on who's talking, the system stands to go bankrupt sometime in the next three or four decades unless something's done. Simply put, there will be too many Americans living longer and becoming eligible for Social Security and too few younger Americans to support their payments. Some believe because we're living longer and healthier lives, the retirement age for becoming eligible for Social Security payments should be raised. Others are vehemently opposed. Some argue there should be no cutoff on the salaries from which Social Security taxes are withheld. Others reject the idea. Still others, including President Bush, believe that privatizing at least part of the program is the answer. Many people are staunchly opposed to this idea.

Suffice it to say the argument will continue and eventually it will be resolved. Kiplinger believes that in the end the system we have now, while modified, will remain largely in place. Whatever the result, we've all got a lot riding on it. In the meantime, here's a rundown of what you get for your Social Security taxes.

Retirement Benefits

You'll get regular monthly checks if you reach a certain age and have worked a certain length of time in a job covered by Social Security. You are considered fully covered if you have worked in a covered job for at least 40 calendar quarters (employees of nonprofit organizations who were forced to join Social Security in 1984 get a more generous schedule). You needn't be fully insured to qualify for benefits. A major appeal of Social Security retirement benefits is that they increase automatically along with inflation.

The earliest you can retire and receive benefits is age 62, but your payments will be reduced if you retire before your full retirement age. The age for receiving full benefits and the reduction for early retirement is increasing. The schedule will add two months each year until 2027, when workers born in 1960 and later

---

WRONG SOCIAL SECURITY NUMBER

Q: *I've discovered that my employer has been using the wrong Social Security number on my payroll account. I've brought this to the attention of the payroll department, but what can I do to make sure this doesn't cost me benefits when I retire?*

A: First, get copies of your W-2 forms for any years affected by the error and take them to the nearest Social Security Administration office. They've seen this problem before and can correct the record quickly. Then wait a few months and call the SSA at 800-772-1213 or log onto its Web site at http://www.ssa.gov and order a "Request for Social Security Statement." Fill it out and send it in. You'll get a printout of your payments record, which you can check to make sure earnings have been credited to the right number.

will have to be 67 years old to qualify for full benefits. Eligibility for reduced benefits at age 62 won't change, nor will the age of eligibility for Medicare, which is 65.

Social Security benefits aren't generous enough to support much of a retirement by themselves, but they're nothing to sneeze at. For workers retiring in 2005, the maximum benefit was about $22,500 per year, and the average was around $14,800. By the year 2020, the maximum is expected to be in the neighborhood of $26,400 a year, with the average benefit about $16,400 in today's dollars. (In inflation-adjusted dollars, the benefits would be about $39,700 and $24,600, respectively.) Those are estimates for a single worker; spousal benefits would boost the amounts. A spouse entitled to benefits from his or her own work record receives whichever is larger: his or her own entitlement, or an amount equal to half of the spouse's.

For most retirees Social Security benefits are still entirely tax-free, and they are at least partially tax-free for the rest. If your adjusted gross income, plus nontaxable interest, plus one-half of Social Security benefits exceeds $25,000 if you're single, or $32,000 if you're married, then up to 50 percent of your benefits can be taxed. And if your income is more than $34,000 on a single return, or $44,000 on a joint return, a different formula takes over that almost always requires 85 percent of your benefits be taxed.

The IRS uses an 18-line worksheet to figure this out. Here, in a nutshell, is how the three-tier taxing system works: Assume that you and your spouse get $10,000 in Social Security benefits. If half that amount plus your adjusted gross income and tax-exempt interest total less than $32,000, none of your benefits would be taxed. If the combination totals $33,000, however, $500 worth of your benefits (one-half of the amount over the threshold) would be subject to tax. The one-half-of-the-excess rule would operate until your income plus half your benefits totaled $42,000. From that point on, half of your benefits—$5,000—would be considered taxable income.

For most retirees, Social Security benefits are still entirely tax-free, and they're at least partially tax-free for the rest.

You can do some paid work after retirement and still collect Social Security, but work too much before you reach full retirement age, and you'll be penalized.

Work and You Weep

You can do some paid work after retirement and still collect Social Security, but work too much before you reach full retirement age, and you'll be penalized. If you are between age 62 and full retirement age, $1 in benefits will be deducted for each $2 in earnings you have above the annual limit ($12,000 in 2005). In the year you reach your full retirement age, your benefits will be reduced $1 for every $3 you earn over a different limit ($31,800 in 2005) until the month you reach full retirement age. The amount is indexed for wage inflation and rises a bit each year. From full retirement age on, you can earn any amount and still receive your full benefits. And note that the limitations apply only to money you earn, not to income from stocks, bonds, real estate, pensions, or other "nonearned" income.

A rule that allows retirees to collect full benefits for the months in which their earnings fall below 1/12th of the annual rate applies only in the year in which they retire.

Although Social Security is thought of mainly as a retirement program, it's really much more than that. It offers several kinds of help.

Disability Income

People who are blind, or disabled in ways that prevent them from working, may receive assistance based on their average earnings under Social Security. The rules are tough, though. Disability is defined as an inability to work because of a physical or mental impairment that has lasted or is expected to last at least 12 months or to result in death. Blindness means either central visual acuity of 20/200 or less in the better eye with the use of corrective lenses, or visual-field reduction to 20 degrees or less (tunnel vision).

Survivors' Benefits

The spouse, children, parents, and, in some cases, grandchildren of a deceased eligible worker may be entitled to cash benefits. Specifically eligible are:

■ **A widow or widower** 60 or older (50 if disabled)

- **A widow, widower, or surviving divorced mother** if caring for the worker's child who is under 16 (or disabled) and who is receiving benefits based on the deceased worker's earnings
- **Unmarried children under 18,** or under 19 if full-time students at a secondary school
- **Unmarried children who were severely disabled** before 22 and who remain disabled
- **Dependent parents** 62 or older
- **If the marriage lasted ten years or more,** checks can go to a surviving divorced spouse of 60 or a disabled surviving divorced spouse of 50.

Medicare

Medicare provides hospital and medical insurance to Social Security recipients. If you're eligible, coverage takes effect automatically when you reach age 65. Part A, which covers bills for hospitals (within limits) and similar institutions (nursing homes and hospices, for example) is automatic. Part B of Medicare, which covers doctors' bills, outpatient treatment at hospitals, prescription drugs, and some other costs, isn't automatic. If you want it, you have to pay for it via monthly premiums deducted from your Social Security checks. A fuller description of Medicare can be found in Chapter 20.

How—and When—to Contact Social Security

It's especially important to contact the Social Security Administration if you're unable to work because of an illness or injury that's expected to incapacitate you for a year or longer, or if you're 62 or older and plan to retire soon. If you're nearing retirement and wonder what your benefits will be, call the SSA at 800-772-1213 and ask for a "Request for Social Security Statement." About two to four weeks after returning the completed form to the SSA, you'll receive your estimate in the mail. You can also request the statement on the SSA's Web site at http://www.ssa.gov, where you'll find a wealth of helpful information, plus a directory to local SSA offices.

Even if you intend to keep working after 65, you should check in with the Social Security people three months before your 65th birthday to enroll in Medicare.

Even if you intend to keep working after 65, you should check in with the Social Security people three months before your 65th birthday to enroll in Medicare, which will become available to you at 65 whether or not you retire.

What to Do with a Lump Sum at Retirement

Lump-sum distributions from retirement plans present retirees with a choice: Should you take the money all at once and pay the taxes on it, or should you look for a way to take the money a little at a time, leaving the rest in the shelter of some kind of tax-

HOW LONG WILL YOUR MONEY LAST? HERE'S A ROUGH GAUGE

This table shows roughly how long it would take to deplete an account at various interest rates and withdrawal amounts, assuming that your returns remain constant. A change in return rate, particularly in the early years, would make a big difference—a steep decline would shorten how long your money will last, while a sizable increase would make it last longer. It is assumed that withdrawals are made at the end of each month, that there are no premature withdrawals or penalties (such as there could be in the case of certificates of deposit), and that interest is compounded continuously. There is no adjustment for inflation.

					Percent of Original Principal Withdrawn Each Year						
Total Return	5% YS MS	6% YS MS	7% YS MS	8% YS MS	9% YS MS	10% YS MS	11% YS MS	12% YS MS	13% YS MS	14% YS MS	15% YS MS
5 %	—	37 0	25 6	19 11	16 5	14 0	12 3	10 10	9 9	8 11	8 2
6		—	33 8	23 7	18 7	15 6	13 3	11 8	10 5	9 5	8 7
7			—	31 1	22 1	17 6	14 8	12 8	11 2	10 0	9 1
8				—	28 11	20 9	16 7	14 0	12 2	10 9	9 8
9					—	27 2	19 7	15 9	13 4	11 8	10 4
10						—	25 7	18 7	15 1	12 10	11 2
11							—	24 4	17 9	14 5	12 4
12								—	23 2	17 0	13 11
13									—	22 3	16 4
14										—	21 4
15											—

— = infinity; **YS** = years; **MS** = months

advantaged vehicle? It's a tough problem, compounded by the fact that the sum involved may be in the six-figure range and a mistake could be very expensive.

The most popular choice is to roll the money into one or more IRAs or annuities. If you do that within 60 days of receiving it, you postpone any tax until you start taking the money out. But better not to take receipt of the lump sum at all. If you do, your employer will have to withhold 20 percent for the IRS, and you won't get the money back until you file your tax return. The best way to avoid this particular pain in the neck is to have your employer transfer the money directly into the tax-sheltered vehicle you choose.

Should You Choose an Annuity?

When you buy an annuity, you pay money to an insurance company and receive in return either a guaranteed income, starting right away or later on, or, less commonly, a lump-sum settlement at some later date.

With an *immediate annuity* the payout begins as soon as you put up your money; with a *deferred annuity* it begins some time later. Deferred annuities can be paid for with a single payment or with installment payments in fixed or flexible amounts.

A *fixed annuity* guarantees a minimum yield, or rate of interest, on premium payments during the accumulation period and a minimum income when payouts begin. A *variable annuity* offers a choice of investments, usually mutual funds. You get the chance at higher returns during the buildup phase and thus the possibility of higher income when you begin taking money out, but a lower guaranteed rate than a fixed annuity. See the description of variable annuities beginning on page 484.

What's appealing about an annuity is that it guarantees you a specified income for life or some other period. You can usually choose one of several ways to receive the income:

- **as a lump sum** you can reinvest;
- **as a guaranteed income** for ten years; or
- **as a guaranteed income** for as long as you live (or for

as long as you and your spouse live). Naturally, the size of the payments will vary accordingly.

Annuity contracts have a tax advantage—no federal or state income taxes are owed on the interest or other investment earnings until the money is withdrawn. Should you die, the contract value would pass directly to your designated heirs without going through probate, although the money wouldn't necessarily escape taxes.

But there are drawbacks. You'll usually pay a 10 percent penalty tax on amounts you withdraw or borrow from an annuity before age 59½. Most variable annuities have stiff charges for surrendering (cashing in) the contract within the first several years of its purchase. And with inflation, any kind of fixed income you sign up for will buy less and less as years go by.

Finally, to make sure that the lifetime income you're promised applies to your life and not to that of an insurance company that unexpectedly becomes insolvent, you'll want to shop carefully for a company, using the procedures outlined in Chapter 19.

You'll probably choose one of the following popular types of payout plans.

LIFE ONLY. It guarantees a stipulated monthly income for life. This provides the highest level of income, but there are no death benefits or surrender values.

LIFE WITH TEN YEARS CERTAIN. This payout plan provides a lifetime income and guarantees that should you die during the first ten years, the payments to your designated beneficiary would continue through the tenth year. Ten years is a common period, but others are available. This type of annuity can maximize income over a period in which you have major financial obligations.

INSTALLMENT REFUND. This guarantees you a lifetime income and provides that should you die before the total of the payouts equals the purchase price, payments will be made to your beneficiary until the payout equals the purchase price. If you want the satisfaction of knowing you (or your heirs) will get your money back, this is one way to do it. Installment-refund annuities can also be a choice if you have reason to believe that you might not live long enough to recoup your purchase price.

JOINT AND SURVIVOR. This guarantees payments over your lifetime and a reduced level of payments for the life of your surviving spouse or other beneficiary. If you are married, this is the payout method you'll be assigned automatically from a defined-benefit pension plan at work unless you choose another and your spouse agrees to it in writing. Joint-and-survivor annuities are a popular way to protect the income stream of a designated survivor after you die. When comparing contracts, watch closely for disclaimers, qualifiers, and ambiguities. Be sure the net income you would receive after payment of any commissions or service charges is clearly stated in the contract. Special taxes could lower your net income, too: Some states collect premium taxes on annuity purchases.

Do It Yourself?

When you buy an immediate annuity, you're betting that you'll live long enough to come out ahead, or at least break even. Suppose you'd rather not take the chance that the insurance company will end up with a lot of your money. In that case, you could set up a retirement fund yourself by putting the money into income-producing investments such as those described in the investment chapters of this book. You wouldn't get the same kind of ironclad guarantees, but neither would you surrender your capital. And the assets would not be lost at your death—they could be willed to whomever you chose.

Another thing: An unscheduled chunk of the principal could be used in an emergency, an option you don't get with an annuity. In fact, you could create your own annuity by drawing out small parts of the principal along with the interest in accordance with a

When you buy an immediate annuity, you're betting that you'll live long enough to come out ahead, or at least break even.

Part of the proceeds from annuities and self-liquidating funds is excluded from tax, since it is a return of your own money.

schedule that would preserve the nest egg for as long as you expect to live. The table on page 494 shows how long your money would hold out using various withdrawal schedules.

To illustrate how to use the table, let's say you're a 65-year-old woman with $50,000 to invest. If your life span is average, you'll be around another 22 years or so.

Now assume you invest the money and it earns 9 percent a year for the foreseeable future. Reading along the 9 percent line, you'll see that the money would last 27 years and two months if you withdrew 10 percent of the original principal each year, or $5,000. That would give you a monthly income of $416.67 and a five-year statistical margin of safety on your anticipated life span.

Whichever type of plan you choose, be sure to factor in the tax consequences. If you invest the money and withdraw interest only, leaving the principal intact, all of the income may be subject to federal income taxes. By contrast, part of the proceeds from annuities and self-liquidating funds is excluded from tax, since it is a return of your own money. Whether this would make a significant difference depends on your tax situation, but it definitely should be taken into account in making income comparisons.

To determine how the proceeds from annuity contracts would be taxed, call the IRS at 800-829-3676 and request a free copy of Publication 575, *Pension and Annuity Income*. Publication 590, *Individual Retirement Arrangements*, describes the tax treatment of employee-benefit rollovers. You can also view these publications on the IRS Web site at http://www.irs.gov.

Using Home Equity for Retirement Income

Many retired people face a common problem after a lifetime of making mortgage payments: Their paid-off home is a substantial asset, but they can't get any income out of it when they need it the most. That's the problem that home-equity conversions were created to solve. Equity conversions take several forms. The most appealing is called a reverse mortgage or reverse-annuity mortgage.

Reverse Mortgages

A reverse mortgage turns the usual lender-buyer relationship upside down. A bank or other institution accepts your house as collateral for a loan, but instead of giving you all the money at once, it doles it out on a monthly basis. One way to look at it is to say the bank is making mortgage payments to you. Meanwhile, you stay in your house and don't have to pay anything back until the term of the loan is up—perhaps 10 to 15 years later, perhaps not until after you die. Presumably you or your heirs pay back the loan by selling the house.

Reverse mortgages are available throughout the United States to people age 62 and over, typically through government agencies, nonprofit groups that work with the aging, and more recently through the Home Keeper program backed by Fannie Mae. But other kinds of home-equity conversion plans are more widely available, including sale-leasebacks and home-equity lines of credit.

For free information on reverse mortgages contact AARP. The contents of the information booklet, *Home-Made Money: A Consumer's Guide to Reverse Mortgages* (#D15601), is available online at its Web site (http://www.aarp.org/revmort) or you can order the booklet by calling 888-687-2277. You can also call the Department of Housing and Urban Development or check its Web site for free information about reverse mortgages (800-217-6970; http://www.hud.gov/buying/rvrsmort.cfm).

Sale-Leasebacks

In this arrangement, you sell your house and rent it back from the buyer. Typically the buyer is your child, who leases the place back to you for life. Because your son or daughter is in effect your landlord, he or she gets all the tax advantages that go with owning rental real estate. Most sale-leasebacks are financed by the seller, who gets an infusion of cash from the down payment and regular income from the mortgage payments.

Home-Equity Loans

The major disadvantage of using this type of loan (described in detail in Chapter 3) as a source of income is that repayment must start immediately.

Where There's a Will, There's an Estate Plan

Writing a will is a sobering act that's easy to put off, which is probably why so many of us never get around to it. But consider for a moment what might happen if you don't leave clear instructions for the distribution of your property after you're gone.

If you die without a valid will, your state will supply a ready-made one that has been devised by its legislature. Like a ready-made suit, it may fit—and it may not. Abraham Lincoln died without a will, and his estate was divided (as an estate still would be in some states) into thirds—one third for his widow and a third for each of their sons. One son was grown and the other was 12 years old, so the arrangement may not have been considered an ideal one by Abe's widow, Mary.

The possibilities for trouble when you leave no will are nearly endless. A hostile relative might be able to acquire a share of your estate, for example, or a relative who is already well fixed might take legal precedence over needier kin.

So you should have a will, and it should be a carefully written one. Oral wills, the procrastinator's deathbed solution, aren't legal in a number of states and they are valid only in narrow circumstances in states where they are legal. Handwritten, or holographic, wills are legal in some states but can create complicated and expensive problems for the people you leave behind. Videotaped wills may make good drama on television, but they have no legal standing in the real world.

Chapter 30

When you want to make a will, don't take shortcuts to save a few bucks. Get a competent lawyer to write the document.

Six Steps to a Good Will

This is not a time to take shortcuts in the hope of saving a few bucks. It makes sense to pay a competent lawyer a reasonable fee to write a document that will lay out your wishes and stand up later to scrutiny by the probate court, your beneficiaries, and anyone you choose not to make a beneficiary. Getting a good will also takes some thinking on your part. Will-writing kits, on paper or computers, can help you focus your thinking and get ready to meet with the lawyer. Two software programs are: *Kiplinger's WILL Power*, a helpful program published by Block Financial Corp. (Windows or Mac download or CD-ROM, $29.95; available at http://www.taxcut.com/products/legal); and *Quicken WillMaker Plus 2005* by Nolo (Windows download or CD-ROM, $79.99 in stores, or $49.99 for the CD or $39.99 for a download at http://www.nolo.com).

1. Size Up Your Estate

Start by drawing up a list of your assets—real estate, bank accounts, stocks, bonds, cars, boats, life insurance, profit-sharing and pension funds, business holdings, money owed to you, and the like. Use the form on page 506.

2. Protect the Children

If you have minor children, you'll have to decide who you want to take care of them if you and your spouse both die. This involves setting up a guardianship, a task that has two principal functions. The first is to provide for the proper care of the children until they reach the age of majority. The second is to manage the money and property you leave to the children and distribute it to them as you would wish.

The same person could fill both roles, but the "guardian of the person" can be different from the "guardian of the property." Choose the former for his or her nurturing abilities and the latter for financial knowledge and money-management skills. If you're divorced, you might be inclined to choose a separate property guardian because the surviving parent typically would get custody of your children. Name backup guardians in case your first choice dies, is incapacitated, or perhaps wants to relinquish the job after a few years.

In addition to your will, it helps to leave detailed instructions on how you want your children raised. In a letter, or even on videotape, you can spell out anything from your views on cars and part-time jobs for teenagers to your priorities on education and religion. These instructions can provide important guidance, but they aren't binding.

3. Distribute Your Property

Next you'll have to decide how you want your estate distributed. This is obvious and straightforward in many instances, such as leaving everything to your spouse, or to your children if both of you die. You needn't account for every piece of jewelry or every stick of furniture (but do account for pets). Making specific bequests of long lists of items like that in a will can needlessly complicate matters and lead to extra costs and delays. Write these up separately and let your executor carry out your instructions.

4. Choose an Executor

You'll have to be prepared to name an executor (sometimes called an administrator), whose job it will be to see to the distribution of your estate and make sure any taxes, debts, and other obligations are paid.

Choose your executor carefully. Naturally, he or she should be someone you trust—a relative, a friend, your lawyer, or anyone you feel is able to take on the responsible task of disposing of your estate. The person should be willing to do the job, so check before you name someone who might later refuse, thus forcing the court to appoint someone you might not have chosen.

A husband and wife can name each other or a mutually agreed-on person as executor for their wills. You'll also have to choose someone who will step in as executor if for some reason your first choice can't do it.

> **Choose your executor carefully. The person should be willing to do the job, so check before you name someone.**

Once your will is written, don't just stuff it in a safe-deposit box. The box may be sealed after your death, making the document unavailable for a time.

5. See the Lawyer

For simple wills a generalist should be able to do the job at a reasonable price. If your estate is substantial, consult a lawyer who specializes in estate planning. Don't conclude hastily that your estate is too small for you to worry about taxes. Insurance policies, company benefits, investments, and home equity could make your estate larger than you think it is.

Depending on where you live, the complexities of the document you need, and the time you've spent sorting things out already, the lawyer's fee can range from as little as $300 or so for a simple will to $200 an hour for the time involved in planning a complex estate. There is no such thing as an average price.

6. Change It If You Want

If your situation changes in the future, you can always amend the will. (Under some circumstances, you should change it, as described later in this chapter.) But don't do it yourself. You could invalidate the entire document in the eyes of the court, thus undoing the good you've done so far. Go to the expense of having the lawyer make the changes.

Once your will is written, don't just stuff it in a safe-deposit box. The box may be sealed after your death, making the document unavailable for a time. Perhaps you can keep it in the lawyer's vault or safe at home with your other important papers. You may also want to give a copy to the executor or the principal beneficiary. Subject to your lawyer's advice, consider including a letter of last instructions that will help your executor gather your affairs together and carry out your wishes.

Estate-Planning Basics

Everything you own is considered part of your estate when you die. To grasp the importance of planning for the distribution of your worldly goods, consider all the things that influence what happens to them.

The Role of Probate

This is the procedure by which state courts validate a will's authenticity, thereby clearing the way for the executor to collect and pay debts, pay taxes, sell property, distribute funds, and carry out other necessary tasks involved with settling an estate. The process can be slow and expensive, and probate fees can absorb 3 to 7 percent of the estate's assets. And if there is a "will contest," costs will skyrocket.

Mindful of criticism and the spread of devices designed expressly to keep assets out of the grip of probate courts, most states have adopted a streamlined procedure for small estates, with informal procedures requiring little court supervision. Sometimes all that's necessary is for the appropriate person to file an affidavit with the court and have relevant records, such as title to property, changed. Formal probate, in which major steps along the way are supervised by the court, is commonly reserved for large estates.

Not all of your estate has to go through probate. Among the items exempted from probate—but not necessarily from taxes—are life insurance payable to a named beneficiary, property left in certain kinds of trusts, and assets such as homes and bank accounts held in joint tenancy with right of survivorship. There's more on avoiding probate later in this chapter.

Joint Ownership

Property jointly owned with a right of survivorship—the form that is commonly used by married couples but can be employed by any two people—automatically passes to the other owner when one owner dies. Tenancy by the entirety, another form of joint ownership, can apply only to married couples and isn't recognized in all states. The pluses and minuses of joint ownership are discussed in detail later on in the chapter. For now, suffice it to say that it is an important estate-planning tool.

Federal Estate and Gift Taxes

After years of squabbling over eliminating what many call the "death tax," Congress passed rules that greatly

Probate is the procedure by which state courts validate a will's authenticity, clearing the way for the executor to carry out the necessary tasks involved with settling an estate.

HOW LARGE IS YOUR ESTATE?

Although you don't have to pay any federal estate taxes until your taxable estate exceeds certain thresholds—$1.5 million in 2005, then $2 million in 2006 through 2008, before rising again to $3.5 million in 2009—the federal estate tax is scheduled to disappear in 2010, but it will reappear in 2011 unless the legislation is renewed before then.

In the worksheet below, the ownership column is included because how you own property is pivotal to how much of its value will be included in your estate when you die. In the "value" column, include the following:

- **the full value of property** of which you are the sole owner;
- **half the value of property** you own jointly with your spouse with right of survivorship;
- **your share of property** owned with others;
- **half the value of community property** if you live in a community-property state.

Also include the value of the proceeds of an insurance policy on your life if you own the policy, your vested interest in pension and profit-sharing plans, and the value of property in revocable trusts.

ASSETS	Value	Who Owns It
Cash in checking, savings, money-market accounts	_____	_____
Stocks	_____	_____
Bonds	_____	_____
Mutual funds	_____	_____
Other investments	_____	_____
Real estate	_____	_____
Personal property, including furniture, cars, clothing, etc.	_____	_____
Art, antiques, collectibles	_____	_____
Proceeds of life insurance policies you own on your life	_____	_____
Pension and profit-sharing benefits, IRAs, etc.	_____	_____
Business interests: sole proprietorship, partnerships, closely held corporations	_____	_____
Money owed to you, such as mortgages, rents, professional fees due	_____	_____
Other	_____	_____
Total Assets	_____	_____
LIABILITIES		
Mortgages	_____	_____
Loans and notes	_____	_____
Taxes	_____	_____
Consumer debt	_____	_____
Other	_____	_____
Total Liabilities	_____	_____
NET ESTATE (total assets minus total liabilities)	_____	_____

increase the threshold that must be reached before there is any federal estate tax and—at least apparently—scheduled the tax's demise in 2010. (We say "apparently" because the law has the tax ending in 2010 but the law expires the following year, unless there's new legislation to extend its provisions.) In 2005, an estate had to amount to more than $1.5 million before it incurred any federal tax at all. In 2006, the threshold increases to $2 million, and it rises again to $3.5 million in 2009. Then it disappears in 2010. Married couples who leave personal property to their spouses can avoid tax on the entire estate of the first spouse to die, no matter how much it's worth. This is called the "marital deduction."

If your estate crosses the increased threshold, the pain can still be intense for your heirs. Federal estate-tax brackets can be as high as 47 percent in 2005, then 46 percent in 2006. Americans who have accumulated substantial assets during their lifetimes need to be careful that they don't hand most of it over to Uncle Sam when they die.

Before you die, you can give away up to $11,000 a year to as many recipients as you want without incurring what's called a gift tax. For married couples the limit is $22,000. The gift tax is designed to prevent people from giving away much of their wealth to prospective heirs and thus escaping the estate tax entirely. The current rules set a lifetime gift-tax exclusion of $1 million. The top rate on taxable gifts drops in tandem with the estate-tax rates until 2010. That's when the estate tax "disappears" and the top gift-tax rate settles in at 35 percent—the same as the highest income-tax rate. Lawmakers kept this tax to stymie lifetime transfers of income-producing property to heirs who are in a lower income-tax bracket to reduce income taxes.

There is no limit on gifts between spouses and no limit on the marital deduction described above. This means that, with proper estate planning, the marital deduction and the estate-tax exclusion can be used to pass estates of any size from one spouse to the other without incurring any federal estate tax. To make sure

Couples who leave personal property to spouses can avoid tax on the entire estate of the first spouse to die.

Well-written trusts can save time, money, and hassles by steering assets away from the probate process and getting them into the hands of people you'd like to have them before you die.

that you take full advantage of this opportunity and to minimize estate taxes upon the death of the second spouse, consult with an experienced estate lawyer familiar with the laws of your state.

Your State Wants a Share, Too

The federal government is not the only authority wanting a piece of your estate when you die. Most state governments levy some form of death taxes that cut into much smaller estates than the federal tax does. Most states levy an inheritance tax. An inheritance tax is paid by each heir out of his or her inheritance unless the will directs that the estate cover it. (This makes an inheritance tax different from an estate tax, which must be paid by the estate before its proceeds can be divided up among the heirs.)

All states and the District of Columbia also had a so-called pickup tax, which applied only to estates owing a federal tax. While the pickup tax didn't actually increase your tax, it claimed for the state an amount that would otherwise be claimed by the feds. As of 2005, the federal credit and all pickup tax revenue it painlessly channeled to the states disappeared because when Congress voted to eliminate the estate tax by 2010, it also phased out the state estate-tax credit—and with it the pickup tax—on an even faster schedule.

So far, about 20 states and the District of Columbia have changed their laws to keep the cash coming in by "decoupling" from the federal law. They continue to demand the same amount of death tax they were entitled to under the old rules. But because the feds won't give back as much via the credit, if you live in a decoupled state, your estate will wind up paying more death tax than if you died in a state whose lawmakers are going along with the program.

Putting Your Trust in Trusts

Essentially, a trust is an arrangement whereby you give assets to a legal entity (the trust) created in a separate agreement to be administered by an individual or institutional trustee for a beneficiary, who may be yourself or some other person. Well-written trusts can save time, money, and hassles by steering assets away from the probate process and getting them into the hands of people you'd like to have them before you die.

An *inter vivos*, or *living trust*, operates while you are alive. A *testamentary trust* goes into effect after your death. A *revocable trust*'s provisions can be changed; an *irrevocable trust* can't be materially modified.

The main attraction of a revocable trust is that you can transfer legal ownership of assets without actually giving up control of them. In most states, you can name yourself both trustee and beneficiary. And you can revoke the trust at any time and take back ownership of the assets. You can also change the agreement if you want, or transfer assets in and out of the trust as you desire.

Trusts can reduce taxes by transferring the ownership of property from a high-tax situation to a lower-tax situation. They also help in instances like the following.

■ **James is the sole support of his elderly father.** If James dies before his father, there is no assurance that the father will be able to care for himself. Therefore, instead of willing his money directly to his father, James set up a testamentary trust with a bank and his sister as cotrustees. In a case like this, with an aging parent, it's a good idea to use both a bank trust department and an individual (a family member or friend) as trustees. The bank's trust department will provide the financial expertise, and the individual can deal with the beneficiary personally. If James dies while his father is still living, the bank will invest the money and work with the sister to use the proceeds for the father's support. When the father dies, the remaining funds will be distributed to James's sister and any another beneficiaries designated in the trust.

■ **Harry and Sally intend to leave a substantial sum** to their son but are concerned about his ability to handle that much money. Rather than give him the entire amount at once, they set up a trust that will generate an annual income for him until he reaches age 25,

Trusts can reduce taxes by transferring the ownership of property from a high-tax situation to a lower-tax situation.

To avoid having some assets distributed under your state's intestacy rules, you need at least a simple will that "pours over" to the trust any property you've left out.

when he'll get half the capital. He'll get the rest when he turns 30.

Banks and professionals such as lawyers commonly administer trusts for a fee. You might prefer to appoint a friend or relative who knows the trust's beneficiary and who might be willing to serve for a smaller fee or even for expenses only. Husbands and wives can sometimes act as trustees for each other's trusts. You should appoint two or more trustees in case one becomes incapacitated, and name a successor who will take over if a trustee dies.

The Overselling of Living Trusts

Living trusts can be valuable estate-planning tools, but they are sometimes oversold to people who don't really need them or who buy them for the wrong reasons. Consider the following claims often made for living trusts. The facts don't always support them.

CLAIM: *A living trust will protect your assets from the hassle, delay, and expense of probate proceedings.*
FACTS: True enough, but assets in a living trust aren't the only ones that skip probate. Property that is owned jointly with the right of survivorship, for example, automatically goes to the survivor. Pension, IRA, and Keogh plan benefits, and life insurance death benefits payable to a named beneficiary go to the one named without passing through probate. So do government bonds and bank accounts with a designated pay-on-death beneficiary. The fewer the assets you have that would have to go through probate, the weaker this argument in favor of a living trust.

CLAIM: *Having a living trust saves money over running a will through probate.*
FACTS: Maybe, but in some cases, this "cure" could cost more than the alleged disease. Here's why:

You still need a will. People often fail to transfer all their assets into the trust initially, and they acquire new assets over time. To avoid having some assets distributed under your state's intestacy rules, you need at least a simple will that "pours over" to the trust any property you've left out. You also need a will to make specific gifts to relatives, friends, and charities, and to name a guardian for minors. Lawyers may charge an extra $1,000 to $2,500 to draw up a living trust and pour-over will.

Changing title to assets is a nuisance and can be expensive. For the trust to work, you must make it the legal owner of your property. You have to complete special forms at banks and brokerage houses. New deeds have to be prepared and recorded for real estate, and you may have to pay a hefty transfer tax. Even after the assets are in the trust, you face potential hassles in dealing with them in your capacity as trustee.

You may not save on administration costs. There are typically three costs associated with probate:
- **Filing and court fees.** A living trust does avoid these costs, which are at least 3 percent of the value of the estate in most states. Most have simplified probate procedures for small estates.
- **Executor's commission.** In most states this is a percentage of the value of the probate estate. But in the majority of cases, the executor is a family member who waives compensation.
- **Lawyer's fees.** Most probates are largely paper-shuffling affairs, so the executor of your estate may be able to handle the entire process with only occasional advice from a lawyer who charges by the hour.

CLAIM: *Your assets can be distributed faster through a living trust than they would if they were to go through probate.*

FACTS: It's possible, but if your assets are uncomplicated and your will doesn't create a postdeath trust, there shouldn't be much difference whether the assets are distributed through a trust or through probate. If you have a complicated estate that requires federal estate-

If your assets are uncomplicated and your will doesn't create a postdeath trust, there shouldn't be much difference whether the assets are distributed through a trust or through probate.

As the circumstances in your life change, take a look at your will and estate plan, and revise them as necessary.

tax planning, a living trust still may not save a significant amount of time or money. A lawyer and accountant will probably be heavily involved and may have to prepare and file two death-tax returns, one state and one federal. That can take months, whether or not the plan is part of a trust.

CLAIM: *You'll save taxes with a revocable living trust.*

FACTS: No, you won't. During your lifetime, there are no income-tax savings attributable to earnings of the trust. Because you retain total control over the assets and can revoke the trust anytime you want, you are taxed on all the income (on your personal tax return if you are the trustee).

You won't automatically save on the federal estate tax, either. Assets in the trust are included in your estate for federal estate-tax purposes and are generally subject to state death taxes as well. However, a living trust can be drafted to include the same tax-saving provisions that can be placed in a will.

Good Reasons to Change Your Will

After you've created your will and an estate plan, you'll most likely need to revisit them at key points in your life as your circumstances change.

You Get Married

Your new spouse doesn't automatically become your chief heir. Most states give a spouse one-third or one-half of an estate. If you don't have any children, your parents or siblings would get the rest. To leave all your property to your spouse, you'll need a will. You cannot disinherit a spouse without his or her consent.

In community-property states (Arizona, California, Idaho, Louisiana, Nevada, New Mexico, Texas, Washington, and Wisconsin), each spouse automatically owns one-half of all community property. Basically, that is property acquired during the marriage by means other than inheritance or gifts. You can leave your half of the property to anyone you want, including your spouse.

If you are living with someone but are not married and you want your significant other to inherit any of your property, you need a will.

You Become a Parent

Obviously, the big question is how your children will be cared for if both you and your spouse die. Now you definitely need a will to name a guardian for your children, as discussed earlier.

- **Consider using trusts,** perhaps in your will, to handle assets that would go to your children.
- **Execute a durable power of attorney** naming your spouse or someone else to act for you in financial matters when you can't. Durable power remains effective even if you become mentally unable to handle your own affairs.

You Approach Middle Age

Your assets are growing, so tax planning could save your heirs thousands in federal estate taxes. The time to act is when you and your spouse have a combined net worth, including house, retirement plans, and insurance proceeds, that approaches the amount vulnerable to the federal estate tax. You can give an unlimited amount to your spouse tax-free, by designating it in your will or by owning all assets jointly, for example. But with a little more planning, a married couple can leave twice the amount of the estate-tax exemption—up to $3 million in 2005, $4 million in 2006 through 2008, and $7 million by 2009—tax-free after the second spouse dies. (See the discussion of changes in the federal estate-tax threshold earlier in this chapter.)

- **Make sure each of you owns enough assets** individually to take advantage of your own tax-free allowance, even if it means splitting jointly owned assets.
- **If your estate is large enough** to warrant limiting jointly owned property for tax purposes (see the box on page 506), consider a revocable living trust. It can

In most states a divorce automatically revokes the provisions of a will that apply to a former spouse.

incorporate the same tax-saving measures that are described above, and its assets bypass probate.

■ **Update your will** to reflect family births, deaths, separations, or divorces. Review guardian, trustee, and personal-representative appointments. Reevaluate the nature of specific gifts to people or groups.

■ **Recalculate how much life insurance you need.** Should the assets of you and your spouse exceed the level protected by the estate-tax exclusion, an irrevocable life insurance trust could be useful to shelter insurance proceeds from the estate tax. A life insurance trust owns a policy on your life. You pay the trust so that the trust can pay the premiums. When you die, the proceeds of the policy are used to pay your federal estate taxes. Because the irrevocable trust owned the policy, not you, the proceeds aren't part of your estate and therefore aren't taxable.

You Get Divorced

Review absolutely everything. The people in your life are changing. So must your estate plan.

■ **Get a new will.** In most states a divorce automatically revokes the provisions of a will that apply to a former spouse. In some states a divorce revokes the entire will.

■ **Set up trusts** to control the assets you plan to leave your children.

■ **Revise any living trusts** to remove your former spouse as a beneficiary or trustee. Do likewise with a durable power of attorney or a living will (see Chapter 18).

■ **Unless restricted by a divorce decree,** change the beneficiaries on your life insurance, pensions, and IRA.

You Remarry

You and your new spouse may have to plan for families from prior marriages and for children you have together.

■ **Consider a prenuptial agreement,** should you want to keep assets separate and nullify your inheritance rights to each other's estates (see Chapter 13).

■ **Provide for your new spouse** and still be certain your children are taken care of. To do this, talk to an estate-planning lawyer about a qualified terminable interest property trust—QTIP, for short. This trust can be set up in a will to give your spouse the income from the trust property and some rights to principal. But when he or she dies, the assets go to beneficiaries you have chosen.

You Retire or Move to Another State

If you retire to another state (or any time you move to a new state, for that matter), have your estate-planning documents reviewed in light of that state's laws and your current needs.

- **Durable powers of attorney** become even more important. For example, if you are stricken with Alzheimer's disease, you may become unable to give the required consent for financial transactions.
- **Life insurance coverage** may not be needed anymore. But if your estate faces an estate-tax liability or if your spouse is dependent on retirement income that will end with your death, consider keeping the coverage.

Your Spouse Dies

This loss can leave you emotionally vulnerable to financial mistakes. For at least several months, avoid selling your house or making other drastic changes.

- **Seek expert advice.** There may be tax benefits to disclaiming some of your inheritance in favor of alternate beneficiaries, such as your children, if your spouse's estate is subject to the federal estate tax and you have enough assets of your own, including liquid assets.
- **Get a new will** and, if needed, a revocable living trust.
- **Execute a new durable power of attorney** and a living will (which expresses your wishes in case of an illness that leaves you permanently incapacitated). Put these in a safe place, and tell people who need to know where they are.

> **If you retire to another state (or any time you move to a new state, for that matter), have your estate-planning documents reviewed in light of that state's laws and your current needs.**

State Securities Regulation Offices

Use the phone numbers and addresses on the following pages to obtain an employment and disciplinary report on a stockbroker. Nearly all 50 states and the District of Columbia say they will send out-of-state investors a report on a broker. So if you live in a state that withholds all disciplinary information, or in a state that deletes some information, call another state's securities department because all have access to the Central Registration Depository data base.

There is usually a charge for a report. In most cases it's nominal, but a few states charge hourly fees as high as $15. The National Association of Securities Dealers (NASD) reports are free. You can contact the NASD (800-289-9999; http://www.nasdr.com) to find out if agents or firms have disciplinary histories with securities regulators or criminal authorities.

Most state reports will include unresolved investor complaints, pending arbitration cases, pending civil lawsuits, criminal charges, and criminal convictions being appealed.

ALABAMA
Office of Securities Commission
770 Washington Avenue, Suite 570
Montgomery, AL 36130
800-222-1253
www.asc.state.al.us

ALASKA
Dept. of Commerce and
  Economic Development
P.O. Box 110807
Juneau, AK 99801
907-465-2521
www.dced.state.ak.us/bsc/bsc.htm

ARIZONA
Arizona Corporate Commission
  Securities Division
1300 West Washington Street
  3rd Floor
Phoenix, AZ 85007
602-542-4242
www.ccsd.cc.state.az.us

ARKANSAS
Securities Division
Heritage West Building
201 East Markham
Little Rock, AR 72201
800-981-4429
www.state.ar.us/arsec

CALIFORNIA
Department of Corporations
1515 K Street, Suite 200
Sacramento, CA 95814-4052
916-445-7205
www.corp.ca.gov

COLORADO
Division of Securities
1580 Lincoln Street, Suite 420
Denver, CO 80203-1506
303-894-2320
www.dora.state.co.us/securities

CONNECTICUT
Dept. of Banking
260 Constitution Plaza
Hartford, CT 06103-1800
860-240-8299
800-831-7225
www.state.ct.us/dob/pages/secdiv.htm

DELAWARE
Dept. of Justice
Division of Securities
820 N. French Street, 5th Floor
Wilmington, DE 19801
302-577-8424
www.state.de.us/securities

DISTRICT OF COLUMBIA
D.C. Public Service Commission
Office of Consumer Services
1333 H St., N.W., 6th Floor, East Tower
Washington, DC 20005
202-626-9161
www.dcpsc.org

FLORIDA
Division of Securities
200 East Gaines Street
Tallahassee, FL 32399
850-413-3100
Toll free in FL: 800-342-2762
www.dbf.state.fl.us

GEORGIA
Division of Securities and
   Business Regulation
Office of the Secretary of State
802 West Tower
Two Martin Luther King, Jr. Dr.
Atlanta, GA 30334
404-656-3920
888-733-7427
www.sos.state.ga.us/securities

HAWAII
Dept. of Commerce and
   Consumer Affairs
Business Registration Division
P.O. Box 40
Honolulu, HI 96810
808-586-2744
www.hawaii.gov

IDAHO
Securities Bureau
P.O. Box 83720
Boise, ID 83720-0031
208-332-8000
www.2.state.state.id.us/finance/sec.htm

ILLINOIS
Illinois Secretary of State
Securities Department
Jefferson Terrace
Suite 300A
300 West Jefferson St.
Springfield, IL 62702
217-782-2256
www.sos.state.il.us

INDIANA
Secretary of State's Office
Securities Division
302 West Washington Street, Rm. E111
Indianapolis, IN 46204
317-232-6681
www.state.in.us/sos

IOWA
Securities Bureau
340 East Maple
Des Moines, IA 50319-0066
515-281-4441
www.iid.state.ia.us/division/securities/
   default.asp

KANSAS
Office of the Securities Commissioner
618 S. Kansas Avenue, 2nd Floor
Topeka, KS 66603
785-296-3307
Toll free in KS: 800-232-9580
www.securities.state.ks.us

KENTUCKY
Dept. of Financial Institutions
1025 Capitol Center Dr., Suite 200
Frankfort, KY 40601
502-573-3390
800-223-2579
www.dfi.state.ky.us

LOUISIANA
Office of Financial Institutions
   Securities Division
8660 United Plaza Blvd., 2nd Floor
Baton Rouge, LA 70809
225-925-4512
www.ofi.state.la.us

MAINE
Securities Division
121 House Street Station
Augusta, ME 04333-0121
207-624-8551
www.mainesecuritiesreg.org

MARYLAND
Division of Securities
200 St. Paul Place
Baltimore, MD 21202
410-576-6360
www.aag.state.md.us/securities

MASSACHUSETTS
Securities Division
One Ashburton Place, 17th Floor
Boston, MA 02108
617-727-3548
www.state.ma.us/sec/sct

MICHIGAN
Financial and Insurance Services
P.O. Box 30222
Lansing, MI 48909
517-373-0220
www.michigan.gov

MINNESOTA
Department of Commerce
85 Seventh Place East,
 Suite 500
St. Paul, MN 55101
651-296-4973
www.commerce.state.mn.us

MISSISSIPPI
Securities Enforcement & Regulations
P.O. Box 136
Jackson, MS 39202
800-804-6364
www.sos.state.ms.us

MISSOURI
Division of Securities
P.O. Box 1276
Jefferson City, MO 65102
800-721-7996
www.sos.mo.gov/securities

MONTANA
Securities Division
Office of the State Auditor
840 Helena Avenue
Helena, MT 59601
406-444-2040
www.state.mt.us/sao

NEBRASKA
Bureau of Securities
Commerce Court
1230 "O" Street, Suite 400
Lincoln, NE 68509-5006
402-471-3445
www.ndbf.org

NEVADA
Sec. of State/Securities Division
555 E. Washington Avenue, Suite 5200
Las Vegas, NV 89101
702-486-2440
www.sos.state.nv.us/securities

NEW HAMPSHIRE
Bureau of Securities Regulation
State House, Room 204
Concord, NH 03301
603-271-1463
www.sos.nh.gov/securities

NEW JERSEY
Bureau of Securities
P. O. Box 47029
Newark, NJ 07101
973-504-3600
www.state.nj.us/lps/ca/bos.htm

NEW MEXICO
Securities Division
2550 Cerrillos Rd.
Santa Fe, NM 87505
505-476-4580
www.rld.state.nm.us/securities

NEW YORK
Investor Protection & Securities
Attorney General's Office
120 Broadway
New York, NY 10271
212-416-8200
www.oag.state.ny.us

NORTH CAROLINA
Sec. of State/Securities Division
P.O. Box 29622
Raleigh, NC 27626-0622
919-807-2000
800-688-4507 (investor hotline)
www.secretary.state.nc.us/sec

NORTH DAKOTA
Securities Commissioner's Office
600 E. Boulevard Avenue, 5th Floor
Bismarck, ND 58505-0510
701-328-2910
Toll free in ND: 800-297-5124
www.sate.nd.us/securities

OHIO
Division of Securities
77 South High Street, 22nd Floor
Columbus, OH 43215
614-644-7381
Toll free in Ohio: 800-788-1194
www.securities.state.oh.us

OKLAHOMA
Department of Securities
First National Center, Suite 860
120 N. Robinson
Oklahoma City, OK 73102
405-280-7700
www.securities.state.ok.us

OREGON
Division of Finance/Corporate
    Securities
P.O. Box 14480
Salem, OR 97309-0405
503-378-4140
www.cbs.state.or.us/external/dfcs/
    index.html

PENNSYLVANIA
Office of the Secretary
1010 North 7th Street, 2nd Floor
Harrisburg, PA 17102
717-787-8061
www.psc.state.pa.us

RHODE ISLAND
Business Regulation/Securities Division
2332 Richmond Street, Suite 232
Providence, RI 02903
401-222-3048
www.dbr.state.ri.us

SOUTH CAROLINA
Attorney General's Office
Securities Division
P.O. Box 11549
Columbia, SC 29211-1549
803-734-9916
www.scsecurities.com

SOUTH DAKOTA
Division of Securities
445 East Capitol Avenue
Pierre, SD 57501-4823
605-773-4013
www.state.sd.us/dcr/securities

TENNESSEE
Tennessee Department of
    Commerce and Insurance
    Securities
Davy Crockett Tower
500 James Robertson Parkway
Nashville, TN 37243-0565
615-741-2241
www.state.tn.us/commerce

TEXAS
State Securities Board
P. O. Box 13167
Austin, TX 78711-3167
512-305-8330
www.ssb.state.tx.us

UTAH
Securities Division
160 East 300 S., 2nd Floor
Salt Lake City, UT 84114
801-530-6600
Toll free in UT: 800-721-7233
www.securities.state.ut.us

VERMONT
Dept. of Banking, Insurance and
    Securities & Health Care Admin.
89 Main Street, Drawer 20
Montpelier, VT 05620-3101
802-828-3420
www.bishca.state.vt.us

VIRGINIA
Securities Division
P.O. Box 1197
Richmond, VA 23218
804-371-9051
Toll free in VA: 800-552-7945
www.state.va.us/scc/division/srf

WASHINGTON
Dept. of Financial Institutions
Securities Division
P. O. Box 9033
Olympia, WA 98507
360-902-8760
www.dfi.wa.gov/securities

WEST VIRGINIA
Securities Division
State Capitol Building 1
Room W-100
Charleston, WV 25305
304-558-2257
www.wvauditor.com

WISCONSIN
Division of Securities
Dept. of Financial
    Institutions, 4th Floor
P.O. Box 1768
Madison, WI 53701-1768
608-266-1064
www.wdfi.org/securities/default.htm

WYOMING
Securities Division
Sec. of State Office
The Capitol Building, Room 109
200 West 24th Street
Cheyenne, WY 82002
307-777-7370
www.soswy.state.wy.us/securiti/securiti.
htm

Federal Reserve Banks

Board of Governors of the Federal Reserve System
20th Street and Constitution Avenue, NW
Washington, D.C. 20551
202-452-3000
www.federalreserve.gov

Federal Reserve Bank of Boston
600 Atlantic Avenue
Boston, MA 02205
617-973-3000
www.bos.frb.org

Federal Reserve Bank of New York
33 Liberty Street
New York, NY 10045
212-720-5000
www.newyorkfed.org

Federal Reserve Bank of Philadelphia
Ten Independence Mall
Philadelphia, PA 19106
215-574-6000
www.phil.frb.org

Federal Reserve Bank of Cleveland
1455 East Sixth Street
Cleveland, OH 44114
216-579-2000
www.clevelandfed.org

Federal Reserve Bank of Richmond
701 East Byrd Street
Richmond, VA 23219
804-697-8000
www.rich.frb.org

Federal Reserve Bank of Atlanta
1000 Peachtree Street, NE
Atlanta, GA 30309-4470
404-489-8500
www.frbatlanta.org

Federal Reserve Bank of Chicago
230 South LaSalle Street
Chicago, IL 60604
312-322-5322
www.chicagofed.org

Federal Reserve Bank of St. Louis
Broadway and Locust Streets
St. Louis, MO 63102
314-444-8444
www.stlouisfed.org

Federal Reserve Bank of Minneapolis
90 Hennepin Avenue
Minneapolis, MN 55401
612-204-5000
www.minneapolisfed.org

Federal Reserve Bank of Kansas City
925 Grand Boulevard
Kansas City, MO 64198
816-881-2000
www.kansascityfed.org

Federal Reserve Bank of Dallas
2200 North Pearl Street
Dallas, TX 75201
214-922-6000
www.dallasfed.org

Federal Reserve Bank of San Francisco
101 Market Street
San Francisco, CA 94105
415-974-2000
www.frbsf.org

Guide to Recordkeeping

As we go through the daily routine of earning and spending money, we generate a blizzard of paperwork—some created by us, some by those we deal with. Some of that paper can be thrown away; some you should keep. In fact, good recordkeeping is an essential part of sound money management. The need to keep some records—a sales receipt to prove a purchase, for instance—is self-evident. Sometimes it isn't clear what you should keep and for how long.

And recordkeeping has been made a little more difficult for those who like to keep their canceled checks. Few firms return canceled checks monthly any more. They send a list of checks processed, or perhaps substitute checks or small reproductions of your checks. If you need actual checks for your records, you must place a special order and pay a per-check fee.

The following is a guide to which records to keep and why.

Appraisal Records

If your home is damaged or destroyed by fire, the claims process will go much more smoothly if your safe-deposit box contains detailed, up-to-date information on your personal possessions, especially collectibles such as antique furniture, paintings, silver, and anything else on the fine-arts rider of your insurance policy. (The same is true in case of a theft from your home.) Make a complete descriptive inventory of your possessions and get periodic professional appraisals of the more valuable items. Include good-quality photographs of each item as well as photos of whole rooms of your home showing things in their usual location. Videotapes can also be useful for this purpose.

Automobile Records

Keep your automobile title certificate in a safe-deposit box. You can probably obtain a replacement from the state motor vehicle department, but that could be difficult, particularly if the dealer who sold the car has gone out of business and you haven't kept the original bill of sale.

Keeping receipts or a running log of work you have done on the car can help you maintain it properly and presumably lengthen its life. Such records are a must for a new car in order to keep the warranty in force, and they can help when it comes time to sell.

Birth, Death, and Marriage Records

These are vital for many legal and financial purposes, so protect them in your safe-deposit box. If you've lost any, apply for a replacement now, before it's needed, because you could run into a long wait. Check your telephone book under the "state government" listing for the name, address, and phone number of the state agency to contact for copies.

Homeownership and Rental Records

When you buy or sell a house, keep all the records you receive. They may not be essential from a legal standpoint, but they may have other important uses.

The deed, for example, doesn't fully protect your ownership of the property until it is recorded at the county or municipal land office. However, it may give a precise description of the property. Similarly, the survey map provided is a convenient reference for locating boundaries when you put up a fence, a shed, or other structures.The payment records of the transaction will probably be needed for tax purposes either that year or at some future time. Your share of the regular real estate tax is deductible the same year you pay it. Special land-transfer taxes are ordinarily not deductible, but they can be added to the cost of the house in calculating the capital gain, if any, when you sell it.

Any permanent improvements you make to property—central air-conditioning, a porch, a patio, a garage, for example—can also be added to the cost of the property when you sell. The canceled or substitute checks to contractors or the receipted bills should be put away for long-term safekeeping. Maintenance costs for painting, papering, and the like do not qualify as permanent improvements.When you rent a house or apartment, your legal and financial relationship with the landlord rests on the lease. You may need it to verify particular provisions from time to time. Keep it handy.

Insurance Policies

Life insurance policies are best kept in a safe place, quickly and easily accessible to your heirs. A safe-deposit box might not always be the best location because there may be a delay before your heirs can get permission to open the box. Ask your bank how long it usually takes to gain access. The insurance company can replace lost policies.

Auto, house, and other property policies should be readily accessible at home so you can verify the provisions when making claims.

Investment Dividends

It's helpful to log dividend payments each year in a separate record to guard against company errors or lost checks. You can discard your tally after matching it against the annual dividend summary the company or the fund sends to you (and the IRS). However, you should maintain an ongoing record of capital-gains dividends, because they have to be figured into the gain or loss reported for taxes when the shares are sold.

Loan Contracts

Even though you may be keeping the list of checks, substitute checks, or reproductions from your bank to document payments on a loan, you might need the contract spelling out the credit terms to settle differences with the lender and for tax purposes. Similarly, when you make a loan to someone, the note constitutes the best evidence of the terms.

Unfortunately, the one loan document borrowers rarely receive before the debt is paid off is their home mortgage and the attached note covering the payments. You should be able to obtain a copy of the note and the mortgage from the lending institution, or a copy of the mortgage and deed from the land office where it was recorded.

Military Service Records

The two key documents for most veterans are the discharge certificate and the service record. If you qualify for disability benefits, retain the original letter from the Department of Veterans Affairs specifying the amount you're entitled to. You might need it if you should have to enter a VA hospital.

Put the discharge, service record, and disability letter in a safe-deposit box, and keep copies for home reference if you like. To replace lost VA records, contact the nearest VA office.

Passports

Don't throw out an expired passport. You can use it to satisfy some of the application requirements for a new one. Keep current passports in a home safe or bank safe-deposit box.

Pension and Profit-Sharing Records

Before retirement, your prospective benefits from a defined-benefit plan are likely to change with your salary and length of service, so you need to keep only the last annual statement issued by your employer or union.

If you leave the company before retirement, with rights to a pension that starts at some future date, make absolutely sure to preserve a record of how much you will receive and when payments will begin. In some plans, the employee is given the annuity policy that will provide the pension payments. In others, your rights may be recorded only in the plan's files and it is up to you to apply for the pension when you're eligible.

As a growing number of companies shift to 401(k) and other defined-contribution plans, it is especially important to hang on to the records of your contributions and the employer's matching contributions, if any.

Savings Passbooks and Certificates

They're not as difficult or costly to replace as stock certificates, but their loss could cause some inconvenience. Bank procedures for handling lost passbooks and certificates vary. You may be given new ones with no fuss. In some cases, though, withdrawals from the account might be temporarily restricted.

Stock and Bond Certificates

These should be kept in your safe-deposit box or, if you prefer, in the brokerage firm's vault.

If you lose a stock certificate, immediately notify the issuing company or its transfer agent (your broker can find the name for you). You will probably be sent a set of replacement forms, including an application for an indemnity bond. The bond insures the company against loss if the missing shares are cashed illegally. You can expect to be charged a fee for the indemnity bond based on the value of the shares. Once the bond is obtained, the company can issue a new certificate.

Stock or Mutual Fund
Purchase and Sale Confirmations

The broker's or fund's statement showing the number of shares you purchased, the date, the price, commission, and taxes, if any, should be kept with the certificates.

You will need that information eventually to figure your gain or loss for tax purposes when you sell the shares. The broker's sales statement goes with your current year's tax material.

Tax Records

Canceled or substitute checks, receipts, and myriad other documents may be required for federal and state income tax purposes, both to calculate how much you owe and to justify deductions, exemptions, and other tax items. You should be prepared to present concrete evidence to the government in case of an audit.

However, you can lighten your files by eliminating superfluous items and discarding records after they have served their purpose. For instance, you can dispose of weekly or monthly salary statements once you have checked them against the annual W–2 wage form. Often, a canceled check or substitute check that relates directly to an entry on your return is sufficient without supplementary documents. The check record for a medical expense doesn't have to be supported by the original bill unless the nature of the expense is ambiguous. A check to a physician leaves little doubt as to the service involved, but you would want to back up a check to a drugstore with a detailed receipt, because the payment could cover either deductible drugs or nondeductible cosmetics.

Sometimes you can and should create a record to protect yourself. If a charity fails to give you a receipt for donated goods, draw up a list with the used-market value of each item, the name of the organization, and the date of the contribution. For noncash donations greater than $500, you'll need detailed information on the cost of the item and how and when you acquired it. Precise records are particularly important for business travel- and entertainment-expense deductions. If you expect to claim business expenses, write to your Internal Revenue Service district office (or check their Web site at http://www.irs.gov) for a copy of Publication 463, *Travel, Entertainment, Gift and Car Expenses,* which explains the regulations and recordkeeping requirements.

How long should you keep tax records? The law allows the IRS three years to challenge a return under ordinary circumstances, and six years when you have understated income by more than 25 percent. In cases of fraud, there is no limit.

Warranties, Service Agreements

Try to assemble in one place all your warranties, appliance instruction booklets, and agreements covering such services as lawn care and termite inspection, and periodically remove the out-of-date ones.

If you buy an appliance without a printed warranty, retain the canceled check, check substitute, or paid bill in case you have to make a claim against the retailer or manufacturer. They could be obligated to correct defects, even without an explicit warranty, under the legal principle that any product should adequately perform its designated function.

Wills

Many people leave the original copy of their will in the custody of their lawyer and keep one duplicate in their own safe-deposit box and another at home. If you don't have a regular lawyer, put the original will in your safe-deposit box and keep a copy at home.

Glossary

Account executive: The title given by some brokerage firms to their stockbrokers. Other variations on the title include registered representative, financial counselor, and financial consultant.

Accrued interest: Interest that is due (on a bond, for example) but hasn't yet been paid. If you buy a bond halfway between interest payment dates, for example, you must pay the seller for the interest accrued but not yet received. You get the money back—tax-free—when you receive the interest payment for the entire period.

Alpha: A mathematical measure of price volatility that attempts to isolate the price movements of a stock or mutual fund from those of the market. A stock with a high alpha is expected to perform well regardless of what happens to the market as a whole. (*See also* Beta.)

American depositary receipts: Certificates traded on U.S. stock exchanges or over the counter, representing ownership of a specific number of shares of a foreign stock.

Annual percentage rate: The method of expressing the cost of credit that takes into account the fact that you owe interest on a smaller and smaller amount as you pay down the loan. The federal Truth in Lending Act requires lenders to use the APR.

Annuity: A tax-favored investment that generates a series of regular payments guaranteed to continue for a specific time (usually the recipient's lifetime) in exchange for a single payment up front or a series of payments. With a deferred annuity, payments begin sometime in the future. With an immediate annuity, payments begin immediately. A fixed annuity pays a fixed income stream for the life of the contract. With a variable annuity, the payments may change according to how successfully the money is invested.

ARM fund: A mutual fund that invests in adjustable-rate mortgages (ARMs).

Asset management account: Offered by brokerage firms and banks, AMAs pay interest and provide a full range of services, including check writing, credit and debit cards, loans, and securities transactions.

At-the-market: A term used when trading a stock or bond. When you buy or sell at-the-market, the broker will execute your trade at the next available price. Your alternative is to name a specific price, called a limit order.

Back office: The support operations of a brokerage firm that don't deal directly with customers. "Back office problems" usually refers to slow paperwork or other bottlenecks in the execution of customers' orders.

Bear: A bear thinks the market is going to go down. This makes bearish the opposite of bullish.

Bearer bond: Also called a coupon bond, it is not registered in anyone's name. Rather, whoever holds the bond (the "bearer") is entitled to collect interest payments merely by cutting off attached coupons and mailing them in at the proper time. Bearer bonds are no longer being issued.

Beta: A measure of price volatility that relates the stock or mutual fund to the market as a whole. A stock or fund with a beta higher than 1 is expected to jump up or down more than the market. A beta below 1 indicates a stock or fund that usually moves up and down less than the market.

Bid/asked: Bid is the price a buyer is willing to pay for a security; asked is the price the seller will take. The difference, known as the spread, is the broker's share of the transaction.

Blue chip: A stock that is issued by a well-known, respected company that has a good record of earnings and dividend payments, and is widely held by investors.

Boiler room: A blanket term used to describe the place of origin of high-pressure telephone sales campaigns, usually involving cold calls to unsuspecting customers who would be better off without whatever is being offered to them.

Bond: An interest-bearing security that obligates the issuer to pay a specified amount of interest for a specified time, usually several years, and then repay the bondholder the face amount of the bond. Bonds issued by corporations are backed by corporate assets; in case of default, the bondholders have a legal claim on those assets. Bonds issued by government agencies may or may not be backed by a specific public project, such as a toll bridge or a stadium. Interest from corporate bonds is taxable; interest from municipal bonds, which are issued by state and local governments, is free of federal income taxes and, usually, income taxes of the issuing jurisdiction. Interest from Treasury bonds, issued by the federal government, is free of state and local income taxes but subject to federal taxes.

Bond rating: An analysis by an independent firm (such as Standard & Poor's Corp. or Moody's Investors Service) of a bond issuer's ability to pay interest on schedule and repay the bond principal when due. The S&P and Moody's rating systems, although slightly different, both use a letter-grade system, with triple-A the highest rating and C or D the lowest.

Book value: The value of a company's net assets (total assets minus all liabilities). That number divided by total outstanding shares gives you the stock's book value per share. If a stock is selling at a low book value relative to similar companies, it may or may not be a bargain.

Brokered CD: A large-denomination certificate of deposit sold by a bank to a brokerage, which slices it up into smaller pieces and sells the pieces to its customers.

Bull: A bull is someone who thinks the market is going to go up, which makes bullish the opposite of bearish.

Call: *See* Option.

Capital gain or loss: The difference between the price at which you buy an investment and the price at which you sell it. Adding the capital gain or loss to the income received from the investment yields the total return. When the asset has been held for more than 12 months, the gain or loss is said to be long term; assets owned fewer than 12 months produce a short-term gain or loss.

Certificate of deposit: Usually called a CD, a certificate of deposit is a short- to medium-term instrument (one month to five years) that is issued by a bank or savings and loan to pay interest at a rate higher than that paid by a regular savings account. There is usually a penalty for early withdrawal.

Charting: Another name for technical analysis.

Check 21: Check 21, shorthand for Check Clearing for the 21st Century Act, was designed to modernize how checks are processed. The bank or company you sent the check to can turn the paper into an electronic image and speed the image and data through the system. In addition to saving the banking industry billions in transportation and processing costs, this avoids situations where transportation grinds to a halt due to weather or other factors. Instead of receiving a canceled check, you may receive a list of checks, substitute checks, or small reproductions with your bank statement.

Churning: Excessive buying and selling in a customer's account undertaken to generate commissions for the broker.

Closed-end fund: A type of mutual fund or investment company that issues a set number of shares, then no more. Shares of the fund trade like other stocks on one of the stock exchanges.

COBRA (Consolidated Omnibus Budget Reconciliation Act): Federal law that states that if you leave a job that provided health insurance, you have the right to continue your coverage for 18 months or more if you pay the premium and an administrative fee. The law does not apply to companies with fewer than 20 employees, or employees of a church, the government of a U.S. territory, or the District of Columbia.

Cold calling: The practice of salespeople making unsolicited telephone calls to people on lists they buy or borrow in an attempt to drum up business. Never make investment decisions based on cold calls.

Commercial paper: Short-term IOUs issued by corporations without collateral. They are bought in large quantities by money-market funds.

Common stock: The most basic type of share ownership in a U.S. corporation. Owners of common stock are entitled to all the risks and rewards that go with owning a piece of the company. In case of bankruptcy, common stockholders' claims on company assets rank behind the claims of bondholders. (*See also* Preferred stock.)

Contrarian: An investor who thinks and acts in opposition to the conventional wisdom. When the majority of investors are bearish, a contrarian is bullish, and vice versa.

Convertible bond: A special type of bond that can be exchanged, or converted, into a set number of common stock shares of the issuing company. The choice of when to convert is up to the bond owner. The appeal of a convertible is that it gives you a chance to cash in if the stock price of the company soars.

Coverdell Education Account (ESA): A tax-deferred account to which eligible parents can contribute up to $2,000 a year earmarked for the education of their children. Contributions are not deductible, but withdrawals are tax-free if used to pay college bills.

Debenture: A corporate IOU that is not backed by the company's assets and is therefore somewhat riskier than a bond.

Debit card: Used at both bank ATMs to obtain cash and retail establishments to make purchases. Debit cards immediately deduct the specified amount from your account, thus eliminating the grace period of a credit card or the "float" of a check.

Defined-benefit plan: A pension plan that uses a mathematical formula to determine the employee's pension, which is usually tied to years of service and salary. It's up to the employer to contribute enough to the fund to provide the retirement income prescribed by the formula.

Defined-contribution plan: A pension plan in which the company (and often the employee) contributes a specified amount each year to a fund that's invested in securities, mutual funds, or some sort of insurance contract. You take the investment risk, and if the investments don't do well, you will have less available at retirement.

Discretionary account: A brokerage account in which the customer gives the broker the authority to buy and sell securities at his or her discretion—that is, without checking with the customer first.

Dividend: A share of company earnings paid out quarterly to stockholders, usually in cash, but sometimes in the form of additional shares of stock.

Dividend reinvestment plan: A program in which the company automatically reinvests a shareholder's cash dividends in additional shares of common stock, often with no brokerage charge to the shareholder. Also called a DRIP.

Dollar-cost averaging: A program of investing a set amount on a regular schedule regardless of the price of the shares at the time. In the long run, dollar-cost averaging results in your buying more shares at low prices than you do at high prices.

Dow Theory: A belief that a major trend in the stock market isn't signaled by one index alone but must be confirmed by two—specifically, a new high or low must be recorded by both the Dow Jones industrial average and the Dow Jones transportation average before it can safely be declared that the market is headed in one direction or the other.

Due diligence: The work performed by a broker or other representative in order to investigate and understand an investment thoroughly before recommending it to a customer.

Duration: When applied to bond mutual funds, duration is a measure of the sensitivity of the fund's portfolio to a one-percentage-point change in interest rates. The portfolio of a bond fund with a duration of six years, for example, can be expected to lose 6 percent of its value if the interest rates on similar bonds rise by one percentage point. By the same token, the fund should gain 6 percent in value if rates on similar bonds decline by one point.

Earnings per share: A company's profits after taxes, bond interest, and preferred-stock payments have been subtracted, divided by the number of shares of common stock outstanding.

ESOP (employee stock ownership plan): A plan by which employees buy stock in their company through payroll withholding or some other way, or the corporation contributes shares of its stock to funds that allocate the shares to employees based on their annual compensation.

Exchange-traded funds (ETFs): ETFs own a fixed portfolio of securities and can be bought and sold any time the stock market is open. Like an index fund, an ETF's portfolio represents a slice of the market—an index, a subsector of an index, or a particular industry. You buy and sell them through a broker, even sell them short or buy them on margin, like ordinary stocks.

Ex-dividend: The period between the declaration of a dividend by a company or a mutual fund and the actual payment of the dividend. On the ex-dividend date, the price of the stock or fund will fall by the amount of the dividend, so new investors don't get the benefit of it. Companies and funds that have "gone ex-dividend" are marked by an X in the newspaper listings.

Fannie Mae: The name under which the Federal National Mortgage Association conducts business, buying mortgages on the secondary market, repackaging them, and selling off pieces to investors. The effect is to infuse the mortgage markets with fresh money.

FDIC (Federal Deposit Insurance Corp.): The government agency that provides $100,000 of insurance per depositor's account. Most banks, savings and loans, and mutual savings banks are members.

Fixed-income investment: A catchall description for investments in bonds, certificates of deposit (CDs), and similar instruments that pay a fixed amount of interest.

Flexible Spending Account (FSA): A fringe benefit that allows an employee to divert part of his or her salary to a special account used to reimburse the cost of medical expenses. Funds channeled through the account escape federal income and Social Security taxes, and, in most states, state income taxes.

401(k) plan: An employer-sponsored retirement plan that permits employees to divert part of their pay into the plan and avoid current taxes on that income. Money directed to the plan may or may not be partially matched by the employer, and investment earnings within the plan accumulate tax-free until they are withdrawn. The 401(k) is named for the section of the federal tax code that authorizes it.

403(b) plan: Similar to 401(k) plans, but set up for public employees and employees of nonprofit organizations.

Freddie Mac: The name under which the Federal Home Loan Mortgage Corp. conducts business, operating a lot like Fannie Mae.

Full-service broker: A brokerage firm that maintains a research department and other services designed to supply its individual and institutional customers with investment advice. Commission rates are higher than those of discount brokers.

Fundamental analysis: Study of the balance sheet, earnings history, management, product lines, and other elements of a company in an attempt to discern reasonable expectations for the price of its stock. For contrast, *see* Technical analysis.

Futures contract: An agreement to buy or sell a certain amount of a commodity (such as wheat, soybeans, or gold) or a financial instrument (such as Treasury bills or deutsche marks) at a stipulated price in a specified future month. As the actual price moves closer to or further away from the contract price, the price of the contract fluctuates up and down, thus creating profits and losses for its holders, who may never actually take or make delivery of the underlying commodity.

Ginnie Mae: A dual-purpose acronym that stands for both the Government National Mortgage Association (GNMA) and the mortgage-backed securities that this government agency packages, guarantees, and sells to investors.

Good-til-canceled order: An order to buy or sell a stock or bond at a specified price, which stays in effect until it is executed by the broker because that price was reached, or until you cancel it.

Guaranteed investment contract (GIC): An investment product—issued by an insurance company—that works like a giant certificate of deposit, but without federal deposit insurance. The contracts generally run one to seven years. Managers of 401(k) plans often put many GICs together into a fund and offer this investment to plan participants.

Health care proxy: A legal document appointing someone to make health care decisions for you if you are unable to do so.

Health maintenance organization (HMO): A medical plan in which you pay in advance for your care. The HMO handles just about all hospital and medical needs.

Health savings account (HSA): A tax-advantaged plan for the self-employed and employees. An HSA combines a high-deductible health insurance policy with a deductible savings account similar to an IRA. Funds contributed to the account are tax-free, earnings grow tax-deferred, and withdrawals are tax-free if used to pay medical bills.

Hope scholarship tax credit: A tax credit worth $1,500 a year for each student for whom a parent pays qualifying college expenses. The Hope credit is available only for freshman and sophomore years.

Individual practice association (IPA): A form of HMO in which the doctors earn a fee based on services rendered, usually in their own offices.

Individual retirement account (IRA): The regular IRA is a tax-favored account designed to encourage retirement saving. The maximum annual contribution is $4,000 for 2005 and will rise to $5,000 by 2008. Tax on earnings is postponed until you withdraw funds. In most cases there is a penalty for withdrawing funds before you're 59½. If your income is below a certain level or you're not covered by a retirement plan at work, you can deduct IRA contributions. (*See also* Roth IRA.)

Initial public offering: A corporation's first public offering of an issue of stock. Also called an IPO.

Institutional investors: Pension plans, mutual funds, banks, insurance companies, and other institutions that buy and sell large quantities of stocks and bonds. Institutional investors account for 70 percent of the market volume.

Junk bond: A high-risk, high-yield bond rated BB or lower by Standard & Poor's, Ba or lower by Moody's, or not rated at all by any agency. Junk bonds are generally issued by relatively unknown or financially weak companies.

Keogh plan: A tax-sheltered retirement plan for the self-employed. Up to 25 percent of self-employment income can be diverted into a Keogh, and contributions can be deducted from taxable income. Earnings in the account grow tax-free until the money is withdrawn, and there are restrictions on tapping the account before age 59½.

Kiddie tax: The nickname given to the rule that says that a certain level of unearned income (such as interest or dividends) received by a child under age 14 will be taxed at the parents' rate, not the child's. The aim is to prevent high-income parents from avoiding taxes by putting assets in their child's name.

Leveraged buyout: The use of borrowed money to finance the purchase of a firm. Often, an LBO is financed by raising money through the issuance and sale of junk bonds.

Leveraging: Investing with borrowed money in the hope of multiplying gains. If you buy $100,000 worth of stock and its price rises to $110,000, you've earned 10 percent on your investment. But if you leveraged the deal by putting up only $50,000 of your own money and borrowing the rest, the same $10,000 increase would represent a 20 percent return on your money, not counting interest on the loan. The flip side of leverage is that it also multiplies losses. If the price of the stock goes down by $5,000 on the all-cash deal, your loss would be 5 percent of your $100,000 investment. On the leveraged deal, your loss would be 10 percent of the money you put up and you'd still have to pay back the $50,000 you borrowed.

Lifetime Learning credit: A tax credit equal to 20 percent of the first $10,000 spent by a taxpayer for tuition in the third or fourth year of college, or for graduate school or continuing education.

Limit order: An order to buy or sell a security if it reaches a specified price.

Limited partnership: A business arrangement put together and managed by a general partner (which may be a company or an individual) and financed by the investments of limited partners, so-called because their liability is limited to the amount of money they invest in the venture. Limited partnerships can invest in virtually anything, but real estate is the most common choice.

They have often been characterized by high fees for the general partners, complicated tax reporting requirements, and elusive payouts for the limited partners.

Liquidity: The ability to quickly convert an investment portfolio to cash without suffering a noticeable loss in value. Stocks and bonds of widely traded companies are considered highly liquid. Real estate and limited partnerships are relatively illiquid.

Living will: A legal document that spells out a person's wishes regarding medical procedures that might be used to prolong life in the event of a terminal illness or accident.

Load: A front-end load is a fee (sales commission) charged when you purchase a mutual fund, insurance policy, or other investment product. A back-end load is a commission charged to mutual fund investors who sell their shares in the fund before owning them for a specified time, often five years. True "no-load" mutual funds charge neither fee.

Margin buying: Financing the purchase of securities partly with money borrowed from the brokerage firm. Regulations permit buying up to 50 percent "on margin," meaning an investor can borrow up to half the purchase price of an investment. (*See* Leveraging.)

Money-market deposit account: Sometimes called money-market investment accounts, these accounts usually pay higher rates than checking accounts. Minimum deposit levels are higher than checking, and access to the account may be limited.

Money-market fund: A mutual fund that invests in short-term corporate and government debt and passes the interest payments on to shareholders. A key feature of money-market funds is that share value doesn't change, making them an ideal place to earn current market interest with a high degree of liquidity.

Mutual fund: A professionally managed portfolio of stocks and bonds or other investments divided up into shares. Minimum purchase is sometimes $500 or less, and mutual funds stand ready to buy back their shares at any time. The market price of the fund's shares, called the net asset value, fluctuates daily with the market price of the securities in its portfolio.

Nasdaq: Pronounced Nazz-dak, it started out as the acronym for the National Association of Securities Dealers Automated Quotations System, a computerized price-reporting system used by brokers to track over-the-counter securities as well as some exchange-listed issues. Now the term refers to the computerized "stock market" on which hundreds of millions of shares trade every day.

Odd lot: A stock trade involving fewer than 100 shares. For contrast, *see* Round lot.

Opportunity cost: The cost of passing up one investment in favor of another. For instance, if you pull money out of a money-market fund, where it is earning 5 percent interest, to invest it in a stock that has promise but yields just 3 percent, your opportunity cost while you're waiting for the price to rise is 2 percent.

Option: The right to buy or sell a security at a given price within a given time. The right to buy the security is called a "call." Calls are bought by investors who expect the price of the stock to rise. The right to sell a stock is called a "put." Puts are purchased by investors who expect the price of the stock to fall. Investors use puts and calls to bet on the direction of price movements without actually having to buy or sell the stock. One option represents 100 shares and sells for a fraction of the price of the shares themselves. As the time approaches for the option to expire, its price will move up or down depending on the movement of the stock price. Options can also be used to wring a little income out of stock you own without selling it.

By writing (selling) a "covered call," you collect the premium and, assuming the stock price stays under the call price, get to keep the stock. The risk, of course, is that the stock will get called away and you will miss out on the price rise.

Over the counter (OTC): The name used to describe a stock or bond transaction that takes place somewhere other than the floor of one of the exchanges, such as the New York Stock Exchange. U.S. Treasury bonds, for instance, are traded over the counter, while major corporate bonds can be found listed on the exchanges. The primary over-the-counter marketplace is the Nasdaq National Market System, which provides a computerized trading mechanism for quite a few major U.S. companies and thousands of minor ones.

Par: The face value of a stock or bond. Also called par value.

Penny stock (also known as microcap stock): Generally thought of as a recently issued stock selling at low prices, often for less than $5 a share, and traded over the counter. Penny stocks are usually issued by small, relatively unknown companies and lightly traded, making them more prone to price manipulation than larger, better-established issues. They are, in short, a gamble.

Point: A one-time fee paid up front to mortgage lenders. One "point" equals 1 percent of the loan amount.

Power of attorney: A legal document that delegates someone of your choosing to make legal, financial, or medical decisions on your behalf.

Preferred-provider organization (PPO): The name given to a collection of doctors, clinics, and hospitals that agree to accept fees determined by the insurance company providing the coverage to their patients.

Preferred stock: A class of stock that pays a specified dividend that is set when it is issued. Preferreds generally pay less income than bonds of the same company and don't have the price appreciation potential of common stock. They appeal mainly to corporations, which get a tax break on their dividend income.

Price-earnings ratio: Usually called the P/E, it is the price of a stock divided by either its latest annual earnings per share (a "trailing" P/E) or its predicted earnings (an "anticipated" P/E). Either way, the P/E is considered an important indicator of investor sentiment about a stock because it indicates how much investors are willing to pay for a dollar of earnings.

Price-sales ratio: The PSR is the stock's price divided by its company's latest annual sales per share. It is favored by some investors as a measure of a stock's relative value. The lower the PSR, according to this school of thought, the better the value.

Private mortgage insurance: Required by lenders for homebuyers getting conventional loans with down payments of less than 20 percent. It is designed to protect lenders from losses in the event of default.

Probate: The procedure by which state courts validate a will's authenticity, thereby clearing the way for the executor to carry out necessary tasks involved with settling an estate.

Program trading: A complex computerized system designed to take advantage of temporary differences between the actual value of the stocks composing a popular index and the value represented by futures contracts on those stocks. To simplify, if the stocks' prices are higher than the futures contracts reflect, computer programs issue orders to sell stocks and buy futures contracts. If the stocks are lower than the futures contracts reflect, program traders buy stocks and sell the futures. The result is virtually risk-free profits for the program traders and more volatility for the market because of the vast numbers of shares needed to make the system work.

Prospectus: The document that describes a securities offering or the operations of a mutual fund, a limited partnership, or other investment. The prospectus divulges financial data about the company, backgrounds of its officers, and other information needed by investors to make an informed decision. It is required by federal securities laws.

Proxy: The formal authorization by a stockholder that permits someone else (usually company management) to vote in his or her place at shareholder meetings or on matters put to the shareholders for a vote at other times.

Put: *See* Options.

Real Estate Investment Trust (REIT): A closed-end investment company that buys real estate properties or mortgages and passes virtually all the profits on to its shareholders. REIT shares trade like stock on the NYSE and other stock exchanges and offer a convenient way for small investors to add a real estate component to their investment portfolio.

Registered representative: The formal name for a stockbroker, so called because he or she must be registered with the National Association of Securities Dealers as qualified to handle securities trades.

Return on equity (ROE): An important measure of investment results that is obtained by dividing the total value of shareholders' equity—that is, the market value of common and preferred stock—into the company's net income after taxes.

Return on investment (ROI): A company's net profit after taxes divided by its total assets.

Reverse mortgage: Allows a homeowner to borrow against a portion of the equity in the home without having to pay back any principal or interest until the home is sold, possibly after the owner's death.

Roth 401(k): An employer-sponsored retirement plan that permits employees to divert part of their after-tax pay. If the money directed to the plan is partially matched by the employer, the matching funds must go into a traditional 401(k). Withdrawals will be completely tax-free in retirement. The 403(b) plans are also eligible for the Roth provisions.

Roth IRA: An individual retirement account in which contributions are not deductible, but withdrawals can be completely tax-free in retirement.

Round lot: A hundred shares of stock, the preferred number for buying and selling and often the most economical unit when commissions are calculated.

Sallie Mae: The name under which the Student Loan Marketing Association conducts business. It buys student loans from colleges, universities, and other lenders and packages them into units sold to investors. Sallie Mae thus infuses the student-loan market with new money in much the same way that Ginnie Mae infuses the mortgage market with new money.

Secondary market: The general name given to stock exchanges, the over-the-counter market, and other marketplaces in which stocks, bonds, mortgages, and other investments are sold after they have been issued and sold initially. Original issues are sold in the primary market; subsequent sales take place in the secondary market. For example, the primary market for a new issue of stock is the team of underwriters; the secondary market is one of the stock exchanges or the over-the-counter market. The primary market for a mortgage is the lender, which may then sell it to

Fannie Mae or Freddie Mac in the secondary mortgage market.

Short selling: A technique used to take advantage of an anticipated decline in the price of a stock or other security by reversing the usual order of buying and selling. In a short sale, the investor (1) borrows stock from the broker and (2) immediately sells it. Then, if the investor guessed right and the price of the stock does indeed decline, he can replace the borrowed shares by (3) buying them at the cheaper price. The profit is the difference between the price at which he sells the shares and the price at which he buys them later on. Of course, if the price of the shares rises, the investor will suffer a loss.

Sinking fund: Financial reserves set aside to be used exclusively to redeem a bond or preferred stock issue and thus reassure investors that the company will be able to meet that obligation.

SIPC (Securities Investor Protection Corp.): A federally chartered body that provides insurance for brokerage firms' customer accounts up to $500,000 on assets in stocks, bonds, or mutual funds, with a $100,000 limit on cash. SIPC insures against the failure of brokerage firms, not against market risks of customers' investments.

Specialist: A member of the stock exchange who serves as a market maker for a number of different stock issues. A specialist maintains an inventory of certain stocks and buys and sells shares as necessary to maintain an orderly market for those stocks.

Spread: The difference between the bid and asked prices of a security, which may also be called the broker's markup.

Stop-loss order: Standing instructions to a broker to sell a particular stock or bond if its price ever dips to a specified level.

Street name: The term used to describe securities that are held in the name of your brokerage firm but that still belong to you. Holding stocks in street name makes trading simple because there is no need for you to pick up or deliver the stock certificates in person.

Technical analysis: An approach to market analysis that attempts to forecast price movements by examining and charting the patterns formed by past movements in prices, trading volume, the ratio of advancing to declining stocks, and other statistics. For contrast, *see* Fundamental analysis.

Tender offer: An offer to shareholders to buy their shares of stock in a company. Tender offers are usually a key element of a strategy to take over, or buy out, a company and thus are usually made at a higher-than-market price to encourage shareholders to accept them.

10-K: A detailed financial report that must be filed with the Securities and Exchange Commission (SEC) each year by all companies whose shares are publicly traded. It is much more detailed than a typical annual report and can be obtained from the company or from the SEC.

Term insurance: The simplest form of life insurance. You insure your life for a certain amount of money for a fixed period of time—say, five years—and pay an annual premium based on your age and the amount of coverage you're buying.

Total return: An investment performance measurement that combines two components: any change in the price of the shares and any dividends or other distributions paid to shareholders over the period being measured. For example, the total return on a utility stock that rose 4 percent over a year and that paid a dividend of 6 percent (calculated as a percentage of your original investment) would be 10 percent. In mutual funds, total return assumes that dividends and capital gains are reinvested into the fund.

Totten trust: A regular bank account with a designated "pay on death" inheritor. It is a simple form of a revocable grantor trust used to avoid probate court and is often used to save for funeral expenses.

Triple witching hour: A phrase made popular by program trading, it is the last hour of stock market trading on the third Friday of March, June, September, and December. That's when options and futures contracts expire on market indexes used by program traders to hedge their positions in stocks. The simultaneous expirations often set off heavy buying and selling of options, futures, and the underlying stocks themselves, thus creating the "triple" witching hour.

Trust: An arrangement whereby you give assets to a legal entity (the trust) created in a separate agreement to be administered by an individual or institutional trustee for a beneficiary, who may be yourself or another person. A living trust, or *inter vivos* trust, operates while you are alive. A testamentary trust goes into effect after your death. A revocable trust's provisions can be changed; an irrevocable trust can't be materially modified.

12b-1 fees: An extra fee charged by some mutual funds to cover the costs of promotion and marketing. In practice, 12b-1 fees are often used to compensate brokers for selling low-load and no-load funds. The effect of the fee is reflected in the performance figures reported by the funds.

Unit trust: A collection of securities, usually bonds, packaged by brokers and sold to investors. Unit trusts offer a steady, known yield and investors recoup their principal as the bonds in the trust mature.

Universal-life insurance: This variation of whole-life insurance lets you decide how much of the premium to use for insurance and how much for investments. Premium payments can be varied, and universal life offers yields on the cash-value portion that may be higher than regular whole-life policies.

Variable-life insurance: Allows you to invest part of your cash value in stocks and other securities, through mutual funds run by the insurance company. Both the death benefit and the cash value depend on the investments you choose; there is no guaranteed minimum interest rate for the cash value.

Vesting: Process through which you become entitled to benefits in a company pension plan. Companies may use either cliff vesting, in which you are 100 percent vested after three years of service, with nothing in the meantime, or gradual vesting, which starts at 20 percent after two years of service and adds 20 percent for each of the next four years so that vesting is complete after six years of employment.

Whole-life insurance: Commonly called cash-value insurance. In its basic form, it charges you the same premium for as long as you keep the policy in force. Part of the premium pays for insurance, part pays the agent's commission and administrative costs, and the rest is credited to your account, where it earns interest.

Yield: In general, the annual cash return earned by a stock, bond, mutual fund, real estate investment trust, or other investment. A stock yield is its annual dividend calculated as a percentage of the share price. For example, a stock priced at $50 per share and paying an annual dividend of $2 per share would have a yield of 4 percent. Bond yields can take several forms. Coupon yield is the interest rate paid on the face value of the bond (usually $1,000). Current yield is the interest rate based on the actual purchase price of the bond, which may be higher or lower. Yield to maturity is the rate that takes into account the current yield and the difference between the purchase price and the face value, with the difference assumed to be amortized over the remaining life of the bond.

Zero-coupon bond: A bond that pays all its interest at maturity but none prior to maturity. These "zeros" sell at a deep discount to face value and are especially suitable for long-term investment goals with a definite time horizon, such as college tuition or retirement.

Index

Index